Lecture Notes in Computer Science 9412

More information about this series at http://www.springer.com/series/7409

Frederick W.B. Li · Ralf Klamma
Mart Laanpere · Jun Zhang
Baltasar Fernández Manjón
Rynson W.H. Lau (Eds.)

Advances in Web-Based Learning – ICWL 2015

14th International Conference
Guangzhou, China, November 5–8, 2015
Proceedings

Springer

Editors
Frederick W.B. Li
Durham University
Durham
UK

Jun Zhang
Sun Yat-sen University
Guangzhou
China

Ralf Klamma
RWTH Aachen
Aachen
Germany

Baltasar Fernández Manjón
Universidad Complutense de Madrid
Madrid
Spain

Mart Laanpere
Tallinn University
Tallinn
Estonia

Rynson W.H. Lau
City University of Hong Kong
Hong Kong
Hong Kong

ISSN 0302-9743 ISSN 1611-3349 (electronic)
Lecture Notes in Computer Science
ISBN 978-3-319-25514-9 ISBN 978-3-319-25515-6 (eBook)
DOI 10.1007/978-3-319-25515-6

Library of Congress Control Number: 2015951516

LNCS Sublibrary: SL3 – Information Systems and Applications, incl. Internet/Web, and HCI

Springer Cham Heidelberg New York Dordrecht London

Printed on acid-free paper

Springer International Publishing AG Switzerland is part of Springer Science+Business Media
(www.springer.com)

Preface

The annual International Conference on Web-Based Learning (ICWL) started in Hong Kong in 2002 and has so far been held in Asia (China, Malaysia, Hong Kong, Taiwan), Australia, and Europe (Estonia, Germany, Romania, UK). ICWL 2015, the 14th edition in the series, was organized by Sun Yat-sen University (China) and the Hong Kong Web Society.

This year's conference was held in Guangzhou, the third largest Chinese city and the capital and largest city of Guangdong province in South China, located near Hong Kong and Macau. In 2012, Guangzhou was identified as a Beta+ World City by the global city index produced by the GaWC. It owns a large tertiary education complex, housing ten higher education institutions that educate up to 200,000 students. We therefore believe the location offered an appropriate educational and technical context for the ICWL conference.

This year we received 79 submissions from 27 countries worldwide. After a rigorous double-blind review process, 18 papers were accepted as full papers, yielding an acceptance rate of 22.8 %. In addition, two invited papers and seven short papers were accepted. These contributions covered the latest findings in various areas, such as: collaborative and peer learning; computer-supported collaborative learning; e-learning platforms and tools; intelligent tutoring and tools; pedagogical issues and learning analytics; personalized and adaptive learning; Web 2.0 and social learning environments.

Moreover, ICWL 2015 featured two distinguished keynote presentations and four workshops, which covered a wide range of active and emerging topics in Web-based learning, complementing the main conference areas. The good number of workshops indicated that ICWL is not only a forum for presenting results, but is also the meeting place for an active community in which new research foci are collectively explored and brought to a new level of maturity.

We would like to thank the entire Organizing Committee and especially the finance chair, Dr. Howard Leung, for his tremendous efforts in communicating with the authors regarding registration matters. We would also like to express our gratitude to the Program Committee members for their timely and helpful reviews. And last but not least, we would like to thank all the authors for their contribution in maintaining a high-quality conference – we count on your continual support for playing a significant role in the Web-based learning community in the future.

August 2015

Frederick W.B. Li
Mart Laanpere
Ralf Klamma
Jun Zhang
Baltasar Fernández Manjón
Rynson W.H. Lau

Organization

Organizing Committee

Conference Co-chairs

Jun Zhang	Sun Yat-sen University, China
Baltasar Fernández Manjón	Universidad Complutense de Madrid, Spain
Rynson W.H. Lau	City University of Hong Kong, SAR China

Program Co-chairs

Frederick W.B. Li	University of Durham, UK
Mart Laanpere	Tallinn University, Estonia
Ralf Klamma	RWTH Aachen University, Germany

Steering Committee Representative

Qing Li	City University of Hong Kong, SAR China

Organization Chair

Wenyin Liu	MERC, City University of Hong Kong, SAR China

Workshop Co-chairs

Zhiguo Gong	Macau University, SAR China
Yiwei Cao	Information Multimedia Communication AG, Germany

Poster Chair

Yi Cai	South China University of Technology, China

Publicity Co-chairs

Elvira Popescu	University of Craiova, Romania
Tianyong Hao	Guangdong University of Foreign Studies, China

Finance Chair

Howard Leung	Hong Kong Web Society, SAR China

Publication Co-chair

Jeff Tang	Caritas Institute of Higher Education, Hong Kong, SAR China

Local Arrangements Chair

Xiaonan Chen	Sun Yat-sen University, China

Conference Secretary

Christina Tai	MERC, City University of Hong Kong, SAR China

Webmaster

Zhangjun Yan	MERC, City University of Hong Kong, SAR China

International Program Committee

Carlos Alario-Hoyos	Universidad Carlos III de Madrid, Spain
Dirk Börner	Open University of the Netherlands
Adolfo Calleja	Tallinn University, Estonia
Yiwei Cao	imc information multimedia communication AG, Germany
Dickson K.W. Chiu	The University of Hong Kong, SAR China
Maria De Marsico	University of Rome La Sapienza, Italy
Yunhua Deng	City University of Hong Kong, SAR China
Michael Derntl	RWTH Aachen University, Germany
Giuliana Dettori	Istituto di Tecnologie Didattiche del CNR, Italy
Erik Duval	K.U. Leuven, Belgium
Maka Eradze	Tallinn University, Estonia
Baltasar Fernández Manjón	Universidad Complutense de Madrid, Spain
Denis Gillet	EPFL, Switzerland
Eelco Herder	L3S Research Center, Germany
Pedro Isaias	Universidade Aberta, Portugal
Malinka Ivanova	Technical University of Sofia, Bulgaria
Mirjana Ivanovic	University of Novi Sad, Serbia
Roland Klemke	Open University of the Netherlands
Tomaž Klobučar	Jozef Stefan Institute, Slovenia
Milos Kravcik	RWTH Aachen University, Germany
Lam-For Kwok	City University of Hong Kong, SAR China
Elise Lavoué	MAGELLAN, Université Jean Moulin Lyon 3, France
Howard Leung	City University of Hong Kong, SAR China
Xiangfeng Luo	Shanghai University, China
George Magoulas	Birkbeck College, UK

Ivana Marenzi	L3S Research Center, Germany
Alke Martens	University of Rostock, Germany
Harald Mayer	Joanneum Research, Austria
Kai Pata	Tallinn University, Estonia
Elvira Popescu	University of Craiova, Romania
Francesca Pozzi	Istituto Tecnologie Didattiche - CNR, Italy
Maria Jesus Rodriguez Triana	EPFL, Switzerland
Demetrios Sampson	University of Piraeus and CERTH, Greece
Olga C. Santos	aDeNu Research Group (UNED), Spain
Hubert Shum	Northumbria University, UK
Sonia Sousa	Tallinn University, Estonia
Marc Spaniol	Université de Caen Basse-Normandie, France
Marcus Specht	Open University of the Netherlands
Gary K.L. Tam	Swansea University, UK
Marco Temperini	Sapienza University of Rome, Italy
Vladimir Tomberg	Tallinn University, Estonia
Stefan Trausan-Matu	University Politehnica of Bucharest, Romania
Lorna Uden	Staffordshire University, UK
Carsten Ullrich	DFKI GmbH, Germany
Carlos Vaz De Carvalho	Instituto Superior de Engenharia do Porto, Portugal
Riina Vuorikari	IPTS, European Commission
Jianxin Wang	Central South University, China
Fridolin Wild	The Open University, UK
Xu Zheng	Shanghai University, China

Additional Reviewers

Marie Lefevre	Université Lumière Lyon 2, France
Kateryna Neulinger	RWTH Aachen University, Germany
Petru Nicolaescu	RWTH Aachen University, Germany
Dominik Renzel	RWTH Aachen University, Germany
Stylianos Sergis	University of Patras, Greece
Mohsen Shahriari	RWTH Aachen University, Germany
Panagiotis Zervas	Centre for Research and Technology – Hellas, Greece

Contents

Intelligent Tutoring and Tools

Pedagogical Issues

Personalized and Adaptive Learning

Web 2.0 and Social Learning Environments

Invited Papers

Discovering Commonly Shared Semantic Concepts of Eligibility Criteria for Learning Clinical Trial Design

Tianyong Hao[1], Xieling Chen[1], and Guimin Huang[2(✉)]

[1] Guangdong University of Foreign Studies, Guangzhou, China
{haoty,20121003351}@gdufs.edu.cn
[2] Guilin University of Electronic Technology, Guilin, China
gmhuang@guet.edu.cn

Abstract. Discovering commonly shared semantic concepts of eligibility criteria can facilitate hospitals in recruiting appropriate target population and empower patients with more effective result ranking of concept-based search, as well as assist researchers in understanding clinical trial design. This study aims to identify commonly shared semantic concepts of eligibility criteria through the identification of eligibility criteria concepts for each disease. An automated approach for extracting semantic concepts from eligibility criteria texts is proposed. For each disease, commonly shared semantic concepts are determined for reviewing the commonly shared concepts of clinical trials. Our experiment dataset are 145,745 clinical trials associated with 5,488 different types of diseases on ClinicalTrials.gov. 5,508,491 semantic concepts are extracted with 459,936 being unique. We further analyze its application on assisting researchers in learning disease-specific clinical trial design.

Keywords: Semantic concepts · Eligibility criteria · Learning

1 Introduction

Clinical trials generate the most rigorous evidence regarding the efficacy of medical interventions in humans [1]. To focus on a specific research question and minimize the influence of co-variates, clinical trials enroll target populations defined by strict eligibility criteria. Failure to meet recruitment targets is one of the biggest obstacles in the conduct of clinical trials [2]. For recruiters, the restrictive nature of eligibility criteria often makes it difficult to recruit enough subjects to achieve the statistical power needed for a study. For patients seeking trials, the large number of trials, the complexity of their eligibility criteria, and the lack of effective search tools make it difficult for them to find suitable trials. For learners, it is not easy to quickly understand commonly used eligibility criteria features from a long list of clinical trial texts as reference for learning how a clinical trial is designed.

In the research of facilitating patients to participate in clinical trials, most available methods focus on improving trial searches using filters. Several have focused on extracting concepts from eligibility criteria text and using these as part of the search [3–7]. Though these methods are helpful in narrowing the search for potential trials, they require users to

F.W.B. Li et al. (Eds.): ICWL 2015, LNCS 9412, pp. 3–13, 2015.
DOI: 10.1007/978-3-319-25515-6_1

come up with effective search criteria, which is a difficult task for non-specialists given the complexity of eligibility criteria and the specialized nature of medical field. Moreover, eligibility criteria are usually written as free text and tend to be grammatically and syntactically complex, making the extraction task difficult. For example, Ross et al. [1] randomly selected 1,000 eligibility criteria texts from ClinicalTrials.gov and identified 93.2 % of criteria to be complex. Consequently, learners have difficulties to understand how the eligibility criteria are designed.

A method that identifies common eligibility criteria semantic concepts for disease-specific clinical trials can potentially fulfill this need. It would be helpful for both research scientists and patients seeking trials sharing the same wanted concepts about the same disease. Moreover, such a method would help with systematic reviews of trials with similar target population requirements. Starting with a common concept of a disease, patients can view all trials having the concept so as to view all potentially fit trials. Starting with commonly used concepts for a disease, learners can explore the eligibility criteria of trials seeking similar study populations, learning the clinical trial design. This not only encourages knowledge reuse but also contributes to standardization of eligibility criteria, both often cited as desired concepts of clinical trial design (e.g., CDISC[1]).

This paper develops an N-gram-based algorithm to extract eligibility criteria concepts from clinical trials for specific diseases. Based on the algorithm, we focus on discovering commonly used eligibility criteria semantic concepts for each different disease. Our experiment dataset are publicly available 145,745 clinical trial texts from 158 counties on ClinicalTrials.gov. Targeting for 5,488 kinds of diseases, our approach identified 5,508,491 semantic concepts with 459,936 being unique. We analyzed the unique concepts sharing degree of all the trials for each disease. Finally, the commonly shared semantic concepts are ranked and compared by diseases to facilitate learners in the understanding of clinical trial design by providing an overall view of semantic concept sharing situation by diseases. The experiments demonstrate that our approach is able to extract commonly shared semantic concepts from large amount of clinical trial texts effectively.

2 Related Work

Despite the rapid proliferation of tools to assist with trial and participant identification, trial recruitment remains a major problem and thus is a fertile area for testing new and innovative methods.

Eligibility criteria data standardization is an essential step for facilitating data sharing to lead to a stronger evidence base for treatment advances ultimately [8]. Aiming at data sharing in a standardized manner, Common Data Element (CDE) has been well recognized for its advantage of helping clinical researchers employ standardized data collection techniques when they design and conduct new clinical studies, or more effectively aggregate information into significant metadata results [9, 10]. CDE is also recognized

---

[1] http://www.cdisc.org/.

as a trend in encoding medical concepts, e.g., inside eligibility criteria, started with Gennari's use of the NCI's CDEs to serve as a medical terminology for oncology clinical trial protocols [11]. Later, ASPIRE and caMatch collaborated with CDISC in developing CDEs for encoding or annotating medical concepts in eligibility criteria. Maas et al. [8] also conducted their work on coding CDEs for Traumatic Brain Injury into three levels of detail, i.e., basic, intermediate, and advanced. However, most of the works were based on domain experts' manual efforts. As a result, CDE is encouraged for uses in clinical research, patient registries, and other human subject research to improve opportunities for comparison and combination of data from multiple studies and with electronic health records.

However, a great barrier remains in CDE achievement as it heavily relies on domain experts to define fine-grained elements. The task is time-consuming, costly, and domain-specific. For example, NINDS [10] launched a CDE project as a long-awaited breakthrough in streamlining trials in 2009 [12, 13]. A group of international experts worked together by tele-conference meeting and used 12–18 months for a domain CDE list achievement [14]. We emphasize that domain experts are irreplaceable but automated extraction can facilitate experts to speed up the process. Automated approach can provide controllable CDE candidates with detailed evidences that can be used for supporting experts in quantitative analysis, reducing overall human cost eventually, as addressed by Luo et al. [15].

To achieve that, in the clinical trial arena, there are some semi- or full-automated concept mining methods for processing clinical texts. For example, Luo et al. [15] proposed a human-computer collaborative approach. The work addressed that computer assisted methods can reduce the workload of human experts, who no longer need to parse large number of clinical documents manually. A most recent work was an unsupervised tag mining method developed by Riccardo et al. [16]. This method was an unsupervised method and it extracted frequent tags from eligibility criteria texts for automated clinical trial indexing and presented positive impact on clinical trial search. Through testing on the texts from ClincialTrials.gov, the method was proved to be more effective by comparing with Unified Medical Language System (UMLS) Metathesaurus[2] [17]. It was evaluated on 137,889 clinical trials from ClinicalTrials.gov and tested the stability of extracted semantic tags. Results were then compared to real patient prescreening questions with UMLS-only approach to examine the meaningfulness of the tags. The results showed that the algorithm can automatically mine a controlled vocabulary of semantic tags and use them to semantically index all the clinical trials. It also reduced the information overload of clinical trial search engines by indexing all clinical trial eligibility criteria. However, most temporal information cannot be identified, leading to the problem that only small part can be mapped to UMLS thus affecting frequency ranking and filtering. Moreover, sentence processing including splitting and cleaning needed to be improved as symbol-based replacement incurred incorrect gram extractions. Therefore, this motivated us to propose a new semantic concept extraction algorithm to overcome these shortcomings.

[2] http://www.nlm.nih.gov/research/umls/quickstart.html.

3 The Semantic Concept Extraction Approach

An eligibility criteria semantic concept is defined as an interpretative layer of semantics over a set of compounds words or phrases, following the notion in [18]. For example, a compound word "p-450aldo" and a phrase "aldosterone-synthesizing enzyme" can be interpreted as the same semantic concept "cyp11b2 protein human" with semantic type as "enzyme". We use "semantic concept" rather than "concept" based on the consideration that most of valuable representations are more than expert-defined medical concepts. For example "proven venom diagnosis", "medical history of hypersensitivity", and "study pharmaceutical preparations".

A common semantic concept therefore is defined as a frequent semantic concept over a specified frequency threshold for a specific disease. Our definitions were derived from our investigation on "common data element candidate" [15], "controlled vocabulary of frequent tag" [16, 19], "common eligibility tag" [20], and "frequent semantic tags" [21].

To identify commonly used eligibility criteria semantic concepts, it is essential to extract eligibility criteria concepts for each of clinical trials. To achieve the semantic concept extraction, we propose an N-gram-based approach by incorporating UMLS. The approach firstly extracts all eligibility criteria texts from clinical trials on ClinicalTrials.gov for specific diseases. By parsing the structured XML texts for each trial and removing the cases where the eligibility criteria text sections are missing or contain only the phrase "Please contact site for information", the eligibility criteria texts are obtained. The texts are further preprocessed by special non-English symbol

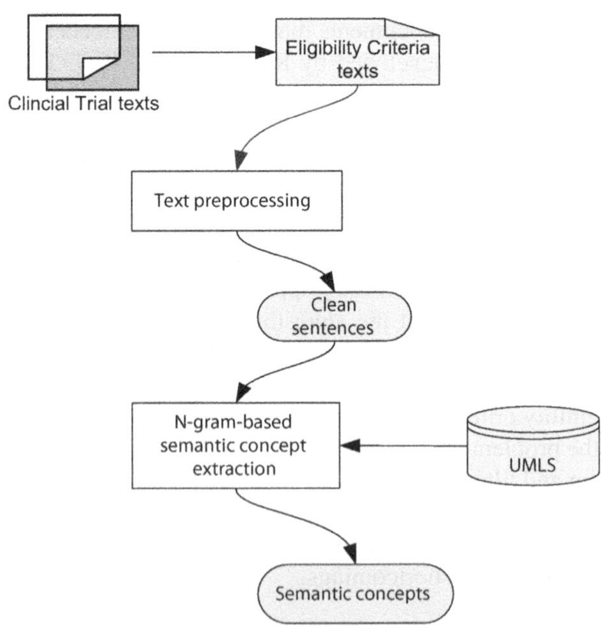

Fig. 1. The flowchart of semantic concept extraction based on the N-gram-based algorithm from clinical trial texts.

replacing, redundant spaces removing, and sentence boundary detecting to obtain sentences. For each word in a sentence, the validity is checked with punctuation and stop word list. Valid words are combined in sequence into grams and are further be standardized through mapping to UMLS. Finally, the grams are checked with frequency and filtered by C-value to achieve frequent and unique ones. Identified semantic concepts from UMLS with frequencies are eventually returned as output. The flowchart of the semantic concept extraction is illustrated in Fig. 1.

For generalization usage, the whole algorithm is designed to contain the following functions: (1) text preprocessing (text cleaning, special symbol replacing); (2) candidate N-gram generation (sentence splitting, phrase splitting, and word tokenization); (3) N-gram generalization by UMLS mapping (preference semantic rule filtering); (4) frequent N-gram extraction; (5) C-value filtering (calculating, filtering, and parameter tuning); and (6) semantic type retrieval. As this paper is neither intended to compare with baselines methods (the algorithm has better performance in the comparison with state-of-the-art methods, as shown in our previous work [21]) nor reviews the sharing in semantic type level (as defined in UMLS) but focuses on application, the C-value filtering and semantic category retrieval will not be described.

Given a collection of eligibility criteria texts as input and a set of parameters, e.g., *n*-gram maximum length, the algorithm firstly initializes and extracts candidate *n*-grams through sentence splitting, phrase splitting, grams generating, stop word checking, and Treebank tags filtering. Mapping with UMLS, the *n*-grams are generalized with identified semantic concepts from UMLS. By checking with a frequency threshold value, frequent *n*-grams can be achieved. The *n*-grams are then calculated and filtered with C-values, while mapped concepts are returned back with corresponding semantic types. The algorithm can output semantic concepts, semantic types, frequent n-grams, matched n-grams (with UMLS), and unmatched n-grams so that the results can be used for different purposes, e.g., reviewing what kind of investigators' words are not formal representations through unmatched n-grams.

In the algorithm, we used NLTK [22] for the sentence splitting and Part-of-Speech tagging. It can be replaced with commonly used parsers, e.g., Stanford Parser [23]. However, eligibility criteria texts are much different from common text format, e.g., news texts. This may cause more errors by directly applying these NLP toolkits. For example, in sentence splitting of clinical trial "NCT00105716"[3], there are diagnosis codes and ICD 9 codes, e.g., "401.1". These codes, special non-English symbols, and numeric values may cause normal NLP toolkits failure. Particularly, there are some editing problems, e.g., "et al." since certain eligibility criteria contains informal text. Our algorithm has designed rules to solve the problems in the preprocessing step accordingly. For example, check each "." symbol to judge whether it is inside a numeric and remove redundant spaces to make sure the symbol is not regarded as splitters by NLTK.

[3] http://clinicaltrials.gov/show/NCT00105716

4 Experiment and Results

We extracted all 145,745 clinical trials from ClinicalTrials.gov (an official service of the U.S. National Institutes of Health - NIH) as of 05/17/2013. By filtering trials missing eligibility criteria text section or containing the phrase "Please contact site for information", 142,948 trials were retained and used as our valid dataset. We further identified 24 disease categories containing 5,488 sub-diseases in total from NIH. After selecting diseases containing at least 10 trials, 102,382 unique trials were eventually kept and used as our experiment dataset.

In the N-gram generation, N is set to be 8 considering the maximum length from UMLS and calculation efficiency. Therefore, any gram with length shorter than 8 words is kept as candidate. For example, both "suspected immunosuppressive agents" and "immunosuppressive agents" are identified as n-gram candidates.

Through pre-processing, 2,770,746 sentences were identified after sentence boundary identification. From the sentences, 5,508,491 semantic concepts, 459,936 being unique, were extracted with 38.5 semantic concepts per trial on average. Among the unique concepts, 160,951 were shared by at least two trials, as shared unique concepts. We therefore calculated the average unique concepts per sub-disease, average shared unique concepts per sub-disease, and average percentage of concept sharing, for each disease. The results for the 24 disease categories are shown as Table 1.

From the result, average semantic concept sharing for the disease categories ranges from 25.65 % to 37.49 %, indicating the slight difference across different disease categories. We further analyzed the semantic concept sharing from two perspectives: (1) the comparison of the proportion of semantic concept sharing for all the sub-diseases; (2) the comparison of the proportion of trials with at least 50 % semantic concepts shared. The first is to view most commonly used semantic concepts across disease and the second is to view sub-diseases with highest semantic concepts sharing degree. From the results presented as Fig. 2(a) and (b), "Hypoalbuminemia", "Hearing loss central", and "Articulation disorders" are three most used semantic concepts. "Foot-and-mouth disease", "Hand foot and mouth disease", and "Meningitis haemophius" are three sub-diseases sharing semantic concepts most. The results indicate these highly shared semantic concepts are more standard as they were frequently used by different clinical trials. Also, this implies the design of a new clinical trial for highly ranked diseases can refer to the existing designs in the same disease as semantic concepts for those diseases were highly shared.

In the application on assisting researchers understand eligibility criteria design, for a specific disease, our approach enables learners to automatically obtain commonly shared semantic concepts from all existing clinical trials in the disease. The concepts can potential help learners in the following three aspects: (1) By reviewing the commonly shared concepts, learners may more systematically understand what types of eligibility criteria should be defined in order to ensure that the clinical trial design covers all required phenotypes; (2) Starting with a commonly shared concept for the disease, learners can explore the relevant eligibility criteria to study how target patient population requirements are defined; and (3) Regarding the commonly used concepts as more standard terms, leaners can study formal eligibility criteria feature representation and use the standard terms in future clinical trial design. Our approach further presents a trial - concept network showing

Table 1. The extracted semantic concepts for the 24 disease categories.

Disease types	# sub-diseases (trials >= 10)	# trials	# average unique concepts/ sub-disease	# average shared unique concepts/ sub-disease	Average concept sharing %
Bacterial and fungal diseases	128	24,589	2294.72	778.98	33.95 %
Behaviors and mental disorders	128	838,578	5623.01	1885.17	33.53 %
Blood and lymph conditions	151	72,152	6510.70	2320.91	35.65 %
Cancers and other neoplasms	359	197,425	7156.74	2521.18	35.23 %
Digestive system diseases	166	84,766	4844.88	1674.35	34.56 %
Diseases and abnormalities at or before birth	234	27,384	1675.59	507.28	30.27 %
Ear, nose, and throat diseases	58	8,101	2256.14	741.14	32.85 %
Eye diseases	122	17,499	1886.74	647.24	34.30 %
Gland and hormone related diseases	95	31,106	3430.56	1146.48	33.42 %
Heart and blood diseases	209	84,848	3938.46	1269.91	32.24 %
Immune system diseases	132	77,950	6389.99	2320.67	36.32 %
Mouth and tooth diseases	77	6,400	2281.61	748.18	32.79 %
Muscle, bone, and cartilage diseases	147	29,368	2771.89	905.82	32.68 %
Nervous system diseases	396	111,907	3268.74	1049.60	32.11 %
Nutritional and metabolic diseases	154	63,397	3392.68	1136.06	33.49 %
Occupational diseases	3	89	574.33	147.33	25.65 %
Parasitic diseases	34	3,302	1121.41	420.38	37.49 %
Respiratory tract (lung and bronchial) diseases	123	62,520	4856.32	1723.98	35.50 %
Skin and connective tissue diseases	152	42,476	3335.39	1146.82	34.38 %
Substance related disorders	29	62,520	1943.90	627.48	32.28 %
Symptoms and general pathology	410	132,371	3372.83	1055.10	31.28 %
Urinary tract, sexual organs, and pregnancy conditions	184	70,395	3959.46	1322.09	33.39 %
Viral diseases	90	57,242	5405.83	2023.83	37.44 %
Wounds and injuries	94	9,449	1727.13	469.54	27.19 %

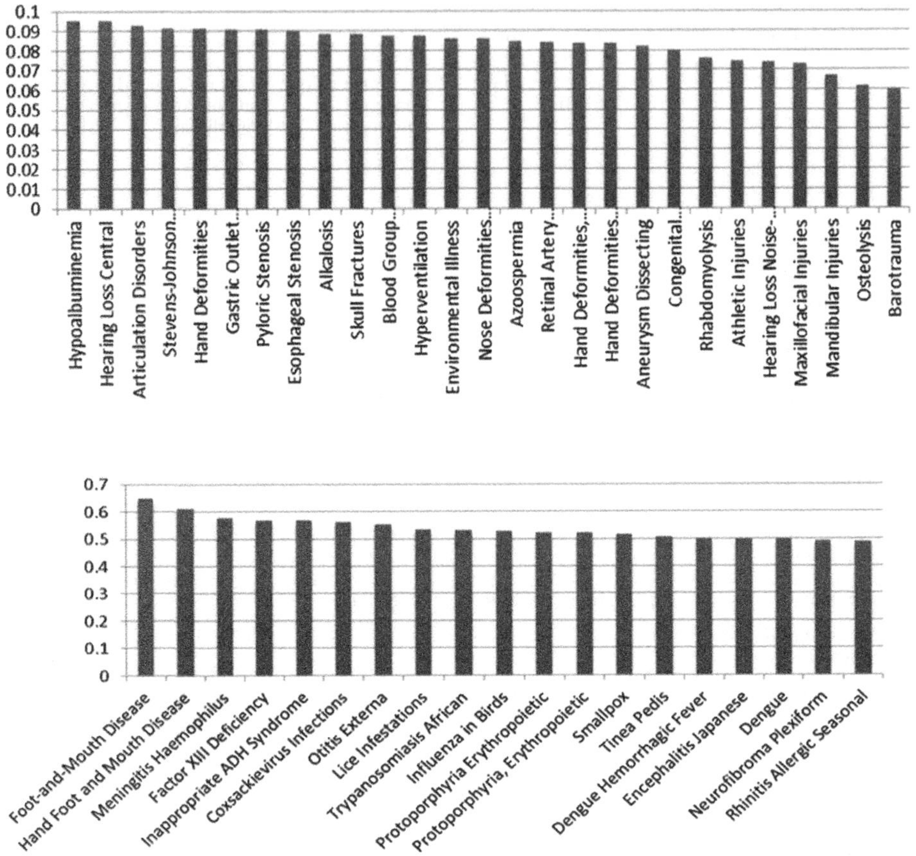

Fig. 2. (a) The ranking of the proportion of semantic concept sharing; (b) The ranking of the proportion of trials with at least 50 % semantic concepts shared.

how the clinical trials are connected and how the semantic concepts are shared. Taking "breast cancer" disease as an example, our approach automatically extracts all the semantic concepts in eligibility criteria text and generates a connection network for the disease, shown as Fig. 3. The yellow big nodes are clinical trials and small blue nodes are shared semantic concepts. The nodes of trials sharing same semantic concepts gather together. More concepts shared, more centralized of trials in the network. Moreover, it enables leaners to dynamically drag and drop to view the relations between concepts and trials and the detailed information as well as the detailed information of the concepts for helping them understand the commonly used eligibility criteria features in the design of a clinical trial. The network for "breast cancer" disease can be accessed from http://www.zhukun.org/haoty/resources.asp?id=network_breast_cancer.

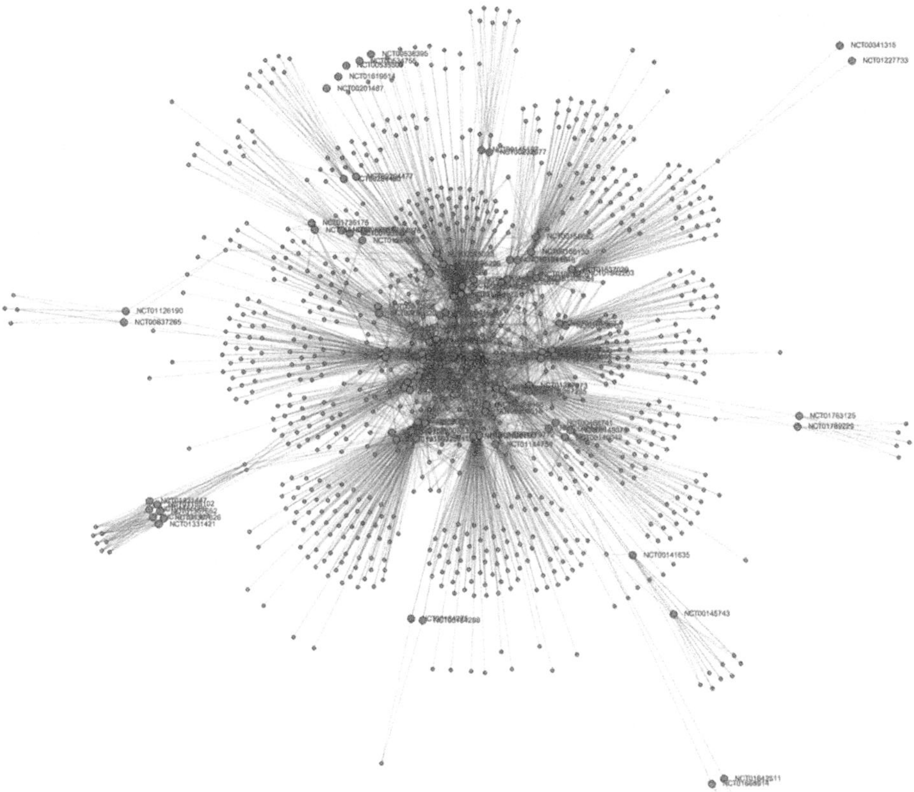

Fig. 3. The trial-concept visualization network help learners in understanding existing clinical trial design for breast cancer disease.

5 Summary

An automated approach is proposed to extract eligibility criteria semantic concepts from clinical trial texts for supporting learners in understanding clinical trial design. The approach identified commonly shared semantic concepts for specific diseases. Based on the 145,745 clinical trial texts obtained from ClinicalTrials.gov, our approach identified 5,508,491 semantic concepts with 459,936 being unique for 5,488 kinds of diseases. In the use case, we applied the approach to the semantic concept extraction for "breast cancer" disease and visualized a trial-concept sharing network for facilitating learners in understanding the design of clinical trials.

Acknowledgements. This work was supported by National Natural Science Foundation of China (grant No. 61403088).

References

1. Ross, J., Tu, S., Carini, S., Sim, I.: Analysis of eligibility criteria complexity in clinical trials. In: Proceedings of AMIA Summits on Translational Science 2010, pp. 46-50 (2010)
2. Vellas, B., Pesce, A., Robert, P.H., et al.: AMPA workshop on challenges faced by investigators conducting Alzheimer's disease clinical trials. Alzheimers Dement. **7**(4), e109–e117 (2011)
3. Campbell, M.K., Snowdon, C., Francis, D., et al.: Recruitment to randomised trials: strategies for trial enrollment and participation study. The STEPS study. Health Technol. Assess. **11**(48), iii, ix–105 (2007)
4. Tu, S.W., Peleg, M., Carini, S., et al.: A practical method for transforming free-text eligibility criteria into computable criteria. J. Biomed. Inform. **44**(2), 239–250 (2011)
5. Weng, C., Wu, X., Luo, Z., et al.: EliXR: an approach to eligibility criteria extraction and representation. J. Am. Med. Inform. Assoc. **18**(Suppl 1), i116–i124 (2011)
6. Milian, K., Bucur, A., Teije A.T.: Formalization of clinical trial eligibility criteria: Evaluation of a pattern-based approach. In: IEEE International Conference on Bioinformatics and Biomedicine, pp. 1–4 (2012)
7. Boland, M.R., Miotto, R., Gao, J., Weng, C.: Feasibility of feature-based indexing, clustering, and search of clinical trials. A case study of breast cancer trials from ClinicalTrials.gov. Methods Inf. Med. **52**(5), 382–394 (2013)
8. Manley, G.T., Diaz-Arrastia, R., Brophy, M., et al.: Common data elements for traumatic brain injury: recommendations from the interagency working group on demographics and clinical assessment. Arch. Phys. Med. Rehabil. **91**(11), 1641–1649 (2010)
9. National institute of health - NINDS Common Data Elements. http://www.ninds.nih.gov/research/clinical_research/toolkit/common_data_elements.htm. Accessed 2015
10. NINDS. http://www.commondataelements.ninds.nih.gov/projreview.aspx. Accessed 2015
11. Fink, E., Kokku, P.K., Nikiforou, S., et al.: Selection of patients for clinical trials: an interactive web-based system. Artif. Intell. Med. **31**, 241–254 (2004)
12. NerveCenter: NINDS common data element project: a long-awaited breakthrough in streamlining trials. Ann. Neurol. **68**(1), A11–A13 (2010)
13. Grinnon, S.T., Miller, K., Marler, J.R., et al.: National institute of neurological disorders and stroke common data element project - approach and methods. Clin. Trials **9**(3), 322–329 (2012)
14. Loring, D.W., Lowenstein, D.H., Barbaro, N.M., et al.: Common data elements in epilepsy research: development and implementation of the NINDS epilepsy FST project. Epilepsia **52**(6), 1186–1191 (2011)
15. Luo, Z., Miotto, R., Weng, C.: A human-computer collaborative approach to identifying common data elements in clinical trial eligibility criteria. J. Biomed. Inform. **46**, 33–39 (2013)
16. Miotto, R., Weng, C.: Unsupervised mining of frequent tags for clinical eligibility text indexing. J. Biomed. Inform. **46**(6), 1145–1151 (2013)
17. UMLS - Unified Medical Language System. http://www.nlm.nih.gov/research/umls/. Accessed 2015
18. Hao, T., Rusanov, A., Boland, M.R., Weng, C.: Clustering clinical trials with similar eligibility criteria features. J. Biomed. Inform. **52**, 112–120 (2014)
19. Lee-Smeltzer, K.H.: Finding the needle: controlled vocabularies, resource discovery, and Dublin Core. Libr. Collect. Acquis. Techn. Serv. **24**(2), 205–215 (2000)
20. Miotto, R., Jiang, S., Weng, C.: eTACTS: a method for dynamically filtering clinical trial search results. J. Biomed. Inform. **46**(6), 1060–1067 (2013)

21. Hao, T., Weng, C.: Adaptive semantic tag mining from heterogeneous clinical research texts. Methods Inf. Med. **54**(2), 164–170 (2015)
22. Extracting key phrases with NLTK in Python, GitHub Gist. https://gist.github.com/alexbowe/879414. Accessed 2015
23. The Stanford Parser: A statistical parser. http://nlp.stanford.edu/software/lex-parser.shtml. Accessed 2015

Strategies in Designing a Media Computing Course to Provide a Discovery-Enriched Curriculum to Students with Diverse Technical Background

Howard Leung[1(✉)] and Yang Yang[2]

[1] Department of Computer Science, City University of Hong Kong, Kowloon Tong, Hong Kong S.A.R
howard@cityu.edu.hk

[2] School of Computer Science and Communication Engineering, Jiangsu University, Zhenjiang, China
yyoung@ujs.edu.cn

Abstract. In this paper, we share our experience in designing a media computing course that aims to teach creative media students who had a diverse technical background. We describe several strategies in the course design and delivery that is aligned with our discovery enriched curriculum. Firstly, we designed the learning materials with visual content that is related to students' real life to stimulate their interest. Secondly, we catered for students' diverse background by designing learning tasks with different levels of difficulty. We also offered different means of help to the students in case they faced any problems. Our design of the learning and assessment tasks encouraged students to make self-discovery and innovation. An empirical study is conducted by analyzing the relationship between several factors for a selected group of students. The relationship between the students' homework grade and their attendance in the laboratory illustrates a positive trend, showing that students who attended our laboratory more often got better scores in the homework. Moreover, the relationship between students' homework grade and their quiz grade also illustrates a positive trend, showing that the design of our laboratory tasks was well aligned with the quiz assessments to help students master the concepts in this course such that we can adjust our focus to put more emphasis on certain topics based on the strength and weakness demonstrated by the students in the homework.

Keywords: Discovery enriched curriculum · Diverse background · Discovery and innovation · Experience sharing

1 Introduction

City University of Hong Kong has been adopting a discovery enriched curriculum (DEC) in developing teaching and learning activities since 2012. With DEC in mind, we would like our students to be able to make original discovery. The slogan of our university is Discover&Innovate@CityU® which clearly aligns with our university mission to nurture and develop the talents of students and to create applicable knowledge in order to support

F.W.B. Li et al. (Eds.): ICWL 2015, LNCS 9412, pp. 14–23, 2015.
DOI: 10.1007/978-3-319-25515-6_2

social and economic advancement. There are three key aspects that we would like our students to develop: attitude, ability and accomplishment. Our students have received a number of awards and generated some intellectual properties as a result of the DEC introduction (http://www.cityu.edu.hk/provost/dec/DEC_awards.htm).

In this paper, we shared our experience in devising strategies to deliver a discovery enriched curriculum in a media computing course. This course includes some programming elements for students to implement some media effects. It was found that a student's motivation and willingness to participate in learning activities is a major determining factor in his/her academic success [1]. As a result, we described how we designed our learning tasks to stimulate students' interest to keep them engaged in class. In fact, Regueras *et al.* examined students' motivation in learning programming in a competitive learning environment [2]. The e-learning communities have explored different aspects of teaching programming. Vesin *et al.* modeled the learners with a programming tutor system [3]. Watson *et al.* proposed to make use of concept visualization together with corrective feedback for students to learn programming in a game-like setting [4]. Hwang *et al.* focused on students' collaborative learning of programming through a web-based system [5]. Choy et al. proposed an automatic assessment system for correcting programming assignments [6]. A virtual education system with a lot of visual content has been implemented to teach C programming [7]. In our previous work [8], we have shared our experience in teaching webpage programming course by including a number of interesting demonstration webpages to be shown to the students in the lectures to ignite students' passion for knowledge and motivate them to come to the lectures. In this paper, we shared our experience in teaching another course on media computing to students with diverse technical background.

This paper is organized as follows. In Sect. 2, we will introduce our course and state our strategies in designing this course to align with our discovery enriched curriculum. In Sect. 3, we include an empirical study to analyze different factors in evaluating some aspects on the design of our course. The conclusion and future work are described in Sect. 4.

2 Course Design and Delivery

In this paper, we would like to share our experience in designing a course that was taken by first year students. It is an introduction course about media computing offered by the Department of Computer Science. On the other hand, this course is offered to our students studying in creative media so many of them do not have strong technical background. It is thus a challenge to design this course to stimulate students' interest and to suit students with diverse background such that students are able to implement some media computing techniques through writing some simple programs. We have developed several strategies towards achieving this goal and they are described in the following subsections.

2.1 Designing Visual Content Related to Real-Life Examples

The course spans a duration of 13 weeks. Every week there are 2 hours of lecture and 2 hours of laboratory. The assessment tasks consisted of 2 individual homework, 1 quiz and 1 group project. Most of our course is focused on two media types: image and audio. We designed the course content to include examples that are closely related to students' real life in order to provide them better motivation to learn about the subject.

For images, we provided HTML5 code to illustrate image manipulation techniques such as color-to-gray conversion, brightness adjustment, flipping and rotation, etc. HTML5 was used because students had already learnt it in the previous semester on web programming. Many students already had experience with Photoshop to manipulate images. In this course we would like to show students how some of these functions can be implemented in practice. In the first homework, students were asked to implement some image effects. They were asked to work with the portrait images containing their own faces since nowadays many students like to take selfies and apply various image effects with their mobile phones. By asking them to work with their own photos, we would like to motivate students to work on the homework to implement the image effects by themselves and get more attached to the interesting results. For example, one of the homework tasks is to identify the centerline of the face region and then flipping the left part of the face horizontally and pasting it to the right part of the face to construct a symmetric face as shown in Fig. 1.

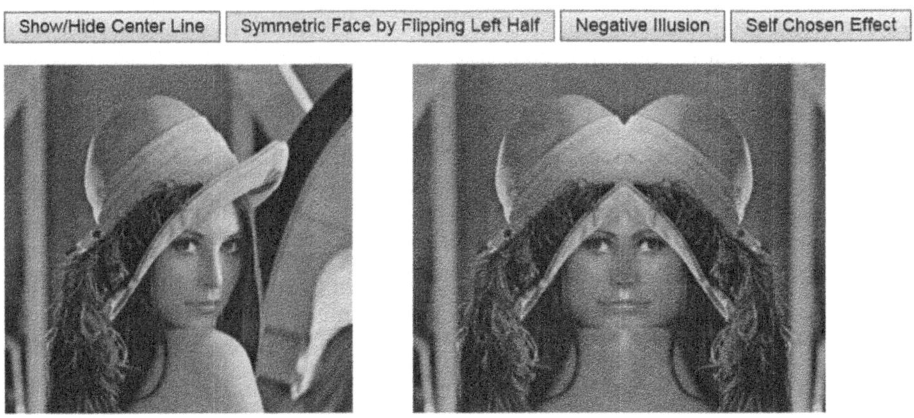

Fig. 1. One of the first homework tasks to construct a symmetric face.

For audio, we used Web Audio API to demonstrate the implementation of various sound effects because it is easy to load an audio file and do some low-level processing by manipulating individual audio samples. With Web Audio API, some javascript code was shown to the students to illustrate how simple audio processing can be implemented such as changing loudness, changing playback speed, fade in/out etc. In one of the laboratory, the tasks were designed to let students simulate a touch tone keypad. First a graphical interface of a mobile phone illustrated in Fig. 2 was provided to the students. They were then guided to implement the touch tone for each key by applying dual-tone multi-frequency signaling, i.e., generating two sinusoids of specific frequencies corresponding to each key. In this way, they were able to create the touch tones similar to the real-life case as if they are pressing a key in their touch tone phone. These touch tones together with dial tone, ring tone and busy tone are introduced in the laboratory such that students can implement these familiar sounds on their own.

Fig. 2. Graphical interface of the second homework to work with touch tones.

2.2 Catering for Students with Diverse Background

As mentioned before, the students in this course were in their first year with diverse technical background. Prior to entering university, some students already had taken some courses in multimedia and programming. On the other hand, some students may have taken information and communication technology while other students had only taken art subjects without any previous experience on computer related subjects. Given the diverse background of students, it is a challenge to design the course content regarding the level of difficulty. If the course content is too difficult, then students with little technical background would not be able to catch up. On the other hand, if the course content is too easy, then students with strong technical background would feel too bored.

The laboratory tasks were designed to cater for students with diverse background. They consist of basic tasks that are relatively easy as well as some more challenging tasks that are optional. During the laboratory, students were given time to solve each basic task. The lab tutor would walk through the solution of the basic task with the students after a while. Students who finished the basic tasks early were asked to carry on to work on the next tasks and continued to do the optional tasks if they finished all the basic tasks. In this way, all students can make accomplishments to a level depending on their abilities. For example, during one of the laboratories, students were asked to add rectangular borders on an image to create the collage effect. The basic task assumes that the rectangular borders are upright so that they do not need to consider rotation (Fig. 3 left) while the optional task asks students to come up with the rotated rectangular borders which correspond to a much more challenging task (Fig. 3 right).

On the other hand, the homework was designed to be an extension of the laboratory tasks. As a result, students who had attended the laboratory sessions should be able to complete the basic tasks of the homework by putting together what they had done from the laboratory. In other words, the laboratory was a preparation step towards other assessment tasks such as homework and quiz.

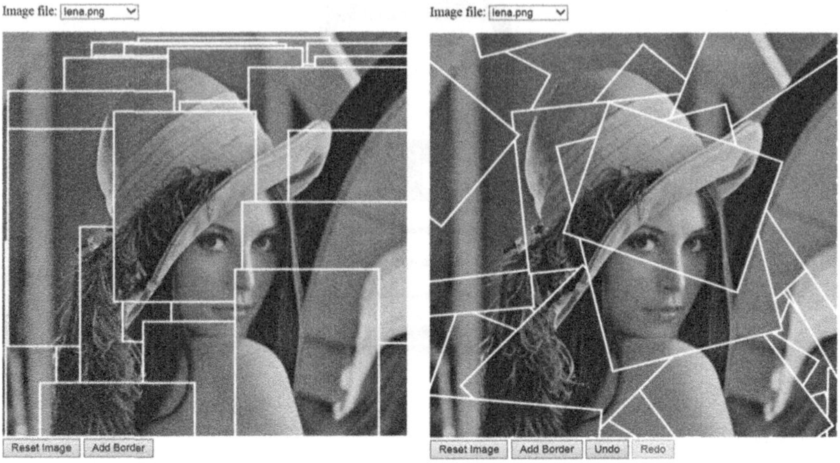

Fig. 3. Outcome from a basic task (left) and an optional task (right) in one laboratory.

2.3 Offering Different Means to Help Students

It is inevitable that students may have questions about the course work. As a result, it is important to provide support to help students in this case. In this course, different means of help were available to support the students. During the laboratory sessions, the lab tutor and the teaching assistant would go around the class to check with the students if they had any problems and answer their questions. Students were asked to form groups during the laboratory to solve problems and work on the project. The classroom where the laboratory was held has chairs equipped with wheels that facilitate students moving them around to form groups quickly. In this setting, students could also get help from their peers which is preferred by most students. During the classes, the instructor also kept reminding the students that they could contact him after class in case they had any questions. The course webpage also includes a discussion board feature where students could post questions for the instructor to answer. In the second homework, one question is posed as follows:

Whenever you have problems in your program, you may have asked your classmate(s). In addition to this option, do you know that there are also other options, for example,

- *Check and post your questions on the discussion board in the Canvas course page?*
- *Ask the instructor/tutor/teaching assistant during or after class?*
- *Schedule an appointment with the instructor and ask him questions and the instructor will be very happy to help you?*
- *Review the related materials from CS1303 which you should have learnt?*

The above question aims to remind students about their options for seeking help in case they face problems in this course.

2.4 Encouraging Students to Discover and Innovate

The slogan of our university is to Discover and Innovate, which indicates what we would like our students to achieve. In the design of this course, students were encouraged to make discovery on their own and be innovative. Near the end of each laboratory session, each group was given some time for them to discuss about issues related to what they had learnt in that class and then they would give a presentation in front of the class. Students were also asked to provide self-reflections about what they had learnt in each homework. For the project, each group is required to describe what the group members have learnt and discovered throughout this project. They were asked to demonstrate their critical thinking by considering various issues such that what problems or challenges they had encountered, how they overcame the difficulties, how they made adjustments and derived the solution, what kind of learning experience they would like to share, etc. From these self-reflections, students can realize better what they have discovered through different learning tasks. For example, one student wrote about her discovery from the first homework: "*I think this homework is the advance level of all lab exercise. I can modify the code which we learned during the lesson. But I try to find another ways to finish the coding. For example, I use the if-else statement instead of Boolean statement to show center line.*"

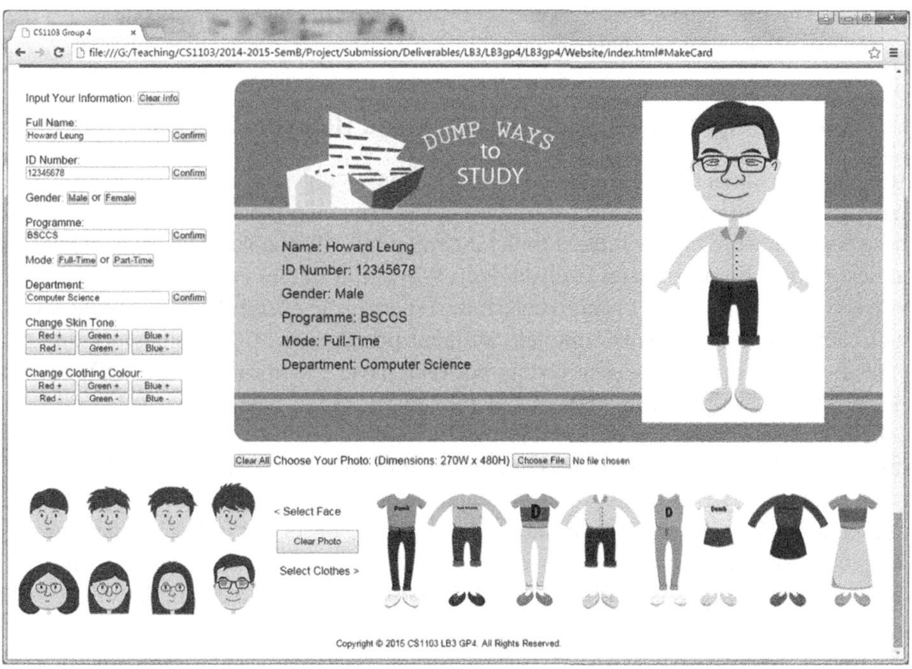

Fig. 4. A group project in the form of a webpage demonstrating creativity.

In each homework, students were asked to come up with their own creative effects. There was a lot of freedom in this task. Some students explored on their own to create interesting media effects. Those students could not come up with novel ideas still could finish this part by putting together the effects that they had learnt in the class. For the project, each group was asked to include any innovative ideas or creative aspects that the group has put into this project. In particular, they were asked to state how their work is different from existing similar webpages/products/platforms and emphasize about the novel aspects of their work. For example, one project group has come up with a creative idea and applied the media computing techniques to implement a webpage that lets the user to have a student card like layout with customized photos and text as illustrated in Fig. 4.

3 Empirical Study

In the course described in this paper, the students were divided into 7 laboratory sessions which are co-taught by 3 lab tutors, with the first author being one of them. The first author has selected two laboratory sessions that were taught by himself for the empirical study reported here. Altogether there were 53 students in these 2 sessions. As mentioned previously, these students had diverse technical background as some of them had taken multimedia and programming subjects before whereas some other students may not have taken science subjects during their senior secondary school. In this study, we mainly examine 3 factors: (1) students' attendance rate during the laboratory sessions; (2) their homework grade; and (3) their quiz grade.

3.1 Relationship Between Attendance Rate and Homework Grade

Attendance is taken during each laboratory session. In this study we counted how many times the students were present during Week 4–11 since the laboratory tasks during these 8 weeks were highly related to the 2 homework. On the other hand, we added the grades of the 2 homework for each student. We would like to examine the relationship between these 2 factors in order to determine whether the design of our laboratory tasks could actually help students complete a higher percentage of the homework and thus achieve a better grade. The relationship between these 2 factors is plotted and shown in Fig. 5. In Fig. 5, the x-axis indicates 4 homework grade categories: [0,15], [15-20], [20,25], [25,30]. Note that each of the two homework carries a maximum of 15 marks thus the sum of the two homework grade has a maximum of 30. Under each of these grade categories, we take the average attendance among students from Week 4–11 (thus a maximum of 8) and show it in the y-axis. It can be observed in Fig. 5 that there is a clear increasing trend showing a positive correlation between these 2 factors. The result shows that in general as students attended more laboratory sessions, they had better performance in their homework. A possible explanation of this trend is that our laboratory task design was effective that it was guiding students to accomplish their homework. One may also argue that better students may attend the classes more often and they may do well in the homework simply because they are better students. We agree that this is true for some students who were already good, on the other hand, we also observed that many students who attended the classes had weak technical background thus it is still beneficial for students to attend the laboratory and get better grade. However, we also believe that we should not force students' attendance by imposing any absence penalty. This is because we believe that although it is important for students to attend classes so that they can learn better, it is also as important for students to learn to be responsible for their own choices and actions. This is the attitude that we would like to train our students in addition to their ability and accomplishment.

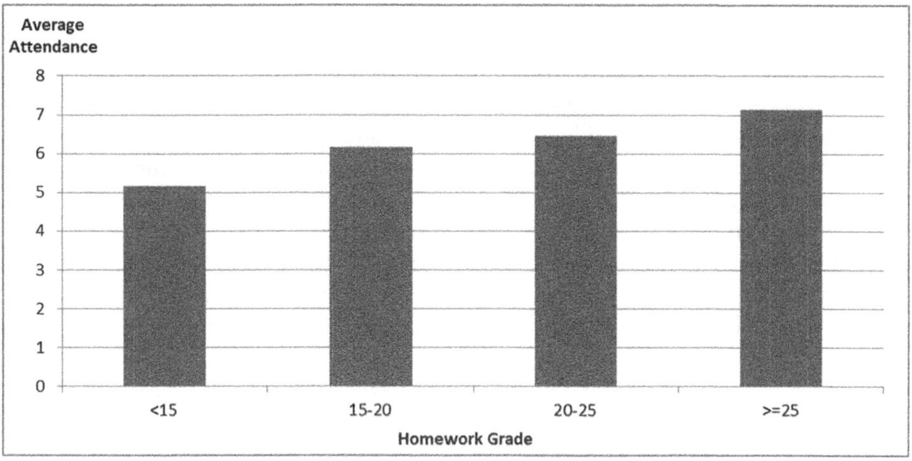

Fig. 5. Relationship between students' homework grade and average attendance during Week 4–11

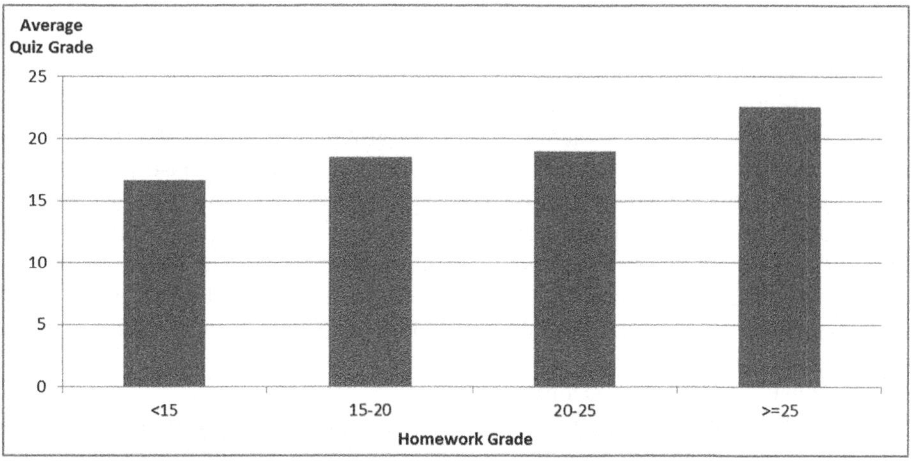

Fig. 6. Relationship between students' homework grade and average quiz grade

3.2 Relationship Between Homework Grade and Quiz Grade

At the end of the semester, the students were given a quiz to test their concepts. The quiz consists of 60 multiple choice questions and students had 1.5 hours to work on it. Each question carries 0.5 mark thus the maximum grade of the quiz is 30 marks. The relationship between the homework grade and the quiz grade is examined to determine if the homework tasks helped students understand the concepts covered by this course. The relationship between these 2 factors is shown in Fig. 6. In Fig. 6, the x-axis is the same as the one in Fig. 5, i.e., the 4 homework grade categories. Under each homework grade category, the quiz grade for those students is averaged and shown in the y-axis. It can be observed in Fig. 6 that there is a positive relationship between the homework grade and the quiz grade, meaning that in general students who got better scores in the homework also performed better in the quiz. The result illustrates that the design of our homework tasks was well aligned with the assessment tasks from the quiz. The homework scores can thus be considered as good continuous assessment indicators to predict the students' performance at the end of the course such that we can adjust the focus to put more emphasis on the concepts with which the students are weak. This will help students accomplish more at the end of the course and enhance their learning experience.

4 Conclusion and Future Work

In this paper, we have shared our experience in designing a media computing course that aims to teach creative media students who had a diverse technical background. We have shown several strategies in the course design and delivery that is aligned with our discovery enriched curriculum. Firstly, we designed the learning materials with visual content that is related to students' real-life to stimulate their interest. Secondly, we catered for students' diverse background by designing learning tasks with different levels of difficulty. We also offered different means of help to the students in case they faced any problems. Our design of the learning and assessment tasks encouraged students to make self-discovery and innovation. We have made an empirical study by analyzing the relationship between several factors in a focus group. The relationship between the students' homework grade and their attendance in the laboratory illustrates a positive trend, showing that students who attended our laboratory more often got better scores in the homework. Moreover, the relationship between students' homework grade and their quiz grade also illustrates a positive trend, suggesting that the design of our laboratory tasks was well aligned with the quiz assessments to help students better master the concepts in this course. We could thus look at the strength and weakness demonstrated by the students in the homework tasks and adjust our subsequent teaching focus to help students make better accomplishments.

One problem that we observed in teaching this course was that some students did not want to take this course but felt that they were forced to take it because it is a compulsory course. As a result, they were not too motivated to learn despite our efforts in designing this course with a lot of interesting content. In the future, we can work with the program leaders to see if we can devise a better way to deliver the message to the students that this course is a fundamental step in their programme and it is crucial for students to learn the programming techniques so that they can handle the courses in their senior years. On the other hand, we will keep an open mind about how to adopt other strategies in this course and explore other factors to enhance the learning experience of the students while following a discovery-enriched curriculum.

References

1. Robey, M., von Konsky, B.R., Ivins, J., Gribble, S.J., Loh, A., Cooper, S.: Student self-motivation: lessons learned from teaching first year computing. In: 36th Annual Frontiers in Education Conference, pp.6–11 (2006)
2. Regueras, L.M., Verdú, E., Verdú, M.J., Pérez, M.Á., de Castro, J.P., Muñoz, M.F.: Motivating students through on-line competition: an analysis of satisfaction and learning styles. In: Li, F., Zhao, J., Shih, T.K., Lau, R., Li, Q., McLeod, D. (eds.) ICWL 2008. LNCS, vol. 5145, pp. 167–177. Springer, Heidelberg (2008)
3. Vesin, B., Ivanović, M., Klašnja-Milićević, A., Budimac, Z.: Rule-based reasoning for building learner model in programming tutoring system. In: Leung, H., Popescu, E., Cao, Y., Lau, R.W., Nejdl, W. (eds.) ICWL 2011. LNCS, vol. 7048, pp. 154–163. Springer, Heidelberg (2011)
4. Watson, C., Li, F.W., Lau, R.W.: Learning programming languages through corrective feedback and concept visualisation. In: Leung, H., Popescu, E., Cao, Y., Lau, R.W., Nejdl, W. (eds.) ICWL 2011. LNCS, vol. 7048, pp. 11–20. Springer, Heidelberg (2011)
5. Hwang, W.-Y., Shadiev, R., Wang, C.-Y., Huang, J.-H.: A pilot study of cooperative programming learning behavior and its relationship with students' learning performance. Comput. Educ. **58**(4), 1267–1281 (2012)
6. Choy, M., Lam, S., Poon, C.K., Wang, F.L., Yu, Y.T., Yuen, L.: Design and implementation of an automated system for assessment of computer programming assignments. In: Leung, H., Li, F., Lau, R., Li, Q. (eds.) ICWL 2007. LNCS, vol. 4823, pp. 584–596. Springer, Heidelberg (2008)
7. Moon, I., Han, S., Choi, K., Kim, D.S., Jeon, C.W., Lee, S., Jeon, H.: Virtual education system for the c programming language. In: Li, F., Zhao, J., Shih, T.K., Lau, R., Li, Q., McLeod, D. (eds.) ICWL 2008. LNCS, vol. 5145, pp. 196–207. Springer, Heidelberg (2008)
8. Leung, H., Li, Z., Zhao, J.: Igniting students' passion for knowledge by incorporating a discovery enriched curriculum. In: Wang, J.-F., Lau, R. (eds.) ICWL 2013. LNCS, vol. 8167, pp. 79–88. Springer, Heidelberg (2013)

Collaborative and Peer Learning

Closing the Circle: Use of Students' Responses for Peer-Assessment Rubric Improvement

Yang Song(✉), Zhewei Hu, and Edward F. Gehringer

Department of Computer Science, North Carolina State University, Raleigh, NC, USA
{ysong8, zhu6, efg}@ncsu.edu

Abstract. Educational peer assessment has proven to be a useful approach for providing students timely feedback and allowing them to help and learn from each other. Reviewers are often expected both to provide formative feedback—textual feedback telling the authors where and how to improve the artifact—and peer grading at the same time. Formative feedback is important for the authors because timely and insightful feedback can help them improve their artifacts, and peer grading is important to the teaching staff, as it provides more input to help determine final grades. In a large class or MOOC when the help from teaching staff is limited, formative feedback from their peers is the best help that the authors may receive. To guarantee the quality of the formative feedback and reliability of peer grading, instructors should keep on improving peer-assessment rubrics. In this study we used students' feedback from the last 3 years in the Expertiza peer-assessment system to analyze the quality of 15 existing rubrics on 61 assignments. A set of patterns on peer-grading reliability and comment length were found and a set of guidelines are given accordingly.

Keywords: Educational peer-review · Review rubric · Peer assessment

1 Introduction

Providing timely formative and summative feedback on students' work is crucial to students' success in a course. Feedback is traditionally provided by teaching staff alone; however, it is only with great dedication and conscientiousness that feedback can have a real impact on students' learning process [1].

Peer assessment serves as an alternative to feedback from teaching staff, and it has several well-known advantages: students have better chance to receive timely feedback, and their understanding levels also improve from giving feedback to their peers [2, 3]. Peer assessment also frees the teaching staff of some of the burden of grading and giving feedback to the students. The time saved by peer assessment may not be appealing enough for small or medium-size class settings, but for large classes and MOOCs, tremendous time can be saved for teaching staff.

One of the daunting aspects of designing a course which supports peer assessment is to design or find an appropriate assessment rubric. In educational settings, a rubric is commonly defined as a "document that articulates the expectations for an assignment by listing the criteria or what counts, and describing levels of quality from excellent to

F.W.B. Li et al. (Eds.): ICWL 2015, LNCS 9412, pp. 27–36, 2015.
DOI: 10.1007/978-3-319-25515-6_3

poor" [4]. Rubrics are believed to be powerful tools for "evaluating and providing guidance" [5]. Recent research has also shown that they can help students understand the goals of assignments [6], provide student authors timely feedback [7] and motivate students to engage more fully in homework [8].

Instructors typically create their own peer-assessment rubrics. As mentioned above, these rubrics are frequently used to provide formative and summative assessment. These qualities of rubrics (e.g. rating reliability and validity, length and tone of comments) are rarely evaluated in the context where they are used.

To test and improve the quality of peer-assessment rubrics, a iterative process should be modeled (Fig. 1). The first stage, *rubric design*, is to create a peer-assessment rubric with the instructors' best knowledge and skill. After a new version of the rubric is ready, an instructor can *deploy it to an online learning management system* (LMS, e.g. Expertiza [9], Coursera [10]) and associate it with online assessment tasks. After one or several task is finished, *data collection* can be done on both formative and summative responses. In *lexical and data analysis*, the students' responses on each rubric criteria are analyzed with statistical and natural language processing techniques. The result can be used by instructors to revise peer-assessment rubrics and the new versions can be deployed again to the LMS.

The short-term product of this iterative process is a set of empirical guidelines on creating peer-assessment rubrics. This paper reports on a pilot study that attempts to "close the circle" and analyze the quality of existing peer-assessment rubrics. We focused our efforts on finding what types of criteria and rubrics have more formative-feedback value and higher peer-grading reliability.

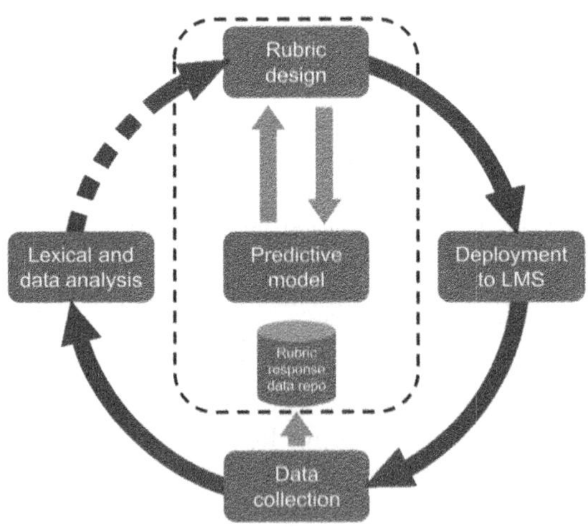

Fig. 1. Rubric improvement cycle

In the long-term, we hope to build a *predictive model* that can be used to predict the feedback validity, peer-grading reliability and overall quality of a peer-assessment rubric even before it is used by any students.

2 Background and Methodology

In this section we provide an overview of our project, including the data set, definitions of different types of criteria and measures used.

2.1 Class Settings

Our data set is generated by students using Expertiza, which is a web-based system developed to facilitate peer assessment on student-generated course content [9].

Sixty-one assignments were used in this research. All of them were from the past 3 academic years (fall 2012–spring 2015) in the NC State University College of Engineering. There were 2 main types of assignments: 10 programming assignments and 51 writing assignments. The programming assignments required students to submit their code; peer assessment focused mainly on functional testing, code review and design patterns. The writing assignments required students to submit their own writings, which could be wiki textbook chapters, case analysis essays or design documentations. The peer assessment tasks for writing assignments focused on a variety of aspects which could help determine the quality of the artifacts, including originality, structure, use of language and examples, etc.

There were 592 students who finished these assignments (490 graduates and 102 undergraduates). Students who dropped the courses were excluded from the data set. According to the syllabi, students were required to do small numbers (for example, 2) of peer assessments for each assignment; however, students were able to request more artifacts to review for extra credits. The instructor could also set a maximum number of peer assessments for each artifact to prevent authors from being overwhelmed by large numbers of reviews.

When doing each peer assessment, students reviewers filled out a peer-assessment rubric. Most of the criteria in these rubrics allowed reviewers to give both textual feedback and Likert-scale scores. Fifteen different peer-assessment rubrics were used in these assignments. More than 200,000 students' responses on different criteria were collected for this research.

2.2 Types of Rubric Criterion

To facilitate later analysis on which kind of criteria are more suitable for educational peer assessment task, we tagged the peer assessment criteria as one of three types: true/false criteria, focused criteria and verification criteria.

True/false criteria can simply be answered "yes" or "no". However, reviewers can add a text response in Expertiza. *Focused criteria* are the ones that require the peer-reviewers to rate and comment on one aspect. The criteria which are not focused are called broad criteria in this paper. *Verification criteria* are the ones that require the peer reviewer to look for specific feature from the artifact and this can be done without having full understanding of the artifacts. The criteria which are not verification criteria are called appraisal criteria in this paper. Table 1 gives examples of those criteria.

Table 1. Examples of different types of criteria

T/F criteria	Focused criteria	Verification criteria
● Is the organization of page(s) logical? ● Is the problem relevant to the material covered in class?	● List any sources that may infringe copyrights. ● What other sources or perspectives might the author want to consider?	● Can an admin assign admin rights to a user? Can an admin delete other users and other admins? ● Does the write-up clearly indicate how to run the project or the tests?

2.3 Measures of Criterion and Rubric Quality

When designing a peer assessment task, instructors are primarily concerned with two issues: validity and reliability.

Validity refers to whether the rubric is measuring what it is supposed to measure. In the context of student peer assessment, this means whether scores given by student peer reviewers are consistent with the grades given by the teaching staff, which is often called "ground truth" [11]. This paper does not consider validity because for part of our data set, the ground truth data was not available, or staff grading was not done by exactly following the rubrics.

Intra-rater reliability—the consistency of grading on the same artifact by the same rater—was not calculated because students cannot review the same artifact twice on Expertiza. Inter-rater reliability refers to the consistency of grades from different reviewers on the same artifact. Two categories of inter-rater reliabilities were used in this paper: agreement and consistency.

Two types of agreements are calculated: exact agreement and adjacent agreement. *Exact agreement* is defined as whether a given grade on an artifact on one criterion is exactly the same as the median on the same artifact on the same criterion. *Adjacent agreement* is defined as a grade within a range of [–1, +1] of the median on the same artifact on the same criterion.

Two types of consistencies were used to measure the grading reliability between one peer assessment and all the peer assessments on the same artifact (using the median): Pearson correlation coefficient and Spearman's Rho.

3 Grading Agreements and Comment Lengths on Each Criterion Type

In this section we investigated the length of the students' text comments, and grading agreement on different types of criteria. We hoped to answer these research questions:

- Do average comment lengths differ between criterion types, or assignment types, or between levels of students (graduate vs. undergraduate)?
- If so, which criterion types have longer comments, and which types have shorter comments?

- Does the percentage of students grading agreements differ between criterion types, or assignment types, or between levels of students (graduate vs. undergraduate)?
- If so, which criterion types have higher agreement percentages, and which types have lower agreement percentages?

3.1 Comment Lengths on Each Criterion Type

We used Student's *t*-test to compare the averages of the independent samples of comment lengths from 3 different criterion types. Our hypotheses are:

H0a: there is no significant difference on the comment length between true/false criteria and non-true/false criteria.
H1a: there is significant difference on the comment length between true/false criteria and non-true/false criteria.
H0b, H1b, H0c and H1c are similar hypotheses but for focused criteria and verification criteria.

We discarded all the empty comments and only used the rest for the tests. From the data analysis in Table 2, all the *p* values are smaller than 0.01, which means that the populations of comment length between each pairs (true/false and non-true/false, focused and broad, verification and appraisal) were different. Those *p*-values, together with the average comment lengths suggested that the true-false criteria, focused criteria and verification criteria may lead to lower average comment lengths.

Table 2. Comparison on comment lengths on each criterion type

	# responses	# responses w/lengths > 0	Avg. comment length	Standard deviation	P value
TF	135763	79945	8.07	11.51	**<0.001**
Non-TF	64669	22139	9.12	12.26	
Focused	146850	70742	7.46	10.65	**<0.001**
Broad	53582	31342	9.08	12.62	
Verification	27505	16641	6.73	10.57	**<0.001**
Appraisal	172927	85443	8.74	11.92	

We further separated the assignments by student levels (graduate or undergraduate) and assignment types (writing or programming). Table 3 shows the statistical results.

From the left part of Table 3 we found that for most of the criterion types, the undergraduate students tended to give more comment than graduate students in most cases, which indicates that in this sample, the undergraduate students tended to give more formative feedback. From the right side of Table 3 we found that artifacts in writing and programming assignments received longer comments on different criterion types. In writing assignment, true/false criteria, focused criteria tended to receive longer comments; in programming assignments verification criteria tended to receive longer comments.

Table 3. Comparison on comment lengths on each criterion type by assignment types

	Stu. level	Avg. comment length	P value	Assgt. type	Avg. comment length	P value
TF	Ugrd.	9.56	**<0.001**	Prgmg.	4.13	**<0.001**
	Grad.	4.77		Writing	6.91	
Non-TF	Ugrd.	N/A	N/A	Prgmg.	5.26	**<0.001**
	Grad.	4.67		Writing	3.14	
Focused	Ugrd.	9.64	**<0.001**	Prgmg.	3.17	**<0.001**
	Grad.	3.80		Writing	6.82	
Broad	Ugrd.	5.06	**<0.001**	Prgmg.	5.78	**<0.001**
	Grad.	5.90		Writing	6.12	
Verification	Ugrd.	N/A	N/A	Prgmg.	4.22	**<0.001**
	Grad.	4.07		Writing	2.44	
Appraisal	Ugrd.	9.56	**<0.001**	Prgmg.	4.34	**<0.001**
	Grad.	5.06		Writing	6.83	

The reason for the "N/A"s in this table is that there was no non-true/false and verification criteria used in any peer-assessment rubric in undergraduate assignments.

3.2 Grading Agreements on Each Criterion Type

We used Student's *t*-test to compare the averages of the independent samples of aggregated grading agreements on each assignment. Our hypotheses are:

H0a: there is no significant difference on the percentages of average adjacent grading agreement between true/false criteria and non-true/false criteria.
H1a: there is significant difference on the percentages of average adjacent grading agreement between true/false criteria and non-true/false criteria.
H0b: there is no significant difference on the percentages of average exact grading agreement between true/false criteria and non-true/false criteria.
H1b: there is significant difference on the percentages of average exact grading agreement between true/false criteria and non-true/false criteria.

The data analysis in Table 4 shows that there are significant differences between each pair on both adjacent and exact measures, except for focused and broad criteria on adjacent agreements. Most of the adjacent agreements are above 90 % and most of the exact agreements are above 70 %, which means the more than 90 % of the grades given by student raters on Expertiza were within the –1 to +1 range of the median grades, and more than 70 % of them gave exactly the same grades as the medians. This is an ideal result meaning most of the student raters on Expertiza did reliable peer assessments. The criterion type which had the lowest agreement level was verification criterion, which was a little surprising. We explored further into the data set and found that "courteous grading" was the reason: the raters, even found the feature asked for in the criterion was missing from the artifact, might not give a 0, but more likely to give a 2 or 3 out of 5. This was also the reason that the agreement levels for true/false criteria were lower than non-true/false criteria.

Table 4. Comparision on grading agreements on each criterion type

	Avg. adjacent agrmt %	Standard deviation	P value	Avg. exactagrmt. %	Standard deviation	P value
TF	0.91	0.065	**<0.001**	0.74	0.13	**0.009**
Non-TF	0.95	0.057		0.79	0.15	
Focused	0.92	0.064	0.063	0.76	0.13	**0.013**
Broad	0.91	0.066		0.72	0.14	
Verification	0.89	0.085	**<0.001**	0.72	0.16	**0.048**
Appraisal	0.93	0.056		0.75	0.13	

We further separated the assignments by student levels (graduate or undergraduate) and assignment types (writing or programming). Table 5 shows the results.

Table 5. Comparison on grading agreements on each criterion type by assignment types

	Stu. level	Avg. adjacent agrmt %	P value	Avg. exactagrmt %	P value	Assgt. type	Avg. adjacentagrmt %	P value	Avg. exactagrmt %	P value
TF	Ugrd.	0.90	0.076	0.74	0.977	Prgmg.	0.89	**<0.001**	0.69	**<0.001**
	Grad.	0.92		0.74		Writing	0.93		0.77	
Non-TF	Ugrd.	N/A	N/A	N/A	N/A	Prgmg.	0.9	**<0.001**	0.66	**<0.001**
	Grad.	0.95		0.79		Writing	0.97		0.85	
Focused	Ugrd.	0.90	**0.001**	0.73	0.131	Prgmg.	0.90	**<0.001**	0.70	**<0.001**
	Grad.	0.93		0.77		Writing	0.94		0.79	
Broad	Ugrd.	0.90	0.835	0.82	0.317	Prgmg.	0.88	**<0.001**	0.67	**<0.001**
	Grad.	0.91		0.72		Writing	0.94		0.77	
Verification	Ugrd.	N/A	N/A	N/A	N/A	Prgmg.	0.87	**<0.001**	0.68	**0.002**
	Grad.	0.89		0.72		Writing	0.96		0.81	
Appraisal	Ugrd.	0.90	**<0.001**	0.74	0.31	Prgmg.	0.90	**<0.001**	0.69	**<0.001**
	Grad.	0.93		0.76		Writing	0.94		0.79	

The reason for the "N/A" in this table is that there was no non-true/false and verification criteria used in any peer-assessment rubric in undergraduate assignments.

From Table 5 we found that the grading agreement (both adjacent and exact) between undergraduates and graduates was not significantly different for most criterion types. We also found that for all criterion types, the agreements on writing assignments were higher than programming assignment.

4 Which Factors Can Influence Average Grading Reliability

We used the Pearson correlation coefficient and Spearman's Rho as measurements of peer-grading reliability between each rater's grade and the median grade on the same artifact. We further aggregated the reliability on each reviewer on the same artifact and got the overall peer-grading reliability on each assignment. The distributions of Pearson correlation coefficient and Spearman's Rho are shown in Fig. 2.

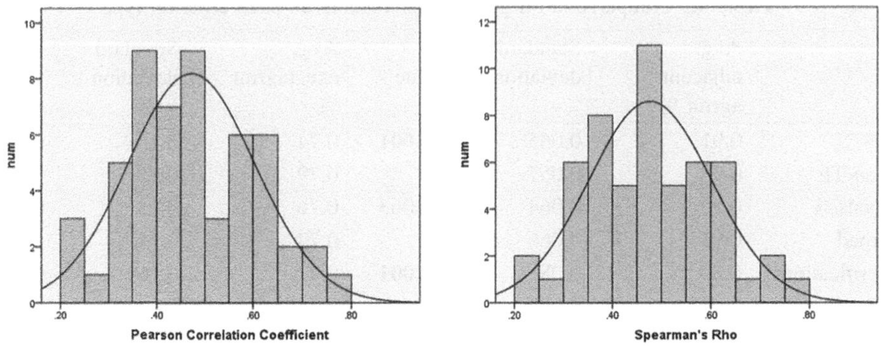

Fig. 2. Distributions of peer-grading reliability measures on all assignments

The average reliabilities of the grading done on Expertiza in past 3 academic years was close to 0.5, which means that peer-grading is moderately dispersed around the median. To determine which factor may influence the overall peer-grading reliability, we applied data analysis to answer the following research questions:

- Does the number of criteria influence the reliability of peer grading?
- Do the percentages of certain criterion type influence the grading reliability?
- If there are such patterns, do they hold for both undergraduates and graduates?
- If there are such patterns, do they hold for both programming and writing assignments?

We applied linear regression to test the influence of number of criteria, the percentages of different types of criteria on the overall peer-grading reliabilities of each assignment. The statistical results are shown in Table 6.

Table 6. Influence of Different Factors on Peer-Grading Reliability

	Pearson			Spearman		
	Ustd. beta	Sig.	Constant	Ustd. beta	Sig.	Constant
Criterion num	–0.012	**0.001**	0.606	–0.011	**0.001**	0.601
TF %	0.114	0.126	0.393	0.100	0.163	0.407
Focused%	–0.043	0.433	0.500	–0.042	0.419	0.504
Verification%	–0.160	0.093	0.487	–0.181	**0.045**	0.493

Table 6 shows that the number of criteria has a negative influence on peer-grading reliability. The unstandardized beta is more than 1 %, which means that, in our data set, with one more criterion added to the rubric, the expected drop in reliability was more than 1 %. Another interesting observation is that the constant value of reliability is roughly 60 %, which means that the expected peer-grading reliability, when there are 1 rubric criterion, is 59.4 % (60.6 %-1.2 % on Pearson correlation coefficient). However, we did not have data to validate this, as there were at least 5 rubric criteria in all our rubrics. Another observation is that the percentage of verification criteria may hinder the reliability. The reason was "courteous grading," as discussed above.

We further separated the assignments by student level (graduate or undergraduate) and assignment type (writing or programming). Table 7 shows the analysis results.

Table 7. Influence of Different Factors on Grading Reliability by Assignment Types

		Pearson		Spearman			Pearson		Spearman	
	Stu. level	Ustd. beta	Sig.	Ustd. beta	Sig.	Assgt. type	Ustd. beta	Sig.	Ustd. beta	Sig.
Criterion num	Ugrd.	–0.005	0.677	–0.004	0.687	Prgmg.	–0.004	0.678	–0.003	0.726
	Grad.	–0.010	**0.007**	–0.009	**0.009**	Writing	–0.012	**0.001**	–0.012	**0.001**
TF %	Ugrd.	0.098	0.677	0.084	0.687	Prgmg.	0.445	0.394	0.292	0.499
	Grad.	0.020	0.814	0.012	0.886	Writing	0.167	**0.031**	0.156	**0.037**
Focused %	Ugrd.	0.201	0.560	0.143	0.643	Prgmg.	–0.100	0.583	–0.061	0.685
	Grad.	–0.122	**0.027**	–0.114	**0.032**	Writing	–0.059	0.306	–0.062	0.260
Verification %	Ugrd.	N/A		N/A		Prgmg.	–0.004	0.678	–0.003	0.726
	Grad.	–0.106	0.254	–0.133	0.138	Writing	–0.012	**0.001**	–0.012	**0.001**

Table 7 shows that the pattern "with one more criterion added to the rubric, the expected drop on peer-grading reliability is more than 1 %" is mainly contributed by graduate students and writing assignments. There was not such a significant pattern for undergraduate students and programming assignments. In addition, the graduate students peer-grading reliability was also sensitive to the percentage of focused criteria. The right side of Table 7 also shows that the more true/false criteria were in favor of the peer-grading reliability of graduate students.

5 Conclusions

Effective peer review requires a well-designed rubric. In this paper we emphasize that rubric development should be iterative and the most important step, "closing the circle", is to analyze students' feedback to figure out how to refine the rubrics.

In our research we collected students' responses to 15 rubrics on 61 assignments. We recorded the comment length for each comment and calculated the grading reliabilities for each assignment. Through statistical analysis, we developed a set of empirical guidelines for designing peer-assessment rubrics for engineering students.

- Students tended to give shorter comment on true/false and verification criteria.
- Students' grading were less consistent on true/false and verification criteria, perhaps due to "courteous grading".
- Undergraduate students tended to give more comments than graduate students.
- Students tended to give more consistent grades for artifacts in a writing assignment than ones in a programming assignment.
- More verification criteria could potentially lower the peer-grading reliability.

- For graduate assignments, more focused criteria could lower the peer-grading reliability.
- The grading reliability tended to drop if the peer-assessment rubrics had more criteria, this pattern was more significant for graduate or writing assignments.
- For writing assignments, more true/false criteria could improve grading reliability.

For future work, we will use the empirical pattern to improve our rubrics and test them in the classes in the next semester. We will also work with other peer-assessment systems, collect more data from different settings and develop more guidelines. After we have collected big enough data, we will build a predictive model which can predict the quality of new peer-assessment rubrics even before it is used by any student. Our long term goal is to make the predictive model a web service which can help more instructors design their rubrics.

Acknowledgments. This project is sponsored by the National Science Foundation, on grant DUE 1432347.

References

1. Kulik, J.A., Kulik, C.-L.C.: Timing of feedback and verbal learning. Rev. Educ. Res. **58**(1), 79–97 (1988)
2. Lundstrom, K., Baker, W.: To give is better than to receive: the benefits of peer review to the reviewer's own writing. J. Second Lang. Writ. **18**(1), 30–43 (2009)
3. Orsmond, P., Merry, S., Reiling, K.: The importance of marking criteria in the use of peer assessment. Assess. Eval. High. Educ. **21**(3), 239–250 (1996)
4. Reddy, Y.M., Andrade, H.: A review of rubric use in higher education. Assess. Eval. High. Educ. **35**(4), 435–448 (2009)
5. Stellmack, M.A., Konheim-Kalkstein, Y.L., Manor, J.E., Massey, A.R., Schmitz, J.A.P.: An assessment of reliability and validity of a rubric for grading APA-style introductions. Teach. Psychol. **36**(2), 102–107 (2009)
6. Allen, D., Tanner, K.: Rubrics: tools for making learning goals and evaluation criteria explicit for both teachers and learners. CBE-Life Sci. Educ. **5**(3), 197–203 (2006)
7. Stevens, D.D., Levi, A.: Introduction to Rubrics: An Assessment Tool to Save Grading Time, Convey Effective Feedback, and Promote Student Learning. Stylus Publishing, LLC, Sterling (2005)
8. Kubincová, Z., Homola, M., Bejdová, V.: Motivational effect of peer review in blog-based activities. In: Wang, J.-F., Lau, R. (eds.) ICWL 2013. LNCS, vol. 8167, pp. 194–203. Springer, Heidelberg (2013)
9. Gehringer, E., Ehresman, L., Conger, S.G., Wagle, P.: Reusable learning objects through peer review: the Expertiza approach
10. Piech, C., Huang, J., Chen, Z., Do, C., Ng, A., Koller, D.: Tuned models of peer assessment in MOOCs. In: 6th International Conference on Educational Data Mining, Memphis, Tennessee, USA (2013)
11. Song, Y., Hu, Z., Gehringer, E.: Pluggable reputation systems for peer review: a web-service approach. In: 45th IEEE Frontiers in Education Conference, 2015, FIE 2015, El Paso, Texas (2015)

The Use of Online Corpora as Reference Resources for Revision Tasks in Writing

Qinqin Luo(✉), Weizhen Huang, and Ying Liao

School of Foreign Languages, Southwest Petroleum University, Chengdu, China
qinqinluo@126.com, 363086681@qq.com

Abstract. The current study reports on an experiment with 60 Chinese college students, aiming to explore the effects of using online corpora BFSU CQP web for revision tasks in EFL writing. Quantitative data about the 60 lower level EFL learners' scores in the post writing test show that there is a significant difference between the experimental group and the control group in terms of the lexical accuracy and the use of cohesion devices, which prove that corpora as reference resources are more useful than the online dictionary in helping learners improve their linguistic competence in writing. The follow-up interviews on the selected participants in the experimental group reveal different learners' perceptions of using online corpora in the process of revising essays and the reasons behind their opinions, which can provide guidance for teachers to apply corpora effectively in teaching writing.

Keywords: Online corpora · Reference resources · Revision tasks · Writing

1 Introduction

The process writing approach that has been prevailing throughout the West in the past thirty years emphasizes the significance of revision. The process of revising is not only helpful to improve the overall writing quality but also crucial to promoting learners' writing competence. But it is found that a considerable number of English as a foreign language (EFL) learners ignore this process and they seldom correct all the underlined errors, leading to the occurrence of similar errors again and again. The reasons for the phenomenon may partly lie in the fact that it is difficult to correct all the errors by learners themselves especially those with lower level of proficiency. However, providing the correct form directly to them may result in learners' over-reliance on teachers. Just as Corder [1, p. 11] states, "making a learner try to discover the right form could often be more instructive to both learners and teachers". That is to say, it is more effective for learners to self-correct errors with the help of some reference resources.

Since Data-driven learning was proposed by Johns [2], corpora have been gradually used as reference resources to assist learners in solving their language problems in writing in western world. Many empirical studies [3–7] have proved the positive effects of using corpora for error correction in writing, but some factors such as error types, learners' training and language proficiency may, to some extent, influence the effects of

F.W.B. Li et al. (Eds.): ICWL 2015, LNCS 9412, pp. 37–46, 2015.
DOI: 10.1007/978-3-319-25515-6_4

corpus use. And it can be also found from studies [8–10] that learners' search behavior and types of corpora also had impacts on the outcome of corpus consultation. Besides correcting errors, Corpora as reference resources could be also used to learn linking adverbials [11, 12], to differentiate synonym adjectives [13], and to assist learners in writing creatively [14]. Thus corpora can be used for various purposes in writing.

However, there are still some limitations of previous studies concerning corpus use in writing. Firstly, the studies concerning lower-level EFL learners in China are relatively few, which is partly due to the fact that corpus tools are not sufficiently user-friendly. Secondly, most studies using corpora for error correction just examine whether the accuracy rate of corrections can be improved but seldom explore the impact of corpus consultation on learners' long-term writing competence. Thirdly, there is still a lack of studies comparing the roles of corpora and traditional resources such as dictionaries in improving learners' linguistic competence in writing. Therefore, the present study focuses on Chinese lower-level EFL learners and selects the user-friendly online corpora as the platform aiming to examine the long-term effects of using corpora for revision tasks, that is, to check whether corpora can play more effective roles in promoting EFL learners' writing than online dictionaries in the following aspects: to improve the linguistic accuracy and lexical complexities, and to make learners more skilled in using cohesion devices such as linking adverbials thus to improve the cohesion of the essay.

2 Method

2.1 Research Questions

In this study, the following research questions are investigated:

(1) Which one is more useful in helping learners improve linguistic competence in free writing, consulting corpora or consulting the online dictionary in the process of revising essays?
(2) What are the differences between learners who make apparent progress and those who make no progress or even behave worse in post-writing test in terms of their attitudes toward corpus use in the process of revising essays?

Learners' linguistic competence is mainly examined in the writing test in terms of the linguistic accuracy, complexity, and the use of cohesion devices. And EFL learners' attitudes are investigated in the form of interview.

2.2 Participants

60 Chinese sophomores with 7 years' experience of learning English participated in the whole experiment, and they finished all the designated writing and revision assignment under the teacher's instruction. Among them, 27 (3 females, 24 males) from one college English class are in the control group and 33 (4 females, 29 males) from another class are in the experimental group. All of them were lower-level learners since their scores in College English Test Band 4 (CET 4 for short) in July 2014 ranged from 350–399 (The total score is 710). At the end of the term they would take CET 4 again thus they

had strong motivation for improving their writing competence, which may guarantee their enthusiasm in continually writing and revising essays. A writing test conducted before the experiment showed no statistically significant difference between the two groups in English writing competence.

2.3 The Online Corpora and Online Dictionary

To supervise them better and confirm they really exploited the reference resources, the two groups were supposed to use the designated online corpora or online dictionary.

The online corpora used by the experimental group was **BFSU CQP web** (http://124.193.83.252/cqp/), which was set up by Mr. Wu and maintained by Dr. Xu and Mr. Wu of the National Research Centre for Foreign Language Education. Compared with other online corpus, BFSU CQP web has the following advantages: Firstly, it is user-friendly and easy to handle enabling technically less competent learners to exploit corpora just like browsing web pages [15]. Secondly, EFL learners can get multiple corpus examples from different corpus. When learners log on to BFSU CQP web, they can have quick access to several native speakers' corpora such as Brown corpus, CLOB corpus. So when one corpus fails to provide sufficient examples about a key word they can conveniently consult another corpus to get more corpus evidence. Thirdly, the 4 parallel corpora can help learners a lot when learners are confused about some new words in the corpus examples or when they are unable to convey what they want to describe in target language.

The control group in this study preferred http://dict.cn/ as the online dictionary because a majority of them have been already accustomed to using it. This dictionary can be stored in mobile phones and it not only provides functions of the monolingual dictionaries but also has the advantages of bilingual dictionaries.

2.4 Procedure

The experiment lasted for a whole term. The procedure was as follows.

Step 1: Training About Corpus Use. Since all the participants had no prior experience in consulting corpus, instruction was given to the experimental groups about how to use corpora on revision tasks before the writing assignment. As Smart [16] states, interacting with corpora directly may be a challenge for learners who are not used to inductive activities and for those who have never used corpora in language learning. Thus the training started from the paper-based materials without requiring learners to access corpora directly. The teacher prepared reference sheets containing concordances selected from BFSU CQP web. For example:

We should always <u>remind</u> ourselves the importance of learning in the university.

Figure 1 provided information for students to correct their mistakes. When they were able to correct errors in this way, they were required to get direct access to corpora to finish some revision tasks. 3 types of revision tasks were included here.

Type 1: Correct the lexico-grammatical errors in the sentences.
More and more people <u>dependent</u> on computers.

Type 2: Find an alternative to the underlined words.
Besides the <u>good</u> effects, it also has <u>bad</u> effects.
Type 3: Use appropriate cohesion devices (linking adverbials).
It is going to rain now. I think we should go back home.

he told himself. She no longer wanted anything about him to	remind	her of the circumstances of their meeting that first night in Parioli
that some of the children, in spite of their color,	remind	him of children he has known and loved, perhaps even of
had mounted it on velvet and hung it over my desk to	remind	me always to use the power of the paper in a Christian
I hung up I was reasonably certain that Francesca had wanted to	remind	me of our town meeting the next evening, and how important
Washington Square seems not part of a free land. It may	remind	one of Russia, China or East Berlin; but it ca
of Russia, China or East Berlin; but it ca n't	remind	one of the freedom that Washington and the Continental soldiers fought for
their proportionate numerical strength would have warranted. We do well to	remind	ourselves that from men and women of New England ancestry also issued
little credit for the invention ". It is hardly necessary to	remind	students of covered bridges that Timothy Palmer was born in 1751 in

Fig. 1. Eight concordance lines of REMIND retrieved from BFSU CQP web

The teacher showed how to do simple queries as well as complex queries in BFSU CQP web in the classroom. If they just conducted the simple query, they may hardly find out the appropriate alternatives. For example, to revise the second type of the errors, learners had to input [pos = "J.*"] "effect", and then they can get the concordance evidence as follows (Fig. 2).

meteorologists the drought has had a	limited effect	on crop production. " Rainfall
, said the extra spending will have a	dramatic effect	. " With these efforts, China w
improve the practice and beef up the	supervisory effect	of the committees, Zhao said.
registration ban is good but of little	significant effect	this year. He said figures from
i Lama 's retirement will only have a	limited effect	on the autonomous region whil
nt document, which has a universal	binding effect	, is not subject to court hearing
dling of international affairs and the	positive effect	the country has had on the pron
China and India will not only have a	profound effect	on our two countries, but also
rosperous Central Asia would have a	positive effect	on China 's underdeveloped Xi
ability and social service will have a	negative effect	on building efficient governme

Fig. 2. Ten concordance lines of EFFECT extracted from BFSU CQP web

After the training, some revision tasks were given to the experimental group to make the participants more skilled in consulting corpora independently. One thing to note is that there was no special training on the control group for they knew how to use the online dictionary to revise their essays.

Step 2: Writing and Revision Assignment. After the training, the participants were required to write 6 essays in total and revise the marked essays based on teachers' requirements. The procedure about every essay was as follows. Firstly, the teacher gave students the writing assignment and provided some cohesion devices (linking adverbials) relevant to the essay for them without telling them the specific usage before writing. Secondly, the participants finished the writing assignment after class and handed in them on time. Thirdly, the teacher underlined all the places that should be revised by consulting corpora or the online dictionaries. Sometimes the teacher also offered some synonyms or words that were easily confused to learners, in order that they could differentiate and use these words or phrase better by consulting reference resources by themselves. Fourthly, the experimental group revised the essays and kept a record of the concordance evidence while the control group finished the revision tasks by referring to the online dictionary. After that, they exchanged their revised essays with each other to examine whether the revision is correct or appropriate and then handed in the essay again to the teacher. Finally, the teacher examined the revised essays and gave a comment in the class based on their correction work.

2.5 Data Collection and Analysis

In order to examine whether the use of corpora have positive effects on learners' linguistic competence in writing, the study employed pre- and post-writing test design. And the topic of the writing tests were both about the internet that the participants were familiar with. Both tests included measures of learners' linguistic accuracy, complexity, and the use of cohesion devices without considering the contents of the essay. The linguistic accuracy was marked by the number and seriousness of the lexico-grammatical errors. The fewer errors they committed, the higher scores they got. The mechanical errors such as spelling errors, capitalization errors were regarded as minor errors which has less negative influence on the score than the serious grammatical errors such as verb forms, tense. The linguistic complexity was assessed in terms of lexical and syntactic complexity. The lexical complexity was measured by the sophistication and array of learners' productive vocabulary [17]. The syntactic complexity was judged by how varied and sophisticated the construction elements or linguistic structures are [18]. The use of cohesion devices was mainly marked globally based on the frequency, variety and appropriateness of the linking adverbials in the essay. Three college English teachers were invited to mark the essays respectively in terms of the above three aspects to ensure the objectivity of the test. The average score of the 3 teachers about each aspect would be calculated, and then we put the data in SPSS17.0. An independent T-test was conducted to examine whether there was significant difference between the two groups in the three aspects of linguistic competence in writing. To know the participants' attitudes toward corpus use in the process of revising essays, a semi-structured interview was conducted on 6 participants in the experimental group.

3 Results Analysis and Discussion

3.1 Results for the Pre-writing Test

It can be revealed from Table 1 that there was no significant difference between the control group and the experimental group in terms of their linguistic accuracy, complexity, and the use of cohesion devices. So the two groups were equivalent in linguistic competence in writing at the beginning of the experiment ($p > 0.05$). The following problems existed equally in both of the two groups' essays: frequently appeared lexico-grammatical errors, lack of cohesion devices such as linking adverbials, an obvious lexical poverty reflected by their use of too many superordinates or general words such as good, bad, important, etc.

Table 1. Comparison between the two groups about the pre-writing test

Category	Group	N	M	Std.	Mean Diff.	t	Sig. (2-Tailed)
Accuracy (5)	Control	27	2.8770	0.5149	0.0228	0.198	0.844
	Ex.	33	2.8542	0.3769			
Complexity(5)	Control	27	2.6974	0.5052	−0.0244	−0.214	0.831
	Ex.	33	2.7218	0.3789			
Cohesion devices (5)	Control	27	2.9267	0.4194	−0.1688	−1.681	0.098
	Ex.	33	3.0955	0.3584			
Total (15)	Control	27	8.4996	0.8814	−0.1719	−0.827	0.412
	Ex.	33	8.6715	0.7296			

3.2 Results for the Post-writing Test

The results of the post-test in Table 2 showed that there were significant differences between the two groups in terms of linguistic accuracy, the use of cohesion devices and the overall writing quality ($p < 0.05$) but no significant difference existed between them in linguistic complexity ($p = 0.121 > 0.05$).

In terms of linguistic accuracy, the experimental group had superior results than the control group, showing that the experimental group made fewer lexico-grammatical errors in essays. In the process of correcting errors, they had to analyze concordance lines and induce the lexical or grammatical rules and eventually applied the rules into the correction work. It's obvious that they were actively involved in the learning process, undertaking the researchers' role, to solve linguistic problems. This time-consuming process may make them deeply aware of the wrong linguistic forms and the repeated linguistic pattern in concordance line may help them master the right usage better. Thus they would try to avoid the previous errors and naturally recalled the right pattern which frequently appeared in corpus examples. This supports Huang's [19] opinion that corpus-based inductive learning helps learners notice and acquire collocational patterns better, which in turn enables learners to generate more accurate patterns. However, the limited examples in the online dictionary were not sufficient to make learners in the control group fully notice the errors. Due to the native language interference, they always committed the similar errors, which could be found in their post-test. This result shows support for a number of papers [3, 4] which study the use of corpora as a reference resource for error-correction.

Table 2. Comparison between the two groups about the post-writing test

Category	Group	N	M	Std.	Mean Diff.	t	Sig. (2-tailed)
Accuracy (5)	Control	27	2.9944	0.4444	−0.6668	−5.521	0.000**
	Ex.	33	3.6612	0.4818			
Complexity (5)	Control	27	2.9937	0.5136	−0.2084	−1.573	0.121
	Ex.	33	3.2021	0.5081			
Cohesion devices (5)	Control	27	3.3707	0.4921	−0.3059	−2.366	0.021*
	Ex.	33	3.6767	0.5033			
Total (15)	Control	27	9.3581	1.3596	−1.1970	−3.318	0.002**
	Ex.	33	10.5552	1.4149			

$^{**}p < 0.001$, $^{*}p < 0.05$

Regarding linguistic complexities, the experimental group also had a higher mean score than the control group, but the difference was not significant. The reasons may be as follows. Firstly, it may take a long time for learners to improve their linguistic complexities. One term's training about writing and revision may not be enough for them to make significant progress. Secondly, some participants didn't know how to skillfully consult corpora to improve the complexities. In most of the cases they had to conduct complex queries or consult the parallel corpus for finding better alternatives to replace the underlined simple word or phrase, but some of them seldom did the complex query and the parallel corpus was not exploited fully.

Concerning the use of cohesion devices, the experimental group also behaved significantly better. They used the linking adverbials more frequently and more skillfully in the post-test. A lot of participants in the experimental group tried to put some linking adverbials such as however in the middle of a sentence as a parenthesis since however was often put in the middle of a sentence in corpus examples. But most participants just habitually put them at the beginning or the end of a sentence. This result is consistent with Boulton's [11] opinion that corpus data as reference resource are more effective in learning linking adverbials than the traditional resources.

3.3 Results for the Interview

The follow-up interview included 3 questions: (1) What are the positive and negative sides of using corpora in revision tasks? (2) Do you think the use of corpora can improve your overall writing competence? (3) Will you keep the habit of using corpora in the future writing activities? There were altogether 6 participants in the experimental group being interviewed. Among them, 3 were randomly selected from those who made apparent progress in the post-test and they were assigned to the first group being interviewed in the first round. The other 3 were the only 3 learners who got lower scores in the post-test and they were assigned to the second group being interviewed in the second round. The two different groups showed divergent opinions about the use of corpora.

The first group generally had a favorable attitude towards corpus use for revision tasks in writing. Firstly, they believed it could help them improve their linguistic accuracy by saying that "it's really helpful for detecting and correcting errors, especially errors about collocation and preposition." This supports O'Sullivan's [20] opinion that corpus consultation can present an opportunity for learners to notice their errors and provide evidence that learners can use to correct their linguistic output. Besides the positive effects on error-correction, they also emphasized some other benefits of using corpora for revision tasks such as "raising the awareness of the importance of collocations", "mastering the usages of words and phrases better", "acquiring new words incidentally", "learning synonyms in a better way" and so on. Although some negative sides such as "too time-consuming" and "failure to understand the incomplete sentences" were also mentioned, they generally agreed that the positive sides outweighed the negative sides and they believed that the use of corpora was beneficial to improving their linguistic competence in writing as long as they could persist in using corpora. Thus when being asked about whether they would keep using corpora, two of them gave a definite answer "Yes", saying that they would firstly consult corpora when they encounter some expressions that they are not sure of. And the other one was a little hesitated by saying "it depends" for he believed that dictionaries and corpora could complement each other. He revealed that he would firstly refer to the dictionary and when the dictionary fail to provide what he wants then he would consult the corpora.

The second group revealed less positive attitudes toward corpus use. Although they all admitted there were some positive effects of using corpora in writing, they expressed their reluctance to use corpora sometimes for they were usually more willing to be told how to correct the errors directly rather than take much time to explore the right form by themselves. They have already been used to being told what to do by the teacher since the primary school. This may be one of the reasons why a small number of students in the experimental group made no improvement. In their eyes, the negative sides outweighed the positive sides, which could be reflected from the following comments: "too many examples in concordance lines", "too much time spent in searching, analyzing and inducing", "too many new words", "unable to induce the right grammatical rules", "failure to get what I want", etc. Due to these factors, while being asked about whether the use of corpora improved their linguistic competence in writing they were not certain. One of them responded that sometimes he consulted corpora just for finishing the teachers' assignment but not for finding out the best alternatives or the most appropriate word. And the other two also expressed the similar meaning that if they could spend more time in learning from corpora and persist in using them, their linguistic competence in writing would be improved. Finally, only one of them implied that he would still keep on using corpora for reference purposes in writing and the other two responded that they will firstly refer to the online dictionary which can save much time and then go to corpora for more detailed information if time permits.

The results of the interviews revealed that the more benefits learners got, the more positive attitudes they had. Thus, to make lower-level learners actively involved in learning from corpus consultation, teachers can start with some simple tasks since the accomplishment of these tasks can help them feel the sense of achievement, which may stimulate them to keep on using corpora. In the meanwhile, appropriate guidance should be offered to them to reduce their anxiety in using corpora especially when they get confused in analyzing the concordances.

4 Conclusion

The present study explored the effects of using online corpora BFSU CQP web in the process of revising essays, finding that the use of corpora is more useful than the online dictionary in improving EFL learners' linguistic competence in writing, especially the linguistic accuracy and the use of cohesion devices. However, the interviews revealed that learners' attitudes toward corpus use were closely related to the benefits learners got from corpora. If they got no progress from using corpora they would naturally show negative attitudes and reluctant to use them in the future. Thus teachers should help them overcome the difficulties technically and psychologically to make them benefit more from using corpora. If learners can skillfully use corpora and get achievements, they will voluntarily exploit corpora for their own purposes, which will definitely promote learner autonomy and improve their writing competence. Nevertheless, there are still some limitations of the present study. Firstly, the learners' essays were merely marked by three teachers, the automated writing assessment system can be used in the further study to ensure more objectivity and transparency in the assessment. Secondly, this study just focused on three aspects of learners' linguistic competence regardless of the contents of the essay, the following study can concentrate on the effects of corpus use on the improvement of content since the content also has great impact on the overall writing quality. Thirdly, the experiment lasted for only one term, a longitudinal study should be conducted to know whether the corpus use can make learners form the habit of using corpora for writing purposes.

Acknowledgements. This work was supported by Southwest Petroleum University Science and Technology Foundation (Grant No. 2012XJR013) and Web Culture Project Sponsored by the Humanities and Social Science Research Base of the Sichuan Provincial Education Department (Grant No. WLWH15-28).

References

1. Corder, P.: Error Analysis and Interlanguage. Oxford University Press, Oxford (1981)
2. Johns, T.: Should you be persuaded: two examples of data-driven learning. In: Johns, T., King, P. (eds.) Classroom Concordancing. ELR, Birmingham (1991)
3. Gaskell, D., Cobb, T.: Can learners use concordance feedback for writing errors? System **32**(3), 301–319 (2004)
4. Gilmore, A.: Using online corpora to develop students' writing skills. ELT J. **11**, 1–10 (2009)

5. Chambers, A., O'Sullivan, Í.: Corpus consultation and advanced learners' writing skills in French. ReCALL **16**(1), 158–172 (2004)
6. O'Sullivan, Í., Chambers, A.: Learners' writing skills in French: corpus consultation and learner evaluation. J. Second Lang. Writ. **15**(1), 49–68 (2006)
7. Tono, Y., Satake, Y., Miura, A.: The effects of using corpora on revision tasks in L2 writing with coded error feedback. ReCALL **26**, 147–162 (2014)
8. Pérez-Paredes, P., Sánchez-Tornel, M., Alcaraz Calero, J.M.: Learners' search patterns during corpus-based focus-on-form activities. Int. J. Corpus Linguist. **17**(4), 483–516 (2012)
9. Chang, J.Y.: The use of general and specialized corpora as reference sources for academic English writing: a case study. ReCALL **26**(2), 243–259 (2014)
10. Lee, D., Swales, J.: A corpus-based EAP course for NNS doctoral students: moving from available specialized corpora to self-compiled corpora. Engl. Specif. Purp. **25**(1), 56–75 (2006)
11. Boulton, A.: Testing the limits of data-driven learning: language proficiency and training. ReCALL **21**(1), 37–51 (2009)
12. Cotos, Elena: Enhancing writing pedagogy with learner corpus data. ReCALL **26**(2), 202–224 (2014)
13. Yeh, Y., Liou, H.C., Li, Y.H.: Online synonym materials and concordancing for EFL college writing. Comput. Assist. Lang. Learn. **20**(2), 131–152 (2007)
14. Kennedy, C., Miceli, T.: Corpus-assisted creative writing: introducing intermediate Italian learners to a corpus as a reference resource. Lang. Learn. Technol. **14**(1), 28–44 (2010)
15. Xu, J.J., Wu, L.P.: Web-based fourth generation corpus analysis tools and the BFSU CQP web case. Comput.-Assist. Foreign Lang. Educ. **5**, 10–15 (2014)
16. Smart, J.: The role of guided induction in paper-based data-driven learning. ReCALL **26**, 184–201 (2014)
17. Wolfe-Quintero, K., Inagaki, S., Kim, H.Y.: Second language development in writing: measures of fluency, accuracy, and complexity (Report No. 17). Second Language Teaching and Curriculum Center, University of Hawai'i, Honolulu (1998)
18. Ortega, L.: Syntactic complexity measures and their relationship to L2 proficiency: a research synthesis of college-level L2 writing. Appl. Linguist. **24**(4), 492–518 (2003)
19. Huang, Z.P.: The effects of paper-based DDL on the acquisition of lexico-grammatical patterns in L2 writing. ReCALL **26**, 163–183 (2014)
20. O'Sullivan, I.: Enhancing a process-oriented approach to literacy and language learning: the role of corpus consultation literacy. ReCALL **19**(3), 269–286 (2007)

E-learning Platform and Tools

Educational Program BigData EduCloud at the Faculty of Informatics and Management

Dagmar El-Hmoudova(✉) and Monika Borkovcova

Faculty of Informatics and Management, University of Hradec Kralove, Rokitanskeho 62, 50003 Hradec Kralove, Czech Republic
{dagmar.elhmoudova,monika.borkovcova}@uhk.cz

Abstract. The current trend of rapid development in the field of BigData brings a new educational direction in teaching Database Servers. Due to our students´ demand in this area the need has arisen to implement teaching NoSQL databases, which are closely connected with BigData. To ensure a highly professional training program the faculty cooperation agreement with IBM started in the summer semester 2015. The aim of the joint training program BigData EduCloud is to provide students with practical professional skills and prepare them for new positions that have recently been created in the labour market. The program consists of lectures, workshops and intensive consultations. Since the face-to-face teaching is organized in blocks, we have created teaching materials for self-study in the Blackboard LMS to support the quality level of the learning environment. The first part of the program is supplemented by multimedia teaching materials, interactive lectures, tests to verify knowledge and by the learning environment created at IBM. Our paper introduces the various parts of the program and their connectivity within an e-learning environment.

Keywords: Bigdata · E-learning · Nosql · Hadoop · Blackboard LMS

1 Introduction

One of the main objectives of the Faculty of Informatics and Management is to facilitate the integration of our students in national and international labor markets by equipping them with the latest theoretical and applied investigation tools for the IT area. In this respect the close cooperation with IBM Company, which created together with the Information Technology and Quantitative Methods Department an educational program called EduCloud, appears to be logical and correct step. The aim of this program, which started in February 2015 (summer semester), is to create a transparent set of multidisciplinary courses, seminars and online practical exercises which give students the opportunity to gain both theoretical and practical knowledge as well as to develop their key skills. The program is of course supported by e-learning course. BigData, which is one of the key topics mentioned in recent IBM study "The IBM Business Tech Trends Study 2014"[1] was the first part of the

[1] http://www-01.ibm.com/common/ssi/cgi-bin/ssialias?htmlfid=XIE12347USEN&appname=skmwww.

F.W.B. Li et al. (Eds.): ICWL 2015, LNCS 9412, pp. 49–58, 2015.
DOI: 10.1007/978-3-319-25515-6_5

EduCloud program - module, which was launched in summer semester 2014/15. It is important to point out that the abovementioned cooperation is the first of this kind in the country and thus our students will be the first to be fully trained for the position of Big Data Analytics. Students participating in this program will get practical experience in a very specific field with a great potential. The added value and one of the advantages of the program is the opportunity to receive globally recognized certifications for free (credited by IBM). Considerably important is also just released publications IBM DB2 Express – C [3] which became inevitable part of the learning and teaching process and which was donated to the university library by the authors. The book has contributed to a more open interest in the database server, is considered to be one of the pillars of the whole issue of big data and brings more effective approach not only to students but also trainers. Generally, we can say that this effective cooperation between the academic and commercial spheres can be developed in the future even for actual applied research.

2 Methods – BigData

The term Big Data has become universal. Owing to a shared origin between academia, industry and the media there is no single unified definition, and various diverse and often contradictory definitions are available [10]. In 2001, industry analyst Doug Laney (currently with Gartner) introduced the now mainstream definition of big data as the three vs of big data: volume, velocity and variety [4]. Sometimes two additional dimensions are considered: variability and complexity. For the needs of this paper we can state that the term Big Data is generally used for large volumes of data that are difficult to process using traditional data processing methods. Every day the world produces 2.5 trillion bytes of data and the volumes have constantly been increasing. 90 % of all the data has been originated only within the last two years and we can imagine them as outputs of sensors measuring the climate, data from social networks, pictures, videos, business transactions, unstructured text, and other formats. Due to the worldwide exponential increase in data and information Big Data is increasingly followed up by commercial companies - whether in terms of data volume and speed of data flow, diversity or reliability. Processing of large amounts of data both structured and unstructured, in the traditional way would mean making huge investments in software and hardware implementations [8]. Thanks to Big Data technologies, data can be stored and analyzed more efficiently and without large upfront investments. The companies understand the great potential in data analysis and their proper usage, on the other hand, the lack of qualified professionals who would be able to handle this data worries them. Figure 1 shows extending data management options enables greater returns on information assets.

2.1 Stakeholders and Their Roles

IBM actively cooperates with the University (Faculty) to create suitable joint curriculum topics in the course of bachelor and master IT studies. IBM, which is the guarantor of the EduCloud program, provides the academia with the latest expected trends and knowledge of the labor market from the perspective of commercial partner proposes the

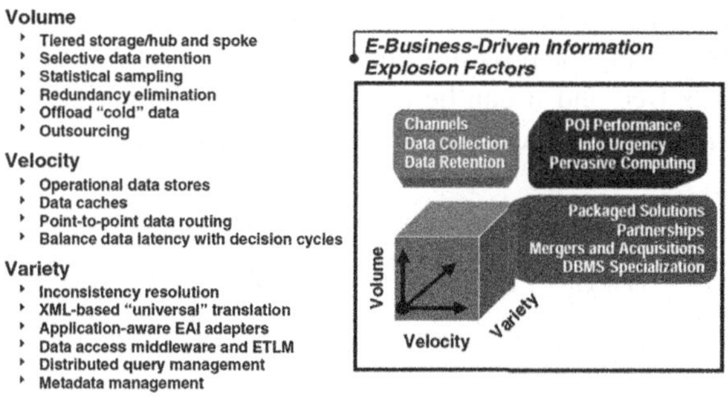

Fig. 1. Data Management Solutions [4]

graduates preparatory materials, implements practice-oriented lectures and provides a software environment for running EduCloud POT workshops. Faculty of Informatics and Management is involved in selected areas of post-graduates training, collaborates with IBM to create the appropriate courses and course modifications with respect to the content consistency in the frame of the EduCloud program. Within this extensive collaboration high level technical co-operation is necessary during the start-ups of EduCloud POT workshops cyber environment. As this program is not included in current syllabi, the Institute for Further Education (IFE) of the Faculty of Informatics and Management deals with the overall organization and communication with students, including the program promotion. IFE arranges and offers the courses, seminar meetings, lectures and other activities connected to further education of professional start. The target group is represented mainly by second and third year students of Applied Informatics and Information Management. There are no special limitations or restrictions which would prevent some students from applying to the EduCloud program.

3 Instruments – The Program Progress

The program is divided into several parts - modules, some of which can be completed during the standard period of semester as accredited courses and some parts have been created solely for the purpose of this program. The University applies the European credit system, which was integrated into this program. An integral part of the EduCloud program implementation to the University educational and credit system was to identify key skills; upgrade corresponding courses; to prepare workshops run by experts from industry and to arrange online exercises on concrete data and technologies.

As already mentioned, the program is composed of individual modules, faculty regular courses, additional seminars and on-line practical exercises. In order to meet the program requirements and get a final certificate of Big Data Analyst, a student must successfully pass all regular faculty courses listed in the curriculum as well as all IBM modules. The price of this certificate is thanks to the IBM sponsorship reduced from $ 200 to $ 30, which is for students a very motivating tool. Students may also be certified in DB2 Fundamentals, focusing on the position of administrator or developer. Those who do not wish to complete the entire course have the opportunity to attend individual modules which they are interested in but without the possibility of obtaining Big Data Analyst certificate. During the program, students can also get certified in DB2 Academic Associate, which is free and it can be achieved after completing the faculty courses, DBS, DBS2 and lectures Hadoop and NoSQL- Introduction.

Table 1. Curriculum of the EduCloud modules

Module Abbreviation	Subject	Type of module	Timing	Credits
A.DBS1	Database systems 1	University acredited course	WS 2014/15	6
A.DBS2	Database systems 2	University acredited course	SS 2014/15	5
L.HAD	Hadoop Introduction	Lectured by the IBM expert	SS 2014/15	1
L.NoSQLDB	NoSQL Introduction	Lectured by the IBM expert	SS 2014/15	1
A.DORDB	DOR database	University acredited course	WS 2015/16	6
L.BigIn	Lecture Big Sheets	Technological lecture	WS 2015/16	2
E.BigIn	PoT BigSheets	EduCloud online exercises	WS 2015/16	
A.APSTA	Applied Statistics	University acredited course	WS 2015/16	6
L.SPSS	SPSS Modeler	Lectured by the IBM expert	WS 2015/16	2
E.SPSS	PoT SPSS Modeler	EduCloud online exercises	WS 2015/16	
E.BigIn/SPSS	PoT SPSS Modeler	EduCloud online exercises	WS 2015/16	2

Note: WS = Winter semester, SS = Summer semester

New courses have also been awarded by credits, the overview of which can be seen in Table 1. As a part of passing module A.DBS1 student´s task was to create a realistic project while within module A.DBS2 students had to attend a mandatory workshop DB2, verify their knowledge by completing e-learning test, and create a real project. Lecture L.HAD aimed at information about Big Data, explained the history and creation of Hadoop, highlighted current trends and prepared students for e-learning test. Next vocational lecture L.NoSQLDB, dealt with detailed introduction to NoSQL database types and their use in practice; acquired knowledge was again examined by e-learning test. In the first academic year, students can obtain a certificate DB2 Academic Associate, which is described in the very part of this chapter entitled “Certificates”.

Another part of the program will take place in the following academic year when L.BigIn will be introduced with the specifications of Hadoop use in the enterprise environment, students will learn about the platform and NoSQL database types and their use in practice. The verification instrument testing students´ knowledge and skills will be an e-learning test, designed by the team of university teachers and IBM specialists. E.BigIn module is aimed at online technology IBS with prepared scenarios of real data. Students will receive IBM Voucher, which entitles them to access directly the IBM environment and the platform consisting of exercises and sub tasks. Within L.SPSS will be performed a real demonstration of the use of selected statistical methods for data processing. E.SPSS and E.BigIn/SPSS modules deal with IBM technology and selected scenarios of real data. Student will receive IBM Voucher, which accesses them directly to the environment and the platform where IBM experts will train our students, who will be expected to perform particular sub tasks. At the end of the program, students may receive the Big Data Analyst certificate, which is described further in this paper. For easier reference see Table 1, that streamlines program modules in the time sequence.

3.1 Certificates

In the course of the program, students can take part in two certifications, which brings them obvious advantages. First, they can use the IBM certificates as part of their CV documents, and second the certificates entitle them to a better starting position in IBM, be it an internship or full-time positions in the company. Of course the certificates officially confirm knowledge of company databases, etc. The first certification can be folded within the Bachelor program and DB2 Academic Associate certificate[2].

3.2 E-learning in the EduCloud Program

An integral part of the whole program implementation has been networking with e-learning lessons. All the study materials were created and uploaded in the Faculty of Informatics and Management LMS system BlackBoard (BB). BB includes a user-friendly environment focusing on presentation of study materials, references, syllabuses etc. and as Poulova et col [6] states in her work there are plenty of strengths and weaknesses some of which are listed below in Fig. 2. The listed advantages and disadvantages of the BB LMS implementation (some of which were taken from the Bradford et co. [1] research work) were taken in mind when the new BigData EduCloud modules were designed. The BlackBoard Learn allows users to manage learning content, digital assets, and ePortfolios in an enterprise learning environment and thus it is very suitable platform for EduCloud program. All students as well as teachers and IBM experts have access to the e-learning course which is designed to give relevant and essential information about the program process. The e-learning courses - modules have been created based on the close cooperation between parties, university teachers and IBM experts, so the connection between academic theory and practical real life aspects are perfectly in harmony here [2, 5], see examples Figs. 3 and 4.

[2] http://www.ibm.com/developerworks/data/events/db2academiccertification/exam.html.

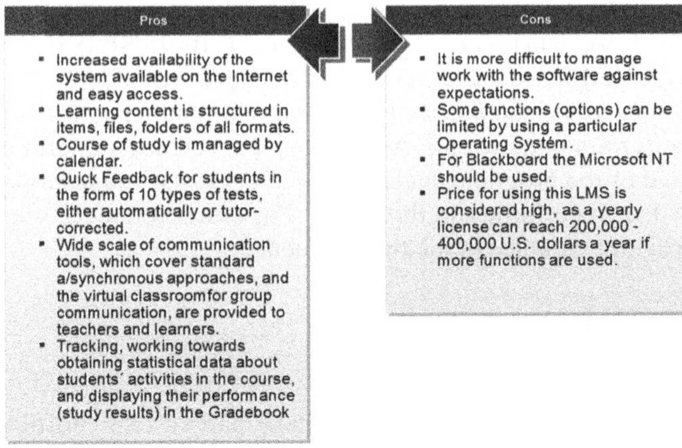

Fig. 2. Pros and Cons of BB LMS

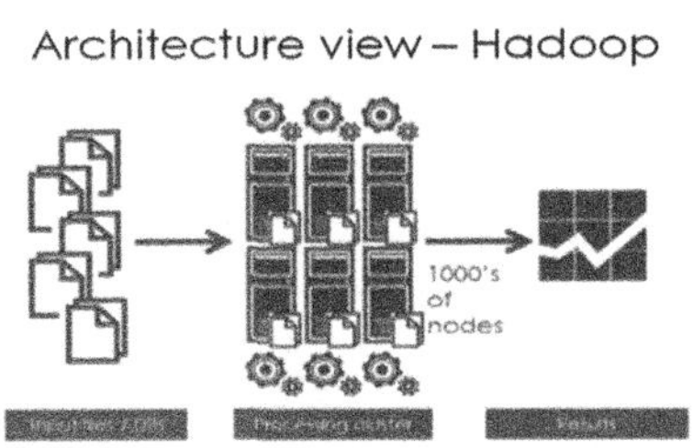

Fig. 3. University e-learning in BB, example of Hadoop lecture

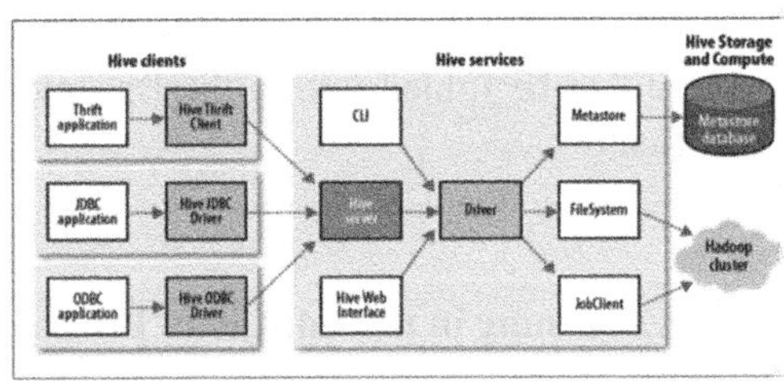

Fig. 4. University e-learning in BB, example of NoSQL databases exercise

In this particular case new practices and strategies that have emerged precisely from direct cooperation with IBM, have been used. The basic idea came from the very conception of the Big Data, which is currently very busy issues - it not only attracted the interest of students and teachers, but also has created a need for some new aspects in subsequent e-learning environment. Tests and teaching materials created during the project acquired another dimension, which would be described as a direct relationship between authors, trainers and students. The outcome of this approach is undoubtedly higher quality education, and especially, better access and cooperation with students. The program therefore is not just about Big Data as a theoretical issue but it also launches practical implementation, supported by specific tests and e-learning supporting material. Each module is equipped with its own guiding instructions, study materials, and modified tests with comprehensive sets of questions. Study materials have been developed not only as standard presentations; they contain audio-visual materials, animations and video instructions. Students´ attendance in the courses and lectures is monitored in order to evaluate not only the results of the individual tests but also to detect the fields of students´ interest.

E-learning and its prospective within the tertiary education courses and programs.

Information technology in teaching and learning environment has created a need to transform the way of university students´ learning and teaching paradigm by using modern, efficient, and effective alternative such as e-learning. E-learning can be viewed as the delivery of course content via electronic media, such as Internet, Intranets, Extranets, satellite broadcast, audio/video tape, interactive TV, and CD-ROM.[7] A lot of projects, authors and managers in higher education institutions see e-learning as offering high potential for quality improvement and key skills development. In practice, e-learning is complex and involves considerable individual and institutional change, beyond the provision of technology [9]. The technological landscape of modern E-Learning is dominated by so-called learning management systems such as Blackboard (BB)[3] WebCT. E-learning at the Faculty of Informatics and Management has a fairly long tradition; it has been almost 11 years since our students can benefit from better access to learning resources. However, e-learning projects often failed to deliver the results expected, mostly because of poor implementation. It is necessary to understand that e-learning is not a technological solution but rather a process with cultural consequences. Successful implementation of e-learning process requires reflection in three main areas people, processes and technology [10]. Based on our research results we can claim that the new BigData EduCloud modules, which have been designed with the support of highly professional teachers and IBM experts, meet even the most demanding requirements for efficient and high quality e-learning course.

4 Results – The Pilot Program Results Assessing

Student's progress in the course of the first academic year of the pilot program BigData EduCloud was detected and analysed, with special focus on students´ reported activities in the program. The results, which appear to be very interesting, will be applied and used for further development of the program in order to increase the quality and consistency of teaching and learning environment in the upcoming semester, as most of modules will be run in winter semester 2015/16 (see Table 1).

Table 2, indicates an overview, which shows high interest of our students in the pilot program. 54 % of students who belong to primary focus group participated in the program. Out of these, 43 % successfully passed the achievement tests and examinations while 57 % failed.

To gain detailed data analysis correlation between participation in Hadoop lecture (L.Hadoop course) and successful relevant test completion in the e-learning environment was initially investigated. Contingency table (Crosstab) designated as Fig. 5, which shows that 11 students who did not attend the lecture as well as 17 students who did participate in the lecture failed in the tests, on the other hand 26 students who attended the lecture actively, passed the test without any particular problems. Considering the measured values the Pearson Chi-square test, which allows to test the independence of the row and column variables, was applied.Asymptotic significance value is, in this case,

[3] http://www.blackboard.com/.

smaller than a given value of alpha confidence level, which leads us to the conclusion that the investigated variables are interdependent. Thus, participation in a lecture directly influences the outcome of e-learning test which is uploaded in the e-learning environment [11]. Once again the well-known statement claiming that supporting e-learning materials should, especially in case of intensive and sophisticated courses, involve face to face lecturing or explanations, is confirmed.

Table 2. Basic program overview in numbers

Total number of students participating in the program:	**54**
Total number of successful students:[a]	**23**
Total number of failed students:	**31**
Total number of successful students in percentage is 42.60 % while 57.4 % of the participating students failed[b].	
Total number of students applying for the certification:	**21**
Successful students:	**13**
Failed students:	**8**
Totally 61.90 % of participating students was successfully certified while 38.1 % were unsuccessful.	
The number of DBS2 students in summer semester2014/2015[c].	**100**
In total, 54 % of students from primary focus group participated in the BigData EduCloud program.	

[a]These are students who have successfully completed modules: A.DBS1, A.DBS2, L.HAD, L.NoSQLDB.

[b]The actual numbers exceeded our expectations and it proves that despite the complexity of the BigData EduCloud program significant interest of our students has been indicated.

[c]This is the primary focus group for the BigData EduCloud program.

Count

		Exam_test_Hadoop		Total
		FAILED	PASSED	
Participation_Lec_Hadoop	NO	11	0	11
	YES	17	26	43
Total		28	26	54

Fig. 5. Participation vs test results – Hadoop module

Count

		Exam_test_NoSQL		Total
		FAILED	PASSED	
Participation_Lec_NoSQL	NO	17	2	19
	YES	13	22	35
Total		30	24	54

Fig. 6. Participation vs test results – NoSQL module

The success of L.NoSQLDB module test was assessed in a similar way. The result can be seen in the contingency Fig. 6. Even in this case the correlation between participation in the lecture and success in e-learning test was confirmed.

5 Implications

The implications of this teaching program from the learning pedagogy pointare manifold. *1. Feedback:* Big Data can be informative from a feedback and context perspective. *2. Motivation:* Students potentially become invested in inputting data to the process because they see the impact of how it works. *3. Personalization:* Big Data will change the way we approach e-learning design by enabling developers to personalize courses to fit their learners' individual needs. *4. Efficiency:* Learning programs which were most effective will be indicated, including the timing. *5. Collaboration*: Specialists from multiple departments must come together to keep a Learning Management System. This encourages cooperation, collaboration, and interdisciplinary thought processes. *6. Tracking:* Big Data can help us understand the real patterns of our students more effectively by allowing us to track their experience in an e-learning course. *7. Understanding the learning process:* By tracking Big Data in e-learning, we can see which parts of an assignment or exam were too easy and which parts were so difficult that the student got stuck.

Still, when discussing BigData educational program, we must consider the risks that it raises e.g. transparency, privacy, and infrastructure, depth of measurement or value to the students. Since BigData educational program is just evolving at our faculty, it is difficult to be prescriptive about such issues at this stage. It will be part of our further research within BigData educational program.

6 Conclusion

The project benefits for faculty development is predominantly in the future employability of the university graduates. In the data analysis and their proper usage see the firms and companies a great potential. What they are concerned about, however, is the lack of qualified professionals who would be able to handle this data. Recently the positions of Big Data architects, Big Data analytics, and lead engi-neer for Big Data have been requested and offered by plenty of IT companies on the labor market. This university program prepares students for key and demanded positions. The close connection of practical insights, teaching practice and students´ interest was the support milestone that resulted in one of the most successful realization and cooperation of such nature in recent years in our region. Although the program is not finished and will continue next academic year as one of the university grant projects, we recommend to implement the new forms of outputs and approaches used in this program into similarly oriented university courses, as it means more open and more direct access to not only solved problems but also to the new resources (authors, companies, etc.). Finally, even modifications of standard university e-learning courses are beneficial not only for students but also for instructors and teachers. Both parties can benefit from greater saturation of what they expect from similar projects and at the same time they can broaden and update their experience and information level. Nevertheless, there era still some questions we shall address in the future e.g. what are the unique features of face-to-face teaching, and for what kinds of learner are these essential; we shall also ask how to achieve an appropriate balance between face-to-face and technology-based teaching. There will always be some aspects of teaching and learning for which face-to-face teaching will be much more appropriate. However, no longer can it be taken as a general assumption that face-to-face teaching is always better. On the contrary, it will become increasingly important to justify it.

References

1. Bradford, P., Porciello, M., Balkon, N., Backus, D.: The blackboard learning system. J. Technol. Syst. **35**, 301–314 (2007)
2. Cerna, M, Poulova, P.: Social software applications and their role in the process of education from the perspective of university students. In: Beldhuis, H. (ed.) Proceedings of the 11th European Conference on E-learning (ECEL), pp. 87 – 96. University of Groningen, Groningen (2012)
3. Chong, Raul F., Hakes, I., Ahuja, R., Šůla, J., Dvorský, B.: Začínáme s DB2 Express-C, IBM Corporation (2014)
4. Laney, D.: 3D Data Management: Controlling Data Volume, Velocity, and Variety. Application Delivery Strategies, file 949, META Group, February 2001
5. Poulova, P., Simonova, I.: Flexible E-learning: Online Courses Tailored to Student's Needs. In: Capay, M., Mesarosova, M., Palmarova, V. (ed.) DIVAI 2012: 9th International Scientific Conference On Distance Learning In Applied Informatics: Conference Proceedings, pp. 251–260. UKF, Nitra (2012)
6. Poulova, P., Simonova, I., Manenova, I.: Which one, or another? comparative analysis of selected LMS. Procedia – Soc. Behav. Sci. **186**, 1302–1308 (2015). doi:10.1016/j.sbspro.2015.04.052
7. Urdan, T.A., Weggen, C.C. Corporate e-learning: exploring a new frontier. WR Hambrecht + Co. (2000)
8. Zentel, P., Bett, K., Meiter, D.M., Rinn, U., Wedekind, J.: A changing process at German universities—innovation through information and communication technologies? Electron. J. e-Learning **2**(1), 237–246 (2004)
9. Zikopoulos, P., Eaton, C.: Understanding Big Data: Analytics for Enterprise Class Hadoop and Streaming Data. McGraw-Hill Osborne Media, New York (2011)
10. Cech, P., Bures, V.: E-learning implementation at university. In: Proceedings of 3rdEuropean Conference on e-Learning, Paris, France, pp. 25–34 (2004). ISBN 0-9547096-7-5
11. Milková, E.: Multimedia applications as an effective complement to the educational process. In: Advanced Educational Technologies, Proceedings of 6th WSEAS/IASME International Conference on Educational Technologies (EDUTE 2010). WSEAS Press, Kantoui, Sousse, Tunisia, pp. 62–67, 3–6 May 2010

Adaptive E-Lecture Video Outline Extraction Based on Slides Analysis

Xiaoyin Che(✉), Haojin Yang, and Christoph Meinel

Hasso Plattner Institute, University of Potsdam,
Prof.-Dr.-Helmert-Str. 2-3, 14482 Potsdam, Germany
{xiaoyin.che,haojin.yang,christoph.meinel}@hpi.de

Abstract. In this paper, we propose an automated adaptive solution to generate logical, accurate and detailed tree-structure outline for video-based online lectures, by extracting the attached slides and reconstructing their content. The proposed solution begins with slide-transition detection and optical character recognition, and then proceeds by a static method of analyzing the layout of single slide and the logical relations within the slides series. Some features about the under-processing slides series, such as a fixed title position, will be figured out and applied in the adaptive rounds to improve the outline quality. The result of our experiments shows that the general accuracy of the final lecture outline reaches 85 %, which is about 13 % higher than the static method.

Keywords: E-learning · Lecture outline · Adaptive slides analysis

1 Introduction

E-lectures are very close to our daily lives today, and video is the core material for most online courses, no matter in traditional tele-teaching or MOOC (*Massive Open Online Course*). But how can learners find the lecture videos or segments exactly what they want among such huge amount of choices? Metadata is so far the best answer. Currently tags and manual descriptions are the main sources of such metadata, but we believe a lecture outline would be a better option.

Some studies suggest that students benefit from the lecture outline when taking online courses [1,2]. And a survey offered with a MOOC course [3] shows that 91 % of the respondents (*90 of 99*) believe an accurate outline could be a positive factor in their learning process. A proper outline contains much more information than tags and is much better structured than descriptions, which enables multiple functions such as preview, navigation, segmentation and retrieval.

It would be an extra burden for the lecturers if we ask them to provide outlines for their courses, and hiring others to create outline manually would cost lots of time or/and money. These facts prompt us to search for automated outline generation possibilities. However, concluding outline from lecture speech transcript [4] is too challenging, while capturing the teacher's writing on the blackboard [5] becomes less practical, because slides have occupied the front of the classroom nowadays [6,7].

F.W.B. Li et al. (Eds.): ICWL 2015, LNCS 9412, pp. 59–68, 2015.
DOI: 10.1007/978-3-319-25515-6_6

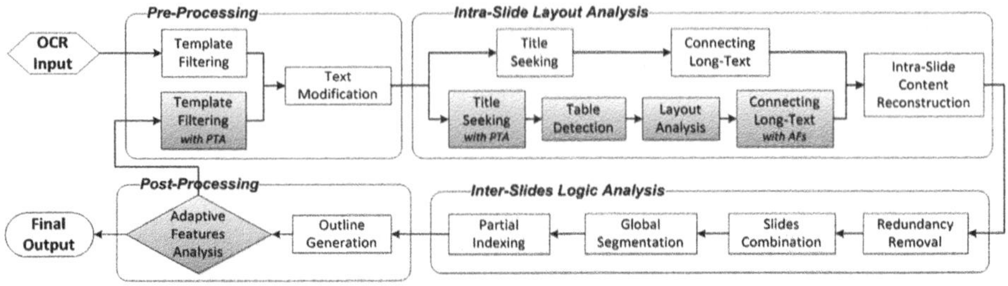

Fig. 1. The framework of proposed solution

Actually most of the lecturers use the slides exactly as the outline of their speeches. Parsing the digital slide files seems to be a good option. But in the purpose of navigation or segmentation, timing information is crucial, which the digital files cannot provide. Instead we will take the slide images extracted from real-time lecture video as the input. Slide images can be located and restored from the projection screen in traditional single-stream lecture video [8,9]. And with double-stream recording systems, such as Tele-TASK, a desktop stream recodes directly from the lecturer's computer. The accuracy of applying OCR (*Optical Character Recognition*) on the high quality slide images extracted from desktop stream reaches 85 % [10], which is available for further use.

Some early efforts have been made with the slides, by exploring the hierarchical semantic concepts [11] or locating the slide title [12]. The first slide-based lecture outline generator has been proposed in 2013 [13]. It explores different components within the slides according to a pre-defined "template" and achieves decent result. But the slide layout could be very diverse due to numerous different slide templates developed by agencies all over the world, the performance of [13] drops drastically when the slides do not fit the pre-defined template.

Therefore we intend to develop a "smarter" outline generator, with the ability to detect the characteristics of the template used by the under-processing slides series and adjust the analyzer adaptively. The initial round of the proposed solution is based on the static method described in [13]. Then four Adaptive Features (AF) describing the differences between slide templates will be analyzed from the output, including Potential Title Area (PTA), General Hierarchical Gap (GHG), Low Case Start (LCS) and Item Bullet (IB). PTA indicates the default title area and the others focus on template characteristics of text-blocks.

The AF-involved steps, along with a few steps implemented in adaptive rounds only, are marked with light blue background in Fig. 1. All AFs will be updated after each round and any change of them will trigger a new round. But the maximum of adaptive rounds has been set to 3, in order to avoid potential "dead loop". The result of slide transition analysis and OCR is taken as system input. Each round can be separated into pre-processing, intra-slide layout analysis, inter-slides logic analysis and post-processing, which will be further illustrated by Sects. 2, 3, 4 and 5 respectively. The evaluation and conclusion come afterwards.

2 Pre-processing

With OCR result as input, each slide can be simplified as a blank background and a group of text-lines. But not all the text-lines should be included in the outline. Since most of the lecturers or presenters will create their slides with affiliation-related templates, logos, names or the presentation titles may appear repeatedly throughout the whole slides series. Thus, a searching scheme is applied to traverse all the slides and mark those repeatedly appearing text-lines with same content and position. If the number of a text-line's accumulated appearances is beyond the threshold, it will be removed from all slides. Sometimes a real slide title, or part of it, might also be shared in multiple continuous slides under the risk of being marked as redundant. So we introduce one adaptive feature, the potential title area, to the pre-processing in adaptive rounds. Any text-lines in the PTA will bypass the pre-processing.

Another task in pre-processing is to modify ill-recognized text-lines caused by OCR errors. Nobody wants to see meaningless strings in the lecture outline, so they need to be deleted. The standards to define meaninglessness include the average word length smaller than 2 characters, extreme text-lines sizes (*either too large or too small*), containing too many same letters or symbols, etc. Moreover, the extra space in the beginning of the text-lines will also be removed here.

3 Intra-slide Layout Analysis

3.1 Title Seeking

Slide title is the most important component in building a lecture outline. We search title candidates in the top 1/3 of the slide. A text-line must have an above-average height and locate not too close to the slide edges. Since the title may occupy multiple rows, including potential subtitle, we accept up to 3 candidates as long as they locate closely. In adaptive rounds, we search prior within the PTA zone. PTA has a strict limitation on vertical position but is quite open horizontally. If a text-line located in this bar-shaped PTA zone, it will be accepted as title candidate and exclude all text-lines out of the zone. With this effort some text components in the slides, which are occasionally near the title, will no longer be mistakenly recognized as the subtitle.

3.2 Table Detection

Table is a type of frequently used data structure in slides. When existing, it contains a lot of detailed information, which we do not need in the outline. We develop a table detection algorithm specialized for slide images. It begins with detecting rows and columns from the text-lines. And then their intersections will be found. An evaluation process comes afterwards to examine whether these intersections belong to a table by analyzing their content, structure and location. When confirmed, these intersections will be considered as a table prototype and further expanded alongside the rows and columns. A final rectangle table area will form and all text-lines inside it will be removed.

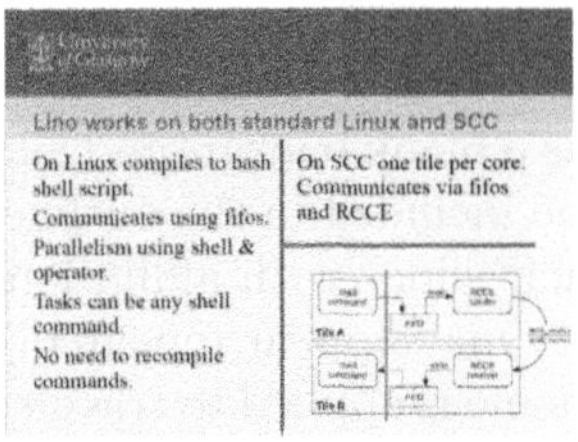

(a) Left-Right-Bottom

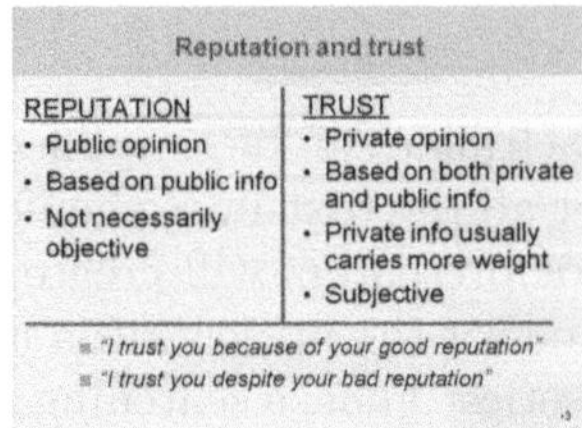

(b) Left-Top-Bottom

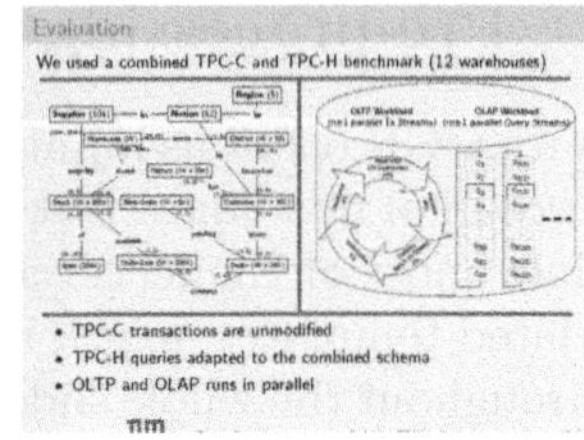

(c) Top-Left-Right-Bottom

Fig. 2. The examples of page layout analysis (Color figure online)

3.3 Page Layout Analysis

The slide layout can be very diverse. Besides the tables, diagrams or multi-column layout may also lead to complex text-lines distribution, which cause a lot of problems in the static method. Detecting them will definitely improve the accuracy of slide content reconstruction. Ignoring the title area, we attempt to split text-lines into groups with proper vertical and horizontal axis, as the red lines shown in Fig. 2[1]. Each group can be represented as a block, either a text block to be further processed, or a diagram block to be deleted. The specific procedures are introduced as follow:

1. Attempt to find a middle line which horizontally divides all text-lines, except for the title, into left and right blocks. If there are more than one option, apply the one closest to the absolute middle. (*Fig.* 2-*a*)
2. For every left-block or right-block, if there is a huge line space inside the block, split it again vertically. (*Right block in Fig.* 2-*a*)
3. If step 1 failed, attempt top-left-right or left-right-bottom layout. In this case no further vertically splitting is applied. (*Fig.* 2-*b*)
4. If step 3 still failed, attempt top-left-right-bottom layout, treat the middle parts as diagram and remove them. (*Fig.* 2-*c*)
5. Any blocks which can be further horizontally split will be removed as diagram. (*Right-bottom sub block in Fig.* 2-*a, with light blue line*)
6. Analyze all remaining blocks by their content. A block contains many digits, single words or not well-aligned will also be considered as a part of diagram or chart and gets deleted.

After removing the blocks supposed to be diagrams, every block left is acknowledged as text block and will be treated as an independent text system in following procedures. For those slides which cannot be split into blocks, all their text-lines is considered as a whole, in other words, an entire block.

[1] The copyright of the example slides belongs to original authors: Mr. Paul Cockshott, Prof. Audun Jøsang & Prof. Thomas Neumann.

3.4 Continuous Text-Line Combination

When several text-lines locating in different rows belong to a long statement, they need to be reconnected. We take the factors like line spaces, horizontal positions and text-line initials under consideration, in addition with some adaptive features. Here we take t_{n-1} and t_n to represent the text-lines supposed to be combined and explain the decisive factors as follow:

◇ When IB is positive, a combination will be suggested if t_{n-1} has a bullet but t_n does not. if t_n has a bullet, the combination will be strongly opposed.
◇ The text-line initial can be upper-case, no-case (*digit e.g.*) or lower-case, with descending values. A combination will be suggested when the value of t_{n-1} is larger than t_n. If LCS is positive, the weight of this factor decreases.
◇ If the line space of t_{n-1} and t_n is way larger than their heights, or obviously larger than the line space of t_n and t_{n+1}, a combination is opposed.
◇ The left-ends of t_{n-1} and t_n should be horizontally close if they belong to same sentence. Please note if the difference of their horizontal starting points fits the GHG, the combination will be vetoed.
◇ All text-lines sharing same horizontal starting point with t_{n-1} will be traversed and the widest one will be taken as reference. Only if the difference between the width of t_{n-1} and the reference is smaller than the width of the first word in t_n, the combination could be suggested.

All above factors will be quantified, with "suggested" into positive values while "opposed" or "vetoed" into negative. Finally if the sum is above 0, a combination will be applied. Please note the combination of multi-rows text-lines is implemented within text blocks, but if a combination is necessary between same-row text-lines, it would be done before the page layout analysis.

3.5 Tree-Structure Outline Reconstruction

The default content reconstruction method, which is the only option in initial round, begins with searching a large enough text-line (*above average height at least*) whose left-end locates in the left-top quarter of the slide. It will be taken as the datum. Then by checking the horizontally aligned and vertically adjacent text-lines of this datum, up to 3 hierarchies will be marked and the tree-structure outline can be generated.

In adaptive rounds more possibilities can be provided. Taking text blocks from the layout analysis as input, a second method specialized for center-aligned situation is applied on such text system which contains less than 5 text-lines. The first text-line is directly set to level-1, and all other text-lines center-aligned to the first will be set to level-2. If there are more than 5 text-lines in the block, a third method is introduced. It traverses all the text-lines to find out the most frequently used left-end as the datum, then locates the 3 potential hierarchies.

By comparing the result of the default method and the alternative, the method that makes more text-lines involved in the system will be adopted. If a slide is divided into several blocks, their content will be combined together according to the order of top-left-right-bottom.

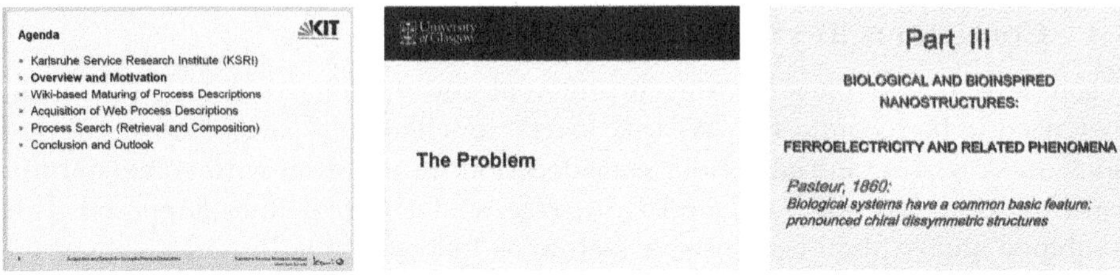

(a) Tag-Page (b) Split-Page (c) Section-Page

Fig. 3. The examples of "border" slides

4 Inter-slides Logic Analysis

4.1 Redundancy Removal and Slides Combination

Redundancy is something that every lecturer attempts to avoid when creating slides. But in real-time presentation, it is quite natural to roll back to a previous slide for further explanation or just misoperate, either of which causes extra slide transitions and results in repeated slides, such as making an original slide sequence 'A-B-C-D' into 'A_1-B_1-C_1-B_2-A_2-B_3-C_2-D'. We use Levenshtein Distance [14] (L.D.) to evaluate how similar two slides are, along with counting the number of same words (S.W.) existing in compared slides. For repeated slides just like A_1 and A_2, L.D. is supposed to be small while S.W. is large. Then the redundancy can be removed.

Slide combination takes place when two adjacent slides share the same title, sometimes with additional numbers, like "(1/3)", "<b>" or "III". There are two possibilities: either a progressive displayed slide is detected as several independent slides, or a key point needs to be discussed in several continuous slides. In such cases the slides will be merged and the text-lines involved in intra-slide content-trees keep their hierarchies unchanged.

4.2 Global Segmentation and Partial Indexing

In many cases a lecture consists of several segments, each of which focuses on a subtopic. Some lecturers mark those segments directly by using special "border" slides, such as a tag-page which is a rough outline of the lecture with a certain highlighted text-line, a split-page which contains only one text-line indicating the subtopic, or a section-page which has special phrases like "Part 1" or "Section two" in its title. Examples can be found in Fig. 3[2]. By confirming these border slides, the whole lecture can be easily segmented globally.

For the lectures without available border slides, or when the globally segmented subtopics are still too general, we propose partial indexing to explore

[2] The copyright of the example slides belongs to original authors: Prof. Rudi Studer, Mr. Paul Cockshott & Prof. Gil Rosenman.

the connections within neighboring slides. Sometimes a slide may act as a preview of several following slides by listing their titles. We address it as index-page, mark it the root node of a partial segment and link previewed slides as its leaves. The range of a partial segment led by an index-page cannot beyond the border of global segments. In extreme instance, a leaf node linked to an index-page inside a global segment can be in level-3.

Besides, we also search for continuous slides with same keyword or prefix in their titles, by which these slides are supposed to illustrate different aspects of a certain topic. If a noun or a phrase repeatedly appears in the floating search interval, a virtual index-page will be created, taking the keyword or prefix as the title. This virtual index-page will be inserted before the interval and act as a real index-page. And virtual index-page searching is only available for slides not included in any global segments.

5 Post-processing

By setting the slide title as level-0 root element in the intra-slide content tree, every text-line has an intra-slide hierarchy ranged 0–3. In addition with an inter-slides hierarchy ranged 1–3, a final hierarchy of each text-line can be calculated by a simple addition, which is ranged 1–6 in tree-structure outline.

Meanwhile, the adaptive features are also achieved or updated. The title position of each slide is recorded and the repeatedly used positions (*1/4 of all slides*) are stored as PTAs. The gap between level-1 and level-2 text-lines within each slide is also recorded. If more than 1/4 slides have similar hierarchical gaps, the value will be saved in GHG. The boolean attributes LCS and IB derive from the statistics of the final outline. When more than 30 % of outline items begin with lower-case letters, LCS will be set to "true". And threshold for IB, which means a subtopic begins with a bullet recognized as single character, just like 'o' or 'u', is 20 %. Any change in AFs will trigger a new round, unless this is already the 3rd adaptive round.

6 Evaluation

In our evaluation session, we select 12 complete e-lectures or academic presentations of 12 different lecturers from Tele-TASK platform to build the test dataset. A total number of 354 pages of original slides are supposed to be extracted from the desktop stream of 437 min of lecture videos, by which the diversity of the dataset could be assured. A lecture ID is used to identify certain lecture, and all these lectures are publicly available[3], in addition with the manually created ground-truth of the lecture outlines[4]. We would like to compare the performances of proposed adaptive solution with the static outline generation method introduced in [13].

[3] The lecture (ID = 'id') is in http://www.tele-task.de/archive/lecture/overview/id/.

[4] https://drive.google.com/folderview?id=0B13Cc1a7ebTufmV6WFRCbmxPYllxR3hYNE1SRUtWN3hxZl9tdHBPaHU0THZwOXVpM29sZEE&usp=sharing.

Table 1. Intra-slide accuracy report

	ID	Character Aspect			Item Aspect					
		Length	L.D.	Precision	G.T.	Hit	Recall	All	Correct	Precision
Static Solution	5626	2305	393	83.0%	66	50	75.8%	82	36	43.9%
	5759	5596	1625	71.0%	208	162	77.9%	215	128	59.5%
	6011	6888	596	91.3%	123	115	93.5%	132	101.5	76.9%
	6031	6103	961	84.3%	158	129	81.6%	139	114	82.0%
	6102	5637	1223	78.3%	162	147	90.7%	184	137	74.5%
	6106	4417	2800	36.6%	107	87	81.3%	169	68.5	40.5%
	6196	7742	2585	66.6%	268	152	56.7%	194	132.5	68.3%
	6201	3381	786	76.8%	118	104	88.1%	133	100.5	75.6%
	6261	4268	1273	70.2%	132	98	74.2%	132	93.5	70.8%
	6266	2569	272	89.4%	65	63	96.9%	81	61	75.3%
	6663	4014	245	93.9%	98	94	95.9%	113	89.5	79.2%
	7314	2820	1352	52.1%	83	63	75.9%	109	60	55.0%
	All	55740	14111	**74.7%**	1588	1264	**79.6%**	1683	1122	**66.7%**
Adaptive Solution	5626	2305	205	91.1%	66	64	97.0%	68	58.5	86.0%
	5759	5596	755	86.5%	208	185	88.9%	205	156	76.1%
	6011	6888	612	91.1%	123	110	89.4%	124	98	79.0%
	6031	6103	515	91.6%	158	154	97.5%	166	146.5	88.3%
	6102	5637	1263	77.6%	162	153	94.4%	184	141	76.6%
	6106	4417	1074	75.7%	107	102	95.3%	139	89	64.0%
	6196	7742	1767	77.2%	268	230	85.8%	257	220	85.6%
	6201	3381	328	90.3%	118	112	94.9%	117	111	94.9%
	6261	4268	506	88.1%	132	115	87.1%	136	105.5	76.1%
	6266	2569	302	88.2%	65	63	96.9%	76	60.5	79.6%
	6663	4014	205	94.9%	98	91	92.9%	94	87	92.6%
	7314	2820	407	66.6%	83	68	81.9%	78	59.5	76.3%
	All	55740	7939	**85.8%**	1588	1447	**91.1%**	1644	1330.5	**80.9%**

First we focus on the intra-slide phase with two aspects: characters and items. In character aspect, the whole content-tree of a slide is connected together as a string, and a Levenshtein distance (L.D.) will be calculated against the ground-truth (G.T.). The smaller the L.D. is, the higher the precision reaches. Then in item aspect, whether a content-tree is hierarchically accurate will be tested. The content and the hierarchy of an outline item value 0.5 respectively. And by comparing with the G.T., both recall and precision can be obtained. Please note minor differences in characters leading no misunderstanding will be ignored here, because they have already affected in character aspect. Statistics can be found in Table 1.

The second phase of evaluation focuses on the inter-slides logic. Slide title will represent the whole slide, with a string and a hierarchy ranged 1∼3. Similar to the item-aspect intra-slide evaluation, the string and the hierarchy weight 50 % each. Table 2 shows the result. Total Slides (T.S.) indicates how many slides have been extracted from the video originally, which in many cases differs from the G.T., due to the logical inter-slides processing.

A final accuracy is calculated generalizing all aspects, as shown in Formation (1). The general intra-slide item-level accuracy is achieved by applying

Table 2. Inter-slides accuracy report

ID	T.S.	G.T.	Static		Adaptive	
			Correct	Accuracy	Correct	Accuracy
5626	17	13	10	76.9 %	10	76.9 %
5759	45	20	5.5	27.5 %	19.5	97.5 %
6011	18	10	5	50.0 %	8	80.0 %
6031	22	20	7	35.0 %	19	95.0 %
6102	36	30	26.5	88.3 %	28	93.3 %
6106	28	28	25	89.3 %	25	89.3 %
6196	81	31	19	61.3 %	21.5	69.4 %
6201	25	25	22	88.0 %	23	92.0 %
6261	27	20	12	60.0 %	14	70.0 %
6266	18	18	12.5	69.4 %	14	77.8 %
6663	20	20	19	95.0 %	19	95.0 %
7314	17	18	12	66.7 %	10.5	58.3 %
All	354	253	175.5	**69.4 %**	211.5	**83.6 %**

Table 3. General accuracies

	Intra-slide (A_1)			Inter-slides (A_2)	A_{final}
	Character (P_C)	Item			
		R_I	P_I		
Static	74.7 %	79.6 %	66.7 %	69.4 %	**71.5 %**
Adaptive	85.8 %	91.1 %	80.9 %	83.6 %	**84.7 %**

F-measure (*harmonic mean*) on recall (R_I) and precision (P_I). Then the G-measure (*geometric mean*) of both item-level accuracy and character-level precision (P_C) represents the general intra-slide accuracy. The final accuracy derives from the G-measure of both intra-slide and inter-slides accuracies (A_1 *and* A_2). From the statistics illustrated in Table 3, we can easily figure out that the general accuracy of proposed solution reaches approximately 85 %.

$$A_{final} = \sqrt{A_2 \cdot \sqrt{P_C \cdot \frac{R_I \cdot P_I}{R_I + P_I}}} \quad (1)$$

7 Conclusion and Future Work

In this paper we introduce our effort in generating outline adaptively for online lectures by analyzing the slides extracted from videos. The proposed solution goes by analyzing and further utilizing the specified features of the certain under-processing slides series. The evaluation shows that the accuracy of final output reached 85 %. In the future we tend to adjust our system for the compromised slide images from single-stream lecture video, enable the digital slide file parsing for accuracy improvement and apply further applications, such as lecture video retrieval, based on the outline generated.

References

1. Grabe, M., Christopherson, K.: Optional student use of online lecture resources: resource preferences, performance and lecture attendance. J. Comput. Assist. Learn. **24**(1), 1–10 (2008)
2. Lonn, S., Teasley, S.D.: Saving time or innovating practice: investigating perceptions and uses of learning management systems. Comput. Educ. **53**(3), 686–694 (2009)
3. Che, X., Luo, S., Wang, C., Meinel, C.: An attempt at mooc localization for chinese-speaking users. Int. J. Inf. Educ. Technol. **6**(2), 90 (2016)
4. Zhang, J., Chan, R.H.Y., Fung, P., Cao, L.: A comparative study on speech summarization of broadcast news and lecture speech. In: Interspeech. pp. 2781–2784. Citeseer (2007)
5. Onishi, M., Izumi, M., Fukunaga, K.: Blackboard segmentation using video image of lecture and its applications. In: 15th International Conference on Pattern Recognition, Proceedings, vol. 4, pp. 615–618. IEEE (2000)
6. Hill, A., Arford, T., Lubitow, A., Smollin, L.M.: Im ambivalent about it the dilemmas of powerpoint. Teach. Sociol. **40**(3), 242–256 (2012)
7. Levasseur, D.G., Kanan Sawyer, J.: Pedagogy meets powerpoint: a research review of the effects of computer-generated slides in the classroom. Rev. Commun. **6**(1–2), 101–123 (2006)
8. Li, K., Wang, J., Wang, H., Dai, Q.: Structuring lecture videos by automatic projection screen localization and analysis. IEEE Trans. Pattern Anal. Mach. Intell. **37**(6), 1233–1246 (2015)
9. Schroth, G., Cheung, N.M., Steinbach, E., Girod, B.: Synchronization of presentation slides and lecture videos using bit rate sequences. In: 18th IEEE International Conference on Image Processing (ICIP), pp. 925–928. IEEE (2011)
10. Yang, H., Siebert, M., Luhne, P., Sack, H., Meinel, C.: Lecture video indexing and analysis using video ocr technology. In: 2011 Seventh International Conference on Signal-Image Technology and Internet-Based Systems (SITIS), pp. 54–61. IEEE (2011)
11. Atapattu, T., Falkner, K., Falkner, N.: Automated extraction of semantic concepts from semi-structured data: supporting computer-based education through the analysis of lecture notes. In: Liddle, S.W., Schewe, K.-D., Tjoa, A.M., Zhou, X. (eds.) DEXA 2012, Part I. LNCS, vol. 7446, pp. 161–175. Springer, Heidelberg (2012)
12. Yang, H., Gruenewald, F., Meinel, C.: Automated extraction of lecture outlines from lecture videos-a hybrid solution for lecture video indexing. In: Proceedings of 4th International Conference on Computer Supported Education (CSEDU), pp. 13–22 (2012)
13. Che, X., Yang, H., Meinel, C.: Tree-structure outline generation for lecture videos with synchronized slides. In: 2013 Second International Conference on e-Learning and e-Technologies in Education (ICEEE), pp. 87–92. IEEE (2013)
14. Levenshtein, V.I.: Binary codes capable of correcting deletions, insertions and reversals. In: Soviet physics doklady, vol. 10, p. 707 (1966)

Design, Model and Framework of e-Learning Systems

Topic-Specific Recommendation for Open Education Resources

Jun Wang[1(✉)], Junfu Xiang[2], and Kanji Uchino[1]

[1] Fujitsu Laboratories of America, Sunnyvale, CA 94085, USA
{jun.wang,kanji}@us.fujitsu.com
[2] Nanjing Fujitsu Nanda Software Technology Co., Ltd., Najing, China
xiangjf.fnst@cn.fujitsu.com

Abstract. Most of the Open Educational Resources are scattered around the Web, and not well described and structured so causing huge problems in their use, search, organization and management. We present a system which can collect and analyze domain-specific contents from massive online learning materials and publications, and automatically identify domain-specific knowledge terms and aggregate them into well-organized topics. The system helps learners who want to learn cutting-edge technology to effectively and efficiently locate appropriate online courses and learning materials using topic-specific recommendation. We further examines the system with real-world data and applications.

Keywords: Open education resources · Topic-specific recommendation · Automated extraction of knowledge terms

1 Introduction

The Web can be described as an ocean of information and knowledge usable for learning. Theoretically, learners can flexibly choose the subjects they want and build up their own curriculum and study schedule which suits their personal needs. However, most of the Open Educational Resources (OERs) are scattered around the Web, and not well described and structured so causing huge problems in their use, search, organization and management. Therefore, it is not easy for learners to locate and judge which learning materials are the right ones for them from massive online learning materials. This is one of the reasons why education done through personalized informal learning is still less effective than through personal interaction in a classroom.

Although some standardized domain knowledge structure like curriculum or ontology exists, they suffer from excessive generalization and only exceptionally fit to the learners' needs at the desired level of granularity [9]. In such cases the domain knowledge structure has to be created "from scratch". Unfortunately, manual construction is a tedious and time-consuming task even for small domains. Compared with traditional and classic courses (such as K12 mathematics), the new and advanced fields (such as machine learning and deep learning)

F.W.B. Li et al. (Eds.): ICWL 2015, LNCS 9412, pp. 71–81, 2015.
DOI: 10.1007/978-3-319-25515-6_7

without mature and stable curriculum have even more serious issues. The success of any e-learning system depends on the organization of learning materials with respect to a domain knowledge structure [8], and practically the domain knowledge structure can be organized into multiple layers: basic concepts represented as domain-specific knowledge terms and high level topics.

In order to address the above issues, we propose a topic-specific recommendation system for OERs, which makes the following main contributions. First, we present a system which can collect and analyze domain-specific contents from massive online learning materials and publications, and automatically identify domain-specific terms and aggregate them into well-organized topics. Second, the system presents an novel approach for topic-specific recommendation, which helps learners who want to learn cutting-edge technology to effectively and efficiently locate appropriate online courses and learning materials. Third, the system is demonstrated and examined with real-world applications.

We organize the remainder of the paper as follows. Section 2 illustrates the general framework of the system we propose. Section 3 presents our experimental results on real-world applications. Section 4 introduces some related work. Finally, Sect. 5 summarizes our work and discuss the future work.

2 System Framework

As shown in the Fig. 1, we briefly describe the system framework.

2.1 Focused Crawling for Domain-Specific OERs

There are a few centralized OCW and MOOC portal sites, such as MIT OCW, Coursera and edX, but most OERs are sparsely distributed on scattered sources

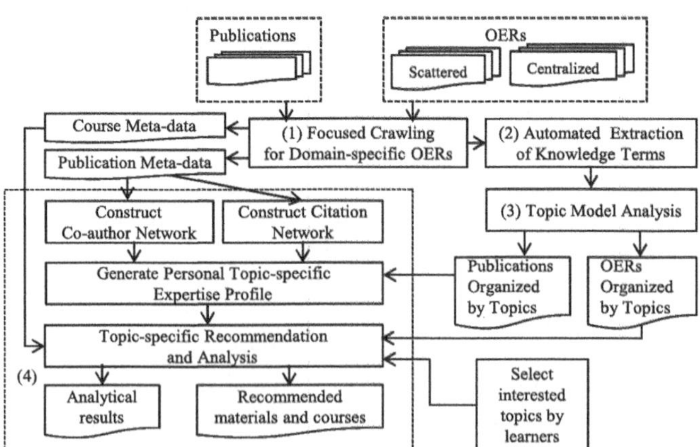

Fig. 1. The system framework.

such as personal home pages of professors [11]. In addition, scientific publications online also can be valuable learning materials, especially for cutting-edge technology domains. The contents in the centralized OER sites usually are generated by templates of content management systems, so we can easily generate site-specific extraction rules based on limited page templates of these sites, and automatically acquire all required information. Since most scientific publications are generally available in specific literature databases with structural meta-data such as DBLP, it is straightforward to collect and extract related information. However, crawling and extracting information from scattered OERs is a much more challenging task, and we create a genre-based focused crawler which can automatically and efficiently discover and identify specific types (or genres) of pages including online courses and corresponding learning materials contained, and collect and extract information from them [11].

During the crawling, we can naturally and simultaneously extract meta-data including names of lecturers or professors offering courses and learning materials, and institution names. Authors and citations can be easily extracted as meta-data from online publications as well.

2.2 Automated Extraction of Knowledge Terms

Although OERs offer abundant and valuable educational contents, most of them usually are not well structured and organized. Ideally, we would like to have a universal knowledge structure which illustrates all basic knowledge units or concepts being taught in a broad range of courses in specific domains, and it is helpful to support decision making such as curricula planning for students, and to support course and curriculum design by teachers based on OER offerings. As shown in Tables 1 and 2, knowledge terms are important artefacts for representing knowledge in and formulating scientific knowledge. Researchers describe knowledge terms as the linguistic representation of the basic knowledge units or concepts in a particular domain [5]. For cutting-edge domains with rapid change, only few domain experts are capable of creating a repository of knowledge terms. Clearly, manual specification is not scalable, and does not adapt over time without the dedication of further expensive resources [5]. So we propose a robust approach to automatically extract knowledge terms of different length without relying on complicated linguistic analysis or hand work.

For crawled web pages or documents of domain-specific learning materials, page format and layout analysis can applied to detect sequence borders such as line breaks, table cell borders, sentence borders and specific punctuations. The pages and documents are segmented into a batch of sequences of tokens (or words) based on the detected borders. With regular pre-processing such as normalizing plurality and removing specific punctuations, all individual sequences are feeded into a generalized suffix tree (GST) [2], which offers an efficient data structure to quickly find repeated sub-sequences (or phrases) as candidates of knowledge terms. Every term instance occurred in the GST contains related information, such as its positions in the source sequence and the source page or document, respectively. Post-processing can be applied to filter out candidate phrases that start or end with auxiliary stop-words (e.g. conjunctions, prepositions, personal pronouns) [5], and acquire statistical information of each candidate phrase. For instance, a frequency threshold can be used to filter rare candidates, and the mutual information and branching entropy can be used to deal with overlapped candidates [6,7]. For instances, "statistical machine learning" and "machine learning" are identified as knowledge terms, but "statistical machine" is invalid. In addition to heuristic rules, specific methods based on machine learning can be applied to estimate parameters of statistical information and refine candidates as well [6].

2.3 Topic Model Analysis

Sometimes navigation and search through keywords or knowledge terms alone are not enough, and we might want to study a topic that we are interested in. Topic models have become a popular method for discovering the abstract topics underlying a collection of documents, and it can help us further refine domain knowledge structure with thematic or topical views, and facilitate understanding, organization and exploration of vast amounts of OER contents. We might "zoom in" and "zoom out" to find specific or broader topics; we might look at how those topics changed through time or how they are connected to each other. Topic models are based upon the idea that documents are mixtures of topics, where a topic is a probability distribution over words [4]. Given a collection of learning material documents and a specified number of topics, a topic model can automatically assign a topic to every word in a document, and further obtain corresponding topic distribution in the document. The conventional topic model is based on the "bag-of-words" assumption, and a list of most probable unigrams is used to describe individual topics, yet these unigrams often provide a hard-to-interpret or ambiguous representation of the topics [3]. The GST constructed in Sect. 2.2 is tracking knowledge term instances in source learning material documents, so the documents can easily be represented as the "bag-of-terms" and feeded into the topic model analysis. As shown in Table 2, augmenting unigrams with knowledge terms provides a more intuitively understandable and accurate description of a topic. Clearly, the knowledge term "Support Vector Machine" is much more interpretable and readable than one single word "machine" or "vector" in a topic representation list.

2.4 Topic-Specific Recommendation and Analysis

In a practical example, if a learner is interested in some topics in machine learning and data mining, and she can easily find dozens of online courses which look similar or with ambiguous course titles, but how should she select appropriate ones without sufficient understanding of courses and learning materials? Or how much do those courses overlap with each other? Traditional educational institutes solve this problem in the old-fashioned way via academic advisors, but it is not suitable for a informal learner. But after we have established domain knowledge structure of online courses and learning materials, which can be represented with basic knowledge terms and well-organized topics, it is possible to offer an efficient facility to recommended appropriate learning materials aligned with specific topics of interest.

Generally, in cutting-edge domains experts with topic-specific expertise are more likely to offer high quality learning contents. Domain-specific publications are valuable sources for evaluating personal expertise and generate corresponding topic-specific profile.

As shown in Fig. 2, a co-author network and a citation network can be constructed based on the publication meta-data MP extracted in Sect. 2.1. If the total number of publications is p, and MP is a vector of length p, and we can extract the total number of unique authors a. The co-author network is a undirected graph, in which each node is representing an author, and an edge between two nodes is representing co-author relation between two authors. The citation network is a directed graph, in which each node is representing a publication, and an edge is representing a citation relation between two publications. We can use centrality metrics, such as betweenness [1], to measure personal influence of authors among the co-author network, and use PageRank [1] to measure influence of publications in the citation network. Topic model analysis in Sect. 2.3 can reveal topic distributions TDP of all p publications, and if k is the number of topics, TDP is a $p \times k$ matrix. As shown in *Algorithm 1*, the topic-specific expertise profile EP of all authors is a $a \times k$ matrix, which can be generated based on TDP and PR (influence of all publications) and CB (personal influence of all authors).

Algorithm 1: Topic-specific Expertise Profile Generation

```
Input: Meta-data MP and Topic Distribution TDP of Publications
Output: Expertise Profile EP
    Authors = GetAllUniqueAuthors(MP)
    a = |Authors| #Authors is a vector of length a
    p = |MP|
    CoAuthorNet = ConstructCoAuthorNetwork(MP)
    CB = Centrality(CoAuthorNet) #CB is a vector of length a
    CitationNet = ConstructCitationNetwork(MP)
    PR = PageRank(CitationNet) #PR is a vector of length p
    Initialize EP with 0
    for i := 1  to a do
        for j := 1 to p do
            if Authors[i] in Publication j
            EP[i] += TDP[j] * PR[j]
        EP[i] *= CB[i]
    return EP
```

Topic model analysis in Sect. 2.3 also recovers topic distributions TDO of all courses and learning materials contained. If there are c courses which contain m learning materials in total, TDO is a $m \times k$ matrix. The course meta-data MO extracted in Sect. 2.1 is a vector of length m. From MO we can extract all unique lecturers into a vector *Lecturers* of length l. Every lecturer is assigned a BASELINE expertise, a constant vector of length k, and if a lecturer is also a publication author, then her corresponding expertise in EP will be added as well. As shown in Fig. 2 and *Algorithm 2*, based on the above information and the author expertise profile EP, we can recommend appropriate OERs including courses and learning materials according to interested topics T of a learner. T is a vector of length k, in which the elements corresponding to the interested topics are 1, and 0 otherwise. Various analysis also can be applied to OER contents for insightful understanding, such as trend or evolution of specific topics.

Algorithm 2: Topic-specific Recommendation and Analysis

```
Input: Meta-data MO and Topic Distributions TDO of OERs
       Expertise Profile EP and Interested Topics T
Output: Recommended learning material list RM and Course list RC
    Lecturers = GetAllUniqueLecturers(MO)
    l = |Lecturers| #Lecturers is a vector of length l
    Materials = GetMaterialList(MO); m = |Materials|
    Courses = GetCourseList(MO); c = |Courses|
    Initialize LEP with 0 #a l*k matrix of Lecturer Expertise profile
    Initialize RM with 0 #a vector of length m
    Initialize RC with 0 #a vector of length c
    for i:=1 to l do
        LEP[i] = BASELINE
        if Lecturers[i] is found in publication authors
            Get corresponding author_id in EP
            LEP[i] += EP[author_id]
    for i:= 1 to m do
        lecturer_id = GetCurrentLecturer(MO,i)
        course_id = GetCurrentCourse(MO,i)
        for j:= 1 to k do
            if T[j] == 0:
                LEP[lecturer_id][j] = 0
        score = LEP[lecturer_id]*TDO[i]
        RM[i] = score
        RC[course_id] += score
    select Top-N of RM, RC by score
    return RM, RC
```

3 Experiments

In this section, the system is demonstrated and examined with real-world data. We begin with the description of datasets. The system mainly focuses on helping informal learners who want to study cutting-edge technology to find appropriate OER contents, and in practice, it can be applied to any scientific domain. We select *machine learning* as the domain for experiments, because it is a rapidly

Table 1. Examples of auto-extracted multi-word knowledge terms.

Length = 2	*Length* = 3	*Length* ≥ 4
Neural network	Support vector machine	Markov chain monte carlo
Graphical model	Hidden markov model	Deep convolutional neural network
Gaussian process	Latent dirichlet allocation	Stochastic dual coordinate ascent
Topic model	Principal component analysis	Alternating direction method of multiplier
Dimensionality reduction	Restricted boltzmann machine	Partially observable markov decision process
...	...	...

changing and emerging domain, and there are relatively abundant domain-specific OERs available online as well. Based on the focused crawling method in Sect. 2.1, we collect a wide range of online courses, from which we find 75 machine learning related courses containing 1672 lecture notes from 49 lecturers of 21 universities. We also collect publication data from top machine learning related academic conferences and journals including 3300 papers of International Conference on Machine Learning (ICML), 5439 papers of Neural Information Processing Systems (NIPS) and 1069 papers of Journal of Machine Learning Research (JMLR) from 10142 authors in total.

In practice, knowledge terms with more than 5 words are very rare, so we set the maximum length as 5 and the frequency threshold as 20, and extract 591 knowledge terms from the above datasets using the heuristic rule-based method in Sect. 2.2. Table 1 shows real examples of auto-extracted multi-word knowledge terms. Abbreviations also can be identified and unified into corresponding original knowledge terms, such as "support vector machine (SVM)", "hidden markov model (HMM)", "latent dirichlet allocation (LDA)", "principal component analysis (PCA)", "markov chain monte carlo (MCMC)", "alternating direction method of multiplier (ADMM)" and "partially observable markov decision process (POMDP)".

Generally, we can use precision and recall to evaluate quality of extracted knowledge terms. The extracted terms are presented to three experienced researchers familiar with machine learning for manually checking if they are correct, and the average precision from the three researchers is 90.4 %. However, we don't have the ground truth of all correct knowledge terms, so recall cannot be measured directly. Recently, two senior researchers took huge efforts and manually curated knowledge term lists[1] including 361 terms in the machine learning domain. We can compare our extracted terms with the curated terms, and evaluate the coverage rate, which is a reasonable alternative of recall. And the experiments show that our auto-extracted terms from OERs and publications achieves coverage of 82.5 %, which is comparable to the state of art [6].

After running experiments with different values of k, we select the topic number $k = 20$. Table 2 shows real examples of auto-discovered topics and corresponding knowledge terms. We present all the discovered topics with the corresponding frequent knowledge terms to the same three researchers, and ask

[1] https://www.metacademy.org/browse.

Table 2. Examples of auto-discovered topics and corresponding representations with knowledge terms.

Topic 1 (learning methods)	Topic 2 (probabilistic graphical models)	Topic 3 (neural network and deep learning)	Topic 4 (brain activity)
Machine learning	Graphical model	Neural network	Neural activity
Reinforcement learning	Topic model	Recurrent neural network	Spiking neuron
Active learning	Hidden markov model	Deep belief network	Visual cortex
Supervised learning	Conditional random field	Deep learning	Firing rate
Unsupervised learning	Latent dirichlet allocation	Convolutional neural network	Neural response
...	...	...	

them to check if a identified topic is informative and corresponding knowledge terms contained are coherent. For example, all 4 topics in Table 2 are informative and coherent, and can be described with succinct labels, respectively. All the three researchers independently find the same one topic containing terms, such as *dynamic programming, global linear models, domain knowledge, prior knowledge*, which are meaningful machine learning concepts but not coherent with each other, so we cannot label the topic with a succinct description. Two researchers identify all other 19 topics as informative and coherent. One researcher agrees on 17 topics with the two other researchers, but identifies 2 topics as coherent and non-informative, because one topic mainly contains terms such as *data sets, training data, labelled data*, and another topic mainly contains terms such as *experimental results, theoretical results, case study*. The results show that a well-organized knowledge structure can be established by the topic model.

Based on *Algorithm 1* in Sect. 2.4, the topic-specific expertise profile of all publication authors can be generated, and Table 3 shows real examples of several influential machine learning researchers, and due to limited space, it only lists some top topic-specific expertise of each researcher. The results are also presented to the same three researchers, and all of them think that the expertise profile data are consistent with their general impressions to top topic-specific experts, which are accumulated from their experiences based on long-term literature reading. The system generates a integrated profile page for every person, which lists personal topic-specific expertise, and topic distributions of all personal publications, courses and learning materials. As shown in Fig. 2(a), the three researchers with the highest expertise scores on the topic of *neural network and deep learning* discovered by the system are exactly the three most famous leaders reviving the topic together.

After generating the topic-specific expertise profile, we can further apply *Algorithm 2* in Sect. 2.4 to the collected OER data organized by topic, and recommend appropriate courses and learning materials based on topics of interest selected by a learner. Table 4 shows some real examples of recommended topic-specific courses, and due to space limit, examples of recommended learning materials are not presented. The topic-specific recommendation results are presented to the three experienced researchers again for evaluation. All of them think recommended courses of over 15 topics are high quality contents suitable for a

Table 3. Examples of personal topic-specific expertise profile.

Person	Total score	Topic-specific expertise
Eric P. Xing	51.91	Graphical model (26 %)
David M. Blei	37.95	Graphical model (48 %)
Michael I. Jordan	117.92	Graphical model (18 %), machine learning (9 %)
Yee Whye Teh	40.93	Graphical model (37 %), inference (11 %)
Joshua B. Tenenbaum	33.91	Graphical model (30 %), machine learning (15 %)
Zoubin Ghahramani	71.93	Graphical model (34 %), inference (10 %)
Geoffrey E. Hinton	67.93	Pattern recognition (16 %), neural network (9 %)
Yoshua Bengio	63.92	Neural network (17 %), graphical model (12 %)
Yann LeCun	34.2	Neural network (16 %), pattern recognition (13 %)
Andrew Y. Ng	69.92	Machine learning (17 %), pattern recognition (13 %)
Tom Mitchell	10.93	Machine learning (22 %)
...	...	...

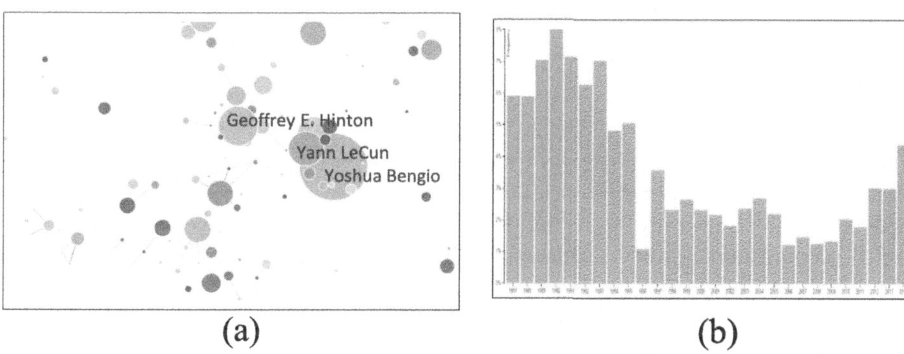

Fig. 2. (a) Influential researchers on neural network (and deep learning). (b) Trend in neural network research.

learner planning to learn the selected topics, and the recommendation results are more compact and informative compared with keyword search results from general search engines. With topic distributions of courses and learning materials, a learner can easily get a high-level overview on knowledge maps, and compare related courses and materials, and it is especially critical for informal learners lack of professional guidance. The system can provide navigation and recommendation by knowledge terms, topics and persons, and in addition, some interesting analytical results can be produced. As shown in Fig. 2(b), based on topic-specific analysis of the publication data set, we can quantitatively measure research activities on neural network in terms of aggregated topic-specific weight of related publications over the last two decades, which reached the peak in the mid-90s and bottomed soon, and recently rebounded due to the deep learning renaissance.

Table 4. Examples of topic-specific recommendation of courses and learning materials.

Topic	Courses	Score
Neural network (deep learning)	CSC321 Introduction to Neural Networks and Machine Learning (Geoffrey E. Hinton)	67.10
	Deep Learning (Yann LeCun)	60.68
	Coursera: Introduction to Neural Networks and Machine Learning (Geoffrey E. Hinton)	56.29
Graphical model	COS597C: Advanced methods in probabilistic modeling (David M. Blei)	86.98
	10708 Probabilistic Graphical Models (Eric P. Xing)	69.06
	STAT/CS 6509: Foundations of graphical models (David M. Blei)	65.53
Machine learning	CS 229 Machine Learning (Andrew Y. Ng)	32.80
	Coursera: Machine Learning (Andrew Y. Ng)	24.66
	10-701/15-781, Machine Learning (Tom Mitchell)	13.90

4 Related Work

ThemePageRank model [5] attempts to automatically generate reading lists of scientific publications for novices, and it also involves topic-specific expertise measurement combining topic model with PageRank. However, it is only trying to recommend quality publications from publications themselves. Our work focuses on topic-specific recommendation of OERs by combining expertise profile generated from scientific publications, and our algorithms are also different due to the different target. Researchers also combined the merits of traditional collaborative filtering and probabilistic topic modeling, and tried to recommend scientific publications to users of an online community [10]. Because most OERs are sparsely distributed, it is hard to create a single online community which can apply collaborative filtering for recommendation. ToPMine also tries to extract quality phrases of different length from scientific publications, and generate more meaningful and readable representations for topic models [3]. But their work mainly focuses on topical phrase mining and doesn't involve topic-specific recommendation.

5 Conclusion and Future Work

This paper presents a novel system for topic-specific recommendation of OERs, which helps learners who want to learn cutting-edge technology to efficiently locate appropriate online courses and learning materials, and the system has been demonstrated and examined with real-world data and applications. A number of open problems still need to be solved in order to establish a more comprehensive domain knowledge structure. For instance, selecting appropriate topic number or granularity, inferring hierarchical and prerequisite relationship among topics and corresponding knowledge terms are all critical for learners who try to create own curriculum and find optimal learning pathways.

References

1. Chakrabarti, D., Faloutsos, C.: Graph mining: laws, generators, and algorithms. ACM Comput. Surv. **38**(1), 2 (2006)
2. Chim, H., Deng, X.: A new suffix tree similarity measure for document clustering. In: Proceedings of the 16th International Conference on World Wide Web, WWW 2007, pp. 121–130. ACM, New York (2007). http://doi.acm.org/10.1145/1242572.1242590
3. El-Kishky, A., Song, Y., Wang, C., Voss, C.R., Han, J.: Scalable topical phrase mining from text corpora. Proc. VLDB Endow. **8**(3), 305–316 (2014). http://dx.doi.org/10.14778/2735508.2735519
4. Griffiths, T.L., Steyvers, M.: Finding scientific topics. PNAS **101**(Suppl. 1), 5228–5235 (2004)
5. Jardine, J.G.: Automatically generating reading lists. Technical Report (UCAM-CL-TR-848), Computer Laboratory, University of Cambridge (2014)
6. Liu, J., Shang, J., Wang, C., Ren, X., Han, J.: Mining quality phrases from massive text corpora. In: Proceedings of the 2015 ACM SIGMOD International Conference on Management of Data, SIGMOD 2015, pp. 1729–1744. ACM, New York (2015). http://doi.acm.org/10.1145/2723372.2751523
7. Magistry, P., Sagot, B.: Unsupervized word segmentation: the case for mandarin chinese. In: Proceedings of the 50th Annual Meeting of the Association for Computational Linguistics: Short Papers - Volume 2, ACL 2012, pp. 383–387. Association for Computational Linguistics, Stroudsburg (2012). http://dl.acm.org/citation.cfm?id=2390665.2390751
8. Roy, D., Sarkar, S., Ghose, S.: Automatic extraction of pedagogic metadata from learning content. Int. J. Artif. Intell. Educ. **18**, 97–118 (2008)
9. Simko, M., Bielikova, M.: Automatic concept relationships discovery for an adaptive e-course. In: Educational Data Mining (2009)
10. Wang, C., Blei, D.M.: Collaborative topic modeling for recommending scientific articles. In: Proceedings of the 17th ACM SIGKDD International Conference on Knowledge Discovery and Data Mining, KDD 2011, pp. 448–456. ACM, New York (2011). http://doi.acm.org/10.1145/2020408.2020480
11. Wang, J., Uchino, K.: Specific online resource identification and extraction. US Patent App. 13/732,036, 3 July 2014

The Web-Based InterUniversity Study

Petra Poulova(✉) and Ivana Simonova

University of Hradec Kralove, Rokitanskeho 62,
500 03 Hradec Kralove, Czech Republic
{petra.poulova,ivana.simonova}@uhk.cz

Abstract. The higher education worldwide is in the period of transition, affected by globalization, the requirement for mass access, changing relationships between the university, state and new technologies and others. Internationalization is one of the major forces impacting and shaping higher education as it evolves to meet the challenges of the 21st century. These were the main reasons why the Run-up InterUniversity Study Project (RIUS) was designed by three Czech higher education institutions. After the successful piloting process the project continued as the InterUniversity Study (IUS) Project, been built on co-operation of eight European universities. Running the R/IUS projects the borderless web-based concept was applied. Several tools were developed for the complex evaluation of the project. The results, presented in this paper, entitle us to state the model of InterUniversity Study designed and verified within the R/IUS projects was successful and can be applied within further on.

Keywords: Web-based learning · Higher education · Interuniversity project

1 Introduction

The higher education worldwide is in a period of transition, affected by globalization, the requirement for mass access, changing relationships between the university, state and new technologies and others [1]. Internationalization is one of the major forces impacting and shaping higher education as it evolves to meet the challenges of the 21st century. Overall, the picture of internationalization is one of complexity, diversity and differentiation. The internationalization of higher education is a process in rapid evolution, both as actor and reactor to the new realities of globalization and to the rather eventful times facing higher education [2–5].

Altbach and Knight cite several motivations universities apply to internationalize. This process may include several approaches, starting from exchange study programmes to the borderless education, i.e. to running the process of instruction online for students of other education institutions. These motivations include profit motivations and the support to increased access and demand for education, improved cultural structure of the student population, competitiveness, prestige, and enhanced strategic alliances with other institutions [6]. To capture the ways in which higher education goes about internationalizing, Arum described international education with three overarching categories: international studies, international educational exchange and technical assistance [7].

F.W.B. Li et al. (Eds.): ICWL 2015, LNCS 9412, pp. 82–91, 2015.
DOI: 10.1007/978-3-319-25515-6_8

There is no one way to be an international scholar or to define international scholarship. The history of internationalization in education is multifaceted [8] and covers administrative and managerial opportunities, teaching/learning opportunities (e.g. cooperation on projects, teaching and curriculum design and revisions, instruction/study abroad participation, or the employment of global, social, economic, political, and educational resources) [8, 9]. Moreover, the participation in international academic activities provides scholars with globalizing academic communities [10]. These communities suggest and create a "ceremonial space" (p. 372) in which scholarship is "played" and "performed" (p. 373) and both "knowledge and academic identities" are produced (p. 377). All these activities may assist individuals to expand and enrich their critical international perspectives, practices, and identities [5].

Therefore, the main objective of this paper is to introduce the concept and feedback from the R/IUS projects as a way towards internationalization through web-based process of instruction.

2 R/IUS Projects Design: Methodology, Tools, Research Sample

The Run-up InterUniversity Study Project (RIUS), supported by European Union funds, was designed by three Czech higher institutions – University of Tomas Bata, Zlin (UTBZ), University of West Bohemia, Pilsen (UWB) and University of Hradec Kralove (UHK). The project been successfully piloted, it continued as the InterUniversity Study (IUS) Project in the next semester. In both EU projects following international institutions, project co-solvers, participated: University of Huddersfield, United Kingdom (UH); Galway-Mayo Institute of Technology, Ireland (GMIT); Savonia University of Applied Sciences, Finland (SUAS); Riga International School of Economics and Business Administration, Latvia (RISEBA) and University of Genoa, Italy (UG). The RIUS project aimed at following fields:

- to create the base of university network in the Czech Republic for the purposes of interuniversity study (IUS);
- to prepare both pedagogical and administrative staff for IUS realization;
- to share teaching/learning aids (mainly those for the hybrid process), educational infrastructure and tools;
- to prepare Czech universities for more intensive co-operation with similar organizations in other EU countries;
- to develop infrastructure, processes, know-how for the connection of created Czech IUS network to similar networks in other EU countries for the purposes of IUS.

The RIUS project design focused on three fields – study, organization and coordination of learning-related activities. The process of instruction was held in the LMS WebCT/Blackboard in tutored distance online courses where only the starting tutorial and final assessment were organized in the face-to-face form. The process of instruction, schedule, quality assessment, administration etc. were agreed and managed by the steering committee consisting of member of all partner institutions. Running the R/IUS projects the 'barrier-free' access to higher education was provided.

The pilot RIUS project been finished and results analyzed, the objectives were applied for the IUS project without any change. Exploiting the distance online learning approach [11] both the RIUS and IUS projects were of identical concepts, i.e. selected European universities provided distance courses in English running in a LMS for students of other universities. In the starting tutorial students were provided with information about the objectives and structure of the subject, ways of communication in the online course, requirements for successful passing exams etc., as well as the access to the course was opened for them. The LMSs WebCT/Blackboard, EDEN and Moodle were used for designing and running the courses. Despite the universities differed in using the LMS, all three learning environments were recognized as standardized and user friendly to provide learners with all tools required for simulating the real process of instruction. The assessment tutorial was organized at the end of the semester where students' knowledge was evaluated by written tests and oral exams. The design of all subjects followed the distance education standards covering both the course design and process of running the instruction (e.g. [12]).

In the RIUS project totally 40 subjects were offered to students, taught by 40 teachers from the above listed institutions; 217 students enrolled in 31 subjects; 102 of them met all requirements and passed the final exams. In the IUS project totally 49 subjects were taught by 46 teachers, 336 students enrolled in 35 of them; 258 of them met all requirements and passed the final exams. Both the teachers (tutors) and students participated on voluntary basis in the project. Detailed data are presented in Table 1.

Table 1. Research sample of the RIUS and IUS projects (n)

		RIUS			IUS		
	Teachers in RIUS + IUS	Subjects offered/ attended	Enrolled students	Passed exam	Subjects offered/ attended	Enrolled students	Passed exams
UH	0 + 5	0	0	0	5	8	4
GMIT	4 + 5	5	51	22	5	49	38
SUAS	5 + 4	5	70	38	5	85	61
RISEBA	5 + 4	5	15	9	6	23	15
UG	5 + 5	5	7	4	5	3	1
TBUZ	8 + 10	7	48	17	8	70	61
UWB	5 + 6	5	18	6	6	19	14
UHK	8 + 7	8	8	6	9	79	64
Total	**40 + 46**	**40/31**	**217**	**102**	**49/35**	**336**	**258**
Success rate				*47 %*			*77 %*

3 RIUS/IUS Projects Evaluation

Despite the provided opportunity of studying at foreign universities was challenging and interesting for many students, only the best ones succeeded in the study, as displayed in Table 1.

The online courses and exams been finished, students' and tutors feedback was collected. Several tools were developed for the complex evaluation in particular subjects during the course of study: written questionnaires (for successful students analyzing their positive and negative experience; for unsuccessful students collecting deeper focus on their problems within the course of study; for tutors) and oral evaluation interview with students and teachers.

Below, the selected results from the evaluation questionnaires and follow-up interviews to make all responses clear are presented.

In Table 2 the amount of those provided feedback is displayed. Under 'failed students' two types of students are included: (1) those who did not meet the course requirements within the semester, i.e. they did not submit assignments in time, stopped studying from any reasons (personal, health reasons, bad time management, low motivation etc.), (2) those who failed the exams.

Table 2. RIUS/IUS participants providing evaluation feedback

Respondents	RIUS (n)	IUS (n)	Total (n)	Provided feedback (n)	Provided feedback (%)
Successful students	102	258	360	332	92
Unsuccessful students	115	78	193	156	81
Tutors	39	47	86	82	95

The process of evaluation ran in two phases: (1) after the RIUS project; (2) after the IUS project. Despite the feedback collected after the RIUS project was implemented in the IUS project design, identical comments, strengths and weaknesses were detected after the IUS project. Therefore, all data were summarized and presented together.

3.1 Course Evaluation by Successful Students

The questionnaire for successful students was structured in two parts covering 64 items relating to didactic and technical (technology-supported) fields of study. Each field was monitored by several items so the collected data were structured to 15 final items. The items were provided in the form of statements and evaluated on the four-level scale (1 - completely agree, 4 - completely disagree). The questionnaire focused on learning objectives, study materials, exam requirements, tutor's work (motivation and stimulation of students, explanation of problems, study materials and teaching methods etc.), quality of methodological instruction on how to study in the distance online course, IT and organizational support, the adequacy of work load during the study and (last but not least) the process of administration. Selected results (ordered from best to worst) are presented in Table 3. The evaluation levels 1 (I completely agree) and 2 (I partially agree) are considered positive, levels 3 (I partially disagree and 4 (I completely disagree) are negative.

Table 3. Successful students' feedback (%)

Statement	Total positive feedback	'I completely agree'	'I partially agree'
Written instructions for assignments were clear and appropriate	80	52	28
Technical requirements were appropriate	79	52	27
Tutor was interested in our learners' opinions	77	58	19
I consider learning within the project beneficial for me	77	47	30
The learning objective was clearly defined	76	38	38
Tutor explained the structure and organization of study	71	40	31
The subjects required an adequate work load for me	71	29	42
The subject documentation was available and clear	70	47	23
Tutor provided sufficient methodological instructions to assignments	70	43	27
I will participate in similar projects in the future	67	41	26
Information on the RIUS/IUS project was clear and provided in time	63	41	22
Learning content was explained in a systematic and comprehensive way	57	28	29
Exam and credit requirements were clear and adequate	59	40	19
In case of technical difficulties efficient help was promptly provided	57	27	30
Applied methods stimulated my learning activity	52	26	26

Despite the above presented evaluation was from successful students, the data are not unambiguously positive. Some features of the course, e.g. definition of learning objectives, tutor's explanation of the structure and organization of study, methodological instructions on how to write assignments, subject documentation, tutor's feedback in learners' opinions, adequate work load etc. received rather positive feedback (above 70 %), whereas others, e.g. methods to support learning activity, should be substantially improved, as well as further advancements could be considered in how to explain the learning content, exam and credit requirements in the distance way, how to provide immediate technical support, how to improve administration of the project etc.

Moreover, most frequent comments were collected in follow-up unstructured interviews. Students would appreciate more frequent communication, information, instructions, from at least two reasons: (1) to have enough information and feedback on how to study, how to prepare assignments, to discuss their problems with other course participants, and (2) to communicate so as not to feel lonely. Despite some problems numerous students stated that way of learning was very motivating for them and exceeded their expectations.

Despite all the above presented, more than two thirds of students are going to participate in another course (other courses) in the future.

3.2 Course Evaluation by Unsuccessful Students

The questionnaire for unsuccessful, i.e. drop-out and failed, students consisted of twelve items covering two sections:

- relating to the process of instruction, i.e. the content and way of learning/teaching the subject, quality of tutor's work;
- relating to technical and administrative problems.

The items were in the form of statements; students were to express complete agreement (1) or complete disagreement (4) with statements on the four-level scale.

In each section three areas of substantial problems were detected where students could state also other reasons of their study drop-out additionally to those listed above. Results (ordered from best to worst) are displayed in Table 4.

As we can see, these statements express students' attitudes from individual points of view. Most of the results are crucial for further running such courses. Despite most tutors were experienced and trained, not all of them performed excellent. On the other side – the question is why students' expectations were different (didn't they read the syllabus carefully?), what (how much) motivation they expected from the tutor in case they voluntarily enrolled in the course they were interested in, what the cause of technical problems was, why they considered the communication complicated (because of technical problems?) etc. More problems seemed to be on students' side. Were students able to study autonomously? Did they have enough capacity (abilities, time management) to complete the subject? Did they expect it would be easier to get credits in a pilot project? However, in follow-up interviews most students explained the main reason(s) of their drop-out in themselves, mostly by inappropriate time management. Problems connected with the content and the teaching/learning of the particular subject were not frequently mentioned. Some students stated they had missed contact with their tutor. Several students discovered the reason(s) of their drop-out in technical problems, e.g. university anti-spam filter marked tutor's e-mail as spam and deleted them, they commented. Other students saw the reason of their drop-out in administrative problems. Moreover, another area relating to tutor's work which was rather criticized by some students (but not by the others) was the proper and early announcement, e.g. instructions were sent late, the starting date was postponed etc.

Table 4. Unsuccessful students' feedback (%)

Statement	Total positive feedback	'I completely agree'	'I partially agree'
Communication in the course was complicated	83	70	13
Bad organization and administration discouraged me from studying	80	70	10
Tutor was not able to establish a good contact with students	79	56	23
This way of study did not suit me	74	52	22
The learning content was different than I expected	71	57	17
Tutor did not enough motivate me to studying	70	57	13
I stopped studying because of technical problems	69	52	17
The organization of lessons was poor for me	61	53	8
The subject was too demanding for me	53	44	9

3.3 Course Evaluation by Tutors

The questionnaire for tutors consisted of 15 items. Tutors provided responses in the form of multiple choice (nine items) and open answers (six items).Their responses focused on teaching, organization, and technical support to the courses. As presented above, totally 66 courses were provided within the RIUS/IUS projects which were tutored by 86 tutors (several courses were tutored by more than one instructor), 82 tutors provided their opinions, experience from running online courses and proposals to implementation in the future. The collected data (ordered from best to worst) are summarized in Table 5.

Nearly all tutors were interested in tutoring the courses despite they considered the work more demanding compared to face-to-face instruction. They did not have any crucial technical problems, as well as they appreciated students had not required support from them very often. Above all, this way of work was very motivating for most of them and they would recommend such experience to other tutors. Despite these facts, only half of them thinks students did excellent work. In other words, from their opinion, students could have worked harder. Tutors also appreciated the opportunity to communicate with foreign students (also with Czech students) in English and the experience in teaching students from other universities, cultures (and thus to get a possibility to teach foreign students and get familiar with different studying cultures.

Problems with communication and motivation, which were mentioned mainly by unsuccessful students, were considered a problem by tutors as well. They often mentioned impersonal contacts and higher possibility of student's cheating, lack of communication, the fact students did not have correct communication manners developed (no or late answers to tutor's emails), and running communication via LMS was considered very time-consuming.

The most frequent students' problem from tutors' views involved writing essays on given topic, working out assignments according to written instructions only, motivating students and keeping them motivated; probably student's level of English knowledge could have been higher.

Table 5. Tutors' feedback (%)

Statement	Total positive feedback	'I completely agree'	'I partially agree'
Was the tutor's work within the project beneficial for you?	100	58	42
Reflecting my experience from this project, I would recommend other tutors to participate in further courses	96	27	67
The project represents a great motivation for my future tutor's work	80	42	38
I was satisfied with the project organization	80	17	63
Do you consider the tutor's work in the project more demanding compared to face-to-face instruction?	71	21	50
Did students make excellent work?	50	33	17
Did you have any crucial technical difficulties?	46	40	6
Did students frequently need your help or support?	16	7	9

Tutors appreciated their students' enthusiasm, high level of work, their real and honest effort and positive attitude, participation in discussions, some of them conducted inter-university team co-operation. On the other hand, tutors disliked rather massive decrease of students at the beginning and during the course, starting study to late which was later reflected in the quality of students' knowledge, some problems in communication, partially caused by problems in understanding English.

4 Conclusions and Recommendations

Latest developments in borderless web-based education are shaped by a number of factors including the emergence of lifelong education and advances in the use of ICT. The traditional area of higher education (universities, colleges) is changing rapidly as new providers and forms of education emerge, thus defining a wider context of changes in education and society in general. The term of web-enhanced education refers to developments that cross the traditional borders of higher education, both geographic and conceptual [11]. In the conceptual framework, we used to operate in, new didactic means should be applied, i.e. organizational forms, methods of instruction and other relating features, at least the competences required from both the tutors and learners to successfully master such an approach to education. The results presented in this paper entitle us to state the model of InterUniversity Study designed and verified within the R/IUS projects was successful and can be applied within the internationalized web-based education.

Reflecting these results, the project of interuniversity study provided positive impact on the involvement of selected Czech universities in the world network of borderless internationalized education, despite in the RIUS project fewer than 50 % of students met the requirements and successfully passed exams (see Table 1). Emphasis must be paid to the fields which have not proved good performance (see Tables 4 and 5 – unsuccessful students' and tutors' feedback), particularly on:

- keeping the teaching methods maximally stimulating the process of learning and steadily increasing their impact in the affective field of the process;
- improving teaching materials, mainly their comprehensiveness, so that the understanding the topic was as complete as possible;
- providing the exam requirements clear and stable, but reflecting latest pedagogical achievements;
- providing fast IT service and methodological support in case of technical difficulties in LMS.

After solving the problem of rather passive partner institutions (see Table 1), possibly by contracting other universities which will be more active project partners and more deeply engaged in the project work, the project would be recommended to further implementation in following academic years. The main strengths were detected in the fields of tutor's work, setting clear educational objectives and applying appropriate methods of instruction, including the communication. Above all, taking the educational contribution of the project into consideration, it definitely provided 'added value' to students' motivation to further education [6].

Acknowledgment. The paper is supported by the project 'Didactic aspects of Blackboard Mobile Learn implementation into the process of instruction at FIM.'

References

1. Knight, J.: Higher education in turmoil. The changing world of internationalization. Global perspectives on higher education, vol. 13. Center for International Higher Education, Boston, USA (2008)
2. Knight, J.: Internationalization of higher education: new directions, new challenges. International association of universities global survey report. International Association of Universities, Paris (2006)
3. Knight, J.: Internationalization: concepts, complexities and challenges. In: Forest, J., Altbach, P. (eds.) International Handbook of Higher Education, pp. 207–228. Springer Academic Publishers, Dordrecht (2006)
4. Trent, J.: The internationalization of tertiary education in Asia: language, identity and conflict. J. Res. Int. Educ. **11**, 50–69 (2012)
5. Coryell, J.E., Durodoye, B.A., Wright, R.R., Pateand, P.E., Nguyen, S.: Case studies of internationalization in adult and higher education: inside the processes of four universities in the United States and the United Kingdom. J. Stud. Int. Educ. **16**, 75–98 (2012)
6. Altbach, P.G., Knight, J.K.: The internationalization of higher education: motivations and realities. J. Stud. Int. Educ. **11**, 290–305 (2007)
7. Arum, S.: International education: What is it? A taxonomy of international education of U.S. universities. CIEE Occas. Pap. Int. Educ. Exch. **23**, 5–22 (1987)
8. Dolby, N., Rahman, A.: Research in international education. Rev. Educ. Res. **78**, 676–727 (2008)
9. Ruther, N.L.: Barely There, Powerfully Present: Thirty Years of US Policy on International Higher Education. Routledge-Farmer, New York (2002)
10. Solomon, N., Zukas, M.: Globalizing academic communities: new ceremonial spaces for academic identities. In: Proceedings of the 36th Annual SCUTREA Conference, Trinity and All Saints College, Leeds, pp. 371–378 (2006)
11. Allen, I.E., et al.: Blending in eduventures. http://files.eric.ed.gov/fulltext/ED529930.pdf
12. NCPSA: Recommended standards for distance education. http://www.ncpsa.org/client_data/files/2010/13_recommendedstandardsforitdistancelearning.pdf

Intelligent Tutoring and Tools

Highlights in the Literature Available in Serious Games for Intellectual Disabilities

Ana R. Cano[1(✉)], Álvaro J. García-Tejedor[2], and Baltasar Fernández-Manjón[1]

[1] Universidad Complutense de Madrid, Madrid, Spain
anarcano@ucm.es, balta@fdi.ucm.es
[2] Universidad Francisco de Vitoria, Madrid, Spain
a.gtejedor@ceiec.es

Abstract. This review examines the literature on Serious Games used as learning tools for people with intellectual disabilities. Although intellectual disabilities are a very broad field where each individual has very specific characteristics, it would be beneficial to have general evidence-based recommendations about how to design videogames adapted to their cognitive requirements. Thus, the purpose of this paper is to identify and review the available literature on Serious Games for intellectual disabilities classifying them according to the learning outcomes associated. Search terms identified 43 papers covering this topic and this review presents the initial results. The final goal is to identify what is working in this kind of games and how this can be generalized into a methodology to simplify the creation of more effective games for people with intellectual disabilities.

Keywords: Serious Games · Intellectual disabilities · Cognitive disabilities · Educational games · Autism spectrum disorder · Down syndrome

1 Introduction

The use of educational or therapeutic videogames (aka Serious Games) in scientific investigations has grown over the past years but their use for people with intellectual disabilities is still a relatively unexplored field. Even though intellectual disabilities are a very broad and diverse field where each individual has very specific characteristics, it would be beneficial to have general recommendations about how to design videogames adapted to their cognitive features. To pursue this goal, the purpose of this paper is to identify and review the available literature on Serious Games for intellectual disabilities and classify the research found according to the learning outcomes associated to them.

Early research on Serious Games for intellectual disabled people is mostly focused on adapting the interface of existing videogames [1, 2] but we consider that the real challenge is to design learning-games identifying the specific needs of intellectual disabilities users to ensure an effective learning outcome.

F.W.B. Li et al. (Eds.): ICWL 2015, LNCS 9412, pp. 95–108, 2015.
DOI: 10.1007/978-3-319-25515-6_9

2 Serious Games for Intellectual Disabilities

The AAIDD (American Association on Intellectual and Developmental Disabilities) describes 'Intellectual Disability' as a disability characterized by significant limitations both intellectual functioning (reasoning, learning or problem solving) and in adaptive behavior, which covers a range of everyday social and practical skills [3]. An individual is considered to have an intellectual disability based on the following three criteria: (a) intellectual level (IQ) is below 70–75, (b) significant limitations exist in two or more adaptive skills areas (like communication, self-care, social skills, home living, leisure, self-direction) and (c) the condition is presented from childhood [4].

Attending to this definition there is a wide range of mental conditions that can be considered intellectual disabilities, depending on its causes, signs and symptoms. Even though the different intellectual disabilities have similarities, it is not possible to standardize the learning mechanisms of all impairments and reflect them in the design of a videogame's mechanics. The result is that not all Serious Games are suitable as learning tools for all disabled game players [5, 6].

Although the search terms used in this review covers most of the intellectual disabilities in general to ensure that the results are representative enough, we are interested in identifying those articles referred to two concrete disabilities: ASD (Autistic Spectrum Disorder) and DS (Down Syndrome) for three reasons:

1. Down Syndrome is the most common genetic disorder found in newborns and the most common intellectual disability associated with mental impairment. The prevalence of Down syndrome has been reported to occur in about 1 out of every 600 live births [7].
2. ASD comprises a group of conditions within the category of developmental disorders. Due to its heterogeneity of symptoms, ASD is the disorder with the largest number of scientific investigations among the intellectual disabilities [8].
3. There are a large number of associations in Spain and US dedicated to ASD and DS (separately) that can provide us advice about the characteristics, skills, attitudes and behavior of each group and provide users for the actual game testing.

3 Method

We applied the same method used by Connolly et al. [9] to examine the available literature in Serious Games.

3.1 Databases Consulted

The databases consulted are relevant in three different fields according to the topic of this article: Computer Science, Psychology, Medicine and Science in general. All of them were accessed in their electronic format and are listed below: **ASSIA**, **BioMed Central**, **EBSCO** (consisting of Psychology and Behavioural Science, PsycINFO, PubMed, SocINDEX, Library, Information Science and Technology Abstracts, CINAHL, ERIC,

IEEE, Medline and Academic Search Premier), **IngentaConnect**, **Science Direct** and **Web of Science**.

3.2 Search Terms

We identified three groups of search terms which combination helps us to perform an accurate search in databases referred to the technology, the subject and our particular interest in game design and development methodologies. The final query used in the databases remains as follows:

("videogame" OR "game") AND ("intellectual" OR "cognitive" OR "disability" OR "behavior" OR "down syndrome" OR "autism") AND ("design" OR "methodology" OR "survey")[1]

3.3 Selection of Papers for Inclusion in the Review

We applied the following selection criteria to the 498 studies found in the databases searched in order to choose which articles include in our review:

1. The purpose of the study is to test the acquisition of knowledge through videogames designed or adapted considering specific needs of a particular intellectual disability or a common feature in people with intellectual disabilities in general.
2. The purpose of the study is to identify patterns and behaviors in the use of videogames in people with intellectual disabilities.
3. The purpose of the study is to apply a methodology in the design or development of videogames for a particular intellectual disability or intellectual disabilities in general.

In addition, we discarded the studies that do not appear in scientific publications and those published before 2005. Those papers that do not report an empirical evidence of the results has been included only when the results show relevant behaviors of the users or when best practices are identified.

Once the inclusion criterion is applied, 43 studies have been included in our review.

The classification of the Serious Games is a controversial issue since there is not a single taxonomy widely accepted by the scientific community [10, 11, 12, 13, 14]. We chose the taxonomy proposed by Wouters et al. [15] who described a classification consisting of four categories of learning outcomes in Serious Games: cognitive, motor skills, affective and communicative. The studies included in our review are classified as follows: First, we determined the purpose of the investigation in accordance to one of our three inclusion criteria. Second, we applied the taxonomy described by Wouters to those studies which purpose is to learn a skill.

[1] Note that each database has its own nomenclature. We adapted the query to each database's search requirements without removing any search term.

4 Studies and Results Classified by Purpose of the Investigation and Learning Outcomes

See Tables 1, 2, 3, 4 and 5.

Table 1. Acquisition of knowledge through the design or adaptation of videogames. Cognitive skills

Author/s	Domain	Control group	Effect	Summary/Results
Brown et al. (2011)	Intellectual disabilities	Young	+	Positive and effective results in planning, rehearsing and travelling routes independently
Chang et al. (2014)	Intellectual disabilities	Adults	+	The participants improved their success rates and maintained their acquired skills after the three phases of the study, suggesting the effectiveness of the developed video game for learning long, complex and difficult recycling tasks
Curatelli et al. (2014)	Intellectual disabilities	Children	+/−	Positive results in manipulating abstract elements in people with mild intellectual disabilities. Medium to severe intellectual disabilities had troubles in the management of memory, recall past events and actions, fix in memory new facts and in the management of attention and concentration
Delavarian et al. (2014)	Mild intellectual disabilities	Young	+	Improvements in visual-spatial, auditory and speaking skills
Gonzalez et al. (2009)	Intellectual disabilities	Children	+/−	Practical example of designing a personalized SG centered in four cognitive processes: motivation, attention, concentration and emotion. Not tested with users yet
Grynszpan et al. (2007)	Autism spectrum disorders (ASD)	Children	+/−	Protocol that studies the influence of the specific constraints of the learning areas (spatial planning versus dialogue understanding) as well as Human Computer Interface modalities for children with Autism

(*Continued*)

Table 1. (*Continued*)

Author/s	Domain	Control group	Effect	Summary/Results
Hussaan et al. (2011)	Intellectual disabilities	General	+/−	System that generates learning scenarios depending on the cognitive abilities and the domain competences of the user. Not tested yet
Jimenez (2008)	Learning disabilities	Children	+	Users showed an improvement in phonological awareness and word recognition during the playing sessions
Lee et al. (2012)	Intellectual disabilities	Old	+	Evolution in game scores during sessions suggest that users improved in performing basic daily activities such as setting the table, peeling a fruit and using the elevator
Ripamonti and Maggiorini (2011)	Down syndrome	Children	+	All participants achieved the purpose of the Learning Game (reading the time) after sessions playing with a custom-developed SG
Sajjad et al. (2014)	Other	Young	+	The game has remained effective in helping psychotherapy by reducing symptoms like depression, anxiety, anger and disruptive behaviour

Table 2. Acquisition of knowledge through the design or adaptation of videogames. Motor skills and affective learning

Motor skills				
Author/s	Domain	Control	Effect	Summary/Results
Elaklouk et al. (2012)	Traumatic brain injury (TBI)	General	+/−	Collection of game design principles to develop therapeutical SGs. Not tested yet
Golomb et al. (2010)	Hemiplegic cerebral palsy	Young	+	Results showed improvement function of the plegic hand in all participants
Karal et al. (2010)	Mild intellectual disabilities	Children	+	Results showed a positive attitude and motivation of the users while playing a SG aimed to assist the psychomotor development

(*Continued*)

Table 2. (*Continued*)

Montani et al. (2014)	Traumatic brain injury (TBI)	Young	+	Results showed that the SG developed enhances mental flexibility, multitasking, attention skills and executive functions
Salem et al. (2012)	Developmental delay	Children	+	Results showed an improvement of the motor skills and motor performance of players using WiiFit
Schoene et al. (2013)	Elderly with cognitive and physical impairments	Old	+	Results showed an improvement of physical and cognitive parameters of fall risk
Affective learning				
Benveniste et al. (2012)	Alzheimer	Old	+	Usability study shows that patients are able to understand and use the interface using Wiimotes. Therapeutic impact is the next step of the investigation
Fernandes et al. (2012)	Autism spectrum disorders (ASD)	Children	+/−	Positive reaction to the game, but it is necessary a context to achieve the goals and the possibility of customization. More research is required
Fernandez-Aranda et al. (2012)	Intellectual disabilities	General	+	Patients started to show new coping styles with negative emotions in normal stress life situations, additional generalization patterns and more self-control strategies after using the SG described in the paper
Isleyen et al. (2014)	Schizophrenic	Adults	+	Use of HE (Heuristic Evaluation) and TA (Think-Aloud) together is useful to identify interface usability problems for patients with Schizophrenia and/or autism

(*Continued*)

Table 2. (*Continued*)

Kostoulas et al. (2012)	Intellectual disabilities	Adults	+	Description of a speech interface (speech recognition and emotion recognition component) implemented on a platform for the development of SGs. Results showed that patients applied the strategies of the game to reality

Table 3. Acquisition of knowledge through the design or adaptation of videogames. Communicative Learning

Communicative learning				
Author/s	Domain	Control	Effect	Summary/Results
Bernardini et al. (2014)	Autism spectrum disorders (ASD)	Children	+	Improvement in social interaction through the VG character in all players
Frutos et al. (2011)	Autism spectrum disorders (ASD)	Children	+	Positive qualitative results in users' pronunciation compared with the pre-established pattern recorded in the game
Gonzalez et al. (2007)	Autism spectrum disorders (ASD)	Children	+	Positive effect in concentration, motivation, attention and better assurance in the learning process.
Silva et al. (2014)	Autism Spectrum Disorders (ASD)	Children	+	Interaction on the multitouch interface and the collaboration patterns encourage the user to interact with other users performing tasks in the interface, guiding the partner, having physical contact, asking for help, answering, rectifying, complaining, smiling and thanking

Table 4. Patterns and behaviors

Blum-Dimaya et al. (2010)	Autism spectrum disorders (ASD)	Children	+	General improvement in the activities proposed in the video game Guitar Hero II. The activities implied: the use of (a) an activity schedule to set up, turn on and turn off the game and system, (b) simultaneous video modeling embedded in the game to teach how to manipulate the game. controller and (c) the training of multiple exemplars of songs
Facoetti et al. (2014)	Learning disabilities	Children	+	Positive results in usability tests. Children have been successfully performed through touch screens connected to a PC and tablets without a previous training session
Foran and Cermak (2013)	Autism spectrum disorders (ASD)	Children	+/−	No differences reported between ASD and TD (Typical Development) children in the use of commercial videogames
Mazurek and Engelhardt (2013)	Autism spectrum disorders (ASD)	Children	+/−	Results showed that daily videogame use was positively correlated with age. Most preferred video game genre is Action, followed by Platform and Shooter. There is a positively correlation between daily hours of video game play, the type of video game preferred and PVGT (Problematic Video Game Playing Test)
Mazurek and Wenstrup (2013)	Autism spectrum disorders (ASD)	Children	+/−	Boys with ASD spend more time playing video games than TD boys. Inattentive symptoms were strongly associated with problematic video game use for ASD
Noor et al. (2012)	Autism spectrum disorders (ASD)	Children	+	Review of articles for Autism children with diverse positive outcomes in therapy and education
Whyte et al. (2014)	Autism spectrum disorders (ASD)	General	−	Limited evidence of generalization from tasks learned in the videogame to the real-world

Table 5. Methodology for game design or development

Author/s	Domain	Control	Effect	Summary/Results
Alaribe (2015)	Mild intellectual disabilities	Young	+/−	Summary of learning strategies and need analysis to create a SG to use public transportation. Game not developed yet
Archambault et al. (2008)	Other	General	+/−	State of the art of accessibility (physical and intellectual) in computer games
Cankaya and Kuzu (2010)	Autism spectrum disorders (ASD)	Children	+/−	Proposal of project for investigating how children with Autism interact with SGs. Presents application stages for the design and development Not tested yet
Elaklouk et al. (2013)	Traumatic brain injury (TBI)	General	+/−	Framework that provides a game tailoring environment customized to therapist and reduces the development cost of the games
Horne-Moyer et al. (2014)	Intellectual disabilities	General	+/−	Provides clinical recommendations to design SGs for cognitive therapeutic purposes based on several studies
Lanyi et al. (2012)	Learning disabilities	General	+/−	Collection of Design principles for SG oriented to cognitive disabilities in general. Not tested yet
Sauve et al. (2015)	Other	Old	+/−	List of recommendations for game design oriented to old people. Aspects like challenge, competition, learning content, feedback, readability and user-friendliness were positively valued by players in a survey
Tome et al. (2014)	Intellectual disabilities	General	+/−	List of design principles to implement in a SG divided by: interface, user control, identification with the game, feedback, transmission of concepts and accessibility.
Torrente et al. (2014)	Other	General	+/−	List of strategies for adapting SGs for players with disabilities classified by disability: blindness, low vision, motor disability, hearing disability and cognitive disability

(*Continued*)

Table 5. (*Continued*)

Author/s	Domain	Control	Effect	Summary/Results
Torrente et al. (2012)	Down syndrome	Young	+/−	General guidelines and lessons learnt for designing VG for people with cognitive disabilities

Note: + = A positive result is reported, − = A negative result is reported, +/− = Results are inconclusive

5 Conclusions and Future Work

We provide an outline of the research available on Serious Games for intellectual disabilities by reviewing and classifying 43 studies according to the purpose of the investigation and the learning outcomes associated to them. This is only a first step to obtain guidelines for creating games for users with intellectual disabilities. We have identified challenges and trends after reviewing the literature.

In general terms, most of the studies are designed for users with a certain disability because of the heterogeneity of the skills that this type of users have. Most of the studies describe methodologies and design guidelines that provide recommendations and best practices for a particular disability, but a large number of them have not tested their effectiveness in an actual development with a relevant cohort of users.

We also observed that the results of the studies seem to be positive. Apparently, disabled users acquire new skills through the use of Serious Games but not many investigations provide qualitative results that prove the efficiency of this type of games in a long-term learning process. The use of learning analytics can fill this gap collecting data about the gameplay and the progress of the user, tracking the selected skills to reinforce the learning process.

As a conclusion we believe that the number of the studies and the results obtained are not enough to ensure general recommendations but is a good start point to identify what is working in this type of games. It would be desirable to identify, compile, implement and test these best practices to systematize the creation of tailored serious games for people with intellectual disabilities into a general methodology to simplify the creation of more effective games.

Acknowledges. The e-UCM research group has been partially funded by Regional Government of Madrid (eMadrid S2013/ICE-2715), by the Complutense University of Madrid (GR3/14-921340), by the Ministry of Education (TIN2013-46149-C2-1-R), by the RIURE Network (CYTED 513RT0471) and by the European Commission (RAGE H2020-ICT-2014-1-644187).

References

1. Torrente, J.: Reusable game interfaces for people with disabilities. In: Proceedings of the 14th International ACM SIGACCESS Conference on Computers and Accessibility (ASSETS 2012), pp. 301–302 (2012)

2. Iacopetti, F., Fanucci, L., Roncella, R., Giusti, D., Scebba, A.: Game console controller interface for people with disability. In: International Conference on Complex, Intelligent and Software Intensive Systems, CISIS 2008, pp. 757–762 (2008)
3. Shalock et al.: Intellectual disability: definition, classification and systems of supports (11th edn.). AAIDD (American Association on Intellectual and Development Disabilities) (2010)
4. APA American Psychiatric Association: DSM-5 2014. http://www.dsm5.org/. Accessed 22 enero 2015
5. Alves, S., Marques, A., Queirós, C., Orvalho, V.: LIFEisGAME prototype: a serious game about emotions for children with Autism spectrum disorders. PsychNology J. **11**(3), 191–211 (2013)
6. Karal, H., Kokoç, M., Ayyıldız, U.: Educational computer games for developing psychomotor ability in children with mild mental impairment. Procedia Soc. Behav. Sci. **9**, 996–1000 (2010a)
7. Davis, A.: Children with Down Syndrome: implications fos asessment and intervention in the school. Sch. Psychol. Q. **23**(2), 271–281 (2008)
8. Lecavalier, L., Snow, A., Norris, M.: Autism spectrum disorders and intellectual disability. International Handbook of Autism and Pervasive Developmental Disorders, pp. 37–51. Springer, Berlin (2011)
9. Connolly, T.M., et al.: A systematic literature review of empirical evidence on computer games and serious games. Comput. Educ. **59**, 661–686 (2012)
10. Zyda, M.: From visual simulation to virtual reality to games. Computer **38**(9), 25–32 (2005)
11. Chen, S., Michael, D.: Serious Games: Games that Educate, Train and Inform. Muska & Lipman/Premier-Trade, USA (2005)
12. Bergeron, B.: Developing Serious Games. Charles River Media, USA (2006)
13. Sawyer, B., Smith, P.: Serious game taxonomy. In: Serious Game Summit at Games Developers Conference, San Francisco (2008)
14. Djaouti, D., Álvarez, J.J.-P.: Classifying serious games: the G/P/S model. Handbook of Research on Improving Learning and Motivation through Educational Games: Multidisciplinary Approaches, pp. 118–136. IGI Global, Hershey (2011)
15. Wouters, P., van der Spek, E., van Oostendorp, H.: Current practices in serious game research: a review from a learning outcomes perspective. Games-Based Learning Advancements for Multi-Sensory Human Computer Interfaces: Techniques and Effective Practices, pp. 232–250. IGI Global, Hershey (2009)

References of the Literature Review

Brown, D.J., McHugh, D., Standen, P., Evett, L., Shopland, N., Battersby, S.: Designing location-based learning experiences for people with intellectual disabilities and additional sensory impairments. Comput. Educ. **56**(1), 11–20 (2011). doi:10.1016/j.compedu.2010.04.014

Chang, Y.-J., Kang, Y.-S., Liu, F.-L.: A computer-based interactive game to train persons with cognitive impairments to perform recycling tasks independently. Res. Dev. Disabil. **35**(12), 3672–3677 (2014). doi:10.1016/j.ridd.2014.09.009

Curatelli, F., Bellotti, F., Berta, R., Martinengo, C.: Paths for cognitive rehabilitation: from reality to educational software, to serious games, to reality again. In: De Gloria, A. (ed.) GALA 2013. LNCS, vol. 8605, pp. 172–186. Springer, Heidelberg (2014)

Delavarian, M., Bokharaeian, B., Towhidkhah, F., Gharibzadeh, S.: Computer-based working memory training in children with mild intellectual disability. Early Child Dev. Care, pp. 1–9 (2014). doi:10.1080/03004430.2014.903941

González, J.L., Cabrera, M.J., Gutiérrez, F.L., Zea, N.P., Paderewski, P.: Design of videogames in special education. New Trends Hum. Comput. Interact. Res. Dev. New Tools Methods, pp. 43–51 (2009). doi:10.1007/978-1-84882-352-5_5

Grynszpan, O., Martin, J.C., Nadel, J.: Multimedia interfaces for users with high functioning autism: An empirical investigation. International Journal of Human Computer Studies **66**(8), 628–639 (2007). doi:10.1016/j.ijhcs.2008.04.001

Hussaan, A., Sehaba, K., Alain Mille: Helping children with cognitive disabilities through serious games: project CLES. In: 13th International ACM SIGACCESS Conference on Computers and Accessibility (ASSETS 2011), pp. 251–252 (2011). doi:http://dx.doi.org/10.1145/2049536.2049592

Jiménez, J.E., Rojas, E.: Efectos del videojuego Tradislexia en la conciencia fonológica y reconocimiento de palabras en niños disléxicos. Psicothema **20**(3), 347–353 (2008)

Lee, C., Park, M., Park, K., Choi, M., Jung, J.: Clinical applications for the Ntelligent geriatric serious games for mild cognitive impairment. Alzheimer's Dement. **8**(4), 480 (2012)

Ripamonti, L.A., Maggiorini, D.: Learning in virtual worlds: a new path for supporting cognitive impaired children. In: Schmorrow, D.D., Fidopiastis, C.M. (eds.) FAC 2011. LNCS, vol. 6780, pp. 462–471. Springer, Heidelberg (2011)

Sajjad, S., Abdullah, A.H., Sharif, M., Mohsin, S.: Current medical imaging reviews. **10**(1), 62–72. 11p (2014)

Elaklouk, A.M., Zin, N.A.M., Shapii, A.: Requirements for game based cognitive intervention system for acquired brain injury. GSTF J. Comput. **2**(3), 25–31 (2012). 7p

Golomb, M.R., McDonald, B.C., Warden, S.J., Yonkman, J., Saykin, A.J., Shirley, B., Burdea, G.C.: In-home virtual reality videogame telerehabilitation in adolescents with hemiplegic cerebral palsy. Arch. Phys. Med. Rehabil. **91**(1) (2010). doi:10.1016/j.apmr.2009.08.153

Karal, H., Kokoç, M., Ayyildiz, U.: Educational computer games for developing psychomotor ability in children with mild mental impairment. Procedia Soc. Behav. Sci. **9**, 996–1000 (2010b). doi:10.1016/j.sbspro.2010.12.274

Montani, V., De Grazia, M.D.F., Zorzi, M.: A new adaptive videogame for training attention and executive functions: design principles and initial validation. Front. Psychol. **5** (2014). doi:10.3389/fpsyg.2014.00409

Salem, Y., Gropack, S.J., Coffin, D., Godwin, E.M.: Effectiveness of a low-cost virtual reality system for children with developmental delay: a preliminary randomised single-blind controlled trial. Physiotherapy (U.K.) **98**(3), 189–195 (2012). doi:10.1016/j.physio.2012.06.003

Schoene, D., Lord, S.R., Delbaere, K., Severino, C., Davies, T.A., Smith, S.T.: A randomized controlled pilot study of home-based step training in older people using videogame technology. PLoS ONE **8**(3), e57734 (2013). doi:10.1371/journal.pone.0057734

Benveniste, S., Jouvelot, P., Pin, B., Péquignot, R.: The MINWii project: renarcissization of patients suffering from Alzheimer's disease through video game-based music therapy. Entertainment Comput. **3**(4), 111–120 (2012). doi:10.1016/j.entcom.2011.12.004

Fernandes, T., Alves, S., Miranda, J., Queirós, C., Orvalho, V.: LIFEisGAME: a facial character animation system to help recognize facial expressions. In: Cruz-Cunha, M.M., Varajão, J., Powell, P., Martinho, R. (eds.) CENTERIS 2011, Part III. CCIS, vol. 221, pp. 423–432. Springer, Heidelberg (2011)

Fernández-Aranda, F., et al.: Video games as a complementary therapy tool in mental disorders: PlayMancer, a European multicentre study. J. Ment. Health **21**(4), 364–374 (2012). doi:10.3109/09638237.2012.664302

Isleyen, F., Gulkesen, K.H., Cinemre, B., et al.: Evaluation of the usability of a serious game aiming to teach facial expressions to schizophrenic patients. Stud. Health Technol. Inf. **205**, 662–666 (2014)

Kostoulas, T., Mporas, I., Kocsis, O., Ganchev, T., Katsaounos, N., Santamaria, J.J., Fakotakis, N.: Affective speech interface in serious games for supporting therapy of mental disorders. Expert Syst. Appl. **39**(12), 11072–11079 (2012). doi:10.1016/j.eswa.2012.03.067

Bernardini, S., Porayska-Pomsta, K., Smith, T.J.: ECHOES: an intelligent serious game for fostering social communication in children with autism. Inf. Sci. **264**, 41–60 (2014). doi:10.1016/j.ins.2013.10.027

Frutos, M., Bustos, I., Zapirain, B.G., Zorrilla, A.M.: Computer game to learn and enhance speech problems for children with autism. In: 2011 16th International Conference on Computer Games (CGAMES). Louisville, KY, pp. 209–216 (27–30 July 2011). doi:10.1109/CGAMES.2011.6000340

González, J.L., Cabrera, M.J., Gutiérrez, F.L.: Using videogames in special education. In: Moreno Díaz, R., Pichler, F., Quesada Arencibia, A. (eds.) EUROCAST 2007. LNCS, vol. 4739, pp. 360–367. Springer, Heidelberg (2007)

Silva, G.F.M., Raposo, A., Suplino, M.: PAR: a collaborative game for multitouch tabletop to support social interaction of users with autism. Procedia Comput. Sci. **27**, 84–93 (2014). doi:10.1016/j.procs.2014.02.011

Blum-Dimaya, R., et al.: Teaching children with autism to play a video game using activity schedules and game-embedded simultaneous video modeling. Educ. Treat. Child. (2010). doi:10.1353/etc.0.0103

Facoetti, A., Franceschini, S., Gaggi, O., et al.: Multiplatform games for dyslexia identification in preschoolers. In: 2014 IEEE 11th Consumer Communications and Networking Conference (CCNC), pp. 1152–1153. Las Vegas, NV (10–13 January 2014)

Foran, A.C., Cermak, S.A.: Active and traditional videogame ownership and play patterns among youths with autism spectrum disorders. Palaestra **27**(1), 42–48 (2013)

Mazurek, M.O., Wenstrup, C.: Television, video game and social media use among children with ASD and typically developing siblings. J. Autism Dev. Disord. **43**(6), 1258–1271 (2013)

Mazurek, M.O., Engelhardt, C.R.: Video game use and problem behaviors in boys with autism spectrum disorders. Res. Autism Spectr. Disord. **7**(2), 316–324 (2013)

Noor, H.A.M., Shahbodin, F., Che Pee, N.: Serious game for autism children: review of literature. World Acad. Sci. Eng. Technol. **64**, 647–652 (2012). http://eprints2.utem.edu.my/1252/1/Serious Game for Autism Children-Review of Literature_HelmiAdly_ICCG-MAT2012[1].pdf

Whyte, E.M., Smyth, J.M., Scherf, K.S.: Designing serious game interventions for individuals with autism. J. Autism Dev. Disord. (2014)

Alaribe, I.: Design a serious game to teach teenagers with intellectual disabilities how to use public transportation. Procedia Soc. Behav. Sci. **176**, 840–845 (2015)

Archambault, D., Gaudy, T., Miesenberger, K., Natkin, S., Ossmann, R.: Towards generalised accessibility of computer games. In: Pan, Z., Zhang, X., El Rhalibi, A., Woo, W., Li, Y. (eds.) Edutainment 2008. LNCS, vol. 5093, pp. 518–527. Springer, Heidelberg (2008)

Cankaya, S., Kuzu, A.: Investigating the characteristics of educational computer games developed for children with autism: a project proposal. Procedia Soc. Behav. Sci. **9**, 825–830 (2010). doi:10.1016/j.sbspro.2010.12.242

Elaklouk, A.M., Zin, N.A.M.: Advances in Visual Informatics. Lecture Notes in Computer Science, vol. 8237, pp. 218–230 (2013)

Horne-Moyer, H.L., Moyer, B.H., Messer, D.C., et al.: The use of electronic games in therapy: a review with clinical implications. Curr. Psychiatry Rep. **16**(12), 1–9 (2014)

Lányi, C.S., Brown, D.J., Standen, P., Lewis, J., Butkute, V.: Results of user interface evaluation of serious games for students with intellectual disability. Acta Polytechnica Hungarica **9**(1), 225–245 (2012). doi:10.1007/978-3-642-14097-6_37

Sauvé, L., et al.: Validation of the educational game for seniors: "live well, live healthy!". Soc. Behav. Sci. **176**, 674–682 (2015)

Tomé, R.M., Pereira, J.M., Oliveira, M.: Using serious games for cognitive disabilities. In: Ma, M., Oliveira, M.F., Baalsrud Hauge, J. (eds.) SGDA 2014. LNCS, vol. 8778, pp. 34–47. Springer, Heidelberg (2014)

Torrente, J., del Blanco, Á., Moreno-Ger, P., Fernández-Manjón, B.: Designing serious games for adult students with cognitive disabilities. In: Huang, T., Zeng, Z., Li, C., Leung, C.S. (eds.) ICONIP 2012, Part IV. LNCS, vol. 7666, pp. 603–610. Springer, Heidelberg (2012)

Torrente, J., del Blanco, Á., Serrano-Laguna, Á., Vallejo-Pinto, J.Á., Moreno-Ger, P., Fernández-Manjón, B.: Towards a low cost adaptation of educational games for people with disabilities. Comput. Sci. Inf. Syst. **11**(1), 369–391 (2014). doi:10.2298/CSIS121209013T

Multilingual Access to Educational Material Through Contributive Post-editing of MT Pre-translations by Foreign Students

Ruslan Kalitvianski[1,2](✉), Valérie Bellynck[2], and Christian Boitet[2]

[1] Viseo Technologies, 4 avenue Doyen Louis Weil, Grenoble, France
ruslan.kalitvianski@imag.fr
[2] LIG-GETALP, Bat. IMAG B, 41 rue des Mathématiques, 38400 Saint Martin d'Hères, France
{valerie.bellynck,christian.boitet}@imag.fr

Abstract. In our teaching practice, we often observe that, due to the lack of prerequisites and limited mastery of a language, foreign students face difficulties in understanding course contents. This especially burdens students from Eastern and South-Eastern Asia, because of the distance between their native languages and the instructional language (French in our case). We propose a quick and cost-effective method for making educational content accessible in the native tongues of the students, through a contributive computer-assisted multilingualization by voluntary participants. The process consists in post-editing MT (Machine Translation) pre-translations via an interactive multilingual access gateway (iMAG), which displays a web page in a selected language. Since 2012, several students have validated the approach by producing in Chinese more than 500 pages (125 K words) of French undergraduate and graduate course material about computer science, at a rate of about 10 min (total time) per standard page. This multilingual resource is freely accessible on the MACAU-Chamilo platform.

Keywords: Multilingual access · Educational material · Computer-assisted translation · Post-editing

1 Introduction

Our university receives each year about 2300 foreign students. Around 650 of our own students spend a part of their studies abroad via student exchange programmes such as Erasmus[1].

Their academic success depends heavily on their mastery of the instructional tongue, in our case French, and, to a lesser extent, English. But, unfortunately, their linguistic skills are often too limited. It is also common for such students to lack scientific prerequisites necessary to follow the courses of the host university, and as a consequence they have to spend additional time acquiring them.

[1] http://ec.europa.eu/programmes/erasmus-plus/index_en.htm.

F.W.B. Li et al. (Eds.): ICWL 2015, LNCS 9412, pp. 109–118, 2015.
DOI: 10.1007/978-3-319-25515-6_10

When faced with difficulties in French, some seek books in English, however they encounter two important problems:

- these books are barely helpful to them if their English skills are no better than their French, a frequent case with our students from East Asia
- the notations in these books often differ from what is taught in our classes, and they don't cover the same topics, with the same level of detail.

Thus, these students need to get access to course material in the tongue they know best, and in sync with what is taught in our university.

Motivated by this observation, we started the MACAU project in 2012, aiming at providing a multilingual access to the educational content produced by professors, lecturers, as well as students, such as books, hand-outs, lecture notes, report papers, exam papers, solutions to exercises, etc.

A naive approach to multilingual access would be to use a free online machine translation (MT) service, such as Google Translate[2] (GT), without any further ado. GT offers a wide choice of language pairs, however it presents important problems.

1. The quality of translations, though quite acceptable for short conversational sentences, deteriorates for narrowly specialized and advanced technical areas that are taught in our university, as well as for many language pairs, and for longer sentences.
2. While GT allows suggesting corrections to translations, these corrections are not displayed upon subsequent visits to the page. They are stored in Google's translation memory and used for retraining later its statistical MT system.
3. GT requires a URL to a file repository where course material would be stored.

Although rough machine translations are of limited usefulness for multilingual access to educational material, they can be very helpful for accelerating human translation [1]. The approach adopted in the MACAU project described in this paper is to immediately give access to the pedagogical material (formatted in html) in the desired access language, using MT "pre-translations", and then to improve the quality of target segments in an incremental and contributive fashion. In other words, if a student is not satisfied with the proposed translation, s/he can correct it directly on the web page, in a seamless manner.

The rest of the paper is organized as follows: in the next sections, we discuss previous and similar work, then describe the platform and its features, and lastly discuss the resources obtained as by-products, as well as the encountered difficulties.

2 Prior Work

There seems to be not much prior work. Two projects that stand out are the EU Bologna project and the more recent SlideWiki contributive project.

[2] https://translate.google.fr/.

2.1 The Bologna Project

The Bologna project[3] was a EU-funded initiative aiming at building “a translation service designed for translation of course syllabi and study programs from 9 languages — Dutch, English, Finnish, French, German, Portuguese, Spanish, Swedish and Turkish — into English”, using computer-assisted translation tools. Chinese was later added as Chinese students often outnumber all other nationalities among foreign students. This three-year project ended in 2013, and offered a demonstrator of the collaborative web platform, however it has not led to a permanent web service. The translation tools were to be specifically adapted to the translation of course syllabi. In 2013, we evaluated the online Bologna demonstrator and found its translations to be of a quality inferior to that of GT. This service has since been discontinued.

Several ideas underlying the Bologna project converge with those of our project:

- collaborative approach to translation and its improvement
- usage of translation memories specialized to each context
- definition of roles and tasks, such as translator, post-editor, moderator, MT developer, etc.
- handling different formats (html, docx, xslx, txt, rtf, URL link).

However, Bologna had both conceptual and implementation flaws.

- The project lacked ambition, as it was limited to translating 9 of 22[4] European languages into English and Chinese. International students arriving in a foreign country are mostly non-native speakers of English and do not have a sufficient mastery of English to really understand translated documents, and even less to contribute to the improvement of machine pre-translations, as one should always post-edit into one’s native tongue.
- The MT systems that were demonstrated produced output of inferior quality. This is due to the use of statistical MT, which can produce useful results only if it is trained on a large or very large corpus of parallel translations of good quality.
- Access to the post-edition interface was restricted to approved users, and the interface itself was cumbersome. In order to elicit contributions, the interface should allow for post-edition directly on the displayed document, and be freely accessible.

2.2 SlideWiki

SlideWiki is a recent project aiming at the online collaborative construction of educational presentations [2]. These presentations can either be built on the website, or be imported from a pptx format. An interesting aspect is the possibility of producing versions in a different language using Google Translate. However, limiting the content type to presentations appears too restrictive, and the lack of a translation memory limits the efficiency of the translation process.

---

[3] http://www.bologna-translation.eu/.

[4] There are now 23 official languages in the EU, but Croatian was added only in 2013.

2.3 Interactive Multilingual Access Gateways

The concept of an interactive multilingual access gateway (iMAG) has been proposed by Boitet and Bellynck in 2006 and has been used in our laboratory since November 2008 [3]. An iMAG is a gateway very much like Google Translate at first sight: one specifies the URL of a web page and the access language, and then navigates in that access language. The iMAG displays the translated web page with the layout preserved. When the cursor hovers over a segment (usually a sentence or a title), a palette displays the source segment and proposes to contribute by correcting the target segment, in effect post-editing an MT result.

Contrary to GT, an iMAG is dedicated to an elected Web site, or rather to the elected sublanguage defined by one or more URLs and their textual content. It contains a dedicated translation memory (TM). Segments are pre-translated not by a unique MT system, but by a (selectable) set of MT systems. Systran and Google Translate are mainly used now, but specialized systems developed from the post-edited part of the TM have also been used, notably for French→Chinese (Fig. 1).

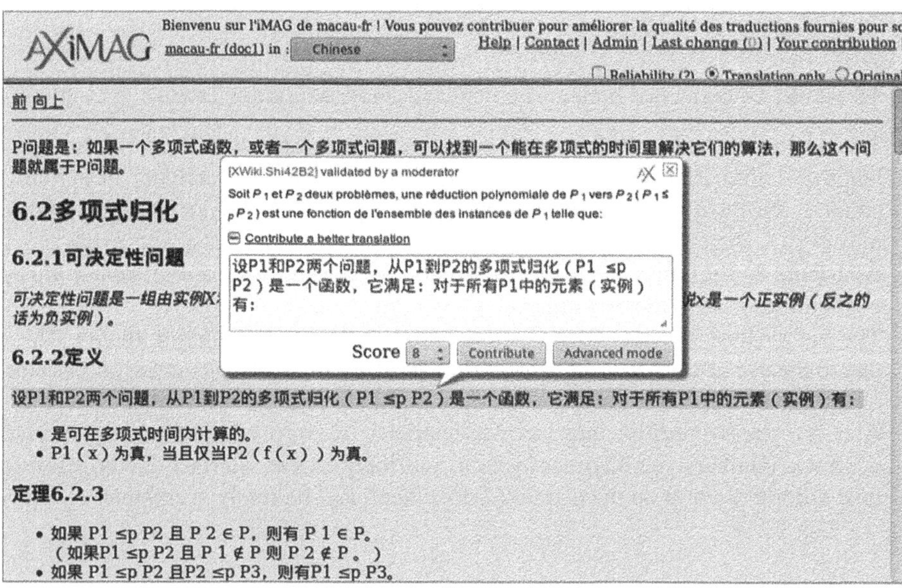

Fig. 1. The post-editing palette on a segment.

While reading a translated page, it is possible not only to contribute to the segment under the cursor, but also to seamlessly switch to an advanced online post-editing environment, equipped with proactive dictionary help as well as filtering and search-and-replace functions, and then return to the reading context.

An MT middleware, TRADOH, allows us to select, parameterize and call the MT systems and define the translation "routes" used for various language pairs. An iMAG-relay is planned to manage users, groups, projects (some contributions may be organized, other opportunistic), and access rights. But, for the moment, these functions are managed by the "back-end" corpus and TM manager, SECTra_w. MT systems tailored to the selected sublanguage can be built and have been built (by combinations of empirical and expert methods) from the TM dedicated to a given elected Web site. That approach inherently raises the linguistic and terminological quality of the MT results, that can sometimes produce *raw* rather than *rough* translations.

Besacier [4] reported in 2014 on an experiment on collaboratively translating into French a short English language novel via an iMAG. In this experiment, which involved non-professional translators, he showed that costless translations of literary texts of acceptable quality can be produced relatively rapidly by post-editing volunteers, even though such translations initially present a certain lack of unity, as well as stylistic inadequacies typical of a beginner translator's work. For our purposes, however, stylistic considerations are less relevant.

3 Proposed Solution

Our aim is to provide a platform allowing users to upload their documents, and to access these documents in the languages of their choice. The translated versions should preserve the layout of the original document, as well as allow users to edit the translations where needed, collaboratively and incrementally, through direct interaction with the concerned segments.

Language learners find it helpful to be able to see both the original text and its translation simultaneously. It allows them to learn sentence to sentence correspondences between languages. We therefore should provide a means to display in parallel the source text and the translation.

Although the access to the content should be open to all, some rights management policy for post-editing should be implemented. The iMAGs can be configured with several modes of control or "moderation", somewhat like Wikipedia.

To support the pedagogical documents, we use an open-source e-learning platform Chamilo, instances of which are widely used by our universities. It features a multilingual interface, and allows users to create courses either by uploading existing HTML documents or by building them online via a WYSIWYG HTML editor. It also allows to communicate via forums or instant messages, as well as to define dictionaries.

We have thus set up a Chamilo platform and equipped it with tools for selecting the access language of a document. The list of languages is defined by the available MT systems or translation memories (Fig. 2).

The default access language of a document is its original language. To access it in another language, one selects it in the "AXiMAG" menu and clicks on "Translate". The resulting course page is reconstituted from the MT results or from the available post-editions, which are both stored in a TM (translation memory) managed by the MACAU iMAG. This works for any HTML content available on MACAU-Chamilo, whether it has been created through the tools of the platform or uploaded by a user. It has to be noted that we are not restricted to Chamilo: iMAGs can be easily integrated with any other platform that provides a URL to its course material.

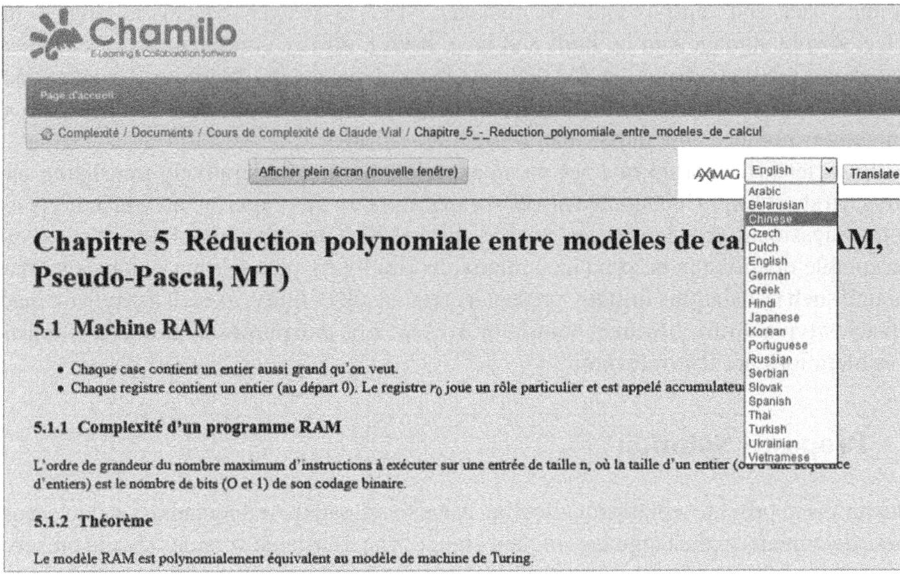

Fig. 2. Multilingual access integrated into Chamilo.

For a course that has not yet been post-edited, the first translation is obtained by MT. The user can correct the translation via the palette that appears when the cursor hovers over the sentences, and these corrections are saved in the translation memory managed by the SECTra_w "backend" of the iMAG. The (system-assigned) reliability level and the (user-assigned) quality score are used for ranking the translations and post-editions in the memory; the post-edition with the highest score is displayed during the visit of the page via the iMAG.

The correction process is called "post-editing", as opposed to "revising". The difference is that it is absolutely necessary to read and understand every sentence before correcting the "pre-translation". This is why we regularly ask good foreign students in the classes where we teach (undergraduates and graduates in computer science) to make the first post-editions.

The user can switch between the parallel view, which displays both the translation and the original, and the translation view, which displays only the translation. The optional "reliability brackets" around segments allow to see at a glance which have been post-edited: green brackets indicate that the segment has been validated by a moderator, yellow brackets that it has been post-edited but awaits moderation (for contributions by users that are not registered), and red brackets enclose MT results (Fig. 3).

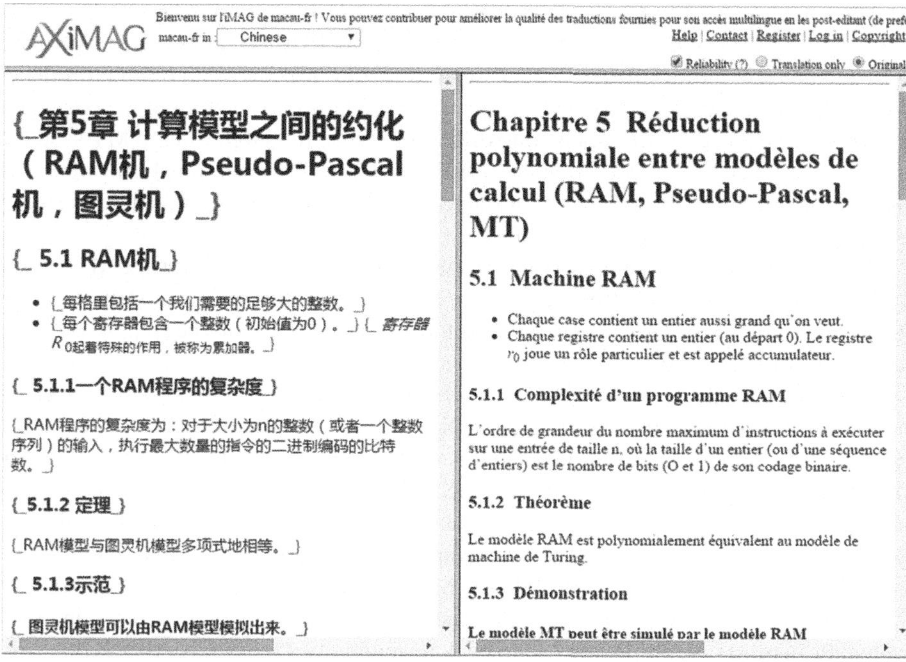

Fig. 3. A parallel presentation of a document, in target and source form, displaying optional reliability brackets around target segments.

4 Method and Results

Our experiments so far confirm the hypothesis that post-editing machine translations of course material by volunteers is a viable way of producing versions of "sufficient quality", even when the MT systems used are not of good quality, if judged by translators. Usage quality does not necessarily correlate with linguistic quality.

The first step is to collect material and convert it into HTML. We have collected educational documents about computer science produced by our teachers and students. These documents include a book on logic ("Logic and automatic demonstration" by S. Devismes, P. Lafourcade, and M. Lévy), lecture notes on computational complexity, as well as various handouts.

Documents came in different formats. The book and lecture notes were in LaTeX and had to be converted into HTML via tools such as HeVeA[5] and LaTeX2HTML[6]. Others were in Microsoft DOCX format, an XML-based format whose conversion into HTML is straightforward and performed well by office suites such as Microsoft Office, LibreOffice and AbiWord.

[5] http://hevea.inria.fr.
[6] http://www.latex2html.org.

The situation was less favorable for PDF files. When this experiment was conducted, there were no tools of acceptable quality for converting PDF into HTML. The available tools either only extracted the text, disregarding the document layout, or produced HTML documents that attempted to preserve the typographical layout of the pages, but in doing so produced HTML code quite difficult to parse for submitting to MT systems. Progress has since been made by Microsoft Word, which now can transform some PDF files into Word documents. This is fortunate, as some teachers are only able to supply us with PDF files, and not their sources.

A second step is the segmentation into pages of convenient size for the MT system we used (GT in this experiment), typically the size of a chapter. This step was done automatically via SegDoc, a segmentation tool for potentially marked-up text that we developed for the purpose.

A further crucial step is normalization, which consists in selecting sections of HTML that should be protected from translation, typically mathematical formulas in their alphanumeric transcription, as well as algorithm code, both susceptible to be treated as text by MT systems. For instance, a variable named '`I`' may be interpreted as a first person pronoun, which is problematic. Other literals may be removed or inverted by the MT system, thus deforming the entity. Protecting these sections consists in inserting the attribute "`translate=no`", part of the HTML5 standard, into surrounding HTML tags.

As for the moment we have no automatic tool for detecting these non-linguistic fragments in most cases, this step had to be done manually. One perspective of this work would be to employ a classifier for automatic detection of such entities.

Once the documents were prepared and uploaded, we incited foreign students (mostly Chinese) to perform some post-editing. As a result, 70 HTML documents, totaling 16069 segments (sentences or titles) of an average length of 8 words per segment, have been post-edited into Chinese. This represents about 514 standard pages. The Table 1 shows the current status of the platform.

All these documents are freely accessible to the public[7]. We are also open to creating new iMAGs for those who are interested in our approach.

A detail worth noting is that post-editing course material into Chinese proved to be quite useful for some students, as it helped them prepare some exams requiring a good and fast understanding of quite lengthy and complex exam papers (in French). A striking example of this is a student who earned excellent marks during the semester in situations where he was able to read the instructions at his own pace and wasn't required to produce lengthy explanations in French on the spot, and yet scored 2.5/20 at the final exam. After post-editing with us, his grade rose to 11/20 and he passed. We conclude that this process helped him make progress both in the subject domain and in expression in French.

With this experiment, going on since 2 years, we have thus

- shown that our approach is a viable way of producing multilingual content from monolingual sources
- produced a significant amount of documents in Chinese, with free access
- seen that post-editing helps understand the subject matter.

---

[7] http://tools.aximag.fr/macau/chamilo-macau/.

As stated in the introduction, Google Translate does not translate well domain-specific terms. Our students solved this problem by creating and "feeding" a specific online multilingual terminological lexicon in a Google Spreadsheets file. This allowed them to maintain inter-translator consistency in their translations.

Table 1. Current status of the MACAU-Chamilo platform

Subject matter	Content type	Pages (html)	Available translations
Introduction to propositional and first-order logic	Full book	45	Chinese (full) English (partial) Russian (partial)
Computational complexity	Lecture notes	13	Chinese (full)
Human-machine interaction	Teacher lectures	7	Chinese (full)
Formal languages and parsing	Teacher lectures, hand-outs	5	Russian (partial)
Modelling of digital systems	Exam paper	2	Chinese (full)
AI and automatic planning	Exam paper	2	Chinese (full)
Introduction to ergonomics	Student report	1	Chinese (full)

As SECTra associates a chronometer to each segment, which measures the *primary PE time* (`Tpe_1`) spent in editing the PE cell of a segment, it is easy to retrieve it, for each segment post-edited in the SECTra PE interface. However, this is not yet possible directly for segments that have been post-edited from the iMAG palette, directly on a Web page. But a recent study indicates that `Tpe_1` can be computed from the combined edit distance[8] between the MT result used and the post-edited segment.

The *total PE time* (`Tpe_tot`) includes `Tpe_1` and the *secondary PE time* (`Tpe_2`), which is the time spent "outside a PE text area" (palette or SECTra cell), in particular on terminological search. In our experiments, we asked the participants to time their time globally, from the start to the end of a PE session. We then obtained a global value for the final ratio `Tpe_tot/Tpe_1` (about 3), from which, assuming proportionality, we got an estimated value for `Tpe_2` and `Tpe_tot` for each segment.

To estimate the gains in overall time, we must compare with the time it would take junior translators to produce comparable final translations in the classical way. The times reported in the profession (by technical translation agencies) are: (1) 1 h/p[9] to produce a first draft and (2) 20 mn/p to do a professional revision (by a senior translator). As what we achieve (and want to achieve) with our method is only the equivalent of a first draft, our basis of comparison is 1 h/p. As `Tpe_tot` is equal to 15–20 mn/p, we can

---

[8] For 2 strings A, B and 2 words u, v, $D_{comb}(A, B) = \alpha\, D_{char}(A, B) + (1\text{-}\alpha)\, D_{words}(A, B)$, where Cost_exchange(u, v) = $D_{char}(u, v)$. This kind of mixed TER has ben introduced in 2004.

[9] h/p = hour per page, mn/p = minute per page, where a standard page has 250 words.

conclude that, in our context, post-editing machine translations is three to four times faster than translating from scratch.

5 Conclusion and Perspectives

We have presented an e-learning platform that allows users to access educational content in many languages, and the method for producing multilingual content from monolingual sources. We have made a set of documents freely accessible on our platform[10] in Chinese (also some in Russian), achieving a satisfactory linguistic quality and a very good usage quality through the contributions of foreign students themselves.

Our perspectives are now:

- to increase the number of subject matters
- to recruit more post-editors and foster international collaborations, and to orchestrate their post-editing activities via the collaboration platform Synaps[11]
- to integrate some lexical and terminological helps, to ensure terminological coherence
- to make it possible to also easily edit the source segments (source post-editing!), to check and modify on screen the segmentation graph (at segment level), and to control the normalization results
- to use the obtained HQ translation memories to train custom statistical machine translation systems — that has already been done for French→Chinese [5]

References

1. Green, S., Heer, J., Manning, C.D.: The efficacy of human post-editing for language translation. In: Proceedings of ACM Human Factors in Computing Systems (2013)
2. Tarasowa, D., Khalili, A., Auer, S., Unbehauen, J.: CrowdLearn: crowd-sourcing the creation of highly-structured e-learning content. In: 5th International Conference on Computer-Supported Education CSEDU 2013 (2013)
3. Boitet, C., Phap, H.C., Nguyen, H.T., Bellynck, V.: The iMAG concept: multilingual access gateway to an elected web sites with incremental quality increase through collaborative post-edition of MT pretranslations. In: TALN-2010, 8 p (2010)
4. Besacier, L.: Traduction automatisée d'une œuvre littéraire: une étude pilote. Traitement Automatique du Langage Naturel (TALN), juillet 2014, Marseille, France (2014)
5. Wang, L., Boitet, C.: Online production of HQ parallel corpora and permanent task-based evaluation of multiple MT systems: both can be obtained through iMAGs with no added cost. In: Proceedings of MT Summit XIV, the 2nd Workshop on Post-editing Technologies and Practice (2013)

[10] http://tools.aximag.fr/macau/chamilo-macau/.

[11] https://synaps.me/.

Pedagogical Issues

Teaching Simulation for Management Students in LMS

Pavel Prazak(✉)

University of Hradec Kralove, Rokitanskeho 62, 500 02 Hradec Kralove, Czech Republic
pavel.prazak@uhk.cz

Abstract. The aim of the paper is to present the role of modelling and simulation in education of future managers. The text reflects the experience that students can learn better when they solve real practical problems. Some of the managerial problems include stochastic variables, and experiments with these models are known as stochastic simulation. The paper presents and focuses on a decision model for a selection of a mobile phone tariff. Since ICT is widely and effectively used in the process of simulation, the paper also presents particular practical steps how to prepare and how to analyse a selected model in MS Excel. All steps are implemented at LMS system. Based on the described method, the paper formulates several recommendations in the area of the model theory and the decision support teaching that can be used in higher education of managers.

Keywords: Computer supported teaching · Decision support · LMS · Simulation

1 Introduction

With regard to the managerial practice, a model can be considered as simplified representation of a real object/organization of their interest, see [9]. Models are usually used to study properties of the given organizing processes in two ways: either to reveal the effect of different policies impact on that organization, or to investigate possible improvements in the organization, see [1]. Typical models constructed by business analysts are used in decision support systems and for comprehension of business rules. Decision support systems can be considered as a part of business analytics component of business intelligence, see [11]. Since a lot of variables within the considered model can have a probability character, computer simulations are widely used to study their properties. In this paper we would like to show that the process of developing of a simulation model is a complex one which uses knowledge and findings from different areas. There are a lot of pedagogical challenges linked with potential ways of explaining the main ideas of modelling and simulation to learners. Firstly, students should be aware of the following essential steps of simulation: (a) formulation of the problem – defining of the problem, acquiring of input data, developing of a simulation model, (b) solution of the problem - running of the computer simulation model including its testing, (c) interpretation of the obtained results – statistical processing and analysing of output data. All these parts of the simulation process are quite complex and long-lasting. Therefore, it is not sufficient to build up only a theoretical framework, but it is also necessary to focus on practical solutions to problems. Moreover, there are a lot of

F.W.B. Li et al. (Eds.): ICWL 2015, LNCS 9412, pp. 121–130, 2015.
DOI: 10.1007/978-3-319-25515-6_11

different approaches how to simulate a given problem, and students should learn which approach is just the best one in the given situation, [9]. Since students usually positively appreciate when a real problem is being solved or when a model is based on real data, we agree with [6, 7] that it is desirable to use models where real data are available. We think that, apart from solutions of simple problems, students should solve more complex problems in their seminar projects. Therefore the aims of this paper are: (a) to introduce a step by step implementation of key learning outcomes (LO) into teaching of the subject called "Stochastic modelling and data", which is offered at our institution; all steps are also implemented at Blackboard Learn LMS (BbL) that is used at our university, (b) to introduce quite a simple but non-trivial model that solves a decision problem when implemented in MS Excel; the main focus will be given on a case study of a decision problem of a small entrepreneur that compares two different mobile phone tariffs and selects the better one, (c) to show that the process of developing a simulation model is complex and that it involves and applies knowledge from different areas of the curriculum, (d) to show that a statistical analysis of output data is necessary for finding a solution of the problem, (e) to present the students' attitudes and opinions concerning each stage of the developing of the simulation model.

2 Methods and Material

The learning objective of the subject "Stochastic modelling and data", which is divided into several modules, is as follows: At the end of the course the student will be able to construct a simulation model for a given managerial problem and to provide an analysis of its solution. In the framework of the seminars in this subject students work out and submit their seminar project. The principal steps of the modelling process are well known, see [9]. They can be briefly presented through the following instructions: analyze and formulate the problem; formulate the model; solve the model or make simulations; verify, interpret and analyze the model's solution; report and present the model. These steps will be introduced as LO of the teaching/learning process in this paper, see [4]. At the end of the course which has been chosen for this case study students were supposed to evaluate the difficulty of each step of their solution process, this evaluation was made through answering the questions included in a short questionnaire.

Since spreadsheets are one of the main tools for modelling in business and management, see [2, 3, 8, 10], the considered model is implemented in MS Excel. Our approach is based on that one used in [1]. When a problem contains at least one variable that exhibits a probability character, the Monte Carlo simulation can be applied. This method of simulation is based on generation of multiple random trials to determine the observation sufficient for finding of the expected value of the output variable. The process can be described in the following steps: First, we find a probability distribution for each parameter that can be represented by a random variable. Secondly, we use a random numbers generator and simulate values from the probability distribution for each random variable. Finally, we repeat the process for series of trials that are usually called replications. Let us remark that symbol $N(\mu, \sigma^2)$ denotes the normal distribution with the mean μ and the variance σ^2, and the symbol $R(a, b)$ denotes the uniform distributions (discrete) between the lower limit a and the upper limit b. MS Excel has two functions to produce random numbers. The function = RAND() produces a (continuous) uniform distribution between 0 and 1. The function = RANDBETWEEN(a;b) provides a (discrete) uniform distribution between *a* and *b*. If we want to use the normal distribution, we have to convert the uniform distribution that is available. One of the possible ways is the following one: Let's remind that function NORM.INV is the inverse of the NORM.DIST function and that it calculates *x* variable given probability *p*. It can be used in the following way: = NORM.INV(p; μ; s), where μ is the mean and s is the standard deviation of the considered normal distribution. Functions RAND() and NORM.INV can be combined to calculate a random number from a normal distribution. The resulting formula is = NORM.INV(RAND(); μ; s).

2.1 LMS Section - Assignments and Tasks

The following problem was assigned to students as their seminar project: an entrepreneur wants to compare his potential costs linked with different phone tariffs. He makes the decision between two possibilities given by the mobile phone operator that are described in Table 1.

Table 1. Selected mobile phone tariffs (source: https://www.t-mobile.cz/dcpublic/Cenik_sluzeb_T-Mobile.pdf)

Tariff	Monthly fee in CZK	Free credit in minutes	Extra free credit in minutes, calling inside T-Mobile	Price in CZK per minute, calling inside the company	Price in CZK per minute	Price per 1 SMS in CZK
Plus 250	250.00	58	25	0.30	4.30	1.00
Plus 450	450.00	136	45	0.30	3.30	1.00

2.2 LMS Section - Input Data, Data Understanding and Data Preparation

During the process of preparation of the input data, the following LO can be considered: A student gathers the input data, makes a simplifying assumption and determines the variables and units of the given problem.

To be able to calculate the costs of phone calls per month, one needs data that are related to the length of calls. For different entrepreneurs we find different input data, and therefore we can gain different results. These data can be collected from the entrepreneur's records taken from his/her former phone calls invoices. The particular approximations of data used in our paper are introduced in Table 2.

Table 2. Random variables of the model and their distributions (source: own observations)

Variable	Distribution
Length of calls inside the company/minutes	$T_1 \sim \mathrm{N}(180, 900)$
Length of calls inside T-Mobile/minutes	$T_2 \sim \mathrm{N}(80, 400)$
Length of calls outside T-Mobile/minutes	$T_3 \sim \mathrm{N}(50, 100)$
Number of text messages (SMS)	$X \sim \mathrm{R}(0, 50)$

2.3 LMS Section - Model

At the stage of formulation of the model, the following LO can be considered: A student establishes relationships among variables and determines equations and functions for them.

Suppose that FC_i is the fixed monthly fee for using mobile phone tariff i, $i \in \{250, 450\}$, where $i = 250$ represents the tariff Plus 250, and $i = 450$ represents the tariff Plus 450. Further, suppose that MC_i are the variable costs of mobile phone calls inside the company, VC_i are the variable costs of mobile phone calls outside the company. Finally, suppose that XC_i are variable costs of text messages (SMS). The total costs TC_i of the services paid are the sum of the fixed costs and the variable costs, which can be formally written as

$$TC_i = FC_i + MC_i + VC_i + XC_i, \tag{1}$$

where $i \in \{250, 450\}$. First, let us consider the variable costs of mobile phone calls outside the company. Since there are free minutes available in this tariff mode, it is necessary to determine the total time T_i, $i \in \{250, 450\}$, that has to be charged in this mode. Further considerations presented in the text are related to the tariff Plus 250 only. Similar considerations can be obviously applied to the tariff Plus 450. According to Table 1 the time T_{MOB} that has to be paid for calling inside T-Mobile is

$$T_{MOB} = \begin{cases} 0, & T_2 \leq 25, \\ T_2 - 25, & T_2 > 25. \end{cases} \tag{2}$$

Similarly, the total time T_{250} that has to be paid for calling outside the firm is

$$T_{250} = \begin{cases} 0, & T_{MOB} + T_3 \leq 58, \\ T_{MOB} + T_3 - 58, & T_{MOB} + T_3 > 58. \end{cases} \tag{3}$$

The above given relations (2) and (3) can be simplified and summarized as follows

$$T_{250} = \max\{0, \max\{0, T_2 - 25\} + T_3 - 58\}. \tag{4}$$

In the same way we could find

$$T_{450} = \max\{0, \max\{0, T_2 - 45\} + T_3 - 136\}. \tag{5}$$

Now we can express the relation for the total costs. According to (1) and Table 1 we can write

$$TC_{250} = 250 + 0.3 \cdot T_1 + 4,3 \cdot T_{250} + 1 \cdot X \tag{6}$$

and similarly

$$TC_{450} = 450 + 0.3 \cdot T_1 + 3,3 \cdot T_{450} + 1 \cdot X. \tag{7}$$

Relations (6) and (7) represent the model of our problem. Although we have found simple expressions for the total monthly costs of calls, we could realize that both quantities TC_{250} and TC_{450} are random variables. When we want to characterize them better, we need to carry out simulations.

2.4 LMS Section - Model Implementation and Simulation

At the level of the implementation of the simulation model we can state the following LO: Students are able to use MS Excel to prepare computations with the given formal model.

We do not present all details of this step here. First, it is necessary to record the input variables given in Table 1. Next we record all parameters of the random variables given in Table 2. The formulas used are summarized in Table 3.

Table 3. Formulas specification for input variables

Description	Cell address	Formula
Length of calls inside the company	H5	=NORM.INV(RAND(); \$H\$2; SQRT(\$H \$3))
Length of calls inside T-Mobile	I5	=NORM.INV(RAND(); \$I\$2; SQRT(\$I\$3))
Length of calls outside T-Mobile	J5	=NORM.INV(RAND(); \$J\$2; SQRT(\$J\$3))
Number of text messages	K5	=RANDBETWEEN(\$K\$2;\$K\$3)

After having prepared all necessary input data, we can proceed to construct a simulation model. Using (6) and (4) we gain the costs of calls and texting with the tariff Plus 250, and similarly, using (7) and (5), we gain the costs of calls and texting with the tariff Plus 450. The formulas used are summarized in Table 4. The formulas in Table 4 use both absolute and relative addresses of some cells. The absolute addresses are used because formulas will be used for replications of the model, and at each step of replication it is necessary to refer to the same input values. Such constant values in the given tariff are: monthly fee, unit prices and number of free minutes, see Table 1. On the other side, relative addresses are used because the formula contains references to random variables that will be freely changed at each replication. Such variables are related to times given in Table 2. Since the constructed simulation model is quite compact, the replications can be performed by copying the model several times. To finish the simulation, the number of replications has to be determined.

Table 4. Formulas specification for output variables

Description	Cell address	Formula
Costs of Plus 250	L5	=\$B\$5 + \$B\$8*H5 + \$B\$9*MAX(0; MAX(0; I5-B\$7) + J5-\$B\$6) + \$B\$10*K5
Costs of Plus 450	K5	=\$D\$5 + \$D\$8*H5 + \$D\$9*MAX(0; MAX(0; I5-D\$7) + J5-\$D\$6) + \$D\$10*K5

The simplest way how to find this number is as follows. The number of replication can be determined in such a way that the relative error of the mean E(TC250) of total costs is less than 2 %. Since the margin of the error e for 95 % confidence interval is approximated by

$$e = 1.96\frac{\delta}{\sqrt{n}}, \tag{8}$$

where δ is the standard deviation and n is the sample size (in the context of simulation it is the number of replications), see [5], the relative error can be estimated as $e/\mu \leq 0.02$. Using the given relations, the number n of replications can be estimated as

$$n \geq \left(1.96 \cdot \frac{\delta}{0.02 \cdot \mu}\right)^2. \tag{9}$$

The unknown values of standard deviation and means can be approximated from the first 100 replications of our model, for instance. In this way it was found that $\mu \approx 540$, $\delta \approx 90$. Using these values and (9) we find that $n \geq 267$. Particularly the number $n = 350$ of replications has been selected.

2.5 LMS Section - Analysis and Interpretation

At the stage of analysing the output data we can consider the following LO: A student applies principles of statistical inference for the output data, analyses them and identifies the potentially best managerial solution. Within the environment of BbL system students then debate the economic effects linked with different solutions of the given managerial problem.

Here we mainly concentrate on comparison of two means: $\mu_1 = E(TC_{250})$ and $\mu_2 = E(TC_{450})$. Since the two considered tariffs, i.e. the tariff Plus 250 and the tariff Plus 450, are different, our research hypothesis is that $\mu_1 \neq \mu_2$. This means that the null and the alternative hypotheses are H_0: $\mu_1 = \mu_2$ and H_A: $\mu_1 \neq \mu_2$. The test will be conducted with the significance level $\alpha = 0.05$. The simulation has been designed in such a way that both values TC_{250} and TC_{450} are computed simultaneously, so the test for paired samples can be used, see [5]. The basic visual characteristic feature of the data analysis is given by box and whisker plots, see Fig. 1.

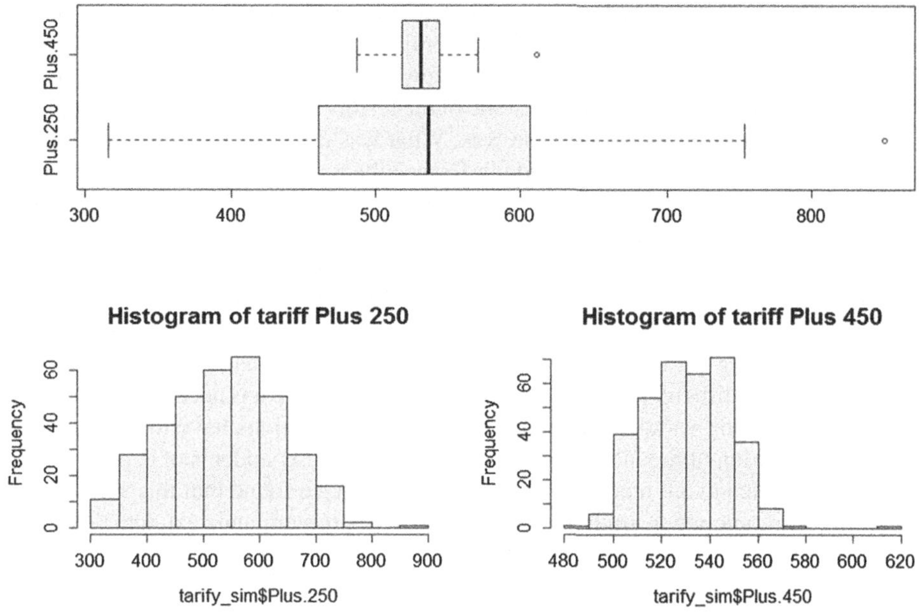

Fig. 1. Box and whisker plots and histograms of data obtained by simulation.

Let $d = TC_{250} - TC_{450}$ be the difference between the costs of calls with the tariff Plus 250 and the tariff Plus 450. Using the replications data of the given simulation model, it was found that the average $\bar{d}$ of the difference d is $\bar{d} = -2.07$ and its standard deviation is $s_d = 97$. The critical value t_{crit} of the rejection region is a quantile of Student's t-distribution. For two tailed test, $\alpha = 0.05$ and $n - 1 = 349$ degrees of freedom, where n is number of replications, it has been found that $t_{crit} = t_{1-\alpha/2}(n - 1) = 1.97$. This value can be found by function T.INV(0.975;349) in MS Excel.

The test statistics is calculated using the following formula

$$t = \frac{\bar{d} - \mu_d}{s_d} \cdot \sqrt{n} = \frac{-2.07 - 0}{97} \cdot \sqrt{350} \doteq -0.4. \tag{10}$$

Due to $|t| < t_{crit}$, we do not reject the null hypothesis. This observation allows us to formulate a conclusion. Based on the input data and on the simulation data, no sufficient statistical evidence exists to conclude that there is a difference between the tariff Plus 250 and the tariff Plus 450. It has to be notified that this result is strongly dependent on the input data given in Table 2. Students should be aware of the fact that working with different input data could bring a different result.

3 Results and Discussion

The essential principles that students of management courses can learn about stochastic simulation in the process of working out their projects were introduced and summarized in this paper. These steps are implemented within the Blackboard Learn system as sections of a module. Having submitted their project in the winter term of academic year 2014/15, the students were asked to answer a few questions in a short questionnaire that was distributed them by BbL system. Some of the results are presented below (a reduced analysis was made). The first question was: What was the most difficult part in developing of the simulation model? 86 students formed the group, 73 answers were gathered. It was found that the distribution for the given question can be characterized as follows: 4.1 % of the students - understanding of the problem, 10.9 % of the students - analysis of the input data, 38.3 % of the students – the model formulation itself, 15.1 % of the students – the implementation of the model, 8.4 % of the students - the simulation itself, 20.5 % of the students – the statistical analysis of the output data, 2.7 % of the students – reaching the decision. From this survey it is clear that in the opinion of our students the most difficult part of the solution is the part where it is necessary to establish relationships among variables and some mathematical relations have to be used. This part of construction of the model is the most critical because students of economics and management often avoid mathematical concepts. We have found that this aversion can be partly overcome when students work with a real problem and real data. This is in accordance with [7]. Quite surprising is the fact that students do not consider the part of preparation and analysis of input data as difficult as it is usually considered, see [1, 11]. We think that the main reason is that the input data were partly given in the assignment of the problem. Another difficult part of the modelling seems to be statistical analysis of the output data. We think that this finding corresponds with the general aversion of students of economics and management to quantitative methods, see [4]. The students also stated that the own implementation of the simulation model in MS Excel was fairly difficult. This is the reason why we deal with this problem in detail in this paper. This issue is quite new for students and we agree with [1] that it is necessary to extend the competences of students in using MS Excel in different areas. In this case we partly modify the approach for Monte Carlo simulation given in [2]. The case study was presented in a detailed way because we want to show how complex the problem of simulation is and which steps are relevant for developing a useful model. A possible way how to simulate a random variable with normal distribution in MS Excel was presented, this simulation allows us to solve a wide range of problems.

Another question that students were asked in the final questionnaire was: Were you interested in the result and impact of the decision made in connection with the given problem? It was found that 67 % of students were interested in the result. Thus we think that solving real problems can motivate our student effectively. These real problems can also support our students' ability to think about and consider the given problem in many different ways. Working on their practical projects, the students can propose different approaches how to reach solutions. They can work in teams and discuss different ideas, which can support their team co-operation. In our practice we have found that the process in which students work out their projects and work with real data is very useful for them as future managers. Working on projects, students learn how to collect data, how to analyze them and how to approximate them. They also learn how to prepare and how to formulate a model for a practical problem and finally how to prepare a computer simulation that enables them to provide an experiment with the given model. During most parts of their work students use ICT. With the help of the simulation model, they can find different phenomena and qualities of the model. These findings do not differ from the findings made by [6], who studied some issues from the sphere of science.

Finally we would like to discuss some advantages of using learning outcomes (LO) that were used in the teaching module. We proposed a concise formulation of LO, which turns the decision about the education strategy away from a teacher to a learner, and tends the orientation of education on its (measurable) outputs as the education purpose, see [4, 12, 13]. Another question the students were asked in the final questionnaire about LO was: Have you found that LO helped you to understand the process of developing a simulation model? The positive answer was stated by 61.6 % of students. We therefore agree with [4] that LO can enhance learning. LO usually provide relevant information about the content to be learned and also about the way in which the student will demonstrate his/her knowledge. It means that if the student has a set of LO he/she can make better choices about study methods and content emphasis. Moreover, LO can also help teachers and instructors to better design and implement their educational intention within BbL system. With LO teacher can better plan and manage their instructions, manage learning or facilitate evaluation activities.

4 Conclusion

Managers and their decisions can be successful only if they work with correct and relevant information. Because it is not possible to implement an experiment with institutions that are to be managed, it is necessary to provide artificial experiments within an appropriate model. This is the way how simulation models are introduced into managerial work. Since we are aware of this reality, we intend to prepare students of management courses in modelling and simulation.

Each model can be enriched, modified and particularized in many ways. The model that was presented in this paper can be also modified, and instead of the monthly costs of phone calls we could compute e.g. the annual costs. Moreover, the statistical analysis can be enriched and can focus on describing of another feature of the output data, for instance that of mapping the difference in the variety of the output data distributions. All these modifications can be discussed with our students. Since modelling and computer simulation provides a useful methodology of the experimental research in the current management and in the university education as well, we would like to aim at the methodological issues in future papers. The intention is to present more detailed description of how to use simulation in business problems and transfer them to our students by BbL LMS.

This paper has been supported by the Specific research project called Models and algorithms for optimization problems in terms of uncertainty II of the Faculty of Informatics and Management of University of Hradec Kralove.

References

1. Balakrishnan, N., Render, B., Stair, R.M.: Managerial Decision Modeling with Spreadsheets. Pearson Prentice Hall, New Jersey (2007)
2. Briand, G.R., Hill, C.: Teaching basic econometric concepts using Monte Carlo. Int. Rev. Econ. Edu. **12**, 60–79 (2012)
3. Findley, T.S.: Using MS Excel to solve and simulate the life-cycle/permanent-income model of consumption and saving. Int. Rev. Econ. Edu. **16**, 129–146 (2013)
4. Gavalcova, T.: Competences in mathematics: involving learning outcomes into teaching/learning. In: Proceedings of the 11th International Conference on Efficiency and Responsibility in Education (ERIE 2014), Prague, pp. 154–161 (2014)
5. Groebner, D.F., et al.: Business Statistics. A Decision-Making Approach. Pearson Prentice Hall, New Jersey (2007)
6. Hubalovska, M., Hubalovsky, S.: Implementation of the systems approach in mathematical modeling, dynamic simulation and visualization using MS Excel spreadsheet. Int. J. Math. Comput. Simul. **7**(2), 267–276 (2013)
7. Milkova, E.: Development of logical thinking in enjoyable way. In: Proceedings of the 11th International Conference on Efficiency and Responsibility in Education (ERIE 2011), Prague, pp. 221–229 (2011)
8. Palocsay, S.W., Markham, I.S., Markham, S.E.: Utilizing and teaching data tools in Excel for exploratory analysis. J. Bus. Res. **63**(2), 191–206 (2010)
9. Pidd, M.: Computer Simulation in Management Science. Wiley, Chichester (2004)
10. Prazak, P.: Discrete dynamic economic models in MS Excel. In: Proceedings of the 11th International Conference on Efficiency and Responsibility in Education (ERIE 2014), Prague, pp. 595–601 (2014)
11. Turban, E., Sharda, R., Delen, D.: Decision Support and Business Intelligence System. Prentice Hall, New Jersey (2011)
12. Luo, X., Xu, Z., Yu, J., Chen, X.: Building association link network for semantic link on web resources. IEEE Trans. Autom. Sci. Eng. **8**(3), 482–494 (2011)
13. Xu, Z., et al.: Mining temporal explicit and implicit semantic relations between entities using web search engines. Future Gener. Comput. Syst. **37**, 468–477 (2014)

Orchestrating Inquiry-Based Learning Spaces: An Analysis of Teacher Needs

María Jesús Rodríguez-Triana(✉), Adrian Holzer,
Andrii Vozniuk, and Denis Gillet

School of Engineering, École Polytechnique Fédérale de Lausanne,
Lausanne, Switzerland
{maria.rodrigueztriana,adrian.holzer,andrii.vozniuk,denis.gillet}@epfl.ch
http://react.epfl.ch/

Abstract. The European Go-Lab project offers Inquiry Learning Spaces (ILSs) as open educational resources to support Inquiry-based Learning (IBL). To successfully exploit ILSs and implement IBL, proper support for orchestration is needed. Researchers have highlighted the complexity of orchestrating Technology Enhanced Learning (TEL) scenarios and the need for supporting participants in this endeavour. In this paper, we address this issue by analyzing the teacher needs when orchestrating IBL and relying on ILSs. Concretely, we have carried out a survey-based study with 23 expert teachers in IBL and four in-depth case studies in authentic classroom scenarios with 2 teachers. The results lead us to a set of needs to be covered regarding the design of the ILS, the learning process and the learning outcomes.

Keywords: Orchestration · Inquiry-based learning · Teachers

1 Introduction

In inquiry learning the main goal is to encourage students to develop their own questioning, figure out their own responses by making proper hypotheses and designing proper experiments, and reflect on the observations. Inquiry learning can be a successful pedagogical approach, provided that effective support is offered to the students [7]. Support can be implemented at various levels. First, activities can be structured in successive inquiry phases (e.g. Orientation, Conceptualization, Investigation, Conclusion, Discussion). Second, within each phase, scaffolding tools can support activities. For instance a concept mapping scaffolding tool can support the Conceptualization phase. Third, relevant cues can be given to the students when necessary. Additionally, in order to conduct a successful learning activity, other authors have highlighted the challenge of providing stakeholders with technologies that support orchestration [14,18]. Since teachers play a crucial role in the orchestration of learning activities, it is necessary to analyze what their orchestration needs are in a IBL scenario to help them in this endeavour.

F.W.B. Li et al. (Eds.): ICWL 2015, LNCS 9412, pp. 131–142, 2015.
DOI: 10.1007/978-3-319-25515-6_12

The Go-Lab European project[1] is an ongoing initiative that precisely aims at providing this kind of support to promote inquiry learning at school for STEM education via *inquiry learning spaces* – ILSs for short. In order to overcome the complexity of orchestration in IBL, this paper addresses the following research question: *What are the teacher orchestration needs when using ILSs?* To better understand this question, this paper presents a survey-based study with 23 expert teachers in IBL and four in-depth case studies in authentic classroom scenarios with 2 teachers.

The remainder of this paper is structured as follows. Section 2 provides an overview of the related work done in orchestration of IBL. Section 3 presents the concept of the ILS in Go-Lab. Section 4 describes the research methodology that guided the studies covered in Sects. 5 and 6. Finally, Sect. 7 discusses the main findings and Sect. 8 wraps up with the conclusions.

2 Related Work

In the field of TEL, the metaphor of *orchestrating learning* is frequently used to reference the challenges that teachers, students, parents, institution, etc. face throughout the learning scenario lifecycle [4]. It covers aspects such as design, management, adaptation and assessment of learning activities, aligning the resources available to achieve the maximum learning effect, informed by theory while complying pragmatically with the contextual constraints of the setting [13]. Technological solutions can facilitate this endeavour by providing adequate support [10]. E.g., Dyckhoff et al. [5] identified a list of teachers information needs to be addressed. The resulting categories were related to the learning process (at individual, group and course level), the learning outcomes generated by the students, and to the teacher (e.g. to improve his/her teaching practice).

In IBL, the main orchestrating challenge is to combine structure and guidance with the freedom of exploring required by the method [16]. Thus, teachers play an essential role in explaining the inquiry process, orienting learners through activities, presenting the inquiry topic and supporting student throughout the inquiry learning process [16].

There are plenty of platforms available on the web to support IBL and many of them address orchestration aspects. In terms of content, we can classify these platforms in three categories from least to most flexible in terms of resource aggregation: standalone tools such as SMILE [15], which do not allow to aggregate external resources; platforms that provide a set of proprietary applications that can be combined, e.g., GreenTouch [19], SAIL [17], and nQuire [12]; and platforms that support the integration of third-party tools, for example WISE [9], SCY [3], weSPOT [11], and Go-Lab [8].

To carry out our studies, we have chosen Go-Lab because apart from supporting IBL, aggregating rich content, and providing orchestration support, it allows to edit collaboratively, reuse and share the ILSs, which supports the complete

[1] Go-Lab project: http://www.go-lab-project.eu.

life-cycle of the learning resource. Go-Lab provides a repository[2] where teachers can find and reuse online labs, applications (a.k.a. *apps*) and existing ILSs. In addition, Go-Lab also offers Graasp[3], an ILS factory where teachers can reuse, modify or create ILSs from scratch.

3 Inquiry Learning Spaces

Figure 1 presents the different stages of an ILS. An ILS supports inquiry learning given that inquiry phases can be structured in tabs, content can be added to each phase and scaffolding apps can be embedded. Figure 1.1 shows an ILS entitled *Anamorphose conique* in edition mode in Graasp. There, the teacher can add or modify resources and apps in each inquiry phase, which can also be modified and renamed. Graasp provides a Standalone View for each ILS, which can be accessed through a secret URL (accessible by clicking the *Standalone View* button). Figure 1.2 shows the login home screen of a Standalone View, which only requires a nickname. Once logged in, students see the ILS in the first inquiry phase as illustrated in Fig. 1.3. Students can then navigate to subsequent phases through the tab-based navigation bar as depicted in Fig. 1.4.

4 Methodology

Contrary to positivist methodological approaches, where all the variables are known in advance and can be controlled, in this work, the factors that impact the research questions are expected to emerge and evolve during the process [2]. Additionally, the multidisciplinary nature of TEL implies a need for mutual understanding among the involved stakeholders, demanding their active participation during the whole development cycle of TEL solutions [6]. Hence, since teachers are our target users, we involved them from the very beginning in the formulation of our proposals. These research context characteristics led us to choose *Design-Based Research* (DBR) [1] as the methodological framework. DBR is a systematic but flexible research approach aimed at improving educational practices through iterative analysis, design, development, and implementation, based on collaboration among researchers and practitioners in real-world settings, and leading to contextually-sensitive design principles and theories [1].

According to the DBR criteria, our research process comprises three iterations. The main purpose of the first and second iterations is to explore the stakeholders orchestration needs in IBL scenarios using ILSs. While the first iteration focuses on teachers, the second, currently in progress, aims at gaining insight on the students' needs. The results of these iterations will lead to the definition and refinement of the solutions which will be applied in the third iteration for their evaluation.

---

[2] Golabz portal: http://golabz.eu.

[3] Graasp: http://graasp.eu.

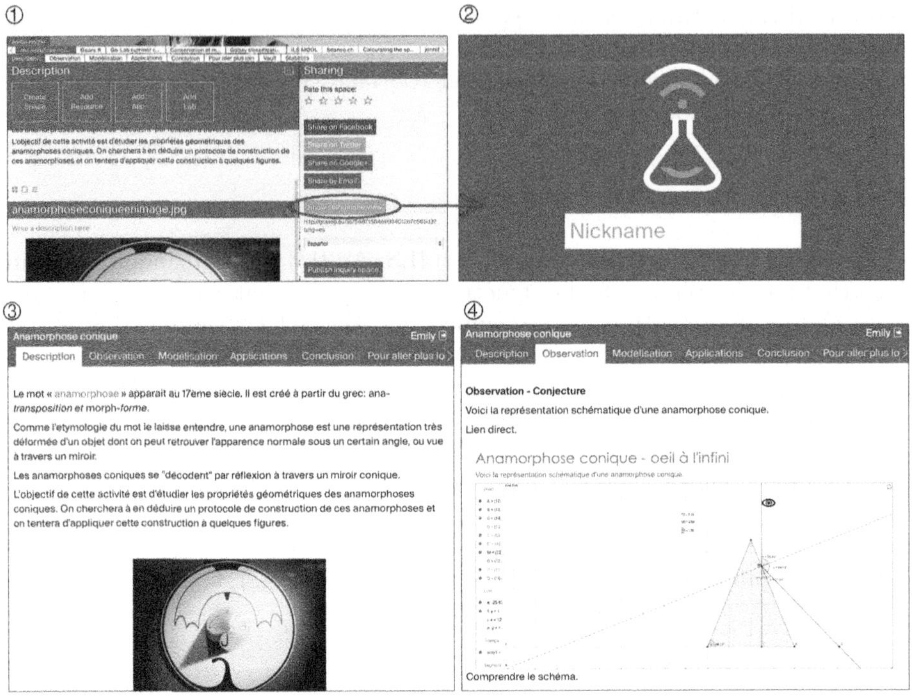

Fig. 1. Inquiry learning space in the authoring view (1) and in the standalone view (2,3,4).

In this paper, we report on the first DBR iteration. To identify the main orchestration needs of teachers when using ILSs, we conducted a survey-based study with 23 expert teachers to reveal what they consider as needs given their current practices. To supplement the survey and to uncover "actual" needs, we carried out 4 in-depth case studies with 2 teachers, helping us to better understand the needs that can emerge during the life-cycle of an ILS. In the following sections we describe these studies.

5 Expert Teacher Survey

To identify the orchestration needs that Go-Lab teachers detect when using Graasp, we conducted a survey from January 30th to March 15th, 2015. We received responses from 23 teachers, including 8 females and 15 males, between 23 and 60 years old from different European countries Cyprus, Estonia, Germany, Greece, Portugal, Spain, and Switzerland). All of them had previous experience applying IBL and using ILSs in their courses. The purposes of this questionnaire were to *better understand the learning scenarios where the teachers use their ILSs* and *identify what additional support could help them orchestrate such scenarios.*

5.1 Learning Context

In order to understand how the participants used their ILSs, we asked them about the characteristics of their learning contexts in terms of number of students, their age, learning mode and social level. As it is shown in Fig. 2, the age range of the students is heterogeneous but the most significant group is between 15 and 16 years old. Regarding the group size, the number of the students involved in the learning scenarios varies from 12 to 140, with an average of 27 students per class. According to the responses, the teachers use their ILSs totally (47.83 %) or mainly (39.13 %) in the classroom, where the students work either individually or in small groups of 2–3 people.

5.2 Teacher Information Needs

To identify what information would help teachers orchestrate their learning scenarios when using ILSs, we asked them an open-ended question where they could express their ideas. Table 1 summarizes their answers. We have classified teacher interest on information needs along three categories: needs related to the *learning design*, the *learning process* and the *learning outcomes*. Table 1 shows the list of 21 needs extracted from the teachers answers, and the number of teachers mentioning a given need. Looking at the number of participants who mentioned needs, there are not many requests regarding the learning design (8.70 %). It appears that teachers are concerned first and foremost about the learning outcomes (73.91 %) and secondly about the learning process (56.52 %).

Learning Design. To improve the design of the ILS, the teachers identified two main needs: getting feedback from experts (e.g., other teachers, app or lab

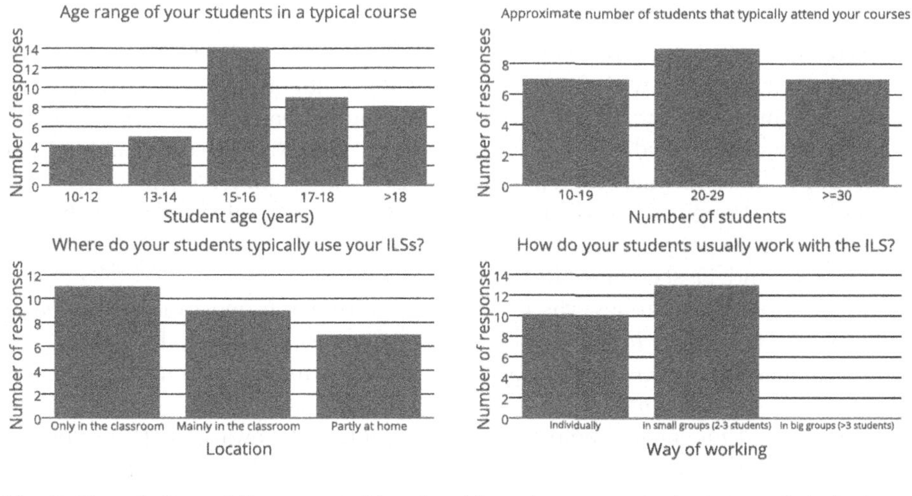

Fig. 2. Description of the surveyed teachers' learning contexts, in terms of student age, number of students, learning mode, and social level.

owners), and having specifications and tips from other teachers who have created/used the ILS.

Learning Process. Certain needs identified by the teachers have *awareness* purposes. Some of them may be covered by Learning Analytics solutions applied to the traces generated by the student's interaction with the ILS (e.g., the current phase where the students are working) and others required the student involvement (e.g., signaling of "stuck students"). This awareness information may help teachers *intervene* and *regulate* the learning scenario. Other needs serve *reflection* purposes, helping the teacher understand how the students use the ILS (e.g., looking at the time spent in the different parts of the ILS). Such information about the learning process may provide relevant feedback for the *refinement* of the ILS (e.g. by adapting the activities to the time available).

Learning Outcomes. Most of the teachers highlighted the importance of having access to students' work: reviewing the intermediate versions of the artifacts may help teachers *intervene* (e.g., by correcting errors or providing feedback) and *regulate* the scenario (e.g., suggesting the students to skip certain activities if they are running out of time); and, accessing the final versions of students' outputs enables the (summative) *assessment* of their work. Whenever the learning activities allow it (e.g., when using quizzes), providing students with automatic evaluation may help them identify their weak points and even offer recommendations to redirect the learning path, if needed. This information is also relevant from the teacher's point of view, since it provides an insight of the individual and whole-class comprehension of the subjects presented in the ILS. Aside from the automatic evaluation, teachers also identified the need of providing support for self, peer, and teacher evaluation of students' work in the ILS.

6 Classroom Case Studies

To better understand the needs that emerge during the orchestration of an ILS, we conducted 4 studies with 2 teachers and their students: Alice[4], with no experience in using ILSs or IBL, and Bob, who had already used ILSs and IBL in his courses. The studies were carried out in Geneva between January and March 2015. Alice's studies took place at the École de Commerce Nicolas-Bouvier involving two groups of 7 and 11 students (18 to 20 years old) respectively. The other two studies were conducted at the Collège Sismondi with Bob and two groups of 15 and 17 students (15 to 16 years old).

The aim of these studies was to address the research question of this paper (*What are the teacher orchestration needs when using ILSs?*) by taking into account orchestration needs that emerge during the learning scenarios. To answer this question we used interviews and observations as main data sources. First, we interviewed the teachers before the experiments to be aware of their expertise on IBL and ILSs. Second, we collected the teachers' needs during the design of the ILS and attended the classroom to observe the learning process. Third, after

[4] Names have been replaced to preserve teachers' anonymity.

Table 1. Teacher information needs classified according to the dimension they refer: learning design, learning process or learning outcome.

Teacher information needs	No. Teachers	L_Design	L_Process	L_Outcome
Expert feedback on the ILS design	1	x		
Specifications and tips from other teachers	1	x		
Current phase per student / students per phase	3		x	
Current actions	1		x	
Current state	1		x	
Time spent (per phase, app, ILS)	4		x	
Followed path	3		x	
Visited phases	1		x	
Used resources, apps, labs	2		x	
Used devices (e.g., phones, tablets, PCs)	1		x	
Statistics per session (filtered)	1		x	
Students questions/ comments	2		x	
Students who required hints	1		x	
Stuck students	2		x	
Evidence of face-to-face interaction	1		x	
Learning outcomes	12			x
Intermediate learning outcomes	2		x	x
Automatic evaluation	5			x
Self-evaluation	2			x
Peer-evaluation	1			x
Teacher-evaluation	1			x
No. indicators per category		2	14	6
No. of teachers mentioning a category		2	13	17
Proportion of interested teachers		8.70 %	56.52 %	73.91 %

the use of the ILSs, the teachers were interviewed about the problems that they faced and the orchestration needs that should be covered.

Learning Design. During the design phase, both teachers elaborated a first draft of their ILSs. In the case of Alice, she required some help to solve *doubts* about the ILS authoring and certain tools, as well as *recommendations* about apps that could satisfy her pedagogical objectives. Once the drafts of the ILSs were ready, the teachers sent them to the expert to get some *feedback* for the refinement of their proposals. The ILSs designed by Alice were for two maths courses. These ILSs contained theoretical descriptions, quizzes, Geogebra resources, a Wolfram Alpha widget[5], and Google Documents where the students had to add the result of their work. The ILS designed by Bob was devoted to two of his physics courses. It was made up by a brief theoretical introduction to the topic, a few tasks to be carried out using the bibliographical resources available in the classroom, and a PhET on-line lab[6]. In the case of Bob, he refined the ILS

[5] http://www.wolframalpha.com/widgets/.

[6] https://phet.colorado.edu/.

he used in his first course to reuse it in the second one. Moreover, the teachers integrated monitoring apps in their ILSs. These apps were supposed to show them the *current students per phase*, *the time spent per phase*, and *the actions registered per app*.

Learning Process. In the two studies carried by Alice, the students were allowed to work individually or in groups. Since Alice was not nearby her computer, she displayed the *monitoring* apps using the projector, so teacher and students could see the visualizations as presented in Fig. 3. She walked around, answering the questions that emerged during the learning activity. After answering the questions, Alice had a look to the apps and, according to the *student distribution across inquiry phases*, chose the next group to visit. At the same time, the students periodically observed the apps to compare their own progress with that of their peers. In the case of Bob, the students worked in groups of 2 to 3 sharing one computer. Since he could access the students' screens from his computer, he controlled the situation from his desk, going to the students just when the students had doubts. Bob mainly used the visualization of the *active users per phase* to monitor whether the students were using the ILS or not, and to be aware of the current phase where they were working on (see Fig. 4). Although both teachers had designed the ILSs to be used in 90-mins, face-to-face sessions, they were also used at home because some students could not attend to the class and others did not finished the activities on time. Thus, they wanted to monitor the on-line work.

For reflection purposes, the teachers considered that the "*time spent per phase*" could be a relevant indicator for better understanding the students' progress. Alice also mentioned that "*the actions registered per app*" could contribute to understand what are the apps that usually attract/discourage the students. Concerning the activity flow, the teachers detected that the students were going back and forth between phases. Therefore, Alice and Bob presented

Fig. 3. Awareness information displayed for Alice and students during the first study.

Fig. 4. Bob monitoring the students from his desktop during the second study.

interest on analyzing the *learning path*, i.e. the sequence of phases and the time spent per phase, to help them improve the flow description of their ILSs. Another functionality requested by Alice was the option of visualizing the *student responses*, especially with the quizzes, to have an quick overview of the class.

Learning Outcomes. Both teachers agreed that their main concern was related to the assessment. According to their rubrics, around 80 % of the marks focus on the *learning outcomes*. Therefore, they need to collect the students productions. In the case of Bob, he normally does it in paper format to have evidence sharable with other teachers, parents and students. Since certain apps and labs embedded in their ILSs did not provide storing features, they decided to collect the production of the students on paper.

7 Discussion

Hereafter we discuss the findings of the studies presented above along the three ILS life-cycle phases, namely learning design, learning process, and learning outcome.

Regarding the learning design, the surveys and the case studies showed that the participants were interested in having feedback from experts, as well as specifications and tips from other teachers who have created or used the ILS. Despite teachers are sometimes seen as working alone on their own projects, these findings suggest that they are actually keen to *collaboratively design and discuss* learning activities in a community of practice. Apart from supporting the collaborative creation of ILSs and providing social functionalities, we envision that offering *recommendations* based on best practices inferred from community (Go-Lab users) could guide the teachers in their designs. For example, applying

Learning Analytics, teachers could know which apps/labs are most frequently used in each IBL phase or how many items are usually added per phase.

Multiple needs detected in the survey and the case studies were related to awareness or reflection on learning process. Although they could be addressed by means of *Learning Analytics solutions* such as the monitoring tools developed in the project, they should take into account the timing and the learning context. For instance, due to the lack of time to pay attention to the apps during the learning activity, the apps should provide simple information that can be interpreted in a glance to support intervention and regulation decisions. Besides, to cover those cases where teachers are not using their computers in the sessions, it is necessary to provide apps that do not require interaction (e.g., for real-time monitoring apps). Furthermore the solutions should be responsive, meaning accessible either through mobile devices or through a public display.

Finally, the survey and the studies revealed that the main teacher concern was to have access to the learning outcomes in final and intermediary versions. Although integrating third-party tools provides multiple design benefits, it also implies important challenges in terms of awareness and assessment because the technological support should *integrate evidence and content coming from heterogeneous sources*. Moreover, as we have seen in the case studies, some apps do not store the student's results or register the user activity. Then, no support for awareness or assessment can be provided in those cases. This issue can be mitigated by promoting the usage of open standards such as Activity Streams or Open Social. To support teachers and students in the collection of learning evidence, one potential solution could rely on the automatic generation of a student portfolio. Additionally, providing ad-hoc apps for self-assessment would help, on the one hand, students to reflect on their work and, on the other hand, teachers to focus not only on a final document but also on the learning methods the student gained.

8 Conclusions and Future Work

This paper investigates the orchestration needs of teachers using ILSs through a survey to 23 expert teachers and 4 authentic case studies with 2 high school teachers. The collected needs have pointed to three main conclusions. First, teachers need and appreciate collaboration support for designing inquiry-based learning activities. Second, teachers request awareness and reflection tools to support and better understand the learning process as well as improve the learning design. Last but not least, the main concern of the teachers was to have access to learning outcomes in their intermediate and final versions, so that they could further guide the students and assess their work.

In the following iterations of the DBR process, we plan to explore *student* orchestration needs and evaluate the solutions created to support the different stakeholders.

Acknowledgements. This research is partially funded by the European Union in the context of the Go-Lab project (Grant Agreement no. 317601). This document does not represent the opinion of the European Union and it is not responsible for any usage made of its content.

References

1. Barab, S., Squire, K.: Design-based research: putting a stake in the ground. J. Learn. Sci. **13**(1), 1–14 (2004)
2. Brown, A.L.: Design experiments: theoretical and methodological challenges in creating complex interventions in classroom settings. J. Learn. Sci. **2**(2), 141–178 (1992)
3. De Jong, T., Van Joolingen, W.R., Giemza, A., Girault, I., Hoppe, U., Kindermann, J.: Learning by creating and exchanging objects: the SCY experience. Br. J. Educ. Technol. **41**(6), 909–921 (2010)
4. Dillenbourg, P., Zufferey, G., Alavi, H., Jermann, P., Do-Lenh, S., Bonnard, Q., Cuendet, S., Kaplan, F.: Classroom orchestration: the third circle of usability. In: International Conference on Computer Supported Collaborative Learning, vol. 1, pp. 510–517. ISLS, Hong Kong (2011)
5. Dyckhoff, A.L., Lukarov, V., Muslim, A., Chatti, M.A., Schroeder, U.: Supporting action research with learning analytics. In: International Conference on Learning Analytics and Knowledge, pp. 220–228. ACM, New York (2013)
6. Häkkinen, P.: Challenges for design of computer-based learning environments. Br. J. Educ. Technol. **33**(4), 461–469 (2002)
7. de Jong, T., Linn, M.C., Zacharia, Z.C.: Physical and virtual laboratories in science and engineering education. Science **340**(6130), 305–308 (2013)
8. de Jong, T., Sotirou, S., Gillet, D.: Innovations in STEM education: the Go-Lab federation of online labs. Smart Learn. Environ. **1**(3), 1–16 (2014)
9. Linn, M.C., Clark, D., Slotta, J.D.: Wise design for knowledge integration. Sci. Educ. **87**(4), 517–538 (2003)
10. Littleton, K., Scanlon, E., Sharples, M. (eds.): Orchestrating Inquiry Learning. Routledge, Abingdon (2012)
11. Mikroyannidis, A., Okada, A., Scott, P., Rusman, E., Specht, M., Stefanov, K., Chaimala, F.: weSPOT: a personal and social approach to inquiry-based learning. J. Univers. Comput. Sci. **19**(14), 2093–2111 (2013)
12. Mulholland, P., Anastopoulou, S., Collins, T., Feisst, M., Gaved, M., Kerawalla, L.: nQuire: technological support for personal inquiry learning. IEEE Trans. Learn. Technol. **5**(2), 157–169 (2012)
13. Prieto, L.P., Holenko Dlab, M., Gutiérrez, I., Abdulwahed, M., Balid, B.: Orchestrating technology enhanced learning: a literature review and a conceptual framework. Int. J. Technol. Enhanced Learn. **3**(6), 583–598 (2011)
14. Roschelle, J., Dimitriadis, Y., Hoppe, U.: Classroom orchestration: synthesis. Comput. Educ. **69**, 523–526 (2013)
15. Seol, S., Sharp, A., Kim, P.: Stanford mobile inquiry-based learning environment (SMILE). World Congress in Computer Science. Computer Engineering, and Applied Computing, pp. 270–276. CSREA Press, USA (2011)
16. Sharples, M., Anastopoulou, S.: Designing orchestration for inquiry learning. In: Littleton, K., Scanlon, E., Sharples, M. (eds.) Orchestrating Inquiry Learning, pp. 69–85. Routledge, Abingdon (2012)

17. Slotta, J.D., Tissenbaum, M., Lui, M.: Orchestrating of complex inquiry: three roles for learning analytics in a smart classroom infrastructure. In: International Conference on Learning Analytics and Knowledge, pp. 270–274. ACM (2013)
18. Sutherland, R., Eagle, S., Joubert, M.: A vision and strategy for Technology Enhanced Learning. Report from the STELLAR Network of Excellence (2012)
19. Valdes, C., Ferreirae, M., Feng, T., Wang, H., Tempel, K., Liu, S., Shaer, O.: A collaborative environment for engaging novices in scientific inquiry. In: ACM International Conference on Interactive Tabletops and Surfaces, pp. 109–118. ACM (2012)

Re-thinking Digital Textbooks: Students as Co-authors

Terje Väljataga(✉), Sebastian H.D. Fiedler, and Mart Laanpere

Centre for Educational Technology, Tallinn University, Tallinn, Estonia
{terje.valjataga,fiedler,mart.laanpere}@tlu.ee

Abstract. The steadily widening access to instruments and services for digital content production allows students and teachers to modify, remix and re-use a wide range of existing artefacts or create new artefacts and assemble them into various content collections. This development holds the potential for shifting patterns of power, roles, and responsibilities of students in digital textbook publishing sector and for supporting the strategic educational vision of "students as creators". However, this vision causes a growing pressure on academic publishers and other learning resource providers, as it tends to intervene and disrupt existing practices and business models of content development and provision. Existing models of interaction analysis are not suitable for the emerging context of mash-up learning resources co-authored by learners. The paper proposes a new analytic framework LoCA for evaluating level of learner's interaction with and co-authorship of digital content.

Keywords: Trialogical learning · Curating · Authorship levels · E-textbooks · Knowledge creation

1 Introduction

An increasing number of everyday activities are enhanced and transformed through the extensive growth of digitisation in our societies. This development has been accelerating by a massive growth of personal mobile device ownership. Thus personal and social computing is becoming truly pervasive and ubiquitous [1], supported by, and supporting, an ever-changing configuration of networked devices, applications and actors [2, 3]. It is becoming the norm that we can all access, interpret and process informational artefacts on the go, transform them into various representational states, or create entirely new ones. We can decouple from, and recouple with, external resources and artefacts of various kinds on a continuous, interactive basis [4]. Be it laptops, smart phones, or tablets - these devices are becoming also increasingly accessible and affordable for our student populations. Thus, a growing number of students experience that the digital realm is gradually penetrating a widening range of activities in their life. In principle this development holds the potential for shifting patterns of power, roles, and responsibilities in educational settings, too. Proponents of such a change vision continue to emphasise that students should be enabled to form their own digital learning ecosystems and design their personal learning environments for various learning purposes [5]. Students can (and should) learn how to take control and responsibility for systematically re-instrumenting their (learning) activities.

F.W.B. Li et al. (Eds.): ICWL 2015, LNCS 9412, pp. 143–151, 2015.
DOI: 10.1007/978-3-319-25515-6_13

From this perspective, mastering a range of digital instruments for working on diverse sets of digital artefacts, is increasingly seen as the pre-requisite for become contributors and (co-)creators of knowledge. By offering their own interpretations, explanations and examples [6], students are shifting ownership of, and control over, knowledge artefacts and the development of their own learning environments.

Current educational policy in Estonia – as formulated in the "Estonian Lifelong Learning Strategy 2020" - is trying to support and stimulate a system-wide change project under the label of "digital turn in schools" that embraces, among other aspects, the idea of "students as creators". Students are expected to collaborate, communicate and connect to ideas in entirely new ways through authoring, remixing, and co-creating digital, networked artifacts of various kinds and of different representational qualities. It is also envisioned that all schools are providing digital resources, making a modern infrastructure available for one-to-one computing, incorporating digital culture in teaching and learning practices and focusing on supporting learners' critical thinking, creativity, knowledge building, and problem solving.

In the context of this ambitious national project of change, existing models and formats of digital textbook production and provision are also scrutinized from the perspective of a future educational practice that would systematically support a shift towards the concept of "student as creator" that we have briefly outlined above. In the remaining paper we want to highlight and discuss some insights and unresolved challenges that we have gathered in the context of Learnmix – an applied research project focusing on the pedagogical and technical re-conceptualisation of the next-generation digital textbook production and provision model in Estonian context.

2 Trialogical Learning and the Concept of Students as Creators

The increasing pervasion of personal and social computing among students offers multiple ways to interact with, reuse, create, and author digital artefacts of all kinds. In consequence, we seemingly need a rather different set of frameworks and metaphors for addressing and capturing this emerging form of learning activity and its mediation. Inspired by Scardamalia and Bereiter's work [7] Paavola et al. [8] propose, for example, a knowledge creation and building metaphor, which they call "trialogical learning". Trialogical learning emphasizes the central role of operations on, and through, knowledge objects. In this view it is essential that students collaboratively create and develop shared, novel (digital) artefacts with the support of (digital) instruments of various kinds. Paavola and Hakkarainen [9] state that "*in trialogues the central aim is not to enhance dialogues but the common ground is provided by jointly constructing external representations, practices and artefacts (dialogues can, of course, help here). In trialogical processes the common ground is deepened (and provided) by modifying those artefacts and practices ("shared objects"), which are objects of joint activity. In trialogues we are not interacting only with words or concepts, but also modifying conceptual artefacts, external representations, and practices*" (p. 12). Knowledge building and creation stresses the importance of idea (conceptual artefact) advancement, expansion and improvement; and the ability of students to develop cultural or conceptual objects. In this manner, students can construct their own knowledge by incorporating and elaborating on artefacts that are, for instance, professionally developed by instructional designers, e-textbook authors, teachers, and so forth or even create their own objects from scratch. According to [9] the objects "*can be knowledge artefacts, practices, ideas, models, representations, etc. but understood as something concrete to be developed collaboratively*" (p. 4).

While the concept of *students as creators and producers* is certainly not an entirely new one, digitisation has transformed existing practices and is stimulating the emergence of new types of creation and production. In this way, it is allowing students to express themselves in a widening range of re-presentational modes. Teachers and students are slowly expanding the boundaries of their respective roles in education. They are becoming (co-)authors of digital content, thus challenging established models and processes of educational content production, its organisation, and provision.

3 Authoring Digital Content Collections

In the context of the Learnmix project, we carried out empirical research on interaction with digital content in 6 schools, where teachers and researchers co-designed 12 lessons where students (age ranging from 8 to 18 years) used personal digital devices to learn through using, editing and creating digital learning resources. All lessons were observed, protocolled and video-recorded by one researcher. Qualitative analysis of lesson protocols and videos showed that when trialogical learning scenarios were successfully implemented, the students were actively engaged in interaction with the content in the role of a creator. The products of the student-centered knowledge creation process were increasingly of an aggregated, collage-like nature. Over time we came to see this practice of combining and aggregating various content items in meaningful ways as yet another, particular aspect of "co-authorship" (see [10]).

In networked environments teachers and students potentially have access to countless content items (images, graphs, videos, tables, text, and so forth) of various quality and origin. Some of them are professionally produced, stored in dedicated repositories, and equipped with different licensing models and metadata. Some of them are freely available, created and designed by "amateurs". This seemingly infinite pool of digital content provides teachers and students with numerous ways to assemble and curate content item collections. Depending on the type of educational scenarios that are initiated and supported, students might even create, collage-like, artefact collections, which may not make use of professionally created artefacts at all.

As part of our work around a series of intervention studies in Estonian K-12 education we traced and modeled the (inter-)action levels with digital micro-content, and various content collections, as they occurred throughout the execution of a variety of scenario based teaching approaches – all designed around the general notion of "students as creators".

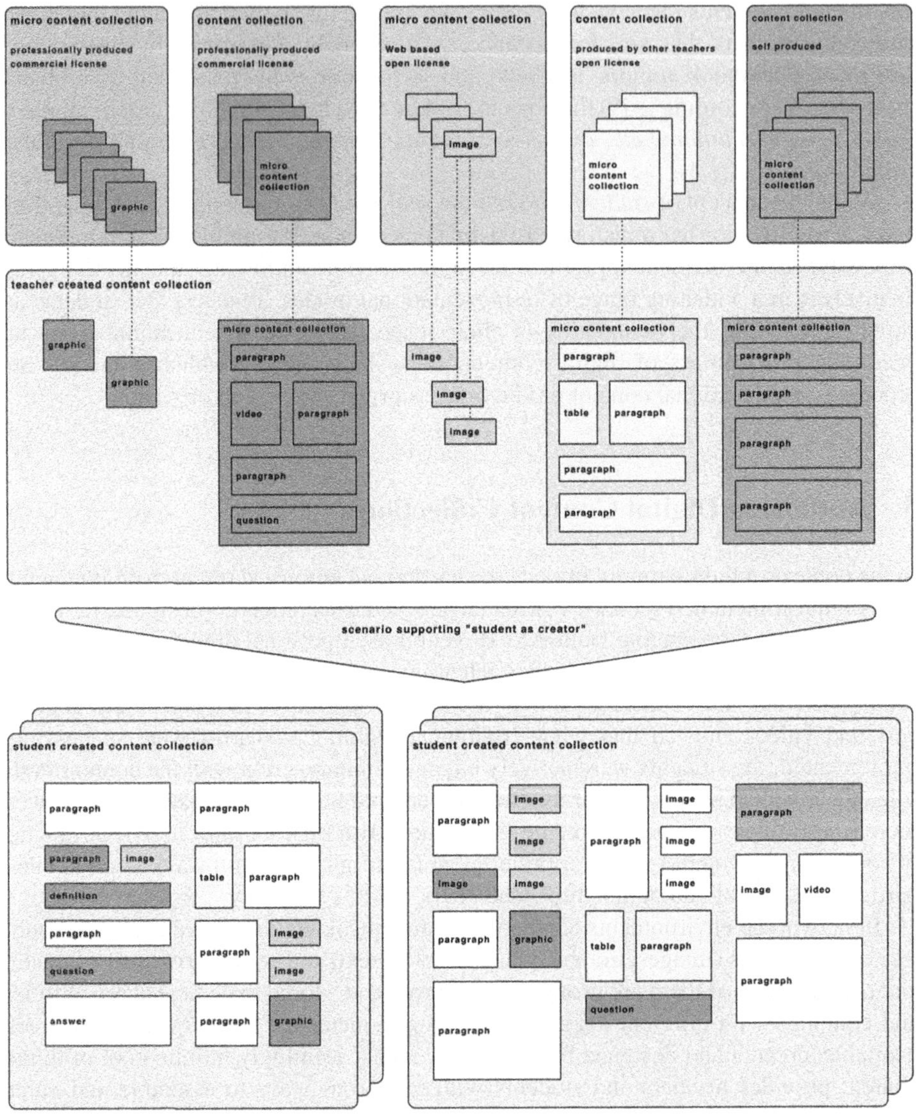

Fig. 1. Illustration of the formation and composition of teacher and student curated content collections

Without going into the details of specific scenarios and their particularities, we would like to emphasise that we were not only able to trace a whole range of individual interactions and authorship levels in relation to specific (micro-)content items, but also the composition and formation of mash-up artifact collections as products of collective knowledge building. Figure 1 on the following page might serve as an illustrative example of such an analytical perspective. The documented case depicts how a teacher pre-selects and arranges a variety of micro-content items or collections of micro-contents in preparation for a particular teaching and learning scenario. The various items sit on a range of repositories. Some graphics and some more elaborated and pre-structured micro-content collections (such as topic based, informational "modules" made of text, graphics, video, questions...) are actually retrieved from professionally produced content repositories that carry some sort of a commercial license. Some additional images come from a Web-based collection offering a range of open licenses. Additional "modules" (of structured and aggregated micro-content) are retrieved from a repository that provides open-licensed content that is created and shared by other teachers. And finally some additional items come from a collection of self-produced, digital content that may only be stored locally by the teacher herself.

If we finally analyse the products that student groups have co-authored while going through a particular scenario (supporting the notion of "students as creators"), we get a rather rich, collage-like image of aggregated content collections that combine various items that were originally provided by the teachers, items that were modified, and items that were created from scratch by the participating students.

It should be rather obvious that this type of educational practice in which students and teachers move beyond simple levels of (inter-)action into the field of content authoring and the creation of content collections, poses further challenges for academic publishers and commercial content providers. Based on the conceptual and empirical work that we carried out within the context of Learnmix project, we see a considerable misfit between the current status quo of contentment provision and production among academic publishers and the importance of supporting the full range of levels of interaction and co-authorship that contemporary educational frameworks such as "trialogical learning" suggest. We see it as an important challenge for educational research and development to design, develop, and test new approaches that potentially align innovative learning and teaching scenarios with the affordances of expanding digital and networked technology, and revised business models for content production, publishing and distribution.

4 Levels of Co-authorship with Digital Content

In the realm of professional and commercial content production for education, however, "interaction" has been promoted as the key added value of digital learning materials. Apparently, it is a widely shared belief among publishing companies, educators, instructional designers and policy makers, that e-textbooks and digital materials need to (and can) be redesigned in ways that enable somewhat more variable modes of interaction with content. Turning e-textbooks and any other digital learning material more interactive in comparison to their printed counterparts is considered to be a significant step further in terms of technical and conceptual development.

However, the bulk of digital learning material and e-textbook solutions currently available are hardly supporting the more ambitious notion of various levels of distributed co-authorship of digital artefacts, as it emphasised within frameworks such as the trialogical learning and knowledge creation that we have mentioned above.

In the context of a national research and development project called Learnmix we attempted to address the changing roles of teachers and students as creators and authors of content. We re-designed learning and teaching practices so that students can become active (co-)constructors of their own knowledge by creating, modifying and integrating various physical, and digital artefacts. In these practices textbooks didn't function as the main references tool and primary means of delivering course content anymore. Instead, participants were making use of various micro content and content collections from a wide range of authors ranging from professional content designers to students and other Internet users interested in the topic at hand. In addition to a descriptive analytical framework, which allows to focus on specific actions, mediating artefacts, and micro-content used or created before and during the learning experience [10], we also extracted 7 distinct levels of co-authorship on digital textbooks to describe how teachers and students worked with artefacts in the context of our intervention studies (Fig. 2). Our taxonomy - Levels of Co-Authorship (LoCA):

0. **Consume** - The lowest and the most static way to interact with content is to simply consume it. This refers to viewing a video clip, listening a podcast or for instance just reading a text. The content item will remain untouched by its users, no changes will be done with the actual content of that artefact.
1. **Annotate** - The next level allows annotation of content with various types of meta-data: e.g. highlights, likes, ratings, tags, comments. Annotation makes content meaningful and personal for the user as he/she carries out some operations with it, mainly at a metadata level. Some annotations (tags, bookmarks) can be shared within online communities.
2. **Manipulate** - This is the most common level of interaction among professional e-textbooks publishers today (e.g. while publishing in iBook, mobi or ePub formats). Although learners are engaged in interacting with some components of the textbook by clicking on hot spots, dragging and dropping some elements to correct location, or filling in some fields in a digital form, they cannot modify or add the content. The software gives immediate personal feedback to learner's interactions with content, while teacher or other learners cannot receive, view or analyse the responses of the learner. The learner's co-authorship remains restricted and temporary, as a digital content of e-textbook is not changed permanently.
3. **Submit** - On this level, the learners are prompted to solve some problems, manipulate interactive content or enter responses to questions. Unlike with the previous level, the results of such interaction or problem-solving will be submitted for review and feedback to the teacher or other participants in the process of learning. The input requested from learners and the feedback given by the teacher will not be included in the textbook itself, but sometimes it is archived as a companion or annex.
4. **Expand** - On the level of expansion a user can edit or complement an artefact, add some micro content to the original artefact, however, the core content of that artefact remains mainly intact. For instance, merging together some video clips, filling in blanks in a self-test, adding a story to a photo etc. While the previous levels of the authorship didn't allow changing the original core content, with this level the original content itself will be complemented with some additions, however, the core parts of the content are still visible and recognisable. We consider this (inter-)action level to mark the starting point for a progressive transition into "authorship".
5. **Remix** - Remixing means altering the original state of the content by adding, removing, and/or changing pieces of the item. In the case of remixing it is difficult

to extract its initial version and parts. The main characteristic of remixing is that it appropriates and changes other materials to create something new. Here, the original author is distanced from her material. The original meaning of the content and the intention of the author might change entirely. The remixer makes the material her own.

6. **Create** - A user can create a totally new artefact from scratch. In this case the user doesn't make use of any other content, but develops his own.

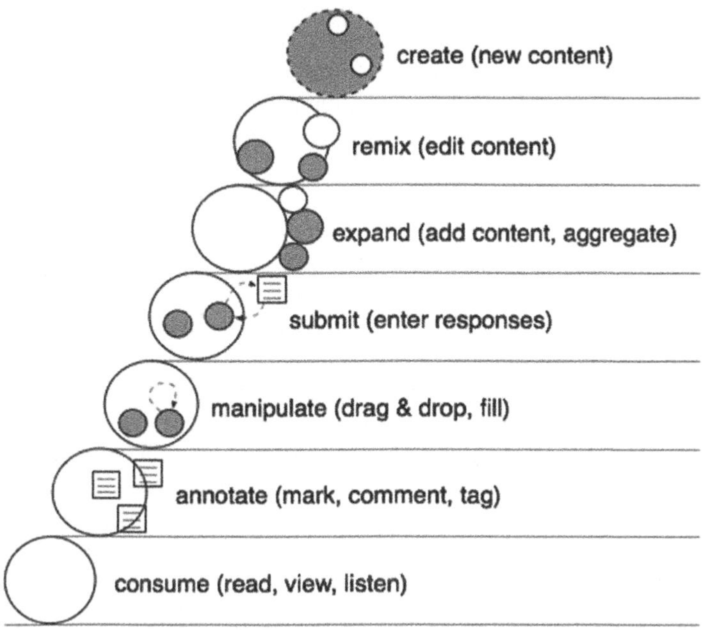

Fig. 2. Levels of co-authorship of digital textbooks

Distinguishing between these different levels of co-authorship of digital textbooks has given us an analytical instrument for describing how particular learning and teaching scenarios support various forms of interaction and co-authorship. It also helps us to explore to what extent a particular scenario allows students to become the author of their own knowledge representations. We have also found it useful to apply this analytical perspective while designing and describing new scenarios.

It is quite obvious that the need to support more advanced forms of interaction, where students and teachers progress into "authorship" territory, put a considerable pressure on academic textbook publishers and other learning material providers.

Digital artefacts are more fluid, unstable and liable to mutate than traditional forms of content provision such as print. In an increasingly networked and digitised world, we all not only have instantaneous access to digital artefacts of various kind, we can also easily produce our own. In consequence, academic publishers and their textbook authors are gradually losing their position as sole authors and owners of authoritative (learning) materials. The steadily widening access to instruments and services for digital content production is increasingly diffusing the power of publishers. Students and teachers already hold the means to modify and compartmentalise a wide range of existing artefacts. They can also produce a variety of digital content items such as photos, video clips, audio recording, and so forth. However, they can also assemble, curate, and share their own collections of micro content according to their desires and needs. The identity of the 'original' author(s) of each fragment often becomes ambiguous or even invisible in the process of this practice.

However, the traditional practices in textbook publishing world have always drawn very clear boundaries between authors and passive users (teachers, students), also between commercially produced (print) content and user-generated (digital) content. Even today, the national legislation in Estonia defines and regulates explicitly the process and quality assurance mechanisms concerning only the printed textbooks and workbooks. While Estonian teachers have been increasingly authoring and using digital learning resources over the last decade, the user-generated digital learning content has existed in completely separate ecosystem than commercially/professionally produced textbooks (e.g.: separate repositories, regulations, delivery channels, legitimacy, pedagogical patterns and platforms of use). The situation is about to change soon, as the Ministry of Education and Research of Estonia has decreed that all newly published textbooks and workbooks have to be available also in the digital format starting from May 2015. As there have been no specifications regarding expected digital formats for upcoming e-textbooks, publishers are pursuing various routes to digital realm. While all textbook publishers acknowledge that digital textbooks cannot be merely static copies of their printed counterparts, the way interaction is introduced in pilot e-textbooks demonstrates the desire of textbook industry to maintain the strict separation of author's and user's roles also in the future. For instance, popular e-textbooks published in the Apple iBook format provide quite limited range of interactivity, as students are allowed merely to fill in or choose the right answer, which will not be shown even to the teacher. Students and teachers cannot add resources to iBook or hide some parts that are not relevant. Yet, some other publishers are experimenting with Web-based textbooks allowing various ways and levels of contributions from teachers and learners. Our agenda behind creating the LoCA analytic framework is helping the textbook publishers, researchers and teachers in comparing, analysing and developing innovative digital textbooks that support trialogical learning. Our next step is validation of the LoCA framework by applying it for comparative analysis of different e-textbooks in Estonia and Finland.

5 Concluding Remarks

It seems obvious that the emerging notion of "students as creators" and related conceptual frameworks like "trialogical learning" and "knowledge building" carry several challenges that go beyond the current state of affairs in the realm of professional and commercial content production, publishing and distribution. If we truly want to support emerging digital practices that augment the productive and creative co-authoring of knowledge artefacts, we need to reconsider what type of models of digital content provision actually make a fit with our emerging vision of education (students as creators) in the digital age.

The changing extent of content and content collection authorships raises a number of particular questions, such as who is the owner of the content; how the ownership is changing in the process of modifying an artefact and who can and should control its distribution in terms of timing, cost, licensing, openness, and so forth. We can witness that alongside a traditional lifespan of a content item, new life cycle paths emerge, as part of the control over content is transferring to students and teachers. Furthermore, this emerging discourse is concerned with further innovations, revenue models, content enrichment, the digital rights management, open-access models, marketing, new sales channels, legal frameworks, formats, pricing, the rise and the possibilities of self-publishing and so on. And this all need to be researched and developed together with emerging educational visions and technological developments.

Acknowledgments. This research has been produced in the context of LEARNMIX project (No RU/3013) funded by Archimedes Foundation.

References

1. McCullough, M.: Digital Ground: Architecture, Pervasive Computing, and Environmental Knowing. MIT Press, Cambridge (2004)
2. Weiser, M.: Ubiquitous computing. In: ACM Conference on Computer Science, p. 418 (1994)
3. Bødker, S., Klokmose, C.N.: The human-artifact model: an activity theoretical approach to artifact ecologies. Hum. Comput. Interact. (Mahwah) **26**(4), 315–371 (2011)
4. Sutton, J.: Distributed cognition. Domains and dimensions. In: Itiel, E., Harnad, S.R. (eds.) Cognition Distributed: How Cognitive Technology Extends Our Minds, pp. 45–56. John Benjamins Publishing Co., Amsterdam (2008)
5. Fiedler, S.H.D., Väljataga, T.: Personal learning environments: a conceptual landscape revisited. eLearning Pap. **35**, 1–16 (2013)
6. Moorefield-Lang, H.: An exploration of e-textbooks. Libr. Media Connection **31**, 18–19 (2013)
7. Scardamalia, M., Bereiter, C.: Knowledge building: theory, pedagogy, and technology. In: Sawyer, K. (ed.) Cambridge Handbook of the Learning Sciences, pp. 97–118. Cambridge University Press, New York (2006)
8. Paavola, S., Engeström, R., Hakkarainen, K.: Trialogical approach as a new form mediation. In: Moen, A., Morch, A.I., Paavola, S. (eds.) Collaborative Knowledge Creation: Practices, Tools, Concepts, pp. 1–14. Sense Publishers, Rotterdam (2012)
9. Paavola, S., Hakkarainen, K.: From meaning making to joint construction of knowledge practices and artefacts - a trialogical approach to CSCL. In: Proceedings of the 9th International Conference on Computer Supported Collaborative Learning, vol. 1, pp. 83–92 (2009)
10. Väljataga, T., Fiedler, S.H.D.: Re-conceptualising e-textbooks: in search for a descriptive framework. In: Cao, Y., Väljataga, T., Tang, J.K.T., Leung, H., Laanpere, M. (eds.) ICWL 2014 Workshops. LNCS, vol. 8699, pp. 264–273. Springer, Heidelberg (2014)

Personalized and Adaptive Learning

Tracing Self-Regulated Learning in Responsive Open Learning Environments

Dominik Renzel[1(✉)], Ralf Klamma[1], Milos Kravcik[1], and Alexander Nussbaumer[2]

[1] Advanced Community Information Systems (ACIS) Group Chair of Computer Science 5, RWTH Aachen University, Ahornstr. 55, 52056 Aachen, Germany
{renzel,klamma,kravcik}@dbis.rwth-aachen.de

[2] Knowledge Technologies Institute, Graz University of Technology, Inffeldgasse 13, 8010 Graz, Austria
alexander.nussbaumer@tugraz.at

Abstract. *Self-Regulated Learning (SRL)* and related meta-cognitive learning competences help to increase learning progress. However, facilitating the acquisition of such competences with learning technologies is challenging. Training requires an individualized approach and the right balance between the learner's freedom and guidance. To support SRL, we applied personalisation and adaptive technologies in the development of an Open Source toolkit for *Responsive Open Learning Environments (ROLE)*. In this paper we present a conceptual foundation for the operationalization of self-regulated learning in personal learning environments as a cyclic process model. Furthermore, we present results of a long-term usage data analysis of the ROLE Sandbox, an open and free Web-based hosting environment for personal learning environments. In particular, we trace self-regulated learning activities in three years of productive operation. We conclude our findings with guidelines for self-regulated learning in personal learning environments.

Keywords: Self-regulated learning · Personal learning environments · Long-term evaluation · Guidelines

1 Introduction

Self-Regulated Learning (SRL) has become a very active research field [2,15,17] with contributions from various disciplines, including pedagogy, psychology and neuroscience. The cyclic phase structure of the SRL process as well as meta-cognitive, motivational and behavioural aspects have been in the focus of educational research. Our main interest is the use of *Personal Learning Environments (PLE)* [13,16] to support SRL processes. PLE support learners in defining their own learning goals and managing their learning contents, tools, and peers with a high degree of autonomy. Pedagogical scaffolding can be provided by suitable recommenders in such community-based adaptive systems [8].

F.W.B. Li et al. (Eds.): ICWL 2015, LNCS 9412, pp. 155–164, 2015.
DOI: 10.1007/978-3-319-25515-6_14

We argue that SRL processes in reality are embedded in many learning settings ranging from formal to informal settings, even within formal educational institutions. We also argue that in many learning situations the learner is not ready for autonomously performed learning processes. Current research underestimates the complexity stemming from differences in technology and learning culture as well from the real learner needs.

We have performed extensive research in realistic learning settings ranging from learning in higher education organizations in different countries, in workplace learning and in self-organized social software-supported learning communities. We found that besides the collection of Web 2.0 tools, learning tools must be integrated into existing learning platforms like organizational or institutional *Learning Management Systems (LMS)*. We also found that learner support must range from total freedom to detailed control of the learning process, contents, tools, and peers. These dimensions have been underestimated in research so far and led to coining the term *Responsive Open Learning Environments (ROLE)* for a new class of SRL-enabled personal learning environments.

This paper makes the following contributions. First, we present our conceptual self-regulated learning process model with an emphasis on its operationalization in PLE. Second, based on usage data sampled from over three years of operation, we analyzed activity in the ROLE Sandbox, a PLE management platform including SRL support. The goal was to trace self-regulated learning over a long time in naturalistic informal learning settings as supplement to rather short-termed controlled laboratory studies. Our results suggest that only a small fraction of ROLE Sandbox users were or have become self-regulated learners. However, these few self-regulated learners are PLE power users in terms of serendipity and repeated frequent use, thus suggesting that the included SRL tools provide appropriate, however yet improvable support for different SRL phases. Third, resulting from our observations, we derive a set of design guidelines for better support of self-regulated learning in PLE.

In Sect. 2 we discuss related work on self-regulated learning and personal learning environments. In Sect. 3 we introduce our SRL Process Model and its operationalization in widget-based responsive open learning environments. In Sect. 4 we present the results of our analysis on SRL activity in the ROLE Sandbox, based on a long-term collection of usage data. In Sect. 5 we conclude five key requirements for PLE management platforms to achieve support for self-regulated learning.

2 Related Work

In the last decades, much research has been conducted in the field of SRL, which overlaps with different disciplines, including pedagogy, psychology, neuroscience, and technology enhanced learning. In particular from a psychological point of view, self-regulated learning is a complex field of research that combines motivational, cognitive and personality theories. Components of SRL are *cognition*, *meta-cognition*, *motivation*, *affects*, and *volition* [10], accompanied by six key processes essential for self-regulated learning [3]. These are *goal setting*, *self-monitoring*, *self-evaluation*, *task strategies*, *help seeking*, and *time management*. A cyclic approach to model SRL has been given by Zimmerman [17]. SRL is a process of meta-cognitive activities consisting of three phases, namely the *forethought phase*, the *performance phase*, and the *self-reflection phase*. According to this model, learning performance and behavior consist of both cognitive activities (e.g. attaining new knowledge) and meta-cognitive activities for controlling the learning process. Aviram et al. [1] extended this model towards a *self-regulated personalised learning (SRPL)* approach by adding a self-profile enabling learners to indicate own preferences.

PLE [13] empower learners to control and arrange their own learning tool sets, contents, and processes [6]. They support individuals to combine own suitable learning environments from a global ecosystem of generic Web 2.0 services, e.g. blogs, links, wikis, social software and RSS feeds. The goal of widget-based PLE platforms is to technically empower learners without strong technical backgrounds to realize such combinations on their own with steep learning curves. In such platforms, learners select multiple widgets from an existing ecosystem (e.g. widget store) and combine them on a desktop surface metaphor. Thereby, widgets are conceived as small-scale Web applications clearly focused on specific simple tasks and activities. However, most existing widget platforms and Web 2.0 tools do not meet the complex needs of self-regulated learners in PLE with respect to planning, learning, and reflection activities. We addressed these shortcomings from conceptual, methodological and technical perspectives with the help of the ROLE SDK, a development environment and management platform for PLE with built-in conceptual and technical support for self-regulated learning. Due to the comparably short existence of widget-based PLE, little research has been conducted to observe and analyze self-regulated learning processes in naturalistic PLE settings over longer periods.

3 Self-Regulated Learning in Widget-Based PLE

From a user (i.e. learner or teacher) perspective, the central concept of the ROLE PLE management platform is the *space*, which also provides the user interface for the learner. A space serves as container context for *widgets*, i.e. small learning tools usually consisting of a Web front-end and a Web-service in the backend. Examples of such widgets are search tools for learning material or tools for planning learning activities. The user can select widgets from a ROLE widget store [4] and add them to a space. The ROLE implementation provides several core features of the space concept on top of plain PLE management. First, it provides a dynamic storage of space and user resources where context and learner-specific information can be stored. Second, it enables both widgets and users in the same space to interact with each other, thus enabling a seamless orchestration of learning tools and real-time communication and collaboration among learners. Third, the platform is augmented with rich logging facilities, thus enabling learning analytics [14]. Altogether, a ROLE space can be defined as a bundle of widgets that includes storage for user and context information and widget data. Spaces can also be pre-configured and shared with others, thus allowing rich re-use of learning environments across learning contexts.

From a conceptual point of view, ROLE spaces are the contexts in which we model self-regulated learning as a cyclic process. Our SRL process model [9] is based on Zimmerman's original SRL conception [17] and the SRPL approach [1]. Our contribution is its adaptation for operationalization in PLE in two ways. First, we introduced an additional phase primarily related to the creation of the own learning environment (preparation phase). Second, the phases are constituted not only on the meta-cognitive level, but also on the cognitive level. These adaptations are necessary to consider active PLE creation and management as part of the SRL process. Our learner-centric SRL process model thus consists of four cyclic phases (*planning*, *preparing*, *learning*, and *reflecting*). Each of these phases is associated with concrete learning strategies, in turn established by *learning activities* on a finer granularity level. Figure 1 depicts our four-phase process model including the related learning strategies. In order to operationalize our model, we defined a taxonomy of *learning strategies* and *techniques* assigned to the learning phases. In this way learning phases are described with clearly defined *learning activities*, thus establishing a connection between the pedagogical constructs and concrete learning tools. Instead of directly assigning pedagogical constructs to widgets, widget functionalities are used as *mediator* construct. This mediator approach has the advantage that widget creators simply describe widget functionality without the need to describe pedagogical purpose. By contrast, pedagogical experts can make the assignment of learning techniques with functionalities without knowing which widgets are available.

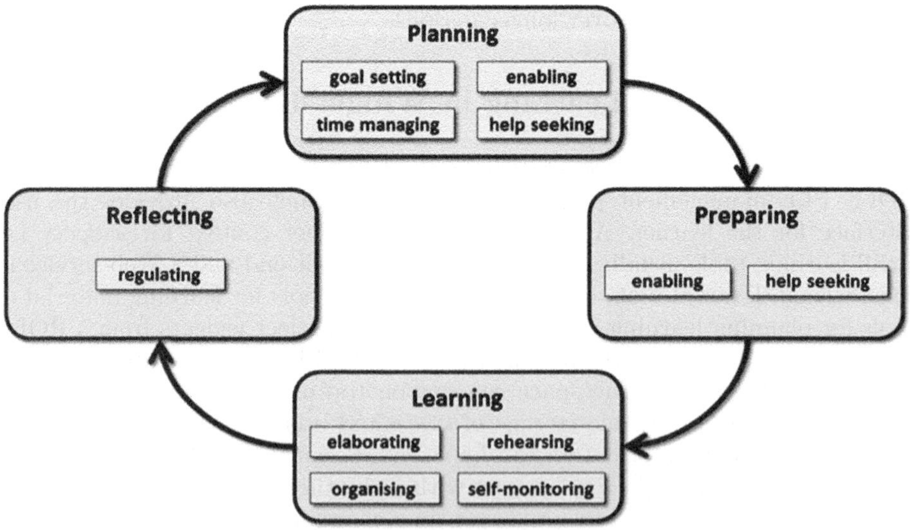

Fig. 1. The ROLE self-regulated learning process model

4 Tracing SRL in the ROLE Sandbox

In 2012, we launched the ROLE Sandbox as a Web deployment of the ROLE SDK with widget and widget-bundle developers being the intended target group. Equipped with usage data collection, cleaning, and enrichment [14], ROLE Sandbox supports the observation of arbitrary human interaction with the system's APIs. Entries in our data set include origin IP address (*who*), timestamp (*when*), request URL and operation (*what*), along with context enrichments. In particular, the data set provides logs of PLE management operations such as *create space*, *join/leave space*, *add/remove widget to/from space*, including context information on widget categories from the ROLE Widget Store [4,12]. Apart from typical repeating patterns of widget development and testing, we found emergent patterns of system interaction indicating learning activity wrt. our operationalization of SRL in PLE (cf. Sect. 3), thus motivating deeper analysis.

We collected our data set over more than three years of operation (2012–2015). For this work, we selected the first 1.5 year sample (03/2012–09/2013) including 1.72 million API requests from >3900 IP addresses in >600 cities and >80 countries. Figure 2 provides an overview of spatio-temporal platform usage distribution. The map on top indicates geospatial usage distribution limited to IPs having accessed the system >10 times. The bottom timeline chart shows temporal usage distribution in terms of request frequency (blue/red graphs) and data transfer (yellow/green graphs).

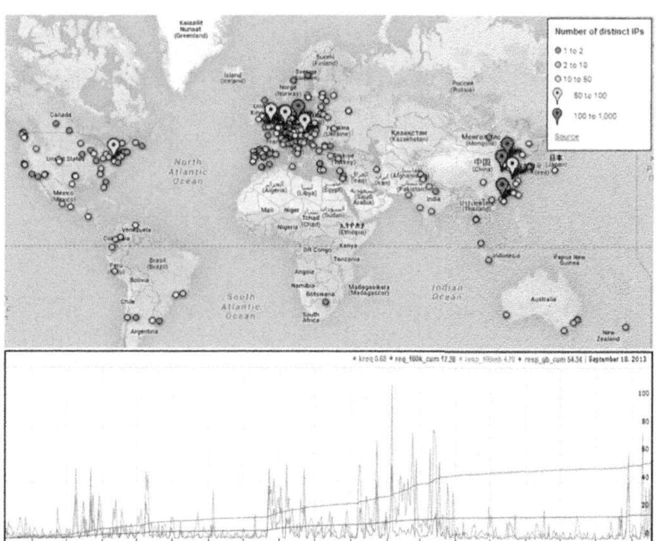

Fig. 2. Spatio-temporal distribution of ROLE Sandbox use from 2012/03–2013/09 (Color figure online)

Dots on the map aggregate amounts of distinct IP addresses resolved to the same geo-coordinates, encoded with different dot symbols and colors. High numbers of IP addresses with same geo-location hint to usage in larger institutions, while low numbers indicate private use by individuals. Thus, we find that the system was used by both individuals and institutions with varying size and varying intensity. Usage mainly concentrates on European countries, but also includes large institutions in both China and the US.

From our data sample we find, that users created 974 spaces in total, where 682 (70 %) can be considered active spaces, i.e. spaces loaded frequently. About 1324 (33.5 %) different users interacted with the ROLE Sandbox in different ways. 178 (4.5 %) users created new spaces, 251 (6.4 %) joined spaces, 320 (8.1 %) added widgets to spaces. 1231 (31.2 %) users loaded spaces designed by others. These statistics confirm the usual observation in social software systems, that only small fractions of users become active in terms of designing learning environments on their own, while most other users only benefit from learning environments previously created by others. According to our SRL process model extension, self-regulated learning includes the design of personal learning environments as well as refinements after repeated self-reflection and evaluation. Thus, we can assume that only a small amount of ROLE Sandbox users are self-regulated learners in that sense.

Furthermore, we analyzed the widgets used in the ROLE Sandbox with regard to SRL. In total, users employed 634 distinct widgets in personal or collaborative learning environments. In order to support self-regulated learning, the ROLE consortium designed and implemented a set of 15 SRL widgets

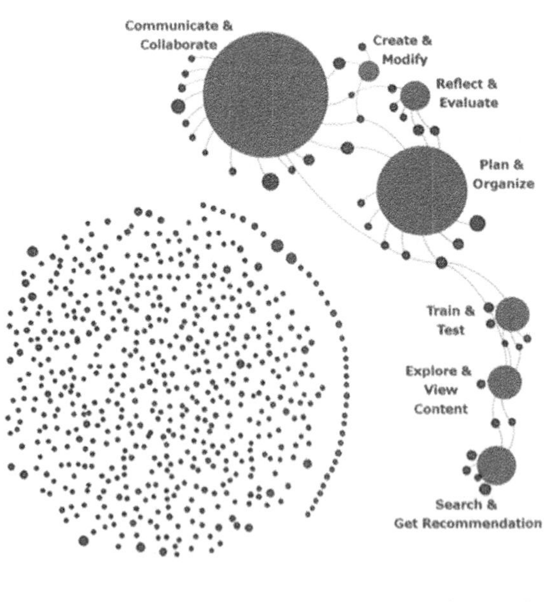

Fig. 3. SRL-related and non-SRL widget categories (Color figure online)

for different purposes such as recommendation, self-assessment, self-monitoring, self-evaluation, and SRL-style work. In our data we found the use of 40 (6.3 %) SRL-related widgets, most of them being further customized deployments of the 15 original SRL widgets. Furthermore, another 40 (6.3 %) widgets were assigned to one or more of the categories *Search & Get Recommendation*, *Plan & Organize*, *Communicate & Collaborate*, *Create & Modify*, *Train & Test*, *Explore & View Content* and *Reflect & Evaluate*, which relate to typical functionality groups assigned to the four phases of our SRL process model. Figure 3 provides an overview of *SRL-related* (red dots) vs. *non-SRL-related* widgets (grey dots) assigned to the categories (blue dots). Widget node size encodes how often the particular widget was added to a space. Category node size encodes the number of widgets assigned to the particular category. Most widgets are not assigned to any category, including the most influential SRL widgets. Most of the assigned widgets are only associated with exactly one category, thus indicating their clear purpose for one of the SRL learning phases. We also find that most of the widgets assigned to categories were used more frequently than those not assigned to any category. This difference is explained by category-based widget recommendations issued to space designers. We conclude that category metadata is helpful for a better overview of the available widget ecosystem and ultimately for improved guidance and tool selection. The majority of unassigned widgets should thus be assigned post-hoc to make them accessible for targeted recommendations.

In order to examine the relation *widget added by user* we constructed a bipartite graph of users and widgets. We thereby distinguished *SRL widgets* vs. *non-SRL widgets* and *SRL widget adders* (i.e. users who added at least one SRL widget to any space) vs. non-SRL widget adders. The resulting graph (not shown due to space restrictions) exhibits 22 connected components with one giant component. Most of the widgets are used by multiple users, and most users added more than one widget. Users in the smaller components mostly represent widget developers working on widget prototypes never used by others. Notably, all SRL widgets and SRL widget adders were part of the giant component. 63 (1.5 %) users added SRL widgets to spaces, 29 (0.7 %) more than one. 123 (3.1 %) users actually used SRL widgets in space contexts, 34 (0.8 %) more than one. In general, we find a correlation between the number of widget add operations and the number of distinct widgets added by a user. This correlation is significantly stronger for SRL-widget adders. At the same time, we find that SRL widget adders are significantly more active in designing own PLE.

We furthermore analyzed our data from the space perspective with the goal to investigate significant differences between SRL spaces, i.e. spaces in which at least one SRL widget was added or loaded, and non-SRL spaces. In total, we found 138 (20.1 %) SRL spaces. In a first step we aggregated widget add frequencies, distinct widget categories, IP addresses and widgets per space. Regarding widget add frequency per space, we clearly observed distribution differences for SRL and non-SRL spaces. Non-SRL spaces span a wider range of widget add frequencies. However, a majority of spaces exhibits very few widget add operations. In contrast, SRL spaces span a closer range, but tend to better distribute widget add frequencies in this range. Regarding the number of distinct categories per space, we again found significant differences. SRL spaces tend to cover more distinct categories to higher extents and less often exhibit widget constellations not assigned to any category. Since categories more or less directly map to the different phases of our SRL model, we can conclude, that SRL spaces tend to cover more learning phases than non-SRL spaces. Again, categories seem to fulfill their role as guidance support.

Regarding the number of distinct IP addresses per space, we find that SRL spaces involve less learner collaboration than non-SRL spaces. The number of SRL spaces with only one learner involved is significantly higher than for non-SRL spaces. The maximum numbers of distinct IP addresses per space also significantly differ with 25 for non-SRL spaces vs. 13 for SRL spaces. Regarding the number of distinct widgets, we find that non-SRL spaces concentrate on lower numbers, while SRL spaces exhibit a larger range with a better distribution. Thus, we can conclude that more exploration of potentially valuable widgets for learning happens in SRL spaces than in non-SRL spaces, again attributable to the SRL recommendation tools we developed.

Finally, we examined widget add operations from the category perspective to receive an overview which categories showed to be most influential in SRL spaces and in spaces in general. Again, we found significant differences, as depicted in Fig. 4. First, a significantly lower percentage of widgets added to spaces belonged to no specific category for SRL spaces (58.8 %) in comparison to non-SRL spaces (64.8 %). Furthermore, we find differences regarding the importance of categories for SRL and non-SRL spaces. While non-SRL spaces put the strongest focus on the category *Collaborate & Communicate*, SRL spaces are stronger in support for SRL-relevant categories such as *Plan & Organize* (13.0 % vs. 8.7 %) and *Reflect & Evaluate* (4.7 % vs. 2.6 %). In other categories, differences between SRL and non-SRL spaces were insignificant.

In total, we found significant differences in terms of PLE management behaviour between SRL-related entities (users and spaces). Category metadata as part of our conceptual SRL process model was helpful for guidance and recommendation. It should be noted that our analysis cannot prove that SRL took place after all. The data merely captures PLE management operations, and not concrete learning activities. However, we consider PLE management operations as integral part of SRL, in particular in planning and exploration phases. We thus see our analysis as relevant evidence that SRL happened in the ROLE Sandbox.

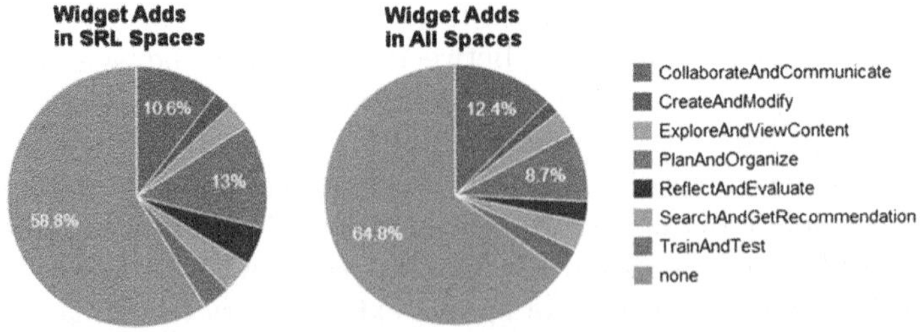

Fig. 4. Categories of widgets added to SRL spaces vs. all spaces

5 Conclusions

From our observations, we conclude five key aspects of self-regulated learning in PLE (cf. [7]): *personalisation*, *guidance & freedom*, *meta-cognition & awareness*, *motivation* and *collaboration & good practice sharing*.

Learners should be empowered to *personalize* and adapt their PLE to own needs and preferred learning techniques, content, tools, services, peers, and communities. The widget space concept provides a context for the creation of own learning environments by adding widgets relevant to respective learning goals. However, personalisation requires an understanding of how to create pedagogically-enabled widget spaces.

The degree of *guidance and freedom* is important regarding optimal learner support. While proficient learners prefer freedom and unobtrusiveness, novice learners need guidance. Therefore, different levels and types of guidance are needed for learners with different SRL skills. Guidance should never be prescriptive, but leave the decision to the learners. Initial guidance helps in assembling or finding widget bundles to build initial PLE. In-learning-process guidance includes support for performing learning activities, using specific widgets, finding content, and developing awareness of their own learning process. In ROLE, such guidance is realized with widgets for personal (i.e. teachers, peers) or algorithmic recommendations, based on usage data and category metadata.

Meta-cognition is a kind of self-monitoring, self-observation and self-regulation related to cognitive and information processing. It is stimulated by engaging learners with the key processes of the self-regulated learning process model. To support meta-cognitive processes, we recommend widgets or widget bundles designed to perform meta-cognitive activities (e.g. reflection or progress visualization) and to give learners feedback about their own learning process, thus stimulating *awareness*. Such feedback requires support for learning analytics.

For stimulation of intrinsic *motivation*, PLE must enable learners to develop autonomy, competence, and relatedness. Motivation is a consequence of the right balance between guidance and freedom, thus being an implicit feature of our framework. However, initial extrinsic motivation facilitated by teachers or peers is advisable in any case.

Collaborative learning comprises extra activities generated by interaction among peers [5]. These collaborative activities trigger additional cognitive mechanisms and appear more frequently in collaborative learning situations than in individual learning [11]. ROLE spaces include a range of ready-to-use collaboration and communication features, including facilities to *share* and *re-use* personal learning environments for arbitrary learner constellations and learning contexts.

ROLE Sandbox will continue to operate and receive improvements in an Open Source manner to even better enable self-regulated learning and analytics thereof in naturalistic informal settings over even longer evaluation periods.

Acknowledgements. This research was supported by the European Commission in the 7th Framework Programme project *Learning Layers*, grant no. 318209.

References

1. Aviram, A., Ronen, Y., Somekh, S., Winer, A., Sarid, A.: Self-regulated personalized learning (SRPL): developing iClass's pedagogical model. eLearning Pap. **9**(9), 1–17 (2008)
2. Cassidy, S.: Self-regulated learning in higher education: identifying key component processes. Stud. High. Educ. **36**(8), 989–1000 (2011)
3. Dabbagh, N., Kitsantas, A.: Supporting self-regulation in student-centered web-based learning environments. Int. J. E-Learn. **3**(1), 40–47 (2004)
4. Dahrendorf, D., Dikke, D., Faltin, N.: Sharing Personal Learning Environments for Widget Based Systems using a Widget Marketplace. In: Pedro, L., Santos, C., Almeida, S. (eds.) The PLE Conference 2012, Proceedings, pp. 17:1–17:7 (2012)
5. Dillenbourg, P.: Introduction: what do you mean by 'collaborative learning'? In: Dillenbourg, P. (ed.) Collaborative-learning: Cognitive and Computational Approaches, pp. 1–15. Elsevier, Oxford (1999)
6. Downes, S.: Learning networks in practice. Emerg. Technol. Learn. **2**, 19–27 (2007)
7. Efklides, A.: The role of meta-cognitive experiences in the learning process. Psicothema **21**(1), 76–82 (2009)
8. Farzan, R., Brusilovsky, P.: Social navigation support in a course recommendation system. In: Wade, V.P., Ashman, H., Smyth, B. (eds.) AH 2006. LNCS, vol. 4018, pp. 91–100. Springer, Heidelberg (2006)
9. Fruhmann, K., Nussbaumer, A., Albert, D.: A psycho-pedagogical framework for self-regulated learning in a responsive open learning environment. In: Hambach, S., Martens, A., Tavangarian, D., Urban, B. (eds.) 3rd International Conference eLearning Baltics Science. Fraunhofer Verlag, Rostock, Germany (2010)
10. Kitsantas, A.: Test preparation and performance: a self-regulatory analysis. J. Exp. Educ. **70**(2), 101–113 (2002)
11. McConnell, D.: Implementing Computer Supported Cooperative Learning, 2nd edn. Kogan Page Limited, London (2000)
12. Nussbaumer, A., Berthold, M., Dahrendorf, D., Schmitz, H.-C., Kravcik, M., Albert, D.: A mashup recommender for creating personal learning environments. In: Popescu, E., Li, Q., Klamma, R., Leung, H., Specht, M. (eds.) ICWL 2012. LNCS, vol. 7558, pp. 79–88. Springer, Heidelberg (2012)
13. Olivier, B., Liber, O.: Lifelong learning: the need for portable personal learning environments and supporting interoperability standards. Technical report, The JISC Centre for Educational Technology Interoperability Standards, Bolton (2001)
14. Renzel, D., Klamma, R.: From micro to macro: analyzing activity in the ROLE sandbox. In: Suthers, D., Verbert, K., Duval, E., Ochoa, X. (eds.) The Third ACM International Conference on Learning Analytics, pp. 250–254. ACM (2013)
15. Sabourin, J., Mott, B., Lester, J.: Utilizing dynamic bayes nets to improve early prediction models of self-regulated learning. In: Carberry, S., Weibelzahl, S., Micarelli, A., Semeraro, G. (eds.) UMAP 2013. LNCS, vol. 7899, pp. 228–241. Springer, Heidelberg (2013)
16. van Harmelen, M.: Personal learning environments. In: Kinshuk, R., Koper, P., Kommers, P., Kirschner, P.A., Sampson, D.G., Didderen, W. (eds.) 6th IEEE International Conference on Advanced Learning Technologies, pp. 815–816. IEEE (2006)
17. Zimmerman, B.J.: Becoming a self-regulated learner: an overview. Theor. Into Pract. **41**(2), 64–70 (2002)

ZhihuRank: A Topic-Sensitive Expert Finding Algorithm in Community Question Answering Websites

Xuebo Liu, Shuang Ye, Xin Li, Yonghao Luo, and Yanghui Rao(✉)

School of Mobile Information Engineering, Sun Yat-sen University, Zhuhai, China
raoyangh@mail.sysu.edu.cn

Abstract. Expert finding is important to the development of community question answering websites and e-learning. In this study, we propose a topic-sensitive probabilistic model to estimate the user authority ranking for each question, which is based on the link analysis technique and topical similarities between users and questions. Most of the existing approaches focus on the user relationship only. Compared to the existing approaches, our method is more effective because we consider the link structure and the topical similarity simultaneously. We use the real-world data set from *Zhihu* (a famous CQA website in China) to conduct experiments. Experimental results show that our algorithm outperforms other algorithms in the user authority ranking.

Keywords: Community question answering · Expert finding · PageRank · Latent topic modeling

1 Introduction

Community Question Answering (CQA) websites are extremely popular in recent years. In CQA websites, users can raise their own questions, answer the questions posted by others and read the corresponding answers to a question. It is interesting that the CQA websites have strong social characteristics, which are different from the traditional ones, such as *Baidu Knows* (https://www.zhidao.baidu.com). Take *Zhihu* (https://www.zhihu.com) as an example, the content read by a user u in his/her home page depend on the people u has followed (i.e., "friends" of u). Therefore, a user is able to see the questions raised by all his/her friends, their answers and their "liked" answers. By allowing the interaction between users, the number of registered users in CQA websites has grown tremendously.

Although the CQA website has attracted many users, it brings several challenges to provide high quality services: (1) **Poor expertise matching:** Many

The research work described in this article has been substantially supported by "the Fundamental Research Funds for the Central Universities" (Project Number: 46000-31610009).

F.W.B. Li et al. (Eds.): ICWL 2015, LNCS 9412, pp. 165–173, 2015.
DOI: 10.1007/978-3-319-25515-6_15

questions are difficult to be recommended to the expert with the best-matching interest and ability to answer them, which results in suboptimal answers and delay of satisfaction [1]. (2) **No answer:** Since it is hard for users to find questions that they are really interested in, there are many questions with no answer. (3) **Similar questions:** If a user can not find a satisfying answer for one question, he/she may post a new similar question. Thus, it is necessary to use expert finding algorithms in CQA websites to solve these problems.

Traditional algorithms of expert finding are based on the relationship between users primarily [2,3], which are insufficient to get a unique user authority ranking for each question. For example, the appropriate users to answer different questions may differ. If we rank the user authority based on the relationship between users only, the user who is a movie star will have many followers and achieve a high ranking. However, he/she may not be appropriate to answer the questions about computers. We here propose a new algorithm based on the link analysis technique and topical similarities between users and questions, which can get a unique user authority ranking for each question. In our algorithm, we consider all answers posted by a user as a document, the description and all answers to a question are also treated as a document, then we apply latent Dirichlet allocation (LDA) [4] to extract topics from both users and questions. After generating these topics, we can measure the topical similarity between questions and answers, and rank users by the relationship between users and the topical similarity between users and questions.

The rest of the paper is organized as follows. Section 2 introduces the relative works on user ranking in social networks. In Sect. 3, the *ZhihuRank* algorithm is described in detail. Section 4 illustrates the dataset used and the experimental results. We conclude our paper and make a future plan in Sect. 5.

2 Related Work

The existing algorithms computed the user authority in CQA websites by the relationship between users primarily. *Bouguessa et al.* [5] proposed a method to dig out the expert user, which is based on the best answer the user posted. *Jurczyk and Agichtein* [6] applied HITS algorithm [3] to their works and compute the user ranking by the followed-following relationship. *Zhang et al.* [7] proposed an algorithm based on the users' specialty. Although the algorithms that analyze the relationship between users have achieved the desired results, there are some challenging problems that are difficult to be solved by these algorithms, e.g., the expert discovered could not give the satisfying answer to the field he/she is not skilled in. Thus, some other algorithms based on topics were proposed. *Guo et al.* [8] proposed an algorithm to explore the similarity between users and the askers by the tags of users. *Liu et al.* [9] used language model and LDA to detect the best answerer.

Recently, there are algorithms that composed the relationship between users and the similarity of topics. *TwitterRank* [10] is a typical algorithm which is able to figure out the influence of Twitter users based on the followed-following relationship and topic similarities. *Zhou et al.* [11] proposed a TSPR algorithm for expert recommendation in CQA websites. In the TSPR algorithm [12], the topics of users were first extracted by LDA, and then experts were recommended by the number of answers a user posted and the similarity between the user and the asker. *Zhao et al.* [13] designed a method to generate experts and topics simultaneously by incorporating the users' contribution dynamically. *Chen et al.* [14] established the user reputation rating system based on user comments. *Pal et al.* [15] proposed an algorithm based on Gaussian mixture models to identify topical authorities in microblogs. *Liu et al.* [16] proposed a new topic model for expert recommendation in CQA websites.

Different from these algorithms, our method considers both the link structure of users and the topical similarity between users and questions, which achieved a competitive performance. To the best of our knowledge, it is the first time that the topical similarity between users and questions for expert recommendation problems in CQA websites has been considered.

3 ZhihuRank Algorithm

ZhihuRank algorithm is able to figure out the user authority ranking in each question, which is based on the relationship between users and the topical similarities between users and questions. Conventionally, the more "likes" a user receives, the higher authority he/she will achieve, which is similar to the ranking approach of websites. It is important to note that the weight of each "likes" given to an answer is different from the others. Assume that both *User B* with higher authority and *User C* with lower authority give "likes" to *User A*, the "likes" from *User B* is often more powerful to improve the authority of *User A* than *User C*. Therefore, we compute of influence of users based on the iteration method of PageRank [2]. In addition, since each question may entail different topics and the topics those users are familiar with may be many, we take also the similarity between users and topics into consideration.

3.1 Topic Extraction from Users

We apply LDA [4] to perform the topic extraction from users. LDA is an unsupervised topic extraction model, which is based on the bag of word assumption. It treats each text as a vector whose characteristic of each dimension is the number of a word that appears in the text. Each text can be expressed as the probability distribution of a series of topics and each topic can be expressed as the probability distribution of a series of words. LDA is a nature model for topic extraction from long text, which has been applied to various areas including social emotion mining [17,18], emotional dictionary construction [19], and emerging event detection [20]. In LDA, the probability distribution of topics for each text and words for each topic can be estimated by Gibbs sampling [21]. The detailed process of user topic extraction in *ZhihuRank* is as follows:

Firstly, we consider all answers of a user posted as a text and the one-to-one mapping between a user and its text is established. Meanwhile, all answers to a question are treated as another text. There is also a one-to-one mapping between a question and its text. Secondly, we use LDA to train the text of all users and question, in which, the probability distribution of the topics corresponding to each text θ and probability distribution of the words corresponding to each topic φ can be estimated. Thirdly, we keep θ unchanged and carry out the Gibbs sampling only with the input of user text. Finally, we get a new φ_{uz} as follows.

Definition 1 φ_{UZ}*: The user-topic matrix, where* U *is the number of users,* Z *is the number of topics.* φ_{iz} *represents the number of words that assigned to topic* z *appearing in all answers posted by User* i.

3.2 User Authority Transition Matrix

In the past researches on social networks, the relationship of following and being followed between users is often used to generate the user authority transition matrix by iterative computation [22]. Different from the traditional social networks, the approval mechanism is introduced into the CQA websites. Conventionally, the more "likes" a user receives, the higher authority he/she will achieve. Meanwhile, the weights of a "likes" given by different users are varied, i.e., the approval by the expert in a certain field is more powerful to improve the authority of the user whom he/she give "likes" to in this field. In addition, the "likes" given by a user who seldom make approval is of higher value in comparison to those who often delivers "likes". Therefore, we consider the users' authority ranking in each topic as a *Markov Chain* [22], and the transition matrix of topic z is defined as follows:

Definition 2

$$T_z(i,j) = \frac{V_{j\to i}}{\sum_{for\ every\ user\ k} V_{j\to k}} \times sim_z(i,j), \tag{1}$$

where T_z *represents the user authority transition matrix of topic* z. $T_z(i,j)$ *represents the influence of User* i *to User* j *in topic* z. $V_{j\to i}$ *represents the number of "likes" that User* j *gives to User* i*, and the denominator is the summation of the number of "likes" that User* j *gives to all users.* $sim_z(i,j)$ *represents the similarity between User* i *and* j *in topic* z.

Definition 3

$$sim_z(i,j) = 1 - 0.5 \times ((\varphi'_{iz} - \varphi'_{jz}) \times ln\left(\frac{\varphi'_{iz}}{\varphi'_{jz}}\right)), \tag{2}$$

where φ' *is the row-normalized form of matrix* φ*, i.e., the* L_1*-norm of each row is 1.* φ'_{iz} *reflects the degree of interest of User* i *in topic* z*. If the degrees of interest of User* i *and* j *in topic* z *are close , both* $ln\left(\frac{\varphi'_{iz}}{\varphi'_{jz}}\right)$ *and* $\varphi'_{iz} - \varphi'_{jz}$ *tend* *to approximate 0 while sim tends to approximate 1,otherwise sim will be small. If there is a huge gap between the degrees of interest of User i and j in topic z, the value of ln* $\left(\frac{\varphi'_{iz}}{\varphi'_{jz}}\right)$ *will be positive infinity. The larger the value of sim is, the more similar User i and j in topic z will be.*

3.3 User Authority Ranking for Each Topic

In Sect. 3.2, we get the user authority transition matrix iteratively. Next, *ZhihuRank* takes the approval relationship between users and the topical similarity into account to compute the authority ranking of users in topic z:

Definition 4

$$UR_z = \lambda T_z \times UR_z + (1-\lambda)\varphi''_z, \tag{3}$$

where UR_z *represents the user authority ranking of topic* z. λ *is a weighting parameter between 0 and 1. A lager value of* λ *indicates that the approval relationship between users has a greater influence on the authority ranking. While a smaller value of* λ *indicates that the degree of interest of the user to topic* z *has a greater influence on the authority ranking.* T_z *is the transition matrix described in Sect. 3.2.* φ''_z *is the column-normalized form of matrix* φ*, i.e., the* L_1*-norm of each column is 1. It represents the degree of interest of each user to topic* z*.*

After convergence, we get the final result of the user authority ranking for each topic.

3.4 Topic Extraction from Questions

We consider all answers to a question as a document. Then we apply LDA trained in Sect. 3.1, i.e., keep θ unchanged and carry out the Gibbs sampling with the input of question document again. Finally, we get ψ_{QZ} as follows.

Definition 5 ψ_{QZ}: *The question-topic matrix, where* Q *is the number of questions,* Z *is the number of topics.* ψ_{qz} *represents the number of words that assigned to topic* z *in all the answers of question* q*.*

3.5 User Authority Ranking for Each Question

Since we get matrix ψ (the topic distribution of every question) and UR (the user authority ranking of every topic), multiply the two matrices (i.e., *Bayes*'s rule) then we get the user authority ranking of each question.

Definition 6

$$QR = \psi \times UR, \tag{4}$$

where ψ *represents the topic distribution of each question.* UR *represents the user authority ranking of each topic. The multiplication result is the user authority ranking of every question.*

4 Experimental Analysis

The previous section introduced the details of our algorithm. In this section, the dataset we used and the experimental results are to be shown.

4.1 Dataset

We use the real-world data from *Zhihu* for experiments. *Zhihu* is one of the most popular question answering communities in China, where all users who "like" an answer are available. Thus, we can get the user authority transition matrix based on users' "like" relationship.

We crawled 576 questions, 9043 users and 209309 answers from *Zhihu*, and employed *Jieba Chinese Text Segmentation* (https://www.github.com/fxsjy/jieba) to perform the Chinese word segmentation. The detail process of preparing the above dataset is as follows:

- For each question, its description, contents of all its answers and the real ranking of all answers were crawled.
- For each user, the number of friends, followers, answers, "likes" received and the contents of all answers he/she posted were crawled.

4.2 Parameters

When applying LDA in topic extraction, the hyper parameters α and β are set to be 0.1 and 0.01, respectively. We selected 50 topics, performed 1000 times of iterations and finally got these topics.

When computing the user authority ranking of each topic, λ is set to be 0.85 based on cross-validation.

4.3 Evaluation Metrics

To measure the accuracy of different algorithms, two evaluation metrics commonly used in information retrieval were chosen:

- *Mean Reciprocal Rank (MRR):* This metric is the multiplicative inverse of the rank of the first retrieved expert for each topic.
- *nDCG:*

$$nDCG@K = \frac{1}{Q}\sum_{q\in Q}\frac{\sum_{j=1}^{K}\frac{1}{log_2(j+1)}score(M_{q,j})}{IdealScore(K,q)}. \quad (5)$$

In the above, Q is the set of questions. $M_{q,j}$ is the j-th expert generated by method M for question q. $score(M_{q,j}) = 2^{v(M_{q,j})} - 1$. $v(M_{q,j})$ is the ground truth score for the expert $M_{q,j}$. $IdealScore(K,q)$ is the ideal ranking score of the top K experts for question q.

4.4 Comparison with Baselines

In this part, we will introduce the baselines and the criterion to measure the experimental results. The baselines used are:

- **In-degree by Number of Followers:** This algorithm measures the authority of users according to the number of followers. The more followers a user has, the higher value of the user authority will be.
- **In-degree by Number of "Likes":** The algorithm measures the authority of users according to the number of "likes" received. The more "likes" a user owns, the higher value of the user authority will be.
- **Topic-sensitive PageRank** [11]**:** The algorithm generates the user ranking of each question according to the following aspects: (1) the user topical similarity between the asker and other users; (2) the number of times that users answered the questions raised by the asker.

For convenience of description, the algorithms are denotes as: *ZhihuRank* (ZR), *In-degree by number of followers* (IDF), *In-degree by number of "likes"* (IDV), and *Topic-sensitive PageRank* (TSPR). The following table shows our experimental results:

Table 1. Performance of expert finding for different methods.

Algorithm	MRR	nDCG
IDF	0.75676	0.85459
IDV	0.74568	0.84730
TSPR	0.63710	0.77037
ZR	**0.84114**	**0.87893**

From Table 1, we can observe that the proposed ZR outperformed other methods for both metrics. The results indicate that it is effective to consider the topical similarity between questions and users when computing the user authority ranking.

5 Conclusion

In the proliferating Web 2.0 communities, the behavior of users is highly influenced by the behavior of their neighbors or community members [23]. This paper proposed an effective algorithm to estimate the user authority ranking in CQA websites, which is based on the relationship between users and the topical similarity between users and questions. We evaluated the algorithm by the dataset from *Zhihu* and experimental results demonstrated the effectiveness of our algorithm when compared to other existing methods. The proposed user authority ranking algorithm has potential applications in Web-based learning [24] and learner profile generation [25].

In the future, we plan to test the algorithm by more data sets, and design a new topic model to cover the shortcomings of LDA in short text topic extraction when there are few answers to a question.

Acknowledgements. The authors are thankful to the anonymous reviewers for their constructive comments and suggestions on an earlier version of this paper. The research described in this paper has been supported by the National Natural Science Foundation of China (Grant No. 61502545), and "the Fundamental Research Funds for the Central Universities" (Grant No. 46000-31121401).

References

1. Agichtein, E., Castillo, C., Donato, D., Gionis, A., Mishne, G.: Finding high-quality content in social media. In: Proceedings of the International Conference on Web Search and Web Data Mining (WSDM), pp. 183–194 (2008)
2. Brin, S., Page, L.: The anatomy of a large-scale hypertextual web search engine. Comput. Netw. ISDN Syst. **30**(1–7), 107–117 (1998)
3. Kleinberg, J.M.: Authoritative sources in a hyperlinked environment. J. ACM **46**(5), 604–632 (1999)
4. Blei, D.M., Ng, A.Y., Jordan, M.I.: Latent dirichlet allocation. J. Mach. Learn. Res. **3**, 993–1022 (2003)
5. Bouguessa, M., Dumoulin, B., Wang, S.: Identifying authoritative actors in question- answering forums: the case of Yahoo! answers. In: Proceedings of the 14th ACM SIGKDD International Conference on Knowledge Discovery and Data Mining (SIGKDD), pp. 866–874 (2008)
6. Jurczyk, P., Agichtein, E.: Discovering authorities in question answer communities by using link analysis. In: Proceedings of the 16th ACM Conference on Information and Knowledge Management (CIKM), pp. 919–922 (2007)
7. Zhang, J., Ackerman, M.S., Adamic, L.: Expertise networks in online communities: structure and algorithms. In: Proceedings of the 16th International Conference on World Wide Web (WWW), pp. 221–230 (2007)
8. Guo, J., Xu, S., Bao, S., Yu, Y.: Tapping on the potential of q & a community by recommending answer providers. In: Proceedings of the 17th ACM Conference on Information and Knowledge Management (CIKM), pp. 921–930 (2008)
9. Liu, X., Croft, W.B., Koll, M.: Finding experts in community-based question answering services. In: Proceedings of the 2005 ACM CIKM International Conference on Information and Knowledge Management (CIKM), pp. 315–316 (2005)
10. Weng, J., Lim, E.-P., Jiang, J., He, Q.: Twitterrank: finding topic-sensitive influential twitterers. In: Proceedings of the 3rd International Conference on Web Search and Web Data Mining (WSDM), pp. 261–270 (2010)
11. Zhou, G., Lai, S., Liu, K., Zhao, J.: Topic-sensitive probabilistic model for expert finding in question answer communities. In: Proceedings of the 21st ACM International Conference on Information and Knowledge Management (CIKM), pp. 1662–1666 (2012)
12. Haveliwala, T.H.: Topic-sensitive PageRank. In: Proceedings of the 11th International World Wide Web Conference (WWW), pp. 517–526 (2002)

13. Zhao, T., Bian, N., Li, C., Li, M.: Topic-level expert modeling in community question answering. In: Proceedings of the 13th SIAM International Conference on Data Mining (SDM), pp. 776–784 (2013)
14. Chen, B.-C., Guo, J., Tseng, B., Yang, J.: User reputation in a comment rating environment. In: Proceedings of the 17th ACM SIGKDD International Conference on Knowledge Discovery and Data Mining (SIGKDD), pp. 159–167 (2011)
15. Pal, A., Counts, S.: Identifying topical authorities in microblogs. In: Proceedings of the Forth International Conference on Web Search and Web Data Mining (WSDM), pp. 45–54 (2011)
16. Liu, Y., Qiu, M., Gottipati, S., Zhu, F., Jiang, J., Sun, H., Chen, Z.: CQARank: jointly model topics and expertise in community question answering. In: Proceedings of the 22nd ACM International Conference on Information and Knowledge Management (CIKM), pp. 99–108 (2013)
17. Rao, Y.H., Li, Q., Wenyin, L., Wu, Q.Y., Quan, X.J.: Affective topic model for social emotion detection. Neural Netw. **58**, 29–37 (2014)
18. Rao, Y.H., Li, Q., Mao, X.D., Wenyin, L.: Sentiment topic models for social emotion mining. Inf. Sci. **266**, 90–100 (2014)
19. Rao, Y.H., Lei, J.S., Wenyin, L., Li, Q., Chen, M.L.: Building emotional dictionary for sentiment analysis of online news. World Wide Web J. **17**, 723–742 (2014)
20. Rao, Y.H., Li, Q.: Term weighting schemes for emerging event detection. In: IEEE/WIC/ACM International Conference on Web Intelligence and Intelligent Agent Technology (WI-IAT), pp. 105–112 (2012)
21. Geman, S., Geman, D.: Stochastic relaxation, gibbs distributions, and the bayesian restoration of images. IEEE Trans. Pattern Anal. Mach. Intell. **6**(6), 721–741 (1984)
22. Norris, J.R.: Markov Chains. Cambridge University Press, Cambridge (1998)
23. Xie, H.R., Li, Q., Mao, X.D., Li, X.D., Cai, Y., Rao, Y.H.: Community-aware user profile enrichment in folksonomy. Neural Netw. **58**, 111–121 (2014)
24. Li, Q., Lau, R.W.H., Wah, B., Ashman, H., Leung, E., Li, F., Lee, V.: Guest editors' introduction: emerging internet technologies for e-learning. IEEE Internet Comput. **13**(4), 11–17 (2009)
25. Zou, D., Xie, H., Li, Q., Wang, F.L., Chen, W.: The load-based learner profile for incidental word learning task generation. In: Popescu, E., Lau, R.W.H., Pata, K., Leung, H., Laanpere, M. (eds.) ICWL 2014. LNCS, vol. 8613, pp. 190–200. Springer, Heidelberg (2014)

Micro Learning Adaptation in MOOC: A Software as a Service and a Personalized Learner Model

Geng Sun[1(✉)], Tingru Cui[1], William Guo[2], Ghassan Beydoun[1], Dongming Xu[3], and Jun Shen[1]

[1] School of Computing and Information Technology, University of Wollongong, Wollongong, Australia
gs147@uowmail.edu.au
[2] School of Engineering and Technology, Central Queensland University, Rockhampton, Australia
[3] UQ Business School, The University of Queensland, Brisbane, Australia

Abstract. Micro learning is gradually becoming a common learning mode in massive open online course learning (MOOC). We illustrate a research strategy to formalize and customize micro learning resources in order to meet personal demands at the real time. This smart micro learning environment can be organized by a Software as a Service (SaaS) we newly designed, in which educational data mining technique is mainly employed to understand learners learning behaviors and recognize learning resource features in order to identify potential micro learning solutions. A learner model with regards to internal and external factors is also proposed for personalization in micro MOOC learning context.

Keywords: MOOC · Mobile learning · Micro learning · Learner model

1 Introduction

Nowadays the quantity of available learning resources is exponentially rocketing. One of the most noticeable trends in that enrichment is, along with many leading universities opening up access to their courses, the massive open online course (MOOC) gains its popularity in the whole higher education sector. It is an online course delivery framework targeting large-scale interactive participation and open access via the Web, which is an important supplement to the traditional distance education [1]. The explosive growth of learning resources leads to a revolution of education and learning [2]. Educational professionals have strived to explore the MOOC format as a regular pedagogical approach for m-learning, however, established studies show that learners using MOOC are currently suffering from low completion rate [3]. Most learners who enrolled in MOOC courses ended up dropping out. As research and development of MOOC are still in infancy, there are evidently many opportunities to improve MOOC courses as well as their affiliations, such as learning platforms and learning support services, to enable easier access and better experience for both providers and learners.

In this paper we introduce a research strategy which targets on supporting smart micro learning in MOOC. We attempt to use a Software as a Service (SaaS) which aims

F.W.B. Li et al. (Eds.): ICWL 2015, LNCS 9412, pp. 174–184, 2015.
DOI: 10.1007/978-3-319-25515-6_16

to give learners opportunities to make the best use of every fragmented piece of time so as to effectively engage in the MOOC learning. We particularly concentrate on delivering learners adaptive learning resources in small chunks that can be learnt in relatively short duration, and modelling the learner and learning context in an extensible manner with respect to the micro learning environment.

2 Micro Learning in MOOC

2.1 The Popularity of Micro Learning in Taking MOOC Courses

MOOC providers try to promote their courses and affiliated educational products by making them available everywhere around the world. They leverage m-learning to enable learners to easily participate in learning activities regardless the restriction of time and location. However, these courses often start with a large number of learners, but many quit halfway. Arguably, this is mainly because learners fail to conduct effective time management, so that they are suffering from time consuming and conflicts with their real life responsibilities [3]. Another crucial factor is that learners deem it is not easy to find appropriate resources they want, or the chosen resources do not always meet their expectation [4]. The third reason is that the types of learners engaged in MOOC courses are more comprehensively diversified. Some MOOC learners do not have a concrete aim to complete an entire course as to get the credits, because they just want to acquire the specific knowledge they actually need. Such knowledge are often enclosed in small course units or passed on during phases going by midway of the course delivery. Therefore, once they are satisfied with the progress they have made, they are possible to quit while leaving assignments or tests unfinished [4].

From a research [5] which analyses the time lasting for young learners' attention in m-learning, the results show that when proceeding m-learning they frequently pause their learning activities and transfer their attention to another thing, so that their attention spans are often limited in 15 min. In addition, by analyzing 6.9 million records of video playing, edX found that the videos with a time length less than 6 min are more attractive, while students' engagements drop sharply after 6 min [6].

These can explain why m-learning in MOOC appears distinct from its traditional forms and modes in on-campus and distance education [9]. It is found that learning activities are off and on frequently during the progress of MOOC course and many learning activities are completed within fragmented pieces of time. In other words, their learning processes become fragmented or of micro size. Hence, it is not surprising that MOOC follows the principles of micro learning to a certain extent and even MOOC is typically designed around the principles of micro learning enabling learners to go through bytes of learning in short duration [6]. For instance, some course materials have been chunked and the units ideally do not exceed 15 min [7].

2.2 Definition of Micro Learning

In literature, "micro learning" processes cover a time span from few seconds (e.g. in mobile learning) to up to 15 min or more. Another definition of micro learning is Web focused: ‘micro learning refers to short-term learning activities on small learning units. In the contemporary mobile/web society, micro learning pertains to small pieces of knowledge based on web resources’ [7]. With mobile devices, quite often learners accomplish learning missions in a short time period. According to the study [8], micro learning can be an assumption about the time needed to complete a relevant learning task. Hence, micro learning booms with the wide use of mobile devices, and it becomes a major learning means in mobile environment. Micro learning shares some similar specialties with mobile learning as they are both individually referable, self-contained, reusable and re-mixable [9].

Micro learning resources can be made available on-demand to facilitate just-in-time learning [10]. These small learning bytes not only aid quick assimilation but also make it possible to learn on the go, thus reducing the dependency on a fixed time slot or the need to take a large chunk of time out of one’s working day [7]. As micro learning evolves, micro-content delivery with a sequence of micro interactions enables users to learn without information overload [10]. It is a key technology to ensure better learning results in terms of retention of propositional content [8].

2.3 Research Challenges

Fragmented learning with mobile devices requires learners’ concentration and reflection. However, being on the go, it is fraught with distractions. Students often find themselves in situations with unpredictable but significant distractions. This leaves the mobile learners with a highly fragmented learning experience.

The operation of MOOC generates a huge amount of data about the learners, courses, educational institutions, networking, and technical details and so on. It could be very difficult for learners to quickly choose the preferred and suitable course chunks in a timely manner. Since the acquirable learning resources become massive, how to set and select the right and appropriate objectives, which stand out from the numerous available resources, brings a challenge for both MOOC providers and customers.

Moreover, there are studies indicating that personality and learning styles play significant roles in influencing academic achievement [11]. As learners commonly do not have sufficient expertise in customizing learning schedules for themselves, and perhaps they are not familiar with their own learning styles, there are high probabilities that they cannot access the right sets of micro content. This may affect them to achieve satisfactory learning outcomes though a lot of time might be spent. In the current situation, learning resources are generally divided and wrapped up by education providers or course lecturers. It considerably lacks flexibilities to fit every specific learner’s time availability so that learner should get accommodated to the time length of course setting and manage to squeeze time to accomplish those learning activities.

3 Micro Learning as a Service-System Framework

In this paper, we attempt to employ design science method to overcome the above challenges so as to deliver learner customized learning resources, in the form of small chunks or fine-grained units. Optimally learners can easily complete the learning process of each unit within fragmented pieces of time. An ideal course module delivered to a learner should be limited in the time length (e.g. 15 min) to ensure a micro but complete learning experience. The framework of the proposed SaaS, Micro Learning as a Service (MLaaS), is shown in Fig. 1.

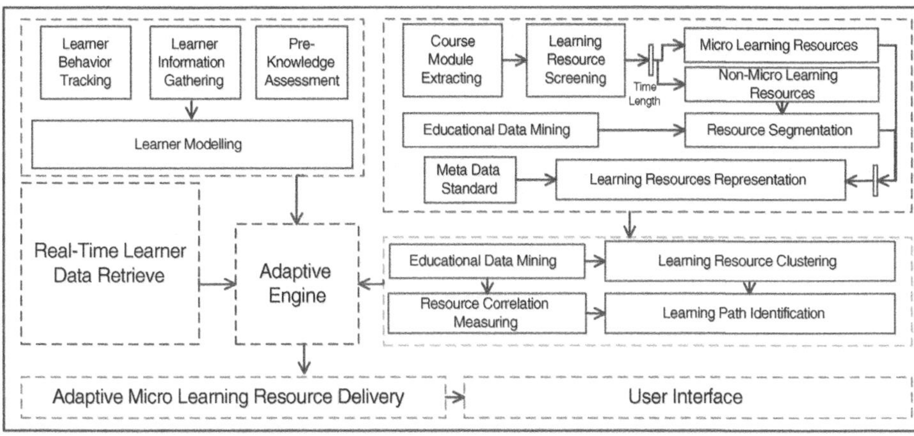

Fig. 1. Framework of adaptive micro learning system for MOOC

The Learner Modelling Service aims to build a specific model for each learner, on the basis of his/her historical information and ongoing learning behavior. Learners' basic information about learning styles, preference and learning purposes is gathered. Based on these data collections, this service assesses the pre-knowledge level for each learner and marks up these features by a set of measurable variables. It is also provided with a function, which tracks learners' behaviors during micro learning process and ensures their models being kept up-to-date once new data are detected or generated.

The Learning Resource Representation Service stores all representations of the available micro learning resources. It extracts course modules from well-developed MOOC courses. Based on their time lengths, they are categorized into micro learning resources (less than 15 min) and non-micro learning resources. Referring to the results of EDM, these longer course modules are cut off programmatically and encapsulated into small units with reasonable time lengths. As this module holds a metadata repository, a metadata standard for describing micro course units is going to be established semantically [12]. According to this standard, all learning resources are represented in terms of discipline, key words, time length, language of instruction, popularity, difficulty and so on [12]. Data related to good-quality and mostly-followed/discussed learner-generated content, can be refilled in to Learning Resource Repository in order to support peer-to-peer learning in MOOC.

For MLaaS, the Real-Time Learner Data Retrieve Service retrieves learners' real-time data, including their learning progress and time availabilities (how many minutes they prefer to use in the moment). Furthermore, in the Learning Resource Repository Service, selected course modules are clustered using text/data mining technologies. This service also measures correlations among chunks, or, if feasible, derives correlations from existing MOOC course modules. It helps to set learning start point and exit point and it also distinguishes the suggested sequences of learning resources and identifies a learning path among them.

Taking inputs from all the above services, the Adaptive Engine acts by providing learners with customized learning resources, which are matching their current micro learning context, personal demands, learning styles and preferences. It is the core of the proposed system, which embeds machine learning technologies to realize the adaptive mechanism [13].

4 Learner Modelling for Micro Learning

Much data generated along with the proceeding of MOOC courses represents learners' behaviors in a form which is longitudinal and fine-grained. Reporting them visually and statistically in order to reveal each learner's learning story is even more crucial. This plays a significant role in conducting study ratiocination, judging learners' study status, estimating learners' study effects and carrying out learning strategy decision making. Finally, a personalized learner model for micro MOOC learning can be established by using these screened and sorted data [14], according to their historical and real-time data. This is the aim of the Learner Modelling Service. As shown in Fig. 2, the learner model consists of two domains of factors (i.e. internal and external), while the internal factors can be classified into personal intelligent and non-intelligent factors. Some components can fall in the intersection of two domains which means these components are multi-correlated to two factors. Also, a component can be overlapped with others which suggest that they are associated and mutually affected.

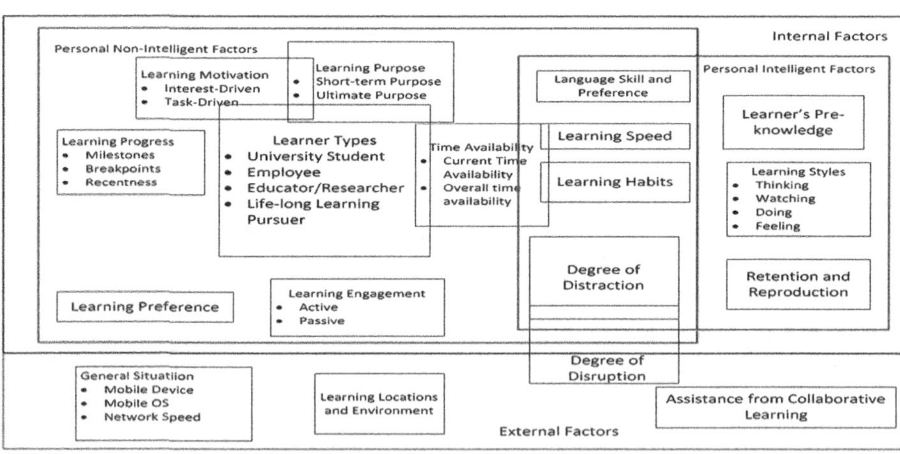

Fig. 2. Personalized learner model for micro MOOC learning

To understand the specific learning pattern of each learner from huge amount of data tracked from daily MOOC usages, EDM is the key technique we employ to explore the common shape and trend of micro learning and set the basis for subsequent adaptation mechanisms. The data collection for building learner model can be realized in two ways: mandatory request and automated extraction. The detailed learner features and learning context we intend to explore through EDM are listed as follows.

4.1 Personal Non-intelligent Factors

Learner Types. The types of MOOC learners vary evidently in accordance with their particular learning purposes and work, learning and life patterns. Their background information cannot always be searched from their registration and logon data [15]. Commonly, they can be university students, educators, researchers, employees or life-long learning pursuers.

Time Availability. EDM performs to clustering similar learners into a cohort. Their disposable time varies to a great extent, which is highly indicative for whether and how often these learners would adopt micro learning modes.
Their current time availability is a mandatory request for them to input before they start each micro learning activity.

Learning Engagement. Mainly it is measured in terms of a learner's total online time length, frequency of logon, submission of required assignments, participation in forums, completion of courses or course chunks, etc.

Learners' engagement can also be categorized into active or passive learning. The former refers to that learners are self-motivated to attend virtual classes in MOOC platform so that they look for and initiatively access MOOC learning resources, which they need when they want; while the latter refers to that learners act as recipients of knowledge through information pushed by MOOC platforms or MOOC affiliated social medias, for example, they might have subscribed electronic reading materials.

Progress Identification. This is basically identified by breakpoints and milestones made by learners. In micro MOOC learning, learning activities become disperse, and the content in two continuous learning phases can be not rigidly restricted in accordance with the sequences in the course curriculum. For this reason, EDM has another significant duty to retrieve back to learners' latest learning content and activities in order to profile a learners learning recentness. Recentness is not confined into particular time points. The recentness of learning categories can be extracted automatically.

Learning Motivation and Purpose. Basically in MOOC learning learners are either interest-driven or task-driven. Their learning purposes are identified by mandatory request data which means learner are suggested to input their learning purpose prior to the commencement of their MOOC learning.

Learning Preference. Learning preference refers to learners' subjective and affective opinion about learning content. It can be sorted out through learners' comments and tags made on resources they have accessed.

4.2 Personal Intelligent Factors

Learner Pre-knowledge Assessment. To build a profile for each learner and customize micro learning strategy for learners with different backgrounds and basis, a measure that is necessary to take in prior is to assess each learner's knowledge in terms of several standards. In micro MOOC learning, it is suggested to investigate and identify their pre-knowledge level in terms of the extent of their education, their historical courses grades in MOOC, and results of pre-course quizzes which are easy to be quantized.

Learning Styles. Individuals differ in how they learn. Learning styles refer to the systematic differences in individuals' natural or habitual pattern of acquiring and processing information in learning situations. According to [16], learning styles can be represented as concrete experience (feeling), reflective observation (watching), abstract conceptualization (thinking) and active experimentation (doing). However, because operations on mobile devices are relatively simple, which are limited in input and output methods, these four learning styles are difficult to be reflected straightway through monitoring learners' operation. Thus, identifying learners learning style requires extra efforts, such as self-evaluation. In addition, if learning activities in other MOOC courses are specified in terms of relevant learning styles, learners' performance in an exact learning activity can indicate their value on the corresponding learning styles.

Memory Ability. Memory ability can impact learning outcomes after the retention and reproduction stage of learning [17]. For MOOC courses in the disciplines of culture, literature, arts, language and history, etc., memory ability is one of the key measures that help learners to transfer the content of online MOOC resources into their own knowledge.

4.3 Intersection of Non-intelligent and Intelligent Factors

Learning Habits. Each individual has a completely isolated structure of available time and learning time. Learning times for on-campus instructor-led learning mostly falls in day time. Unlike that, the mobile/micro MOOC learning time spread over all 24 h of the day. By analyzing the distribution of hotspots of frequently used learning time, EDM serve as to discover whether there are regular patterns of time organization among learners in or across cohorts, and to set up a unique learning habit summary for each learner. Their personal situations affect their learning habits, which refer to, in this paper, how learners utilize their time on MOOC learning, in what way they get learning resources passed on, how often they make pause and repetition, after how long they take a review, whether they learn several MOOC courses in parallel, during what time stages in a day they are more often to make MOOC learning happen, and among those time stages, when they are more often intending to adopt micro learning means.

Learning Speed. This feature simply refers to the extent they have spent to go through a course chunk and finish related tasks in average, estimated from their historical learning record.

Language Skill and Preference. Learners' language skills and preference should be taken into consideration to opt their learning resources. Because most MOOC courses are taught in English so that identification for learners' level of English skills is essential. Alternatively, this service investigates whether they prefer to learn in their native languages or second languages other than English.

Degree of Distraction. Internally it concerns a learner's mood and emotion, and it is highly correlated to the degree of disruption which is a component of the external factors.

4.4 External Factors

Learning Locations and Environments. The ways that learners get connected to Internet apparently reveal their learning locations and surrounding environments. Generally in micro learning scenarios, they are brought to Internet through wireless networks by two means, namely Wi-Fi or mobile cellular network (e.g. 4G, 3G, and GPRS). Simply, connecting to internet through mobile network means learners are taking on learning activities ad hoc, the strength changes of the mobile signals can reflect their statuses of being on-the-go. The logon data of Wi-Fi portal may also determine learners' exact indoor learning places. Normally connecting Internet via Wi-Fi provided in public places rather than homes indicates learners are possible to experience higher frequency of interruptions as their surrounding environments can be more noisy and complicated.

General Situation. General situation regarding learning context partially affects their learning experiences and achievements. Information regarding the mobile devices and mobile OSs the learners utilized to carry out micro MOOC learning must be specified in order to determine devices capabilities, features and limitations [18].

Assistance from Collaborative Learning. Encouraged by the nature of how MOOC is structured and its pedagogical concept, learners can get helpful information from collaborative learning, virtual social activities over social network and content generated by other learners.

Degree of Disruption. The degree of disruption depends on the noise and interference factors from their surroundings, conflicts with their daily works, comfortableness with the setting and layout of the MOOC platforms and course design and so on [19].

5 Micro MOOC Learning Resources Process and Measurement

Given some micro learning resources are provided within short time length (i.e. 15 min), they are normally delivered right away. However, most achievable MOOC contents are non-micro learning resources, which need to be refined properly. These contents need further processing and revision to fulfill micro learning demands. The ultimate shapes of resources after processing are summarized as follows:

- Visual encyclopedia: Learning key points are listed out in terms of the knowledge structure of the entire course. For each key point, a video or textual material is set out without time limit to clearly illustrate the contained content. Because the content contained solely cover a particular scale, accordingly the time length to go through it is short.
- Logical segmentation of course videos: Herein each unit covers the complete information of a learning section, which includes the conditions of beginning and ending, carries coherent content, and can be studied individually.
- Course-related and educational information in affiliated social media: This is a ramification of learning resources and also rich in educational values. This resource can be found not only in forums or blogs embedded in MOOC platforms, but also in other popular social media, where learners, educators or external experts publish course-related materials [20]. A noticeable feature of this kind of resource is that its amount increases from time to time while some of the content may contain pseudoscience or incorrect information. EDM serves as to distinguish such information, which can be useless, harmful and may cause time wasted for learners. EDM can also screen well-recognized information in order to recommend to learners as their learning augmentation besides the materials from course providers [21].
- Two-way interactive contents or activity settings, ranging from feedback, assessment, review for contents generated by other learners, peer-to-peer learning, cooperative writing, collaborative work, and flipped classroom, etc.…

Additionally, for learners who are usually involved in passive learning, EDM has another role to make the decision of when is the best timing to push information to learners and remind them, if needed.

For modelling purpose, a learning resource chunk is considered to be measured with regards to the following features: (1) Time length; (2) Suitability for mobile learning (inferred from frequency of historical records or instructor); (3) Shape of expression; (4) Difficulty (level of knowledge); (5) Completeness; (6) Requirement of attention; (7) Preferred learning styles; (8) one-way imparted or two-way interactive; (9) Requirement of input or hands-on practice.

6 Conclusion and Future Work

Building and optimizing learning path are undertaken by the Learning Resource Repository Service, and the Adaptive Engine provides a learner with proper educational resources, contents or activity settings to meet his demands and all sorts of features and context as clarified in the personalized learner model. Technical details of these two functional services are beyond the scope of this paper and we will report them in future.

In this paper we describe a research strategy which is underpinned by using adaptive micro learning as a cornerstone of the learning support SaaS. Multiple functions in the SaaS target on tailoring personalized learning schedule, specific to every fragmented time piece, for each learner. The SaaS will be finalized and implemented and implemented in the near future while we will carry out case studies focusing on finding out how our proposed system can facilitate micro learning in MOOC and how it can, qualitatively and/or quantitatively, help learners achieve their learning expectations.

References

1. King, C., Robinson, A., Vickers, J.: Online education: targeted MOOC captivates students. Nature **505**, 26 (2014). doi:10.1038/505026a
2. Baggaley, J.: MOOC rampant. Distance Educ. **34**(3), 368–378 (2013)
3. Nawrot, I., Doucet, A.: Building engagement for MOOC students, introducing support for time management on online learning platforms. In: Proceeding of WWW 2014 Companion (2014)
4. Khalil, H., Ebner, M.: MOOCs completion rates and possible methods to improve retention - a literature review. In: Proceedings of World Conference on Educational Multimedia, Hypermedia and Telecommunications (2014)
5. Stockwell, G.: Investigating learner preparedness for and usage patterns of mobile learning. ReCALL J. Camb. Univ. **20**(3), 253–270 (2008)
6. Guo, P.J., Kim, J., Rubin, R.: How video production affects student engagement: an empirical study of MOOC videos. In: The 1st ACM Conference on Learning at Scale (L@S), Atlanta, Georgia, USA (2014)
7. Kovachev, D., Cao, Y., Klamma, R., Jarke, M.: Learn-as-you-go, new ways of cloud based micro-learning for the mobile web. In: 10th International Conference on Web-Based Learning, Hongkong, December 2011
8. Bruck, P.A., Motiwalla, L., Foerster, F.: Mobile learning with micro-content: a framework and evaluation. In: Proceeding of BLED (2012). http://aisel.aisnet.org/bled2012/2
9. Hug, T., Lindner, M.: ML: emerging concepts, practices and technologies after e-learning. In: Proceedings of Micro Learning 2005, Austria, June 2005
10. Souza, M.I., Amaral, S.F.D.: Educational microcontent for mobile learning virtual environments. Creative Educ. **5**, 672–681 (2014)
11. Sun, G., Shen, J.: Facilitating social collaboration in mobile cloud-based learning: a teamwork as a service (TaaS) approach. IEEE Trans. Learn. Technol. **7**(3), 207–220 (2014)
12. Beydoun, G.: Formal concept analysis for an e-learning semantic web. Expert Syst. Appli. **36**(8), 10952–10961 (2009)
13. Al-Hmouz, A., Shen, A.J., Al-Hmouz, R., Yan, J.: Modelling and simulation of an adaptive neuro-fuzzy inference system (ANFIS) for mobile learning. IEEE Trans. Learn. Technol. **5**(3), 226–237 (2010)
14. Al-Hmouz, A., Shen, A.J., Yan, J., Al-Hmouz, R.: Enhanced learner model for adaptive mobile learning. In: The 12th International Conference on Information Integration and Web-Based Applications and Service, Paris, France, November 2010
15. Kay, J., Reimann, P., Diebold, E., Kummerfeld, B.: MOOCs: so many learners, so much potential. IEEE Intell. Syst. **28**(3), 70–77 (2013)
16. Kolb, A.Y., Kolb, A.D.: Learning styles and learning spaces: enhancing experiential learning in higher education. Acad. Manage. Learn. Educ. **4**(2), 193–212 (2005)
17. Bui, D.C., Myerson, J.: The role of working memory abilities in lecture note-taking. Learn. Individ. Differ. **33**, 12–22 (2014)
18. Tortorella, R.A.W., Graf, S.: Personalised mobile learning via an adaptive engine. In: The 12th IEEE International Conference on Advanced Learning Technologies, Roma, July 2012

19. Christensen, C.M., Aaron, S., Clark, W.: Disruption in education. In: Devlin, M., Larson, R., Meyerson, J. (eds.) The Internet and University, pp. 19--44. Boulder, Colorado: EDUCAUSE Review. https://net.educause.edu/ir/library/pdf/erm0313.pdf
20. Mark, S., Williams, R., Mackness, J.: Blogs and forums as communication and learning tools in a MOOC. In: The 7th International Conference on Networked Learning, Aalborg, Denmark, May 2010
21. Romero, C., Ventura, S.: Educational data mining: a review of the state-of-the-art. IEEE Trans. Syst. Man Cybern. C Appli. Rev. **40**(6), 601–618 (2010)

Web 2.0 and Social Learning Environments

A Microservice Approach for Near Real-Time Collaborative 3D Objects Annotation on the Web

Petru Nicolaescu(✉), Georgios Toubekis, and Ralf Klamma

Advanced Community Information Systems (ACIS) Group,
RWTH Aachen University, Ahornstr. 55, 52074 Aachen, Germany
{nicolaescu,toubekis,klamma}@dbis.rwth-aachen.de
http://dbis.rwth-aachen.de

Abstract. Web-based collaborative learning environments enable groups of learners to negotiate meaning around shared digital artefacts, e.g. by annotating them collaboratively. This particularly applies for complex digital artefacts such as multimedia or 3D objects and is mostly achieved by using metadata description standards, understandable to both user and machines for queries, context detection and retrieving relevant details. However, current approaches lack the ability to rapidly prototype courses by using lightweight Web technologies on the server and the browser side. In this paper, we present a customizable and lightweight approach for designing and performing Web-based collaborative courses using 3D Objects in the medical domain. These artefacts and the annotations are shared using *near real-time* updates between learners and tutors. In principle, we solve the problem of different annotation standards that can be used in the same environment by providing an API for using simple contextualized annotations. The evaluations and collected user feedback show that our collaborative browser-based approach simplifies access to digital artefacts and enables more collaboration.

Keywords: 3D objects · Learning environments · Near real-time collaboration · Semantic annotation · Community information systems

1 Introduction

In order to support learning efficiently it is necessary to find a balance between guidance and freedom regarding the appropriate learning strategies for learners. New approaches such as "hybrid learning", "mixed learning" or "multi-method-learning" are challenging methods especially in formal education scenarios that still rely very much on conventional teacher-centered approaches. Applications from the Technology-Enhanced Learning domain aim to achieve optimal communication and information transfer between tutors and learners with integration of specific technologies and media artifacts. Such a learning arrangement combines didactic methods that have been selected for a specific learning purpose and

F.W.B. Li et al. (Eds.): ICWL 2015, LNCS 9412, pp. 187–196, 2015.
DOI: 10.1007/978-3-319-25515-6_17

for a certain environment. Even though several approaches exist, the mixture of personal and collaborative systems that can adapt to formal and informal needs of learners –also in *near real-time* (NRT)– still offers a rich field for research. Courses of Anatomy in classical medical education may serve here as a scenario representing diverse teaching methods such as teacher-centered lectures. Such lectures can take place in the dissection hall with hundreds of students, or the learning can take place individually or in small groups. In both cases, the vast amount of factual knowledge that is to be processed by medical students requires education resources highly adaptive to needs of learners and tutors alike. In conventional medical education a broad variety of anatomical models either generalized or highly detailed exist to address this need. In particular physical anatomical models originating from human beings are essential examples used in medical education, since they provide real-world experience that is not possible to gain from abstracted models. Furthermore, with the digitalization of medical objects, education has far progressed and anatomical 3D graphics are nowadays almost ubiquitous available. Applications scaffolding learning that make use of 3D objects and multimedia are subject to many changes due to the appearance of new fast and reliable protocols and the emergence of new standards that make the Web the most suitable environment for hosting such applications. In the same time, these changes drive innovation and improve the experience of learners, that can benefit from a faster learning. While such Web applications render quite generalized manipulable 3D anatomical models of the human body, techniques that can be employed to capture and transform real world physical artifacts (3D scanning) into digital artifacts are becoming more affordable. Such "digital twins" of real world objects are offering a rich immersive experience and overcome difficulties such as restricted accessibility or fragile handling associated with the original physical object. In this context, driven by the near real-time Web, research efforts are needed to investigate which Web technologies enable seamless integration of collaborative technologies on 3D Objects for learning scenarios and how rendering of 3D Objects on the Web and their collaborative consumption can foster learning processes for specialized domains such as medicine.

In this paper, we present a Personal Learning Environment(PLE) [1] that allows the NRT collaborative visualization of 3D objects on the Web and the instant generation of annotations on these objects. Annotations are created collaboratively and correspond to specific needs of the tutors and learners in terms of what information needs to be captured and retrieved. In contrast with the existing specific 3D exploration and annotation tools, our system is optimized for the Web and does not use dedicated environments or over-specialized solutions. We propose a lightweight approach based on standards such as HTML5, x3dom for 3D Objects visualization and a microservice oriented architecture for storing the annotations. Conceptually, our approach is based on the learner-centric self-regulated learning process model, consisting of four cyclic phases (planning, preparing, learning, and reflecting) [1].

The above mentioned scenario for medical students has been selected to demonstrate the relevance that NRT collaborative approaches can have on student learning behavior in terms of activation and self-regulation by direct feedback loops and ubiquitous access to learning resources. The service has been implemented in the context of a blended learning project in education involving Anatomy classes at RWTH Aachen University Clinic providing access to digital 3D objects of physical models and prosected specimens available in the Anatomy department and that are only usable in the department room due to their fragile nature. The system provides digital learning environments in which the annotation service can be used to create descriptions and terminologies collaboratively on the 3D objects, which can be explored and annotated either in self-learning or group-learning scenarios. The next section presents related work and systems used for 3D Objects. In Sects. 3 and 4 we present the main concepts behind our learning approach and the information system used to technically realize the learning environment and foster collaboration. After the presentation of the evaluation results in Sect. 5, we conclude the paper and offer a summary of future work.

2 Related Work

Digital representations of real world objects offer a cost-efficient and effective way to enable access to information in learning settings. In this context, 3D Objects can be used effectively for collaborative exploration of certain artefacts that would otherwise be hard to procure, expensive, hard to maintain, etc. (e.g. parts of human body, cultural heritage objects, expensive construction equipment and others).

Such digital content requires a semantic enrichment to reveal the relevant relationships and information such as the history, provenance, specific characteristics, etc. Annotating 3D objects has therefore become popular in research, where most 3D annotation applications are directed at niche markets, like biology, engineering or science. This is partially also due to the increase in hardware capabilities and the browser-based technologies. As such, *WebGL*[1] enables the usage of 3D graphics in all contemporary browsers. Based on OpenGL, this cross-platform Web standard in combination with HTML5 uses natively the capabilities of graphic cards by means of HTML5 Canvas and DOM interfaces. *X3D* is an open ISO standard for handling 3D computer graphics [2]. The standard (ISO/IEC IS 19775-1:2013) is the further development of Virtual Reality Modeling Language (VRML). There are initiatives that try to make X3D elements supported natively in HTML5, like *x3dom*[2] open source Javascript library developed by Fraunhofer IGD, which allows the integration of X3D elements as part of the HTML5 DOM tree.

The existing standards and frameworks have already been adopted for application development in different domains. 3D environments were considered for

[1] https://www.khronos.org/registry/webgl/specs/1.0/.
[2] http://www.x3dom.org/.

modern pedagogy, more specifically in virtual worlds [3]. In the referenced work, the authors present a model-view-controller framework for collaborative virtual environments for learning, based on the X3D standard. Here, users can meet and interact with other users, agents, virtual objects and virtual environments. Landro et al. [4] present a Web portal design for academic communities in scientific information exchange. Teachers and learners can use 3D learning objects in a simulation of virtual laboratories to engage in face-to-face learning sessions with thematic Web-seminars. However relevant might the digital content be, the size of the available information can be overwhelming for users. This is why metadata can be used for searching and cataloging the information. There have been various approaches trying to solve the problem of multimedia retrieval and classification [Rui et al. 1999][Lew et al. 2006]. The prominent solutions are content-based search or include user generated metadata, like annotations. Here, we make use of a context-aware multi-granular tagging model, which was developed based on a PLE for Chinese Classic Poems and which associates the learner and the learning content's context [5].

In the Cultural Heritage domain there is a new trend to expose 3D content to a broad audience, the example of the SmithsonianX3D[3] being the most prominent here to date. Enrichment of such 3D content with useful metadata is the challenge for the future, addressed exemplary in the 3DSA project[4]. The system provides a Web-based interface for semantic annotation of 3D objects originating from museum collections [6] based on the Open Annotation Core Data Model[5].

ToBoA-3D is a tool that tries to combine top down and bottom up annotation strategies in dedicated virtual environments. Free form tagging is combined with annotations deriving from ontology based OWL classes [7].

All last examples demonstrate that the semantic enrichment of 3D objects is a rather complex process requiring specific domain knowledge. We propose a rather lightweight approach for both the process of annotating 3D objects based on community practice [5,8] as well the associated storing and parsing of this information. This approach allows a fast deployment of evaluation prototypes that are able to engage profound community involvement required for in-depth enrichment of 3D artifacts.

3 A Lightweight Collaborative Annotation Approach for 3D Objects

We concentrated our efforts in achieving a usable Web platform where learners can interact collaboratively on the Web with 3D Objects, in NRT. Therefore, for a specific course (e.g. from medicine curricula) users can collaborate on and explore 3D Objects in a PLE. By entering the corresponding learning environment, learners can browse 3D Objects directly in browser in two modes:

[3] http://3d.si.edu.
[4] http://www.itee.uq.edu.au/eresearch/projects/3dsa.
[5] http://www.openannotation.org/spec/core/.

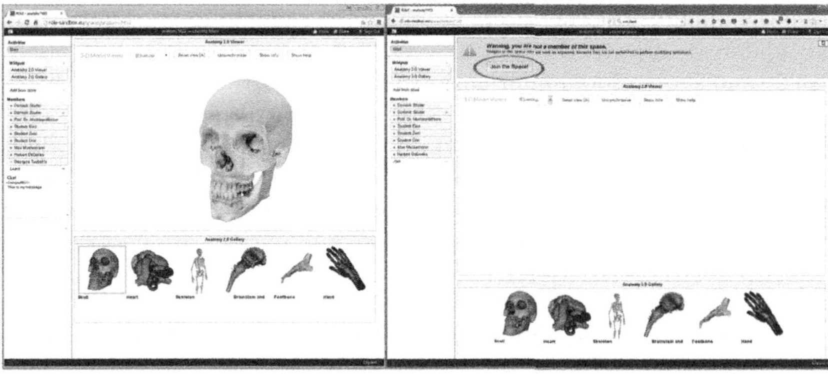

Fig. 1. Shared PLE for exploring 3D anatomical models

a personal mode, where they can explore the objects independently and a collaborative mode where an object of focus is available to all learners and all interactions upon the object are synchronized in NRT. The interaction with the 3D object allows zooming and rotation from arbitrary views, the synchronization function allows the tutor to share a specific view to all the participants of the virtual space. They are also allowed to collaboratively annotate the objects they are currently exploring. The PLE simulates the real world experience both in terms of freedom of interaction with the 3D model and awareness of the participants among each other, a stimulus regarded essential in conventional classroom learning.

For this purpose, we have used ROLE SDK, a development kit for the implementation of PLEs [1,9]. The framework simplifies the development and deployment of widget-based applications. Web widgets are embedded in containers called "Spaces". Essentially, each space is a widget container that has an unique URL and can be joined by multiple users, engaging in collaboration. A space also offers authentication, authorization, user account management and data storage mechanisms [10]. The NRT collaboration feature is enabled by the usage of Inter-Widget Communication (IWC) [10], on top of the XMPP standard protocol [11]. An example for our annotation interface is presented in Fig. 4.

The courses and 3D Objects are managed on a dedicated Website [6], that links to the PLEs which are dedicated for the collaborative study of the objects. As such, the Website offers functions for managing the courses, the spaces, uploading the 3D Objects and assigning them to specific courses. Figure 1 shows a PLE used for an Anatomy course, according to the above described scenario.

As it can be observed, the space is composed from two widgets, one being a repository of existing 3D Objects to be explored and a visualization widget, that can display one 3D Object at a given time. The 3D Object Viewer is built using the x3dom library and features various examination modes of the objects (e.g. examine, walk, fly, etc.). Learners or tutors can synchronize (receive and

[6] http://dbis.rwth-aachen.de/3dnrt/Anatomy2.0/.

visualize the updates of other users based on the same object) or unsynchronize (ignore updates) objects. They can reset the view to its initial position and view angle and show x3dom information about the current object, e.g. hardware rendering, number of nodes, number of points, etc. All participants in a course that have the synchronized mode enabled will have the same view on the same object and each participant can interact with the object of focus.

During the annotation process, tutors (or learners) can use certain annotation types in order to describe the 3D Object. The annotations are performed at the meso level (i.e. at the 3D Object level) in the PLE [5]. The community uses the annotations in order to exploit knowledge (annotations are used as a method of underlining relevant or interesting aspects of an object) and as reflection possibility for the case where a learner explores others' annotations [1]. As can be observed in the figure, we use simple text annotations containing a title, author and a description. Furthermore, our annotation approach also provides a range of basic meso-level annotations that can be used to disambiguate meaning [12]. From the expressiveness point of view, we achieve a highly customizable tagging structure that can be used for rapid prototyping and can guarantee a good and expressive annotation experience for learners and tutors involved in the process.

4 Infrastructure and Architecture

Our technical approach focuses on achieving a collaborative environment that can easily scale with the number of learners and that can be also used in different contexts (e.g. extension of annotation for videos, images, etc.). We therefore consider the architecture instance presented in Fig. 1.

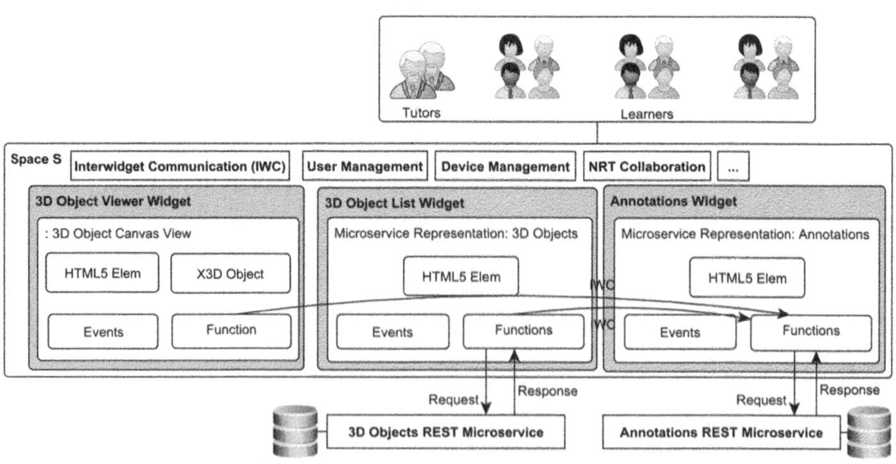

Fig. 2. Architecture instance for rapid prototyping and lightweight annotation services

The lightweight approach proposes dedicated microservices for fulfilling clear functionality such as multimedia annotation or multimedia storage (i.e. of 3D Objects). The microservices are reflected on the interface level using widget components, such as the 3D Object List seen in Fig. 1 or the Annotations widget. These can be composed with other widgets, which leads to an environment that suits well the expectations of the collaborative learning process.

We use JSON[7] for storing metadata, because it offers a lightweight and extensible interchange format which is both human and machine readable. Our architecture reflects a methodological approach where widgets are considered to be clear-cut Web interfaces for microservices. The microservices are all implemented as RESTful Web Services. As such, the backend platform used for storing the objects and the metadata is composed of multiple microservices, each one fulfilling a clear-cut functionality and having its own database. The microservice approach was introduced by Fowler[8] and represents an agile solution to Service Oriented Architectures (SOA). As depicted in Fig. 2, our environment uses 2 microservices: a 3D Object List microservice and an annotations microservice. The 3D Object List microservice uses a MySQL database to store information about the 3D Objects such as title, description, URL, learning environment address to which they belong, etc. The annotation microservice uses ArangoDB, a non-SQL hybrid (i.e. graph, document, relational) database written in Javascript. The annotations are stored inside the service as a graph, using a JSON format. We use two main graph vertex types (i.e. collections), which have unique object identifiers (e.g. for the 3D Objects data stored in the 3D Object List database) that represent objects and annotations, with their full JSON representation. If an annotation is added to an object, a vertex will be added to the graph and an edge will be created to link the annotation with its corresponding 3D Object. The contextual data concerning the annotation and the respective object (i.e. annotation time, absolute coordinates of the 3D Object, where the annotation is added, rotation and translation information, etc.) is stored in the edge, also as a JSON representation. Annotation types can be easily added upon learner's needs and rapidly included into the user interface. Since standardization for annotations is still an open issue, we propose to achieve interoperability by specialized conversion microservices, that can transform the unstructured JSON annotation representation into more structured standards such as MPEG-7, DublinCore, etc. This is how a transformation between an existing annotation and a dedicated standard (e.g. with the goal to include annotations as native labels in X3D) can be achieved.

Finally, the 3D Object Viewer does not have any connection to a microservice, but it listens via IWC to the other widget events in order to get information regarding its state (e.g. object to display, annotations related to current view, etc.). The other widgets are displaying information coming from the microservices. The widgets are composed from events, functions and HTML5 elements.

---

[7] http://json.org/.

[8] http://martinfowler.com/articles/microservices.html.

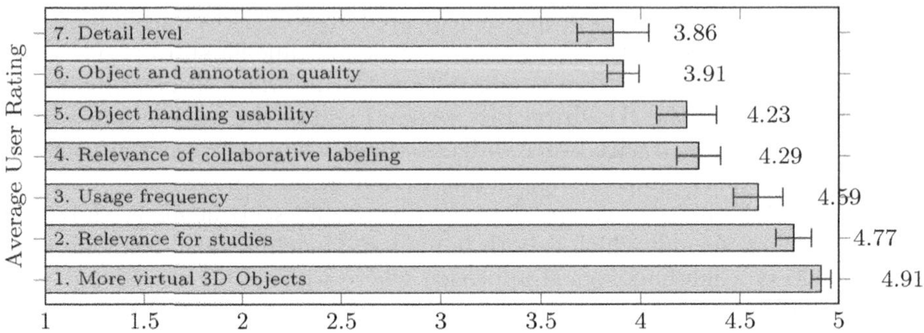

Fig. 3. Evaluation results

5 Evaluation

We are currently evaluating our approach within our blended learning project providing access to 3D anatomical models presented in Sect. 3. The evaluation is ongoing and taking place parallel to the development of the system.

In order to test the feasibility for learning and the usability of our approach, we performed two study sessions with students from the medicine faculties of two different universities. 24 participants from Aachen and Maastricht used the PLE to visualize the 3D Objects and annotate the non-obvious information of the

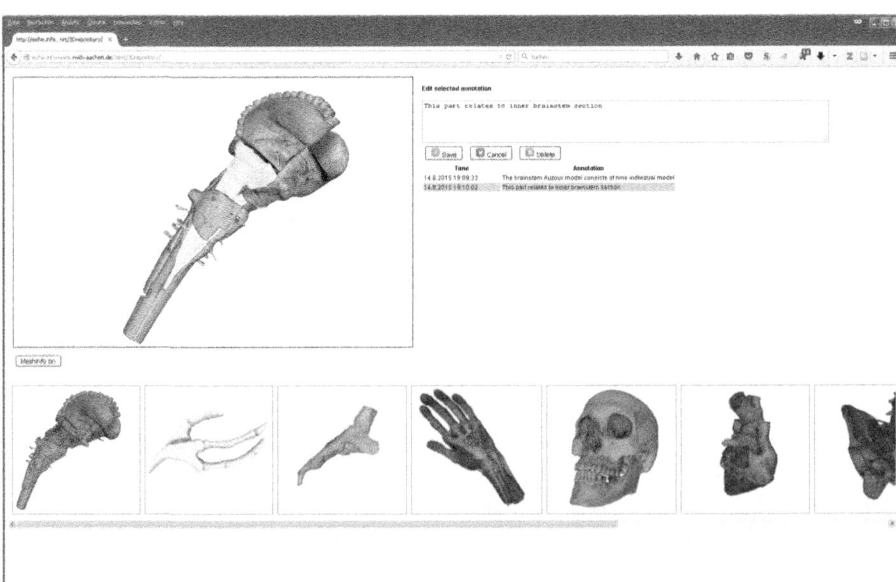

Fig. 4. Annotations for 3D objects used for evaluation with medical students

anatomical models. First, a tutor provided information on certain 3D Objects by using the synchronized view. Then, students were allowed to visualize and annotate independently or collaboratively the objects.

Figure 4 shows contextual text in form of attached annotations to a 3D object. This setting was created in order to test the performance of the annotations service and how the 3D Objects are perceived in the browser by the users.

Finally, we measured the acceptance of the system using questionnaires based on a five points Likert scale (cf. Fig. 3). The overall acceptance towards the current version of our prototype was very good and the usage of the models where characterized as helpful. However, the relevance to the subject requirements still remain unclear. Based on the available system, the evaluation will be extended in the near future with more scenarios.

6 Conclusion

In this paper, we present a lightweight approach for collaborative exploration of 3D Objects on the Web, using annotations and NRT mechanisms. We have opted for an accessible and open Web platform to be used as a PLE and a combination between 3D technologies, annotations and NRT collaboration in order to facilitate learning in Web browser. The evaluation performed using anatomical artifacts showed the relevance and the power of these technologies for learning.

As future work, we plan to develop further our tool using the gathered evaluation results and the tutor's and learners' requirements. We plan to enhance our platform with synchronization mechanisms and NRT shared editing functionality, for the annotations and the exploration of 3D Objects.

Moreover, we plan to support more annotation techniques and explore the vocabulary formed by the communities during the evaluation process. Because the approach is very general, we plan to research how to provide a more domain-specific annotation process, by also keeping the lightweight characteristic.

We are also currently exploring how can the distribution of different widgets on multiple devices and a seamless experience can influence learning in such collaborative settings. Based on the good early evaluation results, the annotation process will be extended for other types of multimedia, such as videos or images. Finally, we plan to perform community monitoring and success measuring [13] methods in order to complete the evaluation of our system for learning communities and to provide self-reflection mechanisms [1,14] for tutors and learners.

Acknowledgments. This research was supported by the European Commission in the 7th Framework Programme project Learning Layers, grant no. 318209.

References

1. Renzel, D., Klamma, R., Kravcik, M., Nussbaumer, A.: Tracing Self-Regulated Learning in Responsive Open Learning Environments. In: Proceedings of the 14th International Conference on Web-based Learning (2015)
2. Liu, J., Su, W., Sun, Y.: 3D model semantic automatic annotation based on X3D scene. In: 2013 Fifth International Conference on Computational and Information Sciences (ICCIS), pp. 282–285 (2013)
3. Settapat, S., Achalakul, T., Ohkura, M.: Web-based 3D medical image visualization framework for biomedical engineering education. J. Comput. Appl. Eng. Educ. **22**(2), 216–226 (2014)
4. Landro, D., De Gasperis, G., Macchiarelli, M.D.G.: A collaborative distance learning portal integrating 3D virtual labs in biomedicine. In: Mascio, T.D., Gennari, R., Vitorini, P., Vicari, R., de la Prieta, F. (eds.) Methodologies and Intelligent Systems for Technology Enhanced Learning. AISC, vol. 292, pp. 149–156. Springer, Heidelberg (2015)
5. Cao, Y., Kovachev, D., Klamma, R., Jarke, M., Lau, R.W.H.: Tagging diversity in personal learning environments. J. Comput. Educ. **2**(1), 93–121 (2015)
6. Yu, C.H., Hunter, J.: Documenting and sharing comparative analyses of 3D digital museum artifacts through semantic web annotations. J. Comput. Cult. Heritage (JOCCH) **6**(4), 18 (2013)
7. Pittarello, F., Gatto, I.: ToBoA-3D: an architecture for managing top-down and bottom-up annotated 3D objects and spaces on the web. In: Proceedings of the 16th International Conference on 3D Web Technology, vol. 57 (2011)
8. Wenger, E.: Communities of Practice: Learning, Meaning, and Identity, Learning in Doing. Cambridge University Press, Cambridge (1998)
9. Govaerts, S., et al.: Towards responsive open learning environments: the ROLE interoperability framework. In: Kloos, C.D., Gillet, D., Crespo García, R.M., Wild, F., Wolpers, M. (eds.) EC-TEL 2011. LNCS, vol. 6964, pp. 125–138. Springer, Heidelberg (2011)
10. Kovachev, D., Renzel, D., Nicolaescu, P., Koren, I., Klamma, R.: DireWolf: a framework for widget-based distributed user interfaces. J. Web Eng. **13**(3&4), 203–222 (2014)
11. Saint-Andre, P.: RFC 6120: Extensible Messaging and Presence Protocol (XMPP), Core (2011)
12. Cao, Y., Renzel, D., Jarke, M., Klamma, R., Lottko, M., Toubekis, G., Jansen, M.: Well-balanced usability and annotation complexity in interactive video semantization. In: 4th International Conference on Multimedia and Ubiquitous Engineering, MUE 2010, pp. 1–8 (2010)
13. DeLone, W.H., McLean, E.R.: The DeLone and McLean model of information systems success: a ten-year update. J. Manag. Inf. Syst. **19**(4), 9–30 (2003)
14. Klamma, R.: Community learning analytics – challenges and opportunities. In: Wang, J.-F., Lau, R. (eds.) ICWL 2013. LNCS, vol. 8167, pp. 284–293. Springer, Heidelberg (2013)

Blogging Activities in Higher Education: Comparing Learning Scenarios in Multiple Course Experiences

Elvira Popescu[1(✉)], Zuzana Kubincová[2], and Martin Homola[2]

[1] University of Craiova, Craiova, Romania
popescu_elvira@software.ucv.ro
[2] Comenius University in Bratislava, Bratislava, Slovakia
{kubincova,homola}@fmph.uniba.sk

Abstract. Blogging has been used in education with various goals and within various contexts. While many benefits of its application have been shown, it is not always clear what kind of blogging tasks should be used, and what is the proper methodology for their implementation, given certain educational goals. In this paper, we provide a large scale experience report on the use of blogs in several courses, run in two universities over multiple years, with more than 1500 students enrolled overall. A catalogue of blogging activities used for learning is provided, outlining their purpose and structure; their integration in four courses (different in terms of curriculum, student background and instructional approach) is also described. A set of findings and practical guidelines are drawn from our experience, which could prove useful to other educators who want to foster student learning through blogging.

Keywords: Social media in education · Blogging · Learning scenario · Experience report

1 Introduction

Various social media services, such as blogs, wikis, microblogging tools or social networking tools, have started to be used as communication and collaboration platforms in educational contexts. There are many reasons behind this, including the ease of use, effectiveness, familiarity and attractiveness of these tools for digital native students [7]. In this paper, we focus specifically on blogs, which have a distinctive position in this area, a large number of applications and are particularly well aligned with modern learning theories such as constructivism, constructionism and connectivism [11,18,20].

Several studies have shown empirical evidence of positive impact of blogging activities on students' learning gain [1,4,9,19]. However, these positive effects are attributable mainly to how blogging is used, and not simply to the technology [8]. Therefore, it is very important to focus on the types of learning activities and

An erratum to this chapter is available at 10.1007/978-3-319-25515-6_28

F.W.B. Li et al. (Eds.): ICWL 2015, LNCS 9412, pp. 197–207, 2015.
DOI: 10.1007/978-3-319-25515-6_18

the pedagogical scenarios in which blogging is integrated. Especially in blended learning settings and in cases where blogging activities are incorporated within organized curricula, there are questions related to how to combine them with more traditional teaching activities, such as lectures, labs, homework etc.

In this paper, we focus on selected blogging activities and their suitability for various learning goals within blended instructional scenarios. We provide a detailed experience report, which builds on a decade of practical use of blogs in two universities from two Eastern European countries. Our situation is specific in that many university students in Eastern Europe are not always well motivated, their engagement patterns with similar activities are often irregular and they require increased teacher guidance [2,5,10]. The blogging activities were integrated in four different courses, which vary in terms of curriculum, student background and instructional approach; a total of more than 1500 students were enrolled in these courses up to the present.

From this large scale experience we abstract a number of observations. Some of them are specific to our context, but many of them are fairly general and we contend that they will be useful to educators who want to use blogging as an effective tool for their teaching. Thus, the rest of the paper brings the following main contributions: (i) a systematic description of blogging activities used for learning in Sect. 2; (ii) an experience sharing from the various courses taught in Sect. 3; (iii) a summary of findings and practical guidelines drawn from our observations in Sect. 4. A short conclusion and future outlook complete the paper.

2 Blogging Activities

In what follows we describe the different blogging activities that we have tried in our courses, outlining their purpose and structure.

2.1 Presentation of Self-acquired Information

Description: After studying resources connected to a certain topic, the students are tasked to write a blog post on that subject. They may either be given both the topic and the references to suitable resources, or they may be required to select the topic and find the resources themselves. The subject matter may be directly part of the curriculum or the task may also be to find some relevant related topic based on the student's interests.

Purpose: The goal is to stimulate higher engagement with a selected theme (either part of or related to the curriculum). This task also allows students to have a higher involvement with a topic of their particular interest. If the activity is combined with reading and commenting on peers' postings, it further widens the students' outlook in the area and allows for exchange of opinions among learners.

Structure: (i) selection of the topic; (ii) looking for and studying of relevant resources; (iii) blog post composition and publishing; (iv) optional comments phase.

2.2 Reflection on the Lectures

Description: The activity is combined with an organized course comprising lectures (or possibly also different types of learning sessions). After each lecture, or just after some selected ones, the students are asked to write a blog post reflecting on the material discussed during the lecture, or their experience learned from the lecture. Optionally, the students may be asked to research and process additional related resources (similar to Activities 2.1 and 2.6).

Purpose: The main purpose is to stimulate reflection, further engagement, and alignment of the knowledge acquired during the lectures (or other educational activities) [12]. The activity may be done individually, but since it is useful for the students to compare their learning experiences and points of view, it is also often combined with commenting on each others' blog posts.

Structure: (i) the activity is preceded by a lecture, exercises, or some other educational activity; (ii) a time period to reflect and organize their knowledge, or optionally to explore further resources on the topic; (iii) blog post composition and publishing; (iv) typically also a comments phase.

2.3 Project Diary

Description: If a project is included among the course activities, blogs can be used as a space for publishing the ongoing report on the project development and/or the project results. This type of project diary is suitable both for individual and group projects. In the former case, the students are asked to regularly post information about their progress in handling the project tasks, about the methods used for problem solving, how well they stick to the schedule, etc. In the latter case, the indicated activities are complemented by dividing the roles in the group and assigning the partial tasks to each group member.

Purpose: One of the most important purposes is to encourage the continuous and regular work of students. The blog helps to maintain a learning log, while also showcasing the project progress and status update. While writing about the project development, the students gain a better insight into their assignment and are able to identify particular sub-problems and the procedures to solve them. Also, reading the reports on peers' projects can help students to work out potential problems in their own project. Furthermore, blog reports enable the teacher to track the activity and progress of students in the project development [3]. In case of group projects, blog posts help the teacher to estimate the share of work per particular group member.

Structure: (i) project assignment; (ii) regular publishing on the blog about the project progress; (iii) optionally, reading and commenting on the peer project reports.

2.4 Professional Blogging

Description: Professional blogging is similar to Activity 2.1 – students are asked to write blog posts on topics related to the course subject. Additionally, they are asked to develop a full professional blog, including their background information, professional interests, etc.; it may also be similar to writing for a company blog. Their articles are required to have all features of a real blog post – the proper form and structure, appropriate formatting, correctly cited resources, respected copyright, etc.

Purpose: Beside encouraging learners' interest in course topics and deepening their knowledge, this activity also aims to raise students' awareness of professional writing and rules of blogging. Furthermore, the purpose is to try the experience of developing their own professional profile via maintaining a professional blog, which some of the students may continue doing also in the future.

Structure: (i) selection of the topic; (ii) study of relevant resources; (iii) blog article writing and publishing; (iv) commenting by instructor; (v) reading and commenting on peers' postings; also, since the blogs are open, external comments should be welcome and the students should be encouraged to react to them.

2.5 Web Content Publishing Practice

Description: This activity is combined with a course that includes web content publishing among its topics. Students are tasked to post content on their blog, however the main focus in the evaluation is not on the content itself, but especially on its form and adherence to quality standards.

Purpose: The purpose is to learn web publishing technology, and the required web content publishing skills such as writing and structuring content for the web, proper formation of titles, usage of links, images and multimedia content. The students may pick the content freely, but some requirements should be in place, regarding number of articles, post length and different types of content that should be present (i.e., images, links, code samples, tables, etc.).

Structure: The activity may be as simple as iterating between (i) publishing a blog posting; and (ii) instructor feedback. But it can also be enhanced by (iii) reading and commenting on peers' postings.

2.6 Gathering and Sharing Learning Resources

Description: This activity complements an assignment or homework, for which students need to autonomously find support resources (e.g., tutorials, algorithms, code samples, software libraries, technology description, etc.). The resources which are considered interesting, useful and relevant to the task can be shared with peers by means of blog posts, which also include a short description or appraisal of the educational material.

Purpose: The collection of resources is not a goal per se, but a means to solving a task or completing a project. The activity fulfills two main roles. First, students benefit from the resources already gathered by peers; these have the advantage of being generally relevant to the students, since they reflect the preference of a relatively homogeneous learning community (i.e., classmates with similar backgrounds, completing the same curriculum and having to solve a similar task) [16]. Secondly, students practice their critical assessment skills by filtering the large number of available resources and providing recommendations and assessments.

Structure: The activity entails three main steps: (i) search for resources of interest; (ii) evaluate the quality and usefulness of the resources; (iii) share and recommend relevant resources.

2.7 Requesting and Providing Help/Feedback

Description: Students can use the blog for describing the problems and difficulties encountered in their work and asking for help; peers can offer solutions and advice based on their own experience. Furthermore, in case of team work, students may present their ideas and proposed approaches on the blog and ask for their teammates' feedback and approval.

Purpose: This activity is based on peer tutoring approach, in which learners help each other and learn by teaching [6]. The goal is to rely on peers' experience, eliciting the wisdom of the crowd for solving a problem. Furthermore, a repository of problems and solutions is created, which is helpful both for other students (who may be faced with the same issues) and for the instructor (who can better understand the learning difficulties encountered by the students).

Structure: The activity involves two basic steps: (i) post a description of the problem encountered; (ii) receive comments with solutions and advice from peers. Additional clarifications may be asked in subsequent comments.

Finally, it should be noted that students can also use the blog as a **communication tool** and many of the activities described above already imply some information exchange between learners. Especially in case of cooperative or collaborative work, the blog serves as a medium for discussing ideas, sharing experience and imparting knowledge. Furthermore, personal interactions through blogging are also encouraged (e.g., expressing emotions and appreciation, congratulating and encouraging peers for their activity); some off topic and small talk posts (e.g., phatics, salutations, greetings, humour) may also be useful, since they foster interaction between students, enhance group cohesion and team spirit.

3 Our Experience

In this section we describe the experience with the above listed blogging activities, as they have been implemented in multiple courses from two different universities – Comenius University in Bratislava, Slovakia and University of Craiova, Romania.

3.1 Experience from Comenius University in Bratislava

Course 1. Since 2006 we have continually used blogging in a Web Design course [2,9,10]. The course was offered in both bachelor and master curricula of Applied Informatics and Computer Science. Throughout these past nine years, more than 800 students were enrolled in this course, the cohort size varying from 54 to 158 attendants per year.

As a practical project, the students were tasked with creating the design of their blog, and then with posting meaningful articles on their blog (as two separate assignments). During 2006–2013 we used professional blogging (Activity 2.4), that is the students were required to maintain a "web design practitioner blog", and post interesting articles related to the topic of the course, their own experiments and projects with web technology, etc. The aim was to reinforce learning outcomes from the project work by providing meaningful content for the blogs, to stimulate further engagement with related topics, and to stimulate social learning via mutual comments.

In the first 3–4 runs the course was voluntary, and the results were encouraging, albeit a smaller number of students participated regularly (the blogging part was not compulsory). In the following years, we tried to attract students to the assignment by allocating it a larger share of evaluation points. While the participation was higher, many students did not have a deep interest in it and they only posted very weak articles to get a few grading points. Furthermore, students were not interested in peers' postings and comments were very sparse. Hence, in the past few years we made a number of changes. We introduced a stricter publishing schedule, with alternating weeks dedicated to publishing and reading respectively, which was further reinforced with structured peer reviews. In the last two years we also deviated from professional blogging, which the students found too demanding, to simple web content publishing practice (Activity 2.5). Both changes brought some positive results – the participation increased from less than 36 % on average in previous years to more than 92 % and learning outcomes also significantly improved (see [2] for more details), however we still have to work on improving the students' satisfaction with the activity.

Course 2. The course on Algorithms and Data Structures (ADS) is an obligatory subject in the bachelor study program of Applied Informatics. Blogging was incorporated into this course in 2009, 2010 and 2012, with the aim to stimulate reflection and engagement with further related topics [10]. The task combined Activities 2.1–2.3. That means students were allowed to choose among the presentation of a new topic related to the course subject, reflection on the lectures or project diary. The first two topics were selected more often, whilst the project diary occurred quite rarely.

The total number of students attending the ADS course in the years in question was 371 (135 in 2009, 124 in 2010 and 112 in 2012). In the first two years, the blogging assignment ran in three rounds, approximately one month each. During each round students were asked to regularly publish several blog posts, which were evaluated by the instructor after the round was over. The activity was voluntary. Although the bloggers were rewarded by some extra points, the number of participating students was low and varied from 5 % to 15 % in different rounds. Moreover, students often participated only partially, just in one or two rounds, and they posted a limited number of articles. We tried to encourage students to read the posts of their peers and to comment on these posts, but our efforts did not bring expected results.

Therefore, we restructured the activity in 2012 and integrated peer review with it. The whole blogging assignment period was divided into six two-week rounds, first week being dedicated to publishing blog posts and the second week to peer reviewing. Similarly to the experience gained in the Web Design course, although the activity remained voluntary, the students' involvement with it increased significantly (to 67 %) and the learning outcomes improved as well.

Course 3. In 2009 we started a new course on using Web Technologies in Education. This subject is offered as a voluntary course in the master study program for Pre-Service Teachers in Informatics. Blogging was introduced as a main learning activity from the first course run. Students were asked to regularly post their subjective view on the topic discussed during each lecture (Activity 2.2); the aim was to stimulate reflection and opinion exchange. This task was mandatory and the score gained for it made up a significant part (one third) of the overall student grading. Since the course is voluntary, only students who agreed with this rule enrolled in it. This is a smaller course, with 3 to 8 attendants per run, giving a total number of 34 students for the whole period 2009–2014.

In the first three runs of the course, students had no previous experience with blogging. Although they were not too enthusiastic about this activity at the beginning, their blog posts brought many interesting and useful ideas and suggestions towards the integration of web technologies into educational process at primary and secondary schools. Starting with 2012, two changes occurred: (i) the students enrolled in this course had some previous experience with educational blogging (from other courses); (ii) peer review was integrated with the blogging activity. The new settings brought an improvement in the blog contributions and an increased number of blog comments, leading also to more fruitful face-to-face discussions between students in subsequent seminars.

3.2 Experience from University of Craiova

Course 4. Our practical experience with educational blogging at University of Craiova took place in the context of a course on Web Applications Design (WAD), taught to 4th year undergraduate students in Computer Science. Blogs were first included as support tools in the instructional scenario in the academic year 2009–2010 and have been used in all subsequent installments (6 course runs up to the present) [13–15]. A project-based learning (PBL) approach was used, in which learning was organized around the development of an authentic web application; students collaborated in teams of 3–6 peers, in order to build their chosen system (e.g., a virtual bookstore, an online auction website, a professional social network, an online travel agency etc.). The PBL scenario was implemented in blended mode, with weekly face-to-face meetings between each team and the instructor complemented by the use of social media tools for communication and collaboration activities between team members. In particular, the blog was used mainly for Activities 2.3, 2.6 and 2.7: reporting the progress of the project, sharing ideas and resources, providing feedback and solutions to peer problems; each team had its own blog, but inter-teams cooperation was encouraged as well. The student assessment took into account both the final product delivered at the end of the semester and the continuous collaborative work carried out by the students, including the blogging activity.

It should be noted that the blog was used in conjunction with other social media tools, such as wiki (for collaborative writing of the project documentation) or microblogging tool (for short news, announcements and status updates). The settings were refined from one course run to the next, to take into account students' feedback and results. Thus, we found out that the introduction of four compulsory intermediary presentations engaged students more and discouraged the practice of activity peak at the end of the semester. Also, students' involvement was increased by introducing a peer evaluation mechanism, both for milestone presentations and for the collaborative activity on the social media tools.

A total of 304 students were enrolled in the WAD course throughout the 6 semesters and were involved in the educational blogging activities. According to the opinion surveys applied at the end of each semester, the majority of the students were satisfied with the use of blogs for their projects; most of them found it easy or very easy to learn how to use the blog as well as actually use it, and did not encounter any technical problems. The main roles fulfilled by the blog (as perceived by the students) were: (i) learn how to use the tool; (ii) exchange experience; (iii) help organize knowledge; (iv) find interesting/useful information; (v) improve writing skills; (vi) receive feedback; (vii) improve collaborative skills; (viii) increase competitiveness. However, several drawbacks of the blogging activity were also revealed: (i) significant variation among students and teams in the number of blog contributions; (ii) relatively low level of interaction between students (as reflected in the lower number of comments compared to the number of posts); (iii) relatively high amount of time and effort necessary for accomplishing the blogging tasks.

4 Findings and Practical Guidelines

In what follows, we summarize the findings from our experience report and we draw some practical recommendations for other instructors interested in using blogs in educational settings.

Student's Acceptance: The proper selection of blogging activity type for the given educational goals is very important; inappropriate tasks can discourage students from blogging. For example, at Comenius University in Bratislava students of Computer Science and Applied Informatics displayed a dislike for professional blogging or lecture reflection. On the other hand, blogging as a reflection on lectures was successfully used for several years with groups of pre-service teachers at the same university. Similarly, Computer Science students at University of Craiova acknowledged the benefits of using blogs in activities such as project diary, sharing ideas and resources, and providing feedback and solutions to peer problems. Hence, *a successful integration of the blog in the educational activity requires a carefully designed instructional scenario, based on a sound pedagogy; the blogging activity should be harmonized with the curriculum and the learning objectives.*

Irregular Engagement: As shown also by other studies [2, 5, 10], some students in Eastern Europe have a reserved attitude towards the use of social media tools in education, which is a different approach from what they are used to do in other courses. They may not perceive the benefits at the beginning, which leads to highly irregular engagement, with activity peaking only towards the end of the semester for many of them. Results from both universities show that this can be greatly amended by *improving guidance and introducing intermediate reporting, deadlines, and stricter structure to the blogging/reading activity.* Furthermore, there are significant disparities between students in terms of involvement with the blogging activity, with highly active learners versus virtually inactive peers. This can be frustrating especially in case of teamwork, where students have to rely on the work of their peers who refuse to collaborate. *A solution would be to try to engage students more uniformly in blogging and learning activity in general, by increasing their accountability through multiple checkpoints during the semester.*

Voluntary vs. Compulsory Activity: The problem of irregular engagement can also be addressed by making the blogging activity compulsory to a certain extent and making it a part of the grading scheme. The experience from the Slovak university shows that the activity should be rewarded by a certain number of evaluation points, but these have to be carefully set. If the blogging activity is completely voluntary, only a small number of students will invest their time into it. On the other hand, if the share of grading points for the activity is perceived as too high by the students, some of them may feel that they are forced to do it; at the same time, some learners may feel they are not evaluated properly, since they regard the blogging activity as secondary to more traditional evaluation approaches. The experience from the Romanian university reinforces the conclusion that *the blogging task should be mandatory and explicitly graded; at the same time, ensuring also an intrinsic motivation is equally important* – this could be done by allowing students to take control over their own learning and by providing a meaningful and authentic task, highly relevant to the student [17].

Instructor's Feedback: Since students are often not experienced in educational blogging, an immediate feedback from the instructor helps them to identify and remove the flaws in their blog posts. It can also serve as support for students who experience difficulties with blogging (both technical and motivational) and boost their activity. According to the surveys, students reported that thanks to the instructor feedback they improved their blog contributions in subsequent rounds, they selected their topics better and they were more aware of copyright issues. *Overall, the recommendation for the instructor is to provide continuous technical support, clear guidelines for interaction as well as adequate feedback to the students.*

Peer-feedback: While blogging can be beneficial also as self-centered reflective activity, its effectiveness is further enhanced by engaging students with each other's postings, encouraging experience and opinion exchange. However, it may not always be easy to involve students in this activity: based on our experience at Comenius University, few students read and commented on peers' postings. We have successfully addressed this issue by *introducing peer reviews, defining a dedicated reading/reviewing period, and explicitly assigning students the postings they are supposed to read and review.* This lead to an enhanced participation in blog reading, better learning outcomes, and an improved perception on the meaningfulness of the reading/reviewing activity. On the other hand, observations from University of Craiova reveal that many students are interested to read other teams' blogs as well, in an attempt to search for information and solutions to problems encountered, but also out of curiosity and for checking out competition. *Therefore, instructors should encourage students to ask for peer help and to share their questions and obstacles encountered; the potential fear of exposure that students may feel when making their ideas public could be alleviated by ensuring a positive group climate and creating an atmosphere of trust and confidence* [15].

5 Conclusions

This paper provided an experience report on using blogging in educational settings, in the framework of multiple courses taught at two Eastern European universities. We introduced blogs as learning support tools a decade ago (the first course running in 2006), and we are still using them in the present, after several refinements of the learning scenarios. Overall, our experience as instructors has been generally positive; we believe the catalogue of blogging activities, the experimental findings and the practical guidelines drawn from our experience will prove useful to other educators who want to foster student learning through blogging.

As future work, we would like to perform a more detailed content analysis of students' blog contributions. Further comparisons with similar educational blogging experiences in other universities are also envisaged.

Acknowledgment. This work was supported from the Slovak national VEGA project no. 1/0948/13. The co-authors carried out part of this work thanks to an Erasmus+ teacher mobility in May 2015.

References

1. Arslan, R.S., Sahin-Kizil, A.: How can the use of blog software facilitate the writing process of English language learners? Comput. Assist. Lang. Learn. **23**(3), 183–197 (2010)
2. Bejdová, V., Homola, M., Kubincová, Z.: Blogging in obligatory course: a bitter victory. In: Popescu, E., Lau, R.W.H., Pata, K., Leung, H., Laanpere, M. (eds.) ICWL 2014. LNCS, vol. 8613, pp. 1–10. Springer, Heidelberg (2014)
3. Chong, E.K.: Using blogging to enhance the initiation of students into academic research. Comput. Educ. **55**(2), 798–807 (2010)
4. El Tantawi, M.M.A.: Evaluation of a blog used in a dental terminology course for first-year dental students. J. Dent. Educ. **72**(6), 725–735 (2008)
5. Felea, C., Stanca, L.: Wiki tools in teaching English for academic purposes - an analysis of student learning behaviour pattern. Proc. ELSE **2013**, 82–91 (2013)
6. Goodlad, S., Hirst, B.: Peer tutoring. Nicholas Publishing, A guide to learning by teaching. New York (1989)
7. Guy, R.: The use of social media for academic practice: a review of literature. Ky. J. High. Educ. Policy Pract. **1**(2) (2012). Article 7
8. Hew, K., Cheung, W.: Use of web 2.0 technologies in K-12 and higher education: the search for evidence-based practice. Educ. Res. Rev. **9**, 47–64 (2013)
9. Homola, M., Kubincová, Z.: Practising web design essentials by iterative blog development within a community portal. Proc. CSEDU **2009**, 181–186 (2009)
10. Kubincová, Z., Homola, M., Bejdová, V.: Motivational effect of peer review in blog-based activities. In: Wang, J.-F., Lau, R. (eds.) ICWL 2013. LNCS, vol. 8167, pp. 194–203. Springer, Heidelberg (2013)
11. Mosel, S.: Self directed learning with personal publishing and microcontent. In: Proceedings of Microlearning 2005 (2005)
12. Oravec, J.: Bookmarking the world: weblog applications in education. J. Adolesc. Adult Lit. **45**(7), 616–621 (2002)
13. Popescu, E.: Students' acceptance of web 2.0 technologies in higher education: findings from a survey in a Romanian university. In: Proceedings of DEXA 2010 Workshops, pp. 92–96 (2010)
14. Popescu, E.: Providing collaborative learning support with social media in an integrated environment. World Wide Web **17**(2), 199–212 (2014)
15. Popescu, E.: Investigating students' blogging activity in project-based learning settings. In: Proceedings of ICSLE 2015 (2015, in press)
16. Popescu, E., Buse, F.: Supporting students to find relevant learning resources through social bookmarking and recommendations. In: Proceedings of ICSTCC 2014, pp. 464–469 (2014)
17. Popescu, E., Maria, C., Udriştoiu, A.L.: Fostering collaborative learning with wikis: extending MediaWiki with educational features. In: Popescu, E., Lau, R.W.H., Pata, K., Leung, H., Laanpere, M. (eds.) ICWL 2014. LNCS, vol. 8613, pp. 22–31. Springer, Heidelberg (2014)
18. Top, E.: Blogging as a social medium in undergraduate courses: sense of community best predictor of perceived learning. Internet High. Educ. **15**, 24–28 (2012)
19. Wong, R.M.F., Hew, K.F.: The impact of blogging and scaffolding on primary school pupils' narrative writing: a case study. Int. J. Web-Based Learn. Teach. Technol. **5**(2), 1–17 (2010)
20. Yang, C., Chang, Y.: Assessing the effects of interactive blogging on student attitudes towards peer interaction, learning motivation, and academic achievements. J. Comput. Assist. Learn. **28**, 126–135 (2012)

Integrating Data Across Workplace Learning Applications with a Social Semantic Infrastructure

Adolfo Ruiz-Calleja[1(✉)], Sebastian Dennerlein[2], Vladimir Tomberg[1], Tobias Ley[1], Dieter Theiler[2], and Elisabeth Lex[2]

[1] Tallinn University, Narva Road 29, 10120 Tallinn, Estonia
{adolfo,vtomberg,tley}@tlu.ee
[2] Graz University of Technology, Inffeldgasse 13, 8010 Graz, Austria
{sdennerlein,dtheiler,elex}@know-center.at

Abstract. This paper presents our experiences using a social semantic infrastructure that implements a semantically-enriched Actor Artifact Network (AAN) to support informal learning at the workplace. Our previous research led us to define the Model of Scaling Informal Learning, to identify several common practices when learning happens at the workplace, and to propose a social semantic infrastructure able to support them. This paper shows this support by means of two illustrative examples where practitioners employed several applications integrated into the infrastructure. Thus, this paper clarifies how workplace learning processes can be supported with such infrastructure according to the aforementioned model. The initial analysis of these experiences gives promising results since it shows how the infrastructure mediates in the sharing of contextualized learning artifacts and how it builds up an AAN that makes explicit the relationships between actors and artifacts when learning at the workplace.

1 Introduction

Informal learning at the workplace is typically connected to current demands of the workers. The knowledge acquired while working is contextualized and it is typically highly dependent on the context where the learning episode happens [1]. These characteristics motivate the learning process and make the knowledge to be easily applicable. However, they hinder individual learning experiences to be further taken up in systematic organizational learning practices [2].

Supporting such unplannable learning processes with technology has proven to be a major challenge. Several authors have already proposed three main approaches to systematize these processes: the first one trusts on adaptive learning technologies to scale workplace learning by supporting the mentorship of an apprentice by a more knowledgeable peer [3]. Other approach uses social technologies to support communities of practice when sharing information and building collective knowledge [4]. Finally, other authors exploit semantic technologies to scale the processes of meaning generation at the workplace [5].

F.W.B. Li et al. (Eds.): ICWL 2015, LNCS 9412, pp. 208–217, 2015.
DOI: 10.1007/978-3-319-25515-6_19

The Learning Layers project[1] focuses on supporting these informal learning processes. This project proposed a conceptual model that integrates the three aforementioned perspectives in a coherent way [2], thus providing basis for the analysis of the domain and the development of applications to scale informal learning at the workplace. In order to support the processes defined in the model many different applications are used. Some of them are developed for a specific domain, such as surgical simulators. Others offer a functionality useful for learning in many domains, such as concept map tools. In addition, there are many other applications that were not specifically developed for educational purposes but have been successfully employed for learning, such as blogs.

The amount of applications employed for workplace learning and their unplannable use by the workers imply that bits and pieces of useful information are manipulated in different moments using different applications, being impossible to foresee when and how it will happen. This information sparsity problem hinders the scalability of the workplace learning since it makes difficult to share information between workers that use different applications but still belong to the same work group, organization or community of practice. For these reasons, the Learning Layers project also proposed an technical infrastructure called Social Semantic Server (SSS) where different applications have already been integrated [6]. Nonetheless, how to support theoretical-compliant learning processes at the workplace using the SSS is still an open question.

In order to illustrate the relationship between theory and workplace learning support, this paper describes two different experiences where the SSS was used in real scenarios in conjunction to four different applications integrated to it. With this aim we firstly present the Integrative Model of Scaling Informal Learning (Sect. 2) and the Social Semantic Infrastructure (Sect. 3). Then, we show in Sect. 4 two experiences where we integrated applications into our infrastructure and end users employed them for workplace learning. The main conclusions of the paper are summarized in Sect. 5.

2 A Conceptual Framework for Scaling Informal Learning at the Workplace

The need for a focus on theory as part of the learning analytics agenda was convincingly argued by [7]. For this purpose, the Integrative Model of Scaling Informal Learning was proposed [2] following a Design Based Research approach [8] and integrating different perspectives of how technology can enhance scaling informal learning settings at the workplace. This model defines the learning processes that occur at workplace and groups them in three perspectives: *task performance, reflection and sense making*, which describes the process of experiencing, reflecting, sharing the reflection and its collaborative validation; *help seeking, guidance and support*, which describes the process of seeking, finding and obtaining help from a collective knowledge; and *emerge and maturing of*

[1] http://learning-layers.eu.

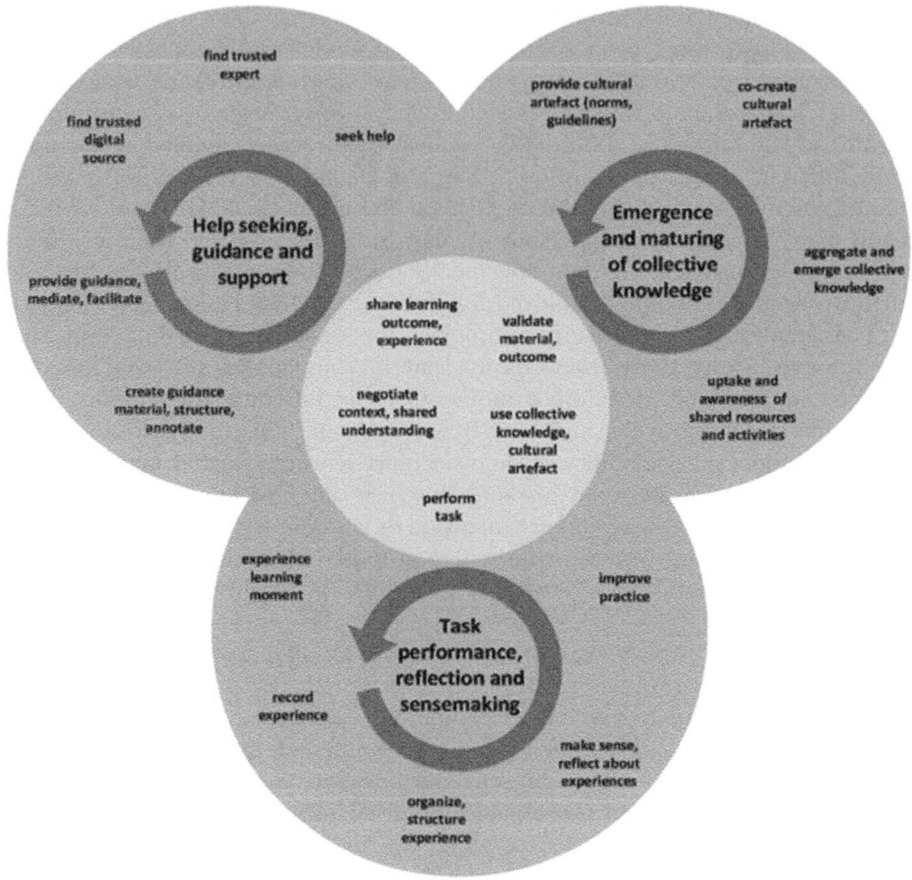

Fig. 1. Integrative model of scaling informal learning, taken from [2].

collective knowledge, which describes the process of how individual experiences, reflections and their related material can be shared to others. In addition the model includes some intersections between the three perspectives that are mediated by shared artifacts. For example, the artifacts that collect the knowledge emerged from a collaborative knowledge process represent sources that individuals trust when seeking for help. It is graphically represented in Fig. 1.

As a distinguishing characteristic, our model focuses on learning practices that go beyond those connected to task performance. In this sense, the model provides an integrated view on learning practices and their support enabling the use of different tools with respect to those practices. So the question arises, how some type of integrated support can be provided. In a first evaluation of the model we conducted in-depth empirical studies in two workplace learning domains: construction and healthcare. These included field observations, several tens of interviews with stakeholders, focus group discussions and panels of experts. All this data was triangulated and analyzed (see [2]) and it was reviewed to further understand learning processes at the workplace.

For example, in the construction domain we found examples of informal networks created with the purpose of discussing particular construction challenges (e.g. what type of concrete to use depending on characteristics of the ground). These challenges often resulted from particular problems and decisions made on the construction site, documented by photos, notes and drawings. Sharing these experiences in a wider network by means of social network technologies allowed the experiences to be discussed in a wider community.

In the healthcare domain, medical guidelines developed in the national health service needed to be implemented locally by a medical practice requiring them to develop an implementation plan that would also recognize local peculiarities (such as the ethnic composition of the local community) and existing experiences made in the practice. While working on this plan for the practice served a collective aim, individuals involved in this initiative would also be able to report these experiences in their revalidation process.

As these experiences show, scaling learning actually involves learning on several interacting levels of analysis (individuals, groups, collectives) and involves the use of a number of different applications and technologies, as well as data shared across these applications. In [6] we proposed a social semantic infrastructure that allows these different perspectives to be integrated by representing a common data layer across different applications. In this paper, we report our initial attempts to integrate four applications through this infrastructure, and hence support and scale informal learning.

3 A Social Semantic Infrastructure

The scenarios collected in our empirical studies show that apprentices and trainers interact with learning artifacts (e.g. text, images or videos) by creating, manipulating, accessing or aggregating them. These interactions occur in specific contexts, which should be taken into account since the relevant information and the way this information is accessed, highly depend on the learning context. Three kind of relationships between actors and artifacts can also be distinguished: actors may be related to artifacts (e.g. an apprentice creates video); actors can be related to other actors (e.g. several workers participated in the same discussion); and artifacts can be related to other artifacts (e.g. an artifact may aggregate some others).

In order to support and analyze the interactions between actors and artifacts we proposed a technical infrastructure called Social Semantic Server (SSS) [6] (see Fig. 2). The SSS relies on a semantically-enriched Artifact-Actor Network (AAN) [9] that combines the social-network (e.g. Facebook) and the artifact-network (e.g. Wikipedia) approaches to describe the relationships among actors and artifacts in different contexts [10]. Thus, it logs the interactions between actors and artifacts - including some meta-data that describes the context where the interactions take place - and then it offers an abstraction of this data as

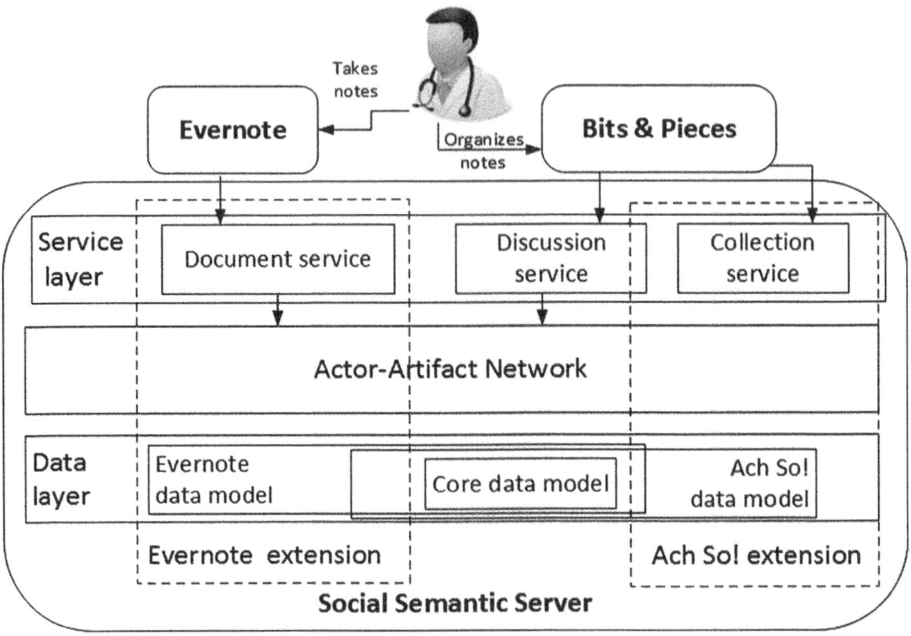

Fig. 2. Integration of evernote and bits & pieces into the SSS.

an AAN that makes explicit the different relationships between its entities. In addition, as the relationships of this AAN have a semantic meaning, they can be based on different characteristics of the entities that may depend on their associated context. For example, two artifacts may be related because they share the same author while other two may be related since they are frequently accessed from the same place (a contextual characteristic).

It is not possible to foresee all the possible applications that can potentially be integrated into this infrastructure. For this reason we developed the SSS as a framework that implements an AAN and a set of core services (such as activity tracking or users and artifacts recommendations) accessible through a REST interface [6]. These services can then be extended to satisfy the requirements of the applications integrated. Additionally, purpose-specific services can also be developed for some applications that require some extra functionality[2].

As Fig. 2 represents, several applications are expected to be integrated simultaneously into the social semantic infrastructure. They may use different services but they will share an AAN. However, it would still not be possible for these integrated application to share information unless they share a common vocabulary to describe the entities of the AAN and their relationships. For this reason the infrastructure includes a core data model (depicted with white background in Fig. 3) that defines a set of high-level concepts useful to describe learning

[2] https://github.com/learning-layers/SocialSemanticServer/releases.

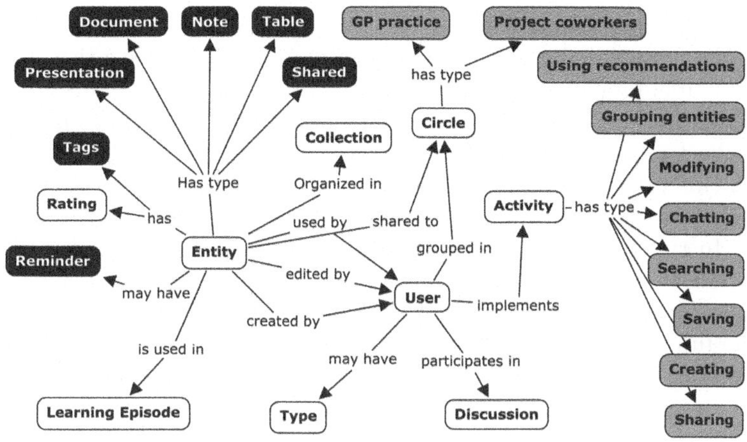

Fig. 3. Core data model of the SSS (white background) and its extensions by Bits & Pieces (grey background) and Evernote (black background) (Color figure online).

practices at the workplace. This core data model does not pretend to fully describe the entities involved in learning activities, but rather to provide some high-level entities and relationships that can then be extended by other applications and services if needed. Thus, the data integration from different applications is possible without heavy restrictions on their data model.

4 Exploiting the Social Semantic Server for Workplace Learning

Several applications are integrated into the SSS or developed on top of this infrastructure. This section describes the integration of two sets of applications into the SSS. One set is devoted to the construction domain, although it has only been tested in a different environment; the other focuses on the healthcare domain and a pilot study with practitioners has already been carried out.

4.1 Wordpress and Chrome for the Construction Domain

In the construction domain it is typical for trainers and managers to collect bookmarks that contain relevant information for their workplace. On the other hand, trainers often offer learning resources to apprentices using blog editors, such as Wordpress[3]. However, in most of the cases these two tasks are disconnected since they lack of a technical solution that makes available the bookmarks collected by trainers and managers when a trainer is writing a blog post. In order to overcome this problem, we proposed to integrate Chrome web browser[4] and WordPress into the SSS by developing both Attacher and Bookmarker [11].

[3] https://WordPress.org.
[4] http://www.google.com/chrome/.

Bookmarker is a simple Chrome extension that allows users to submit bookmarks to the SSS while browsing. Each bookmark may include a title and a set of tags to describe it. Attacher[5] is a WordPress plugin that integrates a blog editor to the SSS. Attacher displays a tagcloud in the blog publishing interface that includes the tags registered in the infrastructure. With this tagcloud the blog publisher can browse the artifacts published in the infrastructure, filter them by their authorship and easily cite them in the blog post using a drag-and-drop interface. In turn, Attacher automatically registers the published blog posts in the infrastructure, including some additional meta-data that contextualizes the publication (authorship, publication time and tags related).

As the functionality of Attacher and Bookmarker is so simple, there was no need to extend the services available on the SSS, nor its core data model. In this sense, they constitute a good example of how a well-known and massively used applications as WordPress and Chrome can easily be integrated into the SSS.

Attacher and Bookmarker have not been used by construction practitioners yet. Nonetheless, they were successfully employed in a master course for training future teachers at Tallinn University with one teacher and 10 students. During the course the students were asked to use Chrome and Bookmarker to collect web resources they considered relevant. Then, they wrote blog posts about their reflections of the subject using WordPress and Attacher.

The SSS registered the bookmarks gathered with Bookmarker, the tags employed by the users to describe and browse such bookmarks, the blog publications written with Attacher and their citations. The events from these two applications were coherently combined by the SSS to create a semantically-enriched AAN that included 11 actors, 53 resources and 116 tags. Analyzing this AAN it was possible to detect several uptake events. For example, most of the users browsed resources from Attacher using the tags created by other users from Bookmarker. There were also examples of users who tag new bookmarks reusing the tags from others, and even an event where a user cited in a blog post a bookmark collected by other.

4.2 Evernote and Bits and Pieces for the Healthcare Domain

Healthcare practitioners commonly collect information taking notes or creating other kind of resources, such as images. During this process they employed well-known applications, such as Evernote[6]. However, they claim that it is sometimes difficult for them to make sense of all the resources collected in a period of time. For this reason we proposed to integrate Evernote into the SSS and to develop a purpose-specific application, called Bits & Pieces[7] [12], on top of the SSS that support the meaning-making process in the healthcare domain. Figure 2 pictorially represents the integration of these two applications into the SSS.

Evernote was integrated into the SSS by developing a new service in the infrastructure that extracts the notes collected by Evernote in conjunction to

[5] https://github.com/learning-layers/Attacher/releases.

[6] https://evernote.com.

[7] https://github.com/learning-layers/BitsAndPieces.

some meta-data about their creation (e.g. authorship or time). This way, many different documents (e.g. images, notes or audio recordings) that are created and modified in Evernote, can be easily imported to the SSS. A different approach was taken to develop Bits & Pieces [12]. In this case, a new service was created and others were extended to satisfy the functional requirements of a collaborative sense-making application for the healthcare domain. Then, a HTML/JavaScript user interface was developed to allow practitioners sorting the information individually or in collaboration to other colleagues.

It is also relevant that the data model of the SSS required an extension to describe the entities managed by Bits & Pieces and Evernote. This extension is depicted in Fig. 3 by the entities with black (Evernote extension) and grey (Bits & Pieces extension) background. Evernote extension mainly required to add several entity types, while Bits & Pieces extension included different activities supported by Bits & Pieces and two domain-specific concepts. However, most of the concepts that describe entities, users and their relations could be directly reused from the core conceptualization of the SSS. In this sense, these two applications constitute an example of how domain-specific and domain-independent applications can be integrated even in the data level using the SSS.

We have conducted a field-testing of both applications with general practice doctors in UK. Eight health care professionals were included into two months trial usage of Evernote for collecting documents. Then, they used Bits & Pieces for individual and collaborative sensemaking. During this period users have collected summarily 563 Evernote documents. From this amount, the practitioners manipulated 98 with Bits & Pieces for sensemaking, sharing 25 of them for collaborative sensemaking with other colleagues.

4.3 Discussion

These pilot studies show how the SSS can be employed for the development of applications that support learning at the workplace and the analysis of the learning process. Attacher and Bookmarker exemplify how a simple plugin is able to relate two well-known applications to this infrastructure, Evernote exemplifies a more complex integration and, finally, Bits & Pieces shows how a domain- and purpose-specific application can make use of the SSS.

In both pilot studies the added value offered by the SSS is twofold. First, the SSS facilitates the contextualization of artifacts and their availability from the workplace, thus supporting the transitions between the perspectives defined in the Model of Informal Learning. In this sense, Attacher shows how the integration of WordPress into the SSS facilitates the access and citation of the learning resources registered on the SSS using other applications (*aggregate and emerge collective knowledge* in the Model of Informal Learning), as well as to register the blog post in such infrastructure (*provide cultural artifact*). Thus, it encourages the creation of documents that aggregate learning outcomes. The healthcare pilot study aims to support all the learning activities related to the perspective *task performance, reflection and sense making*. Note how Evernote can support some of the tasks related to this perspective (see Fig. 1) while the rest of them are supported by Bits & Pieces.

The second added value of the SSS is that it coherently combines data from multiple applications and creates a semantically-enriched AAN out of it. In the experiment that involved Attacher and Bookmarker the meta-data related to the artifacts was reduced to tags, but still an AAN that integrates tags, bookmarks and actors was defined. The semantic nature of the AAN allows to define different kind of relationships between the entities. For example, "published by" or "cited by" are two relationships that link actors and artifacts, while "assigned by" and "browse" are relationships that link actors to tags. Other implicit relationships can be easily extracted exploiting these semantic relationships. For example, it can be possible to define a social network that makes explicit which users browse the tags published by other users. These networks can be very useful to analyze the workers behavior using social network analysis techniques, thus making learning analytics at the workplace [11].

5 Conclusions and Future Work

This paper reports the integration of several applications into the SSS to support informal learning at the workplace. These applications were used, in conjunction to the SSS, in two pilot studies that show the technical viability of our approach and the advantages of using an infrastructure that manages a context-aware and semantically-enriched AAN.

It should be noted that the SSS support is key in the learning processes described. Not only does it allow the sharing of data and learning artifacts among applications, but it also enriches such data and artifacts by relating them to learning contexts, other artifacts and actors. Thus, the transitions between the perspectives defined in the Model of Informal Learning can be supported and overall learning-sense can be extracted out of all the data collected by the applications.

The research presented in this paper can be seen as an iteration in the research done under the Learning Layers project. In the future we will focus on exploring how the relationships registered in the AAN can be further exploited to understand the learning processes that occur at the workplace. Specifically, our plan is to exploit the data collected by the SSS to provide context-aware automatic recommendations of learning resources and to support learning analytics at the workplace [11].

Acknowledgements. This research has been partially funded by the FP7 ICT Workprogramme of the European Community: "Learning Layers - Scaling up Technologies for Informal Learning in SME Clusters" (http://www.learning-layers.eu/, grant no: 318209).

References

1. Eraut, M.: Informal learning in the workplace. Stud. Continuing Educ. **26**(2), 247–273 (2004)
2. Ley, T., Cook, J., Dennerlein, S., Kravcik, M., Kunzmann, C., Pata, K., Purma, J., Sandars, J., Santos, P., Schmidt, A., Al-Smadi, M., Trattner, C.: Scaling informal learning at the workplace: a model and four designs from a large-scale design-based research effort. Br. J. Educ. Technol. **45**(6), 1036–1048 (2014)
3. Lindstaedt, Stefanie, Kump, Barbara, Beham, Günter, Pammer, Viktoria, Ley, Tobias, Dotan, Amir, de Hoog, Robert: Providing varying degrees of guidance for work-integrated learning. In: Wolpers, Martin, Kirschner, Paul A., Scheffel, Maren, Lindstaedt, Stefanie, Dimitrova, Vania (eds.) EC-TEL 2010. LNCS, vol. 6383, pp. 213–228. Springer, Heidelberg (2010)
4. Schmidt, A., Hinkelmann, K., Ley, T., Lindstaedt, S., Maier, R., Riss, U.: Conceptual foundations for a service-oriented knowledge and learning architecture: Supporting content, process and ontology maturing. In Pellegrini, T., Auer, S., Tochtermann, K., Schaffert, S., eds.: Integrating Knowledge Management, New Media Technologies and Semantic Systems. Springer (2009) 79–94
5. Siadaty, M., Gasevic, D., Jovanovic, J., Pata, K., Milikic, N., Holocher-Ertl, T., Hatala, M.: Self-regulated Workplace Learning: A Pedagogical Framework and Semantic Web-based Environment. Educational Technology & Society **15**(4), 75–88 (2012)
6. Kowald, D., Dennerlein, S., Theiler, D., Walk, S., Trattner, C.: The social semantic server a framework to provide services on social semantic network data. In: Proceedings of the I-SEMANTICS 2013 Posters & Demonstrations Track co-located with 9th International Conference on Semantic Systems. Volume 1026, Graz, Austria, Citeseer (2013) 50–54
7. Shum, S.B., Ferguson, R.: Social Learning Analytics. Educational Technology & Society **15**(3), 3–26 (2012)
8. Plomp, T.: Education design research: An introduction. In: Plomp, T., Nieveen, N. (eds.) An Introduction to Educational Design Research, pp. 9–35. Netherland Institute for Curriculum Development, Enchende, The Netherlands (2009)
9. Reinhardt, W., Moi, M., Varlemann, T.: Artefact-Actor-Networks as tie between social networks and artefact networks. In: Proceedings of the 5th International Conference on Collaborative Computing: Networking, Applications and Worksharing, Washington, USA, IEEE (2009) 1–10
10. Dennerlein, S.: Understanding and Supporting Intersubjective Meaning Making in Socio-Technical Systems: A Cognitive Psychology Perspective. In: Proceedings of the Doctoral Consortium at the European Conference on Technology Enhanced Learning (EC-TEL), Paphos, Cyprus, CEUR (2013) 14–19
11. Ruiz-Calleja, A., Dennerlein, S., Tomberg, V., Pata, K., Ley, T., Theiler, D., Lex, E.: Supporting learning analytics for informal workplace learning with a social semantic infrastructure. In: Proceedings of the 10th European Conference on Technology Enhanced Learning (EC-TEL 2015), Toledo, Spain, Springer (2015) In press
12. Dennerlein, S., Rella, M., Tomberg, V., Theiler, D., Treasure-Jones, T., Kerr, M., Ley, T., Al-Smadi, M., Trattner, C.: Making sense of bits and pieces: A sensemaking tool for informal workplace learning. In: Proceedings of the 9th European Conference on Technology Enhanced Learning (EC-TEL 2014), Graz, Austria, Springer (2014) 391–397

Applying Speech-to-Text Recognition with Computer-Aided Translation to Facilitate a Web-Based Cross-Cultural Project

Rustam Shadiev[1(✉)], Yueh-Min Huang[1], Ting-Ting Wu[2], and Wu-Yuin Hwang[3]

[1] Department of Engineering Science, National Cheng Kung University, No. 1, University Road, Tainan City 70101, Taiwan
rustamsh@gmail.com, huang@mail.ncku.edu.tw

[2] Graduate School of Technological and Vocational Education, National Yunlin University of Science and Technology, Douliu City, Taiwan
danytingting@gmail.com

[3] Graduate Institute of Network Learning Technology, National Central University, Zhongli City, Taiwan
wyhwang@cc.ncu.edu.tw

Abstract. In this study, speech-to-text recognition with computer-aided translation were applied to a web-based educational project. With such approach, we aimed to enable participants from two different cultures who do not share common communication language to interact and share information with each other. Speech-to-text recognition system generated text from a speaker's voice input in one language and computer-aided translation system simultaneously translated it into another one. We aimed to test the feasibility of our approach to enhance students' cross-cultural learning. Results of our study demonstrated that applying speech-to-text recognition with computer-aided translation have a potential to enhance cross-cultural learning. Particularly, application of these technologies helps participants from two different cultures and without common language of communication to interact and to share culture-related information with each other.

Keywords: Speech-to-text recognition · Computer-aided translation · Educational project · Cross-cultural understanding

1 Introduction

Culture was defined as the history, customs, etc. of a particular society and it is formed over many years [1]. Understanding others' culture is very important in today's global society [2, 3]. It is therefore vital for educators to teach learners to understand and value others' culture. Furthermore, learners need to amass a certain level of global competence to understand the world they live in and how they fit in this world.

Cultural convergence theory explains cross-cultural understanding [4, 5]. According to this theory, cross-cultural understanding takes place through communication and information sharing of learners from different cultures when they reach a mutual understanding of each other culture. That is, experiences and insights of other cultures that

F.W.B. Li et al. (Eds.): ICWL 2015, LNCS 9412, pp. 218–227, 2015.
DOI: 10.1007/978-3-319-25515-6_20

learners communicate and share enables them to expand their cultural awareness and behaviors [4, 5].

In cross-cultural learning process, learners acquire knowledge and skills related to different cultures and they also absorb new attitudes and values as a result of the experience and participation [6]. Traditionally, cross-cultural education in school is based on textbooks and an instructor's knowledge and experiences. However, neither source can provide a thorough and authentic cross-cultural education [7]. Firstly, textbooks are often biased and mostly present the views of the dominant class. Secondly, teachers may be biased towards other cultures, or they may have only limited cross-cultural knowledge and experiences. Therefore, it is suggested that cross-cultural programs needs to be administered as united, connected events, and as a knowledge-building continuum [6, 7]. The following essential learning behaviors are underlined in the literature that lead to cross-cultural understanding [6]: (a) building relationships – interacting with members of the host culture regularly; (b) valuing people of different cultures – expressing interest and respect for the host culture; (c) listing and observing – spending time observing, reading about, and studying the host culture; (d) coping with ambiguity – understanding ambiguous situations and making sense of new experiences; (e) translating complex information – translating personal thoughts into the language of the host culture.

To facilitate these essential behaviors, various learning activities were proposed in the literature. *Self-introduction* is one activity that enables learners to become acquainted with one another and their cultures [8, 9]. This activity reinforces the comfort level in a classroom and encourages more social interactions among learners [10]. Self-introduction helps learners to identify and examine their own and peers' cultural values [11]. *Creating media content and sharing it with others* is another activity. It enables peer-to-peer learning, diversification of cultural expression, a more empowered cross-cultural understanding, and respect of multiple perspectives across diverse communities [12, 29]. In addition, learners are able to discern important concepts from shared content and then synthesize it with information from other sources during this activity [12]. *Performance and appropriation* activity enables learners to adopt alternative identities and sample and remix media content meaningfully for the purpose of improvisation and discovery [12]. Through performance and appropriation learners from various cultures can introduce their own culture, share their ideas, artifacts and perspectives about it, and experience peers' foreign culture [7]. Finally, *reflecting on foreign culture* activity enables learners to share their reflections and experiences with peers. This activity also allows learners to gain a better cross-cultural understanding and the strengths and weaknesses of cross-cultural project [9].

It is suggested to frame learning activities in a specific topic [30]. Therefore, cooking was selected as a topic for our project. Cooking is defined as the preparation of food for consumption [13] and associated with a specific culture, environment, and history. Therefore, it is distinctive in terms of ingredients, methods, and dishes [14]. Following this notion, "National Cuisine" term was proposed [15] which refers to food cultures that are practiced in terms of production and consumption in the specific ethnic communities and places. "Stinky tofu" is one distinct example of Chinese national cuisine. It is a kind of fermented tofu and it has a very strong unpleasant odor. Stinky tofu was a favorite food of Chinese in the period from the Wei Dynasty to the Qing Dynasty [16]. Despite an unpleasant smell, many develop an increased appetite for Stinky tofu and it is a popular local food in Taiwan and many regions of China nowadays [16].

We believe that learners from different countries may understand each other's cultures better if they perform learning behaviors discussed in [6] by participating in learning activities proposed in [7–12]. Furthermore, if learning activities are framed in a specific topic, such as "National Cuisine," we assume that learners will be more interested in cross-cultural learning and the topic will draw their attention, and stimulate their motivation [30].

However, how to ensure that learners from different cultures who speak different languages communicate and share culture-related information with each other is a question that concern most educators and researchers. One possible solution is an application of computer-assisted technologies. For example, Speech-to-text recognition (STR) technology synchronously transcribes text streams from speech input [17]. According to related studies, STR technology is a potential learning tool and it was successfully applied to many educational studies [18, 19, 31]. For example, this technology was used to assist learners with cognitive or physical disabilities and of those who attend speeches given in their non-native languages [20, 21]. Computer-aided translation (CAT) allows translating texts into different target languages [22]. Related studies suggest that CAT technology have a great potential to aid learning, especially in foreign language learning. For example, CAT was applied to assist learners to write texts in the target foreign language and correct grammatical and lexical errors in texts [23]. EFL learners had an online discussion for which they utilized CAT to translate and search for appropriate words to express their opinions and ideas and to check grammar and spell check [24]. Therefore, in this study we applied speech-to-text recognition with computer-aided translation to facilitate cross-cultural understanding of learners from two different cultures who do not share common communication language. Speech-to-text recognition system generated text from a speaker's voice input in one language and computer-aided translation system simultaneously translated it into another one. We aimed to explore how an application of these technologies to an educational project may facilitate learners' cross-cultural understanding.

2 Method

Ten students from the age of 14 to the age of 18 voluntarily participated in an online cross-cultural educational project. Six participants were Chinese native speakers from Taiwan and four participants were Russian native speakers from Uzbekistan. All participants had no experience with STR use but they had two to three-year experience with CAT. Besides, participants had more than 5 years' computer and Internet experience. According to participants, none of them had any prior knowledge about the food introduced by their foreign counterparts and related culture. In addition, the participants never participated in any cross-cultural projects.

Two experienced in online cross-cultural educational projects instructors, one Chinese native speaker and one Russian native speaker, guided participants during a project. At the beginning, participants were explained by the instructors all steps of a project and how to communicate information to foreign counterparts more efficiently in order to enhance foreign counterparts' cross-cultural understanding and to avoid any culture-related misunderstandings and miscommunications. In addition, the instructors trained participants how to use speech-to-text recognition and computer-aided translation. Participants then practiced to use speech-to-text recognition and computer-aided translation to generate texts in native language and then translate them into another language simultaneously. During a project, an instructor guided participants on using technologies and offered instant support for technology-related questions.

We aimed to enhance participants' cross-cultural understanding through participation in an online cross-cultural project. Our project was carried out in four weeks. In the first week, participants were asked to make self-introductions, explain where they are from, and their interests. Participants introduced their favorite local food and recipes in the second week. In the third week, participants cooked food according to recipes introduced by participants from other culture. Finally, in the fourth week, all participants shared their experiences related to cooking food and reflected upon learning related culture.

STR and CAT systems were introduced to participants to assist their participation in the project. We employed Android based Google voice recognition system as the STR tool and Google Translate system was employed as the CAT tool. Figure 1 shows communication flow among participants. Participants from Taiwan spoke into a microphone and STR system generated speech input into Chinese texts. Texts then were translated from Chinese into Russian. After that, translated texts in Russian were posted online so that participants from Uzbekistan could read them. Participants from Uzbekistan communicated in the same way; their speech in Russian was transcribed into texts and texts were translated into Chinese. Then texts in Chinese were posted online for participants from Taiwan to read.

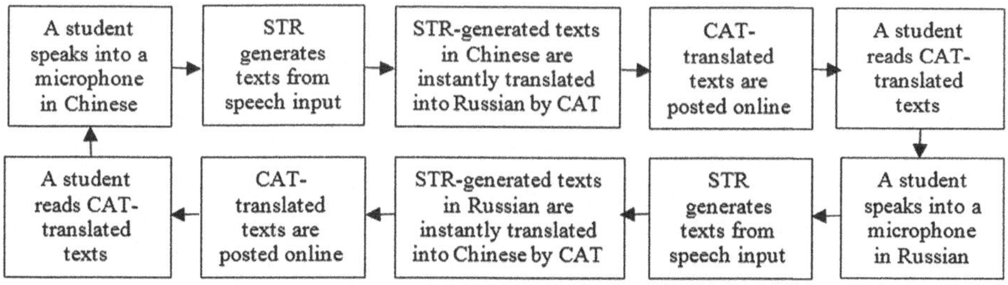

Fig. 1. Communication flow among participants

It is suggested that texts produced by STR and CAT systems may contain mistakes and ambiguities [17, 25, 31]. Therefore, two instructors corrected inaccuracies in texts that were produced either by STR or CAT and they prepared free of errors texts for participants.

The data for our analysis was collected from participants' online communication (i.e. their self-introductions, introductions of local food and recipes, experiences to cook food, and reflections upon learning related culture) and one-on-one semi-structured interviews. This data enabled us to explore and understand the process of cross-cultural educational project, to measure participants' cross-cultural understanding, and to learn about participants' opinions related to facilitating cross-cultural understanding with the project:

Understanding how the project was carried out. We adopted a concept as a coding unit. Text segments that met the criteria for providing the best research information were highlighted and coded. Codes were then sorted to form categories; codes with similar meanings were aggregated together. Established categories produced a framework for reporting research findings. Three raters were involved in the coding process, and big differences in the coding were resolved through raters' discussions and by consensus. Cohen's kappa was adopted to evaluate the inter-rater reliability; the result exceeded 0.90, which indicates high reliability.

Measuring cross-cultural understanding. We analyzed participants' reflections upon learning related culture. Particularly, we evaluated text segments extracted from their reflections that represented their cross-cultural understanding. The evaluation included three dimensions: (1) a foreign food, (2) related history, and (3) traditions. We carried out the evaluation by employing Anderson and Krathwohl's [26] taxonomy. Specifically, we employed the following two rubrics of the taxonomy for the evaluation: (1) Remember - retrieve relevant knowledge from long-term memory and (2) Understand - construct meaning from instructional messages, including oral, written, and graphic communication. A score of "1" was given if participants remember but do not understand how to cook a foreign food and related history and traditions whereas a score of "2" was given if participants both remember and understand how to cook a foreign food and related history and traditions. Participants got a score of "0" if they did not remember and understand either how to cook a foreign food and related to its history and traditions. Three raters were involved in the evaluation process. The inter-rater reliability coefficients among them were calculated using Cohen's kappa. The mean inter-rater reliability among the three raters exceeded 0.90, which demonstrates excellent agreement beyond chance.

Exploring participants' project-related opinions. At the end of the project we carried out in-depth, one-on-one semi-structured interviews with all students and the instructors. The interviews contained open-ended questions in which students and the instructors were asked about their experiences during the project and opinions about facilitating cross-cultural understanding with the project. Each interview took approximately 30 min. Interviews content was audio-recorded with participants' permission and then fully transcribed for analysis. Transcribed texts were coded and categorized to produce a framework for reporting research findings. Three raters were involved in the coding process, and big differences in the coding were resolved through raters' discussions and by consensus. Cohen's kappa was adopted to evaluate the inter-rater reliability; the result exceeded 0.90, which indicates high reliability.

3 Results and Discussion

The data analysis revealed that the project was implemented in four steps. In the first step, participants introduced themselves: participants mentioned were they are from, what they like to do, and what their favorite local food is. In the second step, participants introduced recipes of their local food. In addition, participants mentioned about history and traditions related to that food. In the third step, participants cooked food that was introduced by their foreign peers. In the fourth step, participants reflected on their experiences to cook and what they learned about related history and traditions.

According to participants, none of them had any prior knowledge regarding food they cooked during the project and history and traditions related to it. After the evaluation, we found that students could both remember and understand how to cook a foreign food and related history and traditions. According to Anderson and Krathwohl [26], *Remember* cognitive level represents the ability to retrieve relevant knowledge from long-term memory while *Understand* level represents the ability to grasp the meaning of the learning material. Our evaluation results shows that participants could recall, interpret, summarize, compare and explain what they cooked and related culture and traditions. This may suggest that cross-cultural learning took place through the project.

In the interviews, participants claimed that all steps of the project were useful for their cross-cultural understanding. For example, the self-introduction enabled them to become acquainted with each other. In addition, participants could learn about each other's interests, hobbies and favorite food and notice some cultural differences between themselves and other participants. When participants posted recipes of their local food or cooked food using recipes posted by peers they could learn more about both peers' and their own food and cultures. To better understand about peers' and their own food and cultures participants also searched for additional information from Internet. The reflection enabled participants to reflect on their experiences of cooking and related cultures. In addition, participants could compare their local food and related culture to that presented by peers and find some similarities and differences.

Interviews with the instructors' data analysis confirmed that participating in the project was beneficial for participants' cross-cultural understanding. According to the instructors, students provided as well as received useful information related to their own or peers' culture during the project. All presented information about food, history, and traditions was well understood by participants from both countries.

Self-introduction is a necessary activity for students to become acquainted with one another and their cultures [8, 9]. Through introductions, students identify and examine some of their own and peers' cultural values [11].

Students admitted that it was easier to communicate with peers with whom they have no common language and whom they had never met before using our approach. According to students, our approach could help them ease anxiety and inhibition, and it motivated disclose of personal information more frequently and more effectively if compared to face-to-face interaction.

In this study, speech-to-text recognition (STR) system generated texts from speech input and computer-aided translation (CAT) system translated texts into another language. Table 1 demonstrates accuracy rates of STR and CAT systems for texts generation and translation with respect to Chinese and Russian. According to the data, self-introduction texts were generated with 99 % accuracy rate when spoken in Chinese and with 100 % when spoken in Russian. Recipes of local food were generated with 91 % accuracy rate when spoken in Chinese and with 96 % accuracy rate when spoken in Russian. Spoken reflections in Chinese were generated with 94 % accuracy rate while in Russian with 98 % accuracy rate. One reason that explains the slight difference between accuracy rates of STR-texts from input in Chinese and Russian (especially 5 % in Step 2 and 4 % Step 3) is that Uzbek participants practiced with STR and CAT technologies more than Chinese students. It is suggested to design STR technology-based teaching and learning activities in such way that encourages users, i.e. instructors and students, to use it more regularly [18, 19]. With such approach, users are able to identify strengths and limitations of the STR through real experience. For example, after noticing that STR technology generates text with errors when speech is too fast or too slow, influent, and in a low voice, speakers try to adapt to the STR recognition capacity. That is, speakers start to speak with moderate speed and volume, less spontaneity, and better fluency.

Table 1. STR and CAT accuracy rate (in percentage)

Input	STR			CAT		
	Step 1	Step 2	Step 3	Step 1	Step 2	Step 3
Chinese	99	91	94	89	76	82
Russian	100	96	98	88	74	80

According to our results, in Step 2, STR technology generated texts from input in Chinese and Russian with lowest accuracy rate. One reason that explain this finding is that sentences used to introduce local food and related culture were longer compared to sentenced in which students introduced themselves (Step 1) or reflected on their experiences (Step 3). Another reason is that sentences in Step 2 contained some specific names of food ingredients or terminologies related to history and culture that STR technology could not recognize.

After STR-texts were ready, and before CAT process, we edited them to make 100 % accurate in order to increase CAT accuracy rate. That is, all errors in STR-texts were corrected and punctuation marks, such as commas and periods, were added. According to the table, self-introduction STR-generated texts were translated from Chinese into Russian with 89 % accuracy rate and from Russian into Chinese with 88 % accuracy rate. Recipes STR-generated texts were translated from Chinese into Russian with 76 % accuracy rate while recipes texts in Russian were translated into Chinese with 74 % accuracy rate. STR-generated texts of reflections were translated from Chinese into Russian with 82 % accuracy rate and from Russian into Chinese with 80 % accuracy rate.

The difference between CAT accuracy rate in Chinese and Russian was only 1–2 %. The lowest CAT accuracy rate occurred in Step 2 for both languages (74 and 76 %). Perhaps, the low CAT accuracy rate was due to the same reasons we mentioned earlier; the first reason is that sentences were longer and they contained some specific names of food ingredients and terminologies related to history and culture. According to researchers in the field [27, 28], current CAT technologies has not been able to deliver high-quality translations. It was further argued that CAT technologies produce better translations when confronted with short sentences compared to longer and more complicated ones because of highly limited linguistic context [28]. That is, the longer the sentence is, the more likely that the CAT technology will be led astray by the complexities in the source and target languages. Researchers [17–19, 21], argued that STR- or CAT-texts with only reasonable accuracy rate is acceptable and useful for students. That is, only texts with accuracy rate of 75–85 % or higher [21] can enhance teaching and learning. Following this suggestion, we may conclude that all STR- and CAT- texts in this study were acceptable and useful for our participants except recipes texts translated from Russian into Chinese (74 % accuracy rate). To address low accuracy rate of CAT-texts, several approaches are proposed in the literature. One of them is to correct errors in CAT-texts (e.g. correct misrecognized words, insert missed words, or delete superfluous wording) by the instructor or students [27, 28]. Therefore, we revised all CAT-texts into 100 % accurate texts so as to make them useful and meaningful for teaching and learning.

Based on our results, we would like to highlight the pedagogical usefulness of STR and CAT systems for cross-cultural learning. First, our approach can facilitate communication between participants with no common language. Participants do not need to rely on translators but communicate independently. Besides, there is no limit in information amount they communicate, i.e. it can be small or large. Second, through communication using our approach, participants learn and understand foreign culture in authentic context as they communicate with the host of that culture. Third, participants not only receive information about foreign culture from host but also are able to ask question they have, share opinion, ideas and reflections to better and deeper understand foreign culture. Fourth, such communication makes the instructors and participants less anxious because no foreign language skills are required during such projects. Therefore, our approach demonstrates significant value and importance of STR and CAT systems utilization in education, especially in cross-cultural learning. As our approach is convenient and independent, it holds great potential for solving problems teachers and students typically encounter when teaching and learning cross-cultural understanding through participating in educational project.

4 Conclusion

Results of this study show that applying speech-to-text recognition with computer-aided translation have a potential to enhance cross-cultural learning. Particularly, application of these technologies helps participants from two different cultures without common language of communication to interact and share information with each other.

Based on our results, we make several implications and suggestions. First we suggest that teachers and students utilize STR and CAT technologies for teaching and learning. Particularly, this approach can be useful for courses on cross-cultural understanding when communication between teachers and students with no common language is required. Teachers and students need to be careful about accuracy rate of texts produced by STR and CAT. To increase accuracy rate of such texts in order to make them acceptable and useful for learning we suggest that students practice with STR and CAT systems more frequently. In this case, they will find strength and limitations of the technologies and then fully utilize them. Making input sentences shorter is also helpful for accuracy rate; one needs to split a long sentence into two or more short sentences. In addition, we suggest training both technologies to easily recognize some specific words and terminologies that are frequently misrecognized. This can be done by adding these words into STR or CAT terminology bank so that they will be remembered and recognized correctly in the future. Finally, we suggest that STR- or CAT-texts need to be edited by teachers or students. That is, mistakes in texts should be corrected to make texts acceptable and useful for teaching and learning.

One limitation of our study needs to be acknowledged. We had a small size and a short period of time was allotted for the project. For these reasons, the obtained results cannot easily be generalized. In the future study, more students will be involved. We are particularly interested in a web-based project in which students from different classrooms around the world representing more than two cultures and languages are communicating and sharing information with one another, especially, in real-time. Furthermore, other methods for bridging cross-cultural differences or enabling cross-cultural understanding will be presented in the future in order to test the feasibility of our approach.

References

1. Merriam Webster. Merriam Webster Dictionary. http://www.merriam-webster.com/dictionary/culture (2015)
2. Bartell, M.: Internationalization of universities: a university culture-based framework. High. Educ. **45**(1), 43–70 (2003)
3. Bernáld, H., Cajander, Å., Daniels, M., Laxer, C.: Reasoning about the value of cultural awareness in international collaboration. J. Appl. Comput. Inf. Technol. **15**(1) (2011). http://www.citrenz.ac.nz/jacit/jacit1501/2011Bernald_CulturalAwareness.html (retrieved September 12, 2015)
4. Gudykunst, W.B., Ting-Toomey, S., Chua, E.: Culture and Interpersonal Communication. Sage Publications Inc., Thousand Oaks (1988)
5. Kincaid, D.L.: The Convergence Model of Communication. East-West Center (1979)
6. Yamazaki, Y., Kayes, D.C.: An experiential approach to cross-cultural learning: a review and integration of competencies for successful expatriate adaptation. Acad. Manage. Learn. Educ. **3**(4), 362–379 (2004)
7. Bloom, K., Johnston, K.M.: Digging into YouTube videos: using media literacy and participatory culture to promote cross-cultural understanding. J. Media Literacy Educ. **2**(2), 113–123 (2010)
8. Liu, Y.: Designing quality online education to promote cross-cultural understanding. In: Edmundson, A. (ed.), Globalized e-learning cultural challenges, pp. 35–59. IGI Global, Hershey, PA (2007). doi:10.4018/978-1-59904-301-2.ch003
9. Tu, C.H.: Online Collaborative Learning Communities: Twenty-One Designs to Building an Online Collaborative Learning Community. Greenwood, Westport, CT (2004)
10. Curtis, D.D., Lawson, M.J.: Exploring collaborative online learning. J. Asynchronous Learn. Netw. **5**(1), 21–34 (2001)
11. Chase, M., Macfadyen, L., Reeder, K., Roche, J.: Intercultural challenges in networked learning: hard technologies meet soft skills. First Monday **7**(8) (2002). http://firstmonday.org/ojs/index.php/fm
12. Jenkins, H., Purushotma, R., Weigel, M., Clinton, K., Robison, A.J.: Confronting the Challenges of Participatory Culture: Media Education for the 21st Century. MIT Press, Cambridge (2009)

13. Katz, H.S., Weaver, W.W.: Encyclopedia of Food Culture, vol. 1. Charles Scribners & Sons, New York (2003)
14. Cusack, I.: African cuisines: recipes for nationbuilding? J. Afr. Cult. Stud. **13**(2), 207–225 (2000)
15. Chuang, H.T.: The rise of culinary tourism and its transformation of food cultures: the national cuisine of Taiwan. Copenhagen J. Asian Stud. **27**(2), 84–108 (2009)
16. Liu, S.N., Han, Y., Zhou, Z.J.: Lactic acid bacteria in traditional fermented Chinese foods. Food Res. Int. **44**(3), 643–651 (2011)
17. Shadiev, R., Hwang, W.Y., Yeh, S.C., Yang, S.J.H., Wang, J.L., Lin, H., Hsu, G.L.: Effects of unidirectional vs. reciprocal teaching strategies on web-based computer programming learning. J. Educ. Comput. Res. **50**(1), 67–95 (2014)
18. Hwang, W.Y., Shadiev, R., Kuo, T.C.T., Chen, N.S.: A study of speech to text recognition and its effect to synchronous learning. J. Educ. Technol. Soc. **15**(1), 367–380 (2012)
19. Kuo, T.C.T., Shadiev, R., Hwang, W.Y., Chen, N.S.: Effects of applying STR for group learning activities on learning performance in a synchronous cyber classroom. Comput. Educ. **58**(1), 600–608 (2012)
20. Shadiev, R., Hwang, W.Y., Huang, Y.M., Liu, C.J.: Investigating applications of speech to text recognition for face to face seminar to assist learning of non-native English participants. Technol. Pedagogy Educ. (2015). doi:10.1080/1475939X.2014.988744
21. Wald, M., Bain, K.: Universal access to communication and learning: the role of automatic speech recognition. Int. J. Univers. Access Inf. Soc. **6**(4), 435–447 (2008)
22. Godwin-Jones, R.: Emerging technologies: mobile apps for language learning. Lang. Learn. Technol. **15**(2), 2–11 (2011)
23. Hermet, M., Désilets, A.: Using first and second language models to correct preposition errors in second language authoring. In: Proceedings of the Fourth Workshop on Innovative Use of NLP for Building Educational Applications, pp. 64–72. Association for Computational Linguistics, June 2009
24. Omar, H., Embi, M.A., Yunus, M.M.: ESL learners' interaction in an online discussion via Facebook. Asian Soc. Sci. **8**(11), 67–74 (2012)
25. ElShiekh, A.A.A.: Google translate service: transfer of meaning, distortion or simply a new creation? An investigation into the translation process & problems at google. Engl. Lang. Lit. Stud. **2**(1), 56–68 (2012)
26. Anderson, L.W., Krathwohl, D.R. (eds.): A Taxonomy for Learning, Teaching and Assessing: a Revision of Bloom's Taxonomy of Educational Objectives. Addison Wesley Longman, New York (2001)
27. Barrachina, S., Bender, O., Casacuberta, F., Civera, J., Cubel, E., Khadivi, S., Lagarda, A., Ney, H., Tomás, J., Vidal, E., Vilar, J.M.: Statistical approaches to computer-assisted translation. Comput. Linguist. **35**(1), 3–28 (2009)
28. Mellebeek, B., Khasin, A., Owczarzak, K., Van Genabith, J., Way, A.: Improving online machine translation systems. In: Proceedings of the X MT Summit, pp. 290–297, Phuket, Thailand (2005)
29. Huang, Y.M., Chen, M.Y., Mo, S.S.: How do we inspire people to contact aboriginal culture with Web2.0 technology? Comput. Educ. **86**, 71–83 (2015)
30. Shadiev, R., Hwang, W.Y., Huang, Y.M.: A pilot study of facilitating cross-cultural understanding with project-based collaborative learning activity in online environment. Australas. J. Educ. Technol. **31**(2), 123–139 (2015)
31. Shadiev, R., Hwang, W.Y., Chen, N.S., Huang, Y.M.: Review of speech-to-text recognition technology for enhancing learning. J. Educ. Technol. Soc. **17**(4), 65–84 (2014)

Short Papers

Investigating Students' Use of Lecture Videos in Online Courses: A Case Study for Understanding Learning Behaviors via Data Mining

Ying-Ying Kuo[1(✉)], Juan Luo[1], and Jennifer Brielmaier[2]

[1] Information Technology Services, George Mason University, Fairfax, VA 22030, USA
{ykuo3,jluo2}@gmu.edu

[2] Department of Psychology, George Mason University, Fairfax, VA 22030, USA
jbrielma@gmu.edu

Abstract. This study investigated students' learning behaviors in a fully online psychology course which offered 76 streaming lecture videos and supplementary resources, as well as individual and group activities. This paper focuses on students' use of lecture videos. Data collection included students' real usage of data on Blackboard Learn 9.1, a course survey, and students' final grades. The analysis applied data mining techniques, including sequential patterns, decision trees, and clustering analysis, as well as inferential statistics using ANOVA and correlations. Based on students' use of lecture videos, their learning behaviors were defined into three groups—adaptive viewer, self-regulating viewer, and infrequent viewer. Statistically significant differences within groups were found in their learning satisfaction, final grades, etc. This case study has shown that students' learning behaviors were varied in the online environment and that their use of course videos affected their learning outcomes.

Keywords: Educational data mining · Instructional design · LMS · Streaming lecture videos · Pattern recognition · K-means clustering · Self-regulation

1 Introduction

Streaming videos have become a prominent feature for online learning, particularly since 2007 [1]. Educators provide videos to promote interactive learning environments, allow students to control their learning activities, and increase engagement in asynchronous online environments [2, 3]. Though the use of lecture videos in online environments is on the rise, their impact on students' learning outcomes is still inconclusive [2–4]. One issue is a lack of consistent objective evidence given that most educational research studies rely heavily on survey studies [4, 5]. Survey studies are usually subjective and may be biased due to the survey design, sample size, or the quality of the answers [6]. Black, et al. advocate using the data derived from students' learning activities, e.g. those stored in learning management systems (LMSs) in data mining [7]. Educational data mining (EDM) is a relatively new approach based on students' real usage of content data that can objectively reflect students' learning strategies and preferences. Learning

F.W.B. Li et al. (Eds.): ICWL 2015, LNCS 9412, pp. 231–237, 2015.
DOI: 10.1007/978-3-319-25515-6_21

analytics give researchers a better understanding of students' learning habits, behaviors, and patterns given the large volume of usage data that can be generated from the online environment [8, 9].

1.1 Contemporary Issues of Students' Video Use in Online Learning

Many empirical studies about video uses in online education applied learning analytics (e.g. counting clicks, numbers of discussion posts and visits, etc. [3, 8]), whereas most studies that examined how students use lecture videos have relied on survey instruments [2, 4, 5]. Some studies of video use have employed EDM but still rely on the analytics data provided by commercial sites such as Google Analytics or YouTube Analytics [3]. As a result, the association between students' video use and their learning outcomes is inconclusive [3–5].

Data mining is a computational process used to detect patterns or relationships among variables from a large amount of data [10]. Typical tasks of data mining, including classifications, clustering, associations, prediction, and anomaly detection, have been applied in different areas such as economics, finance, health, image processing, and education [11]. Most LMSs, such as Blackboard, Canvas, or Moodle, track all students' learning records— every single click by each student will generate a record as a line of text in the web server. Even though real usage data is saved in structured database tables, retrieving meaningful information directly from those tables is not straight forward. Educators are not able to obtain meaningful learning analytics if the data is not cleaned and recoded in pre-processing stage as well as transformed based on pedagogical context.

1.2 Purpose of Study

This study investigated students' learning in a fully online course where students could apply their own study strategies to view streaming videos, access any content pages, and complete required assignments and tasks. The course was taught in the fall semester of 2014 in the eastern region of the United States. Due to space limitations this paper reports students' behaviors pertaining to the use of streaming lecture videos. Research questions included, but were not limited to:

1. How did students use lecture videos? Did students display individual differences in their study strategies and learning behaviors?
2. How were students' learning outcomes (e.g. satisfaction and final grades) associated with their use of lecture videos and/or other content materials?

2 Design and Methods

2.1 Course Design

The fully online physiological psychology course is primarily lecture-based and includes weekly individual assignments, group activities, and quizzes. Grading is based on 15 quizzes (15 %), 21 group activities and individual assignments (35 %), a paper (10 %), and two exams (40 %). The entire course is comprised of 7 units in 16 lessons and was released to students at the beginning of the semester. The course design had learner-control features and non-linear navigation. A total of 76 streaming lecture videos were offered and students had full control over how they viewed the video lectures. Students needed to complete required tasks (e.g. assignments, quizzes, and exams) by the due dates in order to receive their grades.

2.2 Data Collection

Data collection included an online course evaluation survey before the final exam, students' actual usage of the course content materials and activities, and students' final grades. Students' real usage of content on the Blackboard course site was extracted from the Advanced System Reporting (ASR) of the backend Blackboard production database in Oracle. The ASR is the statistical database into which a subset of the tables of the production database is transferred every evening. Students' usage information, extracted from the backend database of Blackboard, had entire records of user interaction with the system. The main table of ASR records the end users' activities/events in the Blackboard Learn system.

2.3 Coding and Classification Process

Each record had unique information about a user who worked on a specific task at a specific time, which mainly consists of fields (columns) of USER_ID, TIMESTAMP, SESSION_ID, and TASK TITLE. A unique SESSION_ID occurred on ASR whenever an end user logged onto the course page and a TIMESTAMP was recorded. The session stays active until the user logs out, the session times out, or the user closes the browser windows. So, a session might contain multiple records that depend on students' study activities. The TASK TITLE is the name of the content page, such as Schedule, Unit, Chapter, or Lecture video, which was defined by the course designer. Note that a study time referred from TIMESTAMP from Blackboard database table could be under-estimated, be over-estimated or be counted as missing. TIMESTAMP data could be missing or over-estimated if students just closed the browser window (instead of logging out) or left the window open until the session was expired (with the default expiration time of 3 h). Blackboard database table did not track the click on a URL embedded on a content web page; consequently, the records could be messed up when a user opens multiple screens on a browser and study time can be under-estimated on TIMESTAMP.

The initial data cleaning included (1) excluding any non-learning related record, e.g. orientation and (2) removing redundant usage information. For example, only one click was recorded and repeatedly clicks on the same pages were removed. Then, the assigned course activity was recorded with keywords. Also, the course design made only one video link available on a video page, and because of this, it was assumed that students would click the video link on the page and watch videos if they stayed on the video page longer than 2 s. Therefore, any visits of video pages less than 2 s were not counted as video views.

A more advanced coding task using data-mining techniques was applied to customize the data in order to disclose the hidden relationship among the records. A sequence pattern was applied to find students' preferred path of access content; decision trees supported the students' video viewing behaviors, and clustering technique was used to identify new categories of study behaviors.

Sequence pattern: the sequence of accessing a content page indicated different study behaviors. Students could access a specific content page via the SCHEDULE page, a UNIT page, or ASSIGNMENTS/GROUP pages, and so on.

Decision trees: a label was assigned based on students' actual access of a lecture video compared to its scheduled date. A decision tree was illustrated to identify students' use of the video in four types:

<u>ON TIME</u>: a lecture video was first visited on the scheduled period (week)
<u>EARLY</u>: a lecture video was first visited earlier than the scheduled period (week)
<u>LATE</u>: a lecture video was first visited later than the scheduled period (week)
<u>REVIEW</u>: a lecture video was visited again after the scheduled period (week)

Clustering analysis: Students' video viewing behavior was identified with clustering technique. Students were grouped based on when the type of viewing videos (on time, early, late, or review).

2.4 Variables

Variables were defined below, based on students' usage records, learning satisfaction from the course survey and their final grades. Descriptive and inferential methods of analysis were employed, including ANOVA and correlations, in hypothesis testing with the alpha level set to 0.05.

USER_ID: a unique identifier of a student's usage record on the Blackboard server
SESSION_ID: The unique number assigned when a student accessed the course site
VIDEO_HITS: The total number of hits on a lecture video per student per session
VIDEO_ACCESS: The type of access video (early, on time, late, review)
DATE: The date of accessing a lecture video
SATISFACTION: Students' self-evaluation of their satisfaction level on a 6-point scale, with 1 (Strongly Dissatisfied) to 6 (Strongly Satisfied)
GRADE: Students' final grade score ranged from 1 to 100
GROUP: Students' behaviors of video use were grouped, a result of K-Means clustering analysis with SPSS 22.2 version.

3 Results and Discussions

A total of 20 students (87 % response rate) voluntarily participated in this research study in Fall 2014. The majority of participants were female (19) and one student was male. Four were juniors (20 %) and 16 were seniors (80 %). Only three were new to online learning, while 17 (70 %) students had taken at least one online course before. Students' usage of content materials was collected from August 20 to December 17, 2014. In total, 30,236 records were extracted from the ARS. After the cleaning and pre-processing steps, 2016 unique sessions associated with 20 subjects' learning activities were retrieved. Within them 1488 video access counts were identified.

All 76 lecture videos were accessed, ranging from 8 to 62 hits. Participants who accessed the lecture videos varied, ranging from 2 to 199 (hits) which indicated that some students did not use most of the lecture videos. Participants reported that they were quite satisfied with their learning ($m = 5.2$), based on their answer on the course survey. No one dropped out of the course, and their final letter grades included 7 A's, 7 B's, 5 C's, and 1 D. With the Pearson correlation analysis, students' video access were statistically significantly related (SSR) to their satisfaction level ($r = .70, p = .001$), final grades ($r = .72, p < .001$), and total session numbers ($r = .70, p = .001$).

3.1 Students' Learning Behaviors

This study was interested in students' learning behaviors in a course that offered a supportive learning environment with streaming lecture videos, assignments, and activities. The first research question explored how students learned in this online course when they had control of their study schedule and access to content materials. Learning analytics revealed three types of video viewers based on whether they watched videos on time, early, or late, or for reviewing purposes.

Adaptive Viewers: Two participants (10 %) did not stick to the course schedule to watch videos. They actively used videos when they needed.

Self-regulating Viewers: 11 participants (55 %) followed the course schedule to watch most lecture videos.

Infrequent Viewers: Seven participants (35 %) rarely watched lecture videos over the course of the entire semester.

Table 1 explains how participants used lecture videos and accessed videos (in hits). Results indicated that not all students took advantage of streaming lecture videos to support their learning. Thirty-five percent of students seldom used lecture videos and most students did not make up a missed viewing. The late views were only 28 video hits; apparently, if participants did not watch a lecture video in the assigned week, they seldom made it up as a late viewer.

Table 1. Descriptive statistics on the numbers of video views in three groups

Viewers	n	ON TIME (Hits)	EARLY (Hits)	LATE (Hits)	REVIEW (Hits)	Video access (Hits)
		Mean (SD)	*Mean (SD)*	*Mean (SD)*	*Mean (SD)*	*Mean (SD)*
Adaptive	2	64.5 (23.3)	66.0 (19.8)	- -	22.0 (31.1)	152.5 (74.2)
Self-regulating	11	82.9 (22.9)	6.1 (8.8)	2.3 (1.6)	9.1 (10.3)	101.3 (17.7)
Infrequent	7	8.0 (4.9)	1.1 (1.7)	0.6 (0.6)	0.1 (0.4)	9.9 (5.4)

3.2 Comparisons of Learning Outcomes in Three Groups of Video Viewers

Another research question was concerned with how students' learning outcomes (e.g. satisfaction and final grades) were associated with their video usage. A one-way ANOVA revealed statistically significant differences (SSD) between the three groups of video viewers for satisfaction level, final grades, and the total session numbers, as shown in Table 2. Post Hoc analyses using Fisher's Least Significant Difference (LSD) test revealed that Infrequent Viewers were significantly lower on all three measures as compared to Self-regulating Viewers and Adaptive Viewers.

Table 2. The ANOVA of students' learning satisfaction, final grades, total sessions, and lecture videos

Viewers	n	Satisfaction**	Final grades **	Total * sessions	Lecture handouts (Hits)	Quizzes taken (Counts)	Exercises completed (Counts)
		Mean (SD)	*Mean (SD)*	*Mean (SD)*			
Adaptive	2	5.5 (.71)	95.1 (7.4)	130.5 (29.0)	16–123	15	21
Self-regulating	11	5.6 (.51)	89.6 (6.9)	109.7 (29.3)	57–229	14–15	16–21
Infrequent	7	4.4 (.79)	77.0 (8.9)	78.4 (14.0)	81–243	11–15	12–21

**: $p < .01$ *: $p < .05$

Among the three groups Infrequent Viewers displayed the greatest diversity in their learning behaviors. For example, one Infrequent Viewer took all 15 quizzes but skipped a few graded exercises (assignments and group activities). One completed all 21 graded exercises, but did not take all quizzes. A few of Infrequent Viewers did not complete all quizzes or graded exercises. They used the lecture handouts quite a lot, but there was no SSD found in using lecture handouts among three groups. Overall, Infrequent Viewers' learning satisfaction level was still relatively high with an average of 4.43. Within them there was 1 A and 1 B final grade.

3.3 Limitation: Visit Hits Versus Time Spent on a Video

Video access was defined by the numbers rather than time spent on a video in this study. Two reasons supported researchers' decision. First, the Blackboard database table did not save time data whenever users clicked on a URL and subsequently went to a new browser window. Thus, TIMESTAMP could not reflect a student's actual time spent. Second, the course design allowed students to decide when and how they used the content. Students could choose to watch a video completely or only watch part of a video by clicking on the "slides" in the table of contents (TOC) of the video. Each click indicated their intention to watch a video. Using the number of visits (hits) for a video overcomes a limitation of data collection on Blackboard Learn.

3.4 Conclusion and Future Work

In contrast to other studies, this study did not merely focus on login counts or time-spent; instead it evaluated students' self-directed use of course videos. By combining EDM and survey data, this study has provided a clear picture of students' study strategies and learning behaviors in an online environment. Results suggest that if a course design provides students with the ability to control their learning activities, individual differences in learning behaviors can be observed. Researchers interpreted students' behaviors based on their frequency of accessing videos instead of the time spent viewing videos; as a result, three types of learning behaviors were identified: Adaptive, Self-Regulating, and Infrequent viewers. Analyses indicated that the use of streaming lecture videos had an impact on students' learning performance and final grades. Students who accessed the lecture videos more frequently had a higher level of learning satisfaction and better grades as compared to those who did not.

Future work is planned to increase the sample size of participants as well as extend this study to other disciplines in online education. Increasing sample size can validate the learning analytics approach that was used in this study. Collecting data from courses in different disciplines help guide the creation of a general model of course design that can further elucidate students' learning behaviors in online environments.

References

1. Giannakos, M.N.: Exploring the video-based learning research: a review of the literature. Br. J. Educ. Technol. **44**(6), E191–E195 (2013)
2. Choi, H.J., Johnson, S.D.: The effect of context-based video instruction on learning and motivation in online courses. Am. J. Distance Educ. **19**(4), 215–227 (2005)
3. Draus, P.J., Curran, M.J., Trempus, M.S.: The Influence of instructor-generated video content on student satisfaction with and engagement in asynchronous online classes. J. Online Learn. Teach. **10**(2), 240–254 (2014)
4. Tantrarungroj, P., Lai, F.-Q.: Effect of embedded streaming video strategy in an online learning environment on the learning of neuroscience. Int. J. Learn. **17**(11), 17–27 (2011)
5. Evans, H.K.: An experimental investigation of videotaped lectures in online courses. TechTrends **58**(3), 63–70 (2014)
6. Gonyea, R.M.: Self-reported data in institutional research: review and recommendations. New Dir. Inst. Res. **2005**(127), 73–89 (2005)
7. Black, E.W., Dawson, K., Priem, J.: Data for free: using LMS activity logs to measure community in online courses. Internet High. Educ. **11**(2), 65–70 (2008)
8. Abdous, M., He, W.: Using text mining to uncover students' technology-related problems in live video streaming. Br. J. Educ. Technol. **42**(1), 40–49 (2011)
9. Ullrich, C., Shen, R., Xie, W.: Analyzing student viewing patterns in lecture videos. In: 2013 IEEE 13th International Conference on Advanced Learning Technologies (ICALT), pp. 115–117. IEEE (2013)
10. Luo, J.: Regression Learning in Decision Guidance Systems: Models, Languages, and Algorithms. Ph.D. Dissertation. George Mason University, Fairfax, VA, USA (2012)
11. Shen, J., Su, P.-C., Cheung, S.C.S.: Virtual mirror rendering with stationary RGB-D cameras and stored 3D background. IEEE Trans. Image Process. **22**(9), 1–16 (2013)

STEM Teachers' Community Building Through a Social Tutoring Platform

Yiwei Cao[1(✉)], Eleftheria Tsourlidaki[2], Rob Edlin-White[3], Diana Dikke[1], Nils Faltin[1], Sofoklis Sotiriou[2], and Denis Gillet[4]

[1] Information Multimedia Communication AG, Saarbrücken, Germany
{Yiwei.Cao,Diana.Dikke,Nils.Faltin}@im-c.de
[2] Ellinogermaniki Agogi, Pallini, Greece
{eleftheria,sotiriou}@ea.gr
[3] University of Leicester, Leicester, UK
rew25@leicester.ac.uk
[4] École Polytechnique Fédérale de Lausanne, Lausanne, Switzerland
denis.gillet@epfl.ch

Abstract. Teachers' knowledge and skills have a great impact on students' learning outcomes. Teachers' vocational training has been a research topic in technology-enhanced learning for years. The Go-Lab project aims to engage school students with STEM topics by bringing online laboratory experiments based on inquiry learning approach into the classroom. In Go-Lab, teachers' knowledge and skills in inquiry learning with online labs are important. Thus, we have launched the Go-Lab Tutoring Platform, a social tutoring platform for teachers' expertise sharing and community building through virtual tutoring sessions. In this paper, we present the first rollout results of the tutoring platform based on five teachers' training events. We explore the practical activities for efficient knowledge sharing between teachers and pedagogical experts, in order to build up teachers' community.

Keywords: Tutoring platform · Lifelong learning · Professional training · Community building · Web-based learning · STEM study · Technology-enhanced learning

1 Introduction

Professional skills and competence development are connected to collaborative activities in a community. A good community of practice is vital for individual's skill and competence acquisition [7]. In schools, students acquire knowledge and develop skills in learning groups. Meantime, school teachers exchange and share teaching experiences in order to improve their teaching skills. Teachers' communities are built up through project collaboration work or training, in which the teachers share their knowledge and skills.

F.W.B. Li et al. (Eds.): ICWL 2015, LNCS 9412, pp. 238–244, 2015.
DOI: 10.1007/978-3-319-25515-6_22

This requirement of community building is also demanded in the research project Go-Lab (Global online science labs for inquiry learning at school)[1] within the European FP7 program. The Go-Lab Portal[2] has been developed to host online labs and inquiry learning spaces for school teachers who teach science, technology, engineering, and mathematics (STEM) [3, 4]. The teachers select appropriate online labs and learning applications and prepare inquiry learning spaces (ILS)[3] for school students between 10 and 18 years old. Thus, teachers' skills and knowledge in STEM as well as inquiry-based teaching techniques have an impact on school students' STEM learning using online labs. Previous research shows the lack of school teachers' ICT skills [1, 6]. Professional development measures need to be taken to improve these skills.

Beyond the Go-Lab Portal, pilot schools are selected and assisted in realizing inquiry-based activities, in order to support teachers' professional skills acquisition. Many teachers' contests and online events are organised together with some offline activities, such as Go-Lab summer schools and workshops. However, it is hard to build the Go-Lab teachers' community only through the on-site workshops. Teachers need a channel to talk with Go-Lab experts and with each other.

The paper presents the Go-Lab Tutoring Platform prototype with the organized five tutoring sessions for teachers to support teachers' professional training and their community building. The use of the tutoring platform is ongoing and further sessions and surveys will be conducted in future. This paper presents very promising results from the early sessions.

2 The Go-Lab Tutoring Platform

The Go-Lab Tutoring Platform aims to support teachers' professional training, as one of the main hubs of communication in the Go-Lab community. More conceptual and technical details can be found in [2, 5]. The users (who can be Go-Lab experts, school teachers, and other interested parties) create user profiles to describe their expertise and their skills. The users offer online training events to each other. In this case, the user organizing a training session becomes a tutor. This way, teachers obtain expertise from the experts and from each other. Tutors' reputation can evolve based on social ranking and commenting by other users. The ranking of the tutors may influence teachers' decision about selecting particular tutor's help. For example, tutor's help session will not be booked by teachers if the tutor receives poor ratings. All webinars and tutoring sessions employ Google Hangouts[4], which is used instead of developing a video-chat tool from scratch. Successively all functionalities of Google Hangouts are in use, including Questions & Answers and a chat room (cf. Fig. 1).

---

[1] The project homepage: http://www.go-lab-project.eu.

[2] The Go-Lab Portal: http://www.golabz.eu.

[3] Inquiry learning spaces (ILS) are learning environments that can contain labs, learning resources and apps to enable inquiry-based learning.

[4] Google Hangouts: http://www.google.com/+/learnmore/hangouts/.

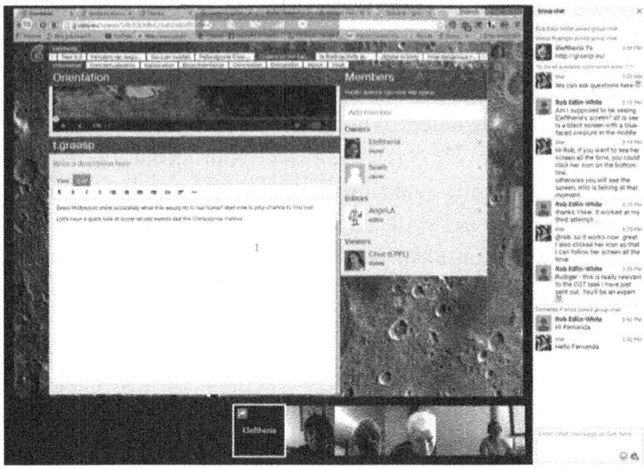

Fig. 1. A tutoring session (Google Hangouts)

The platform is self-organized. Each user in the Go-Lab Tutoring Platform (e.g. an experienced teacher) is encouraged to offer a tutoring session to teachers. We avoid using pre-defined roles to differentiate a teacher from a tutor in the platform.

3 Tutoring Sessions for STEM Teachers' Community

The Go-Lab project offers a set of services to support the Go-Lab pilot teachers and build the Go-Lab teachers' community around them. Aside from supporting the Go-Lab pilot teachers, the community tools aim to foster interaction between teachers and encourage them to exchange ideas and share their experiences. Meanwhile, the communication between teachers, Go-Lab experts, and online lab owners is also encouraged. To further support these interactions, Go-Lab experts, lab owners and teachers are all invited to participate in the social tutoring platform by offering and taking part in the tutoring sessions.

The first four tutoring sessions were offered solely by the Go-Lab experts on the tutoring platform, in order to tackle specific needs of the teachers like creating ILS and publishing them in Go-Lab Inquiry Learning Platform. The first two sessions were organized in the framework of the Go-Lab 2015 contest[5]. They aimed to demonstrate the Go-Lab Portal (Go-Lab Repository and Go-Lab Inquiry Learning Platform) to the contest participants. The sessions helped the participating teachers prepare their submission entries for the contest.

The first tutoring session (Feb. 13th) targeted at teachers who had also attended the 2014 Go-Lab summer school. New features of the Go-Lab Portal were demonstrated, e.g. how to publish ILS which the teachers had prepared during the summer school.

---

[5] Information about the contest: http://www.go-lab-project.eu/teacher-contest.

The second tutoring session (Feb. 26) was the first webinar for Go-Lab contest participants, a recorded session through Google Hangouts on Air[6]. The Go-Lab experts demonstrated to the participants how to publish their work in the Go-Lab Portal. Teachers asked about Java-enabled labs, how to use the inquiry space authoring platform, reuse resources in Moodle etc. The questions were well clarified in the session. Moreover, the teachers did not check the tutorials available in the Go-Lab Portal, but they chose to directly ask the tutors for support. After this session, participants sent fewer e-mails to ask for help on publishing their ILS.

The third session (Apr. 13th) was organized in response to contest participants' e-mails requesting help in publishing their inquiry spaces. This session aimed to help the developers figure out the real problems the teachers have encountered during their ILS publishing process. Two technical experts took the tutor role: one for the Go-Lab Repository, the other for the Go-Lab Inquiry Learning Platform. Five participants joined in, while two of them addressed their questions very frequently during the session. This session managed to solve some technical problems related to the portal for the participants.

The fourth session (Apr. 15th) entitled "How to use Golabz Tutoring" was offered by the tutoring platform technical experts to help participants use the tutoring platform itself. The participants have addressed questions about the Go-Lab Portal instead of the tutoring platform. It showed that teachers grasp the opportunity to talk with the tutors about their use of the Go-Lab Portal and the problems they have met with.

After the Go-Lab experts offered the four sessions, a Go-Lab pilot teacher from Spain initiated a tutoring session entitled "Stage Conceptualisation Terminology in Interactive" on Apr. 27th, 2015. This teacher was active in the offline Go-Lab community by attending different events. She initiated a tutoring offer after she attended one of the previous sessions. She was supported by the project's team in order to prepare her session on inquiry learning methods. The recorded video reached 20 views as of middle of August 2015. As an ICT teacher, she has got some problems with the Google Hangouts, since it was the first time for her to use this Google service.

4 After-Session Survey Results

Based on the five tutoring sessions, we organized an online survey for ca. 15 min consisting of nine questions using Google Form[7]. There were 26 unique users who attended the sessions in total (some users attended more than one session). Among them, there were teachers active in attending the Go-Lab contests and summer schools (except four users). Thirteen of the teachers also registered in the Go-Lab Portal in order to publish their ILS.

Most of the teachers graded the tutoring platform as "easy to use", with four teachers saying "very easy" (30.8 %), four "easy" (30.8 %), and three "average" (23.1 %). Only two out of thirteen graded the use as hard (15.8 %). Eight teachers confirmed the helpfulness of the tutoring platform for their further use of the Go-Lab Portal. This moderate

[6] Google Hangouts on Air: http://www.google.com/+/learnmore/hangouts/onair.html.

[7] The survey is available at http://goo.gl/forms/rDexYxiSdY.

reply reflects that the visibility and the usability of the tutoring platform still need some improvement. We conclude that a user-friendly easy-to-use tutoring platform could encourage more users. In addition, most teachers were not familiar with Google Hangouts, which could lead to some negative rating of the easiness of the tutoring platform, though we observed the participants using the platform more smoothly in the latter part of the tutoring sessions.

There was also a question on the incentives to help other teachers, which reflects the interactions among teachers' communities (see Fig. 2). Eleven teachers rated both of the questions "Tutors get other tutors' help sessions in return" and "Any user has the opportunity to become a tutor" as appropriate and very appropriate. Ten teachers agreed with the statement "teachers like sharing their experiences".

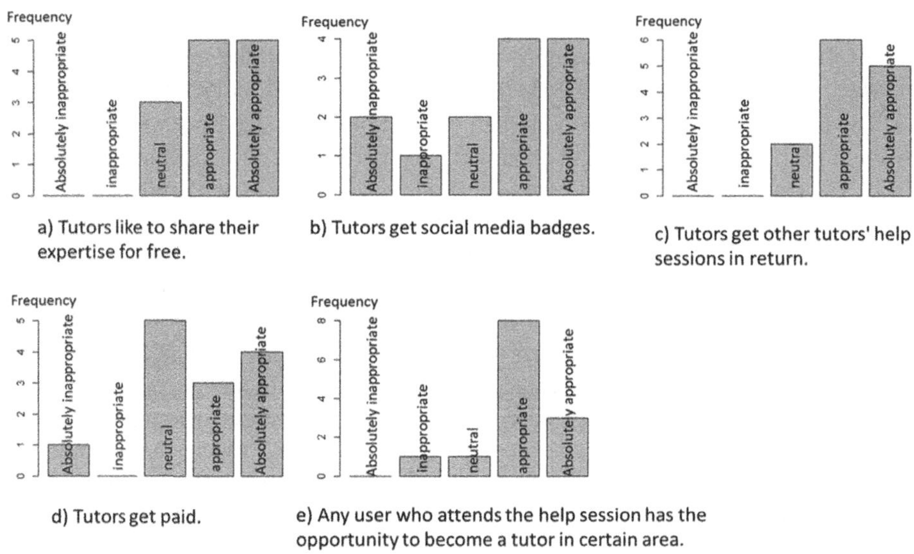

Fig. 2. Teachers' opinions on the incentives to motivate them help other teachers

Via the tutoring sessions on the Go-Lab Tutoring Platform, the teachers often contacted the Go-Lab team. They wrote e-mails and used the tutoring platform and the Go-Lab Portal more frequently. Although the results are still limited due to the small number of participants, it is important for us to use the platform to support community building at its early prototype development phase.

5 Conclusions and Future Work

With the launch of the prototype of the Go-Lab Tutoring Platform, we have hosted five tutoring sessions with 26 teachers. The preliminary results show that the tutoring platform encourages teachers' interactions and community building. From the session booking and session attendance data, we have identified the teachers being active in both the Go-Lab Portal and the tutoring platform. More important, cross-platform comparisons help us learn more about the Go-Lab community building. We have tracked those users' roles and activities in Go-Lab offline events, e.g. the contest. In total, 35 Go-Lab Contest participants have created an ILS in the Go-Lab Inquiry Learning Platform. Around 10 ILS have been published in the Go-Lab Repository by the tutoring session participants.

The tutoring platform also helps the Go-Lab team explore the deficit of knowledge by new users and support their skill development. Since the teachers come from different countries across Europe, some teachers faced communication problems due to the lack of English language skills. The participating teachers were not familiar with Google services. We noticed that their skills in using the Go-Lab Portal grew via the sessions. The teachers have requested more tutoring sessions. The teacher who gave her own session showed her initiative and engagement for community building.

The current results are promising, while the research still need be further conducted with more sessions and more participants. Teachers' community building is a complex task. In future, more research will be done to compare the activities of the participating teachers in the Go-Lab Portal and on the Go-Lab Tutoring Platform, as well as in the Go-Lab offline events. Teachers having different ages and teaching backgrounds may act in a different way in the communities, which also needs exploring. Above all, further tutoring sessions are in plan to attract more teachers' participation.

Acknowledgment. This research is partially funded by the European Union in the context of the Go-Lab project (Grant Agreement no. 317601) under the Information and Communication Technologies (ICT) theme of the 7th Framework Programme for R&D (FP7. This document does not represent the opinion of the European Union, and the European Union is not responsible for any use that might be made of its content.

References

1. Breuer, R., Klamma, R., Cao, Y., Vuorikari, R.: Social network analysis of 45,000 schools: a case study of technology enhanced learning in Europe. In: Cress, U., Dimitrova, V., Specht, M. (eds.) EC-TEL 2009. LNCS, vol. 5794, pp. 166–180. Springer, Heidelberg (2009)
2. Cao, Y., Govaerts, S., Dikke, D., Faltin, N., Gillet, D.: Helping each other teach: design and realisation of a social tutoring platform. In: Journal of Immersive Education (JiED) - Proceedings of 4th European Immersive Education Summit, Immersive Education Initiative, Austria (2014)
3. De Jong, T., Sotiriou, S., Gillet, D.: Innovations in STEM education: the Go-Lab federation of online labs. Smart Learn. Environ. **1**, 3 (2014)
4. Govaerts, S., Cao, Y., Vozniuk, A., Holzer, A., Zutin, D.G., Ruiz, E.S.C., Bollen, L., Manske, S., Faltin, N., Salzmann, C., Tsourlidaki, E., Gillet, D.: Towards an online lab portal for inquiry-based STEM learning at school. In: Wang, J.-F., Lau, R. (eds.) ICWL 2013. LNCS, vol. 8167, pp. 244–253. Springer, Heidelberg (2013)
5. Govaerts, S., Cao, Y., Faltin, N., Cherradi, F., Gillet, D.: Tutoring teachers - building an online tutoring platform for the teacher community. In: Ebner, M., Erenli, K., Malaka, R., Pirker, J., Walsh, A.E. (eds.) EiED 2014. CCIS, vol. 486, pp. 39–51. Springer, Heidelberg (2015)

6. Vuorikari, R., Berlanga, A., Cachia, R., Cao, Y., Fetter, S., Gilleran, A., Klamma, R., Punie, Y., Scimeca, S., Sloep, P., Petrushyna, Z.: ICT-based school collaboration, teachers' networks and their opportunities for teachers' professional development - a case study on eTwinning. In: Leung, H., Popescu, E., Cao, Y., Lau, R.W.H., Nejdl, W. (eds.) ICWL 2011. LNCS, vol. 7048, pp. 112–121. Springer, Heidelberg (2011)
7. Wenger, E.: Communities of Practice - Learning, Meaning, and Identity. Cambridge University Press, Cambridge (1998)

Optimizing Student and Supervisor Interaction During the SciPro Thesis Process – Concepts and Design

Preben Hansen(✉) and Henrik Hansson

Department of Computer and Systems Sciences, Stockholm University, Stockholm, Sweden
{preben,henrik.hansson}@dsv.su.se

Abstract. In order for students to complete their bachelor, master and Ph.D. theses they need feedback, cues, guidance and supervision. Common problems perceived by students are too little instructions as well as infrequent and insufficient supervisor feedback. At Stockholm University, the SciPro (Supporting the **Sci**entific **Pro**cess) system has been developed to tackle these problems. This paper describes, analyze and discuss the interaction between students and supervisors using the SciPro system. The results show high level of interaction between students and supervisors in the thesis handling process. However, six special groups of needs were identified: support for (1) language(s), (2) research methods, (3) self-study, (4) creativity, (5) "How to write", and (6) inspiration and motivation. The collaborative stage of group-supervision may be one possible way to deal with the different type of support for the process of managing student theses.

Keywords: Supervision · Learning support system · Scipro

1 Introduction and Aim

The development of different kinds of Learning Management Systems (LSSs), for higher education has dramatically increased. Many university and college institutions require LSSs to ensure that the learning processes meet the learners' demands and higher education purposes. Even though different kinds of ICT solutions have been suggested in education, specific and sufficient structured resources for thesis courses at Bachelor's and Master's levels is generally lacking. It is true that learners may have access to different kinds of LSSs, virtual learning environments, blogging and wiki engines, and other online resources as well as Facebook groups handling group work. However, there is a need for structured e-resources, made for, directed or adjusted to the thesis courses, in order to support learning process with less instructors' involvements and improving students' individual and independent learning process. In most of the institutions courses, learning still rely much on instructors' teaching and guiding. This also concerns the thesis courses that reflect and provide the same opportunities but also have similar problems and barriers as a distance course [1]. Most problems deal with finding relevant information in the right phase of the thesis process and in that way act independently in their work. Also, the consequence is that teachers and supervisors need to spend a lot of time to administer these resources. In order to reduce these problems, the department

F.W.B. Li et al. (Eds.): ICWL 2015, LNCS 9412, pp. 245–250, 2015.
DOI: 10.1007/978-3-319-25515-6_23

of Computers and Systems Sciences, at Stockholm University, has developed a LSS, called SciPro (Scientific Process). SciPro is a support system for the thesis courses to facilitate independent information access to a set of structured e-resources as well as providing structured step-by-step stages for the students during the thesis project. The aim of this study is to describe and discuss the interaction between students and supervisors using this system.

2 Learning Support System (LSS) – SciPro

The SciPro system supports students, supervisors and administrators in many various ways, such as a peer review system [2], the Idea Bank and matching process and the conceptual design of SciPro [3]. However, the focus in this article is about the student interaction. Students interact with content in SciPro such as basic instructions in texts and videos about the thesis process, requirements and a frequently asked question section. This information relieves the supervisor from communicating many hours of basic information to the student. Templates for thesis layout and templates for opposition reports in two language versions (English and Swedish) are also easy available for the students. The "SciPro projects" provides supervision support for each unique thesis and Fig. 1 below, illustrates some basic interactions provided by the system. Initially the student post a thesis idea in the online Idea Bank and a supervisor select this idea and thereby the student for supervision, or the process is reversed, that is, a supervisor post a thesis idea in the Idea Bank and a student select this idea and are matched with that supervisor. Normally, the connection between student and supervisor is based on a mutual interest, the thesis idea. This matching takes place before course start. When the course start, a first meeting, the first course week is mandatory. There are checklists for what to be communicated in the first meeting and there are checklists for student and supervisor to guide through the whole process. A particular kind of checklist is the 'Milestones', these are sub tasks for each student to do in order to complete their thesis course.

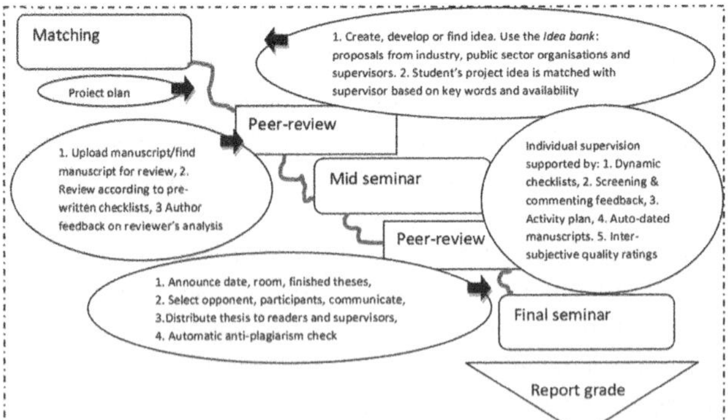

Fig. 1. The SciPro thesis management system.

For instance, they have to do peer reviews, facilitated through the system, and be active participants at two final seminars, do a written and oral opposition on another thesis at a final seminar. The system supports this with instructions, templates and auto-semi-auto check of these milestones when done. The supervision overview contains a summary graph of answered checklist and a progress bar of how many milestones are done. Most of the students at the department are campus students and the SciPro system adds value as the major ICT part in a blended learning mode of education. Users prefer to manage all their communication and administration via forum messages, to files, final seminar administration, anti-plagiarism control and grading. SciPro standardize the initial phase, allocation of supervisors (matching), and the final phase, the grading process, but not they journey from the start to finish. The communication between supervisor and student is basically up to the two interacting persons. There are differences on how supervisors decide to use SciPro. In order to provide a view on how different these supervision strategies can look like, we will describe two use cases of supervising and discuss how SciPro was used through using the concepts reflection on action and reflection in action [4]. Reflective practices is now common within the education field often combined with action research [5–7].

3 Two Case Scenarios

These two case scenarios covers totally 38 bachelor and master students and Table 1 shows the overall percentage of thesis completion.

Table 1. Percentage of completed thesis during spring 2015 for 2 supervisors

2015 thesis completion	Supervisor 1 (25 students)		Supervisor 2 (13 students)	
	Master (12)	Bachelor (13)	Master (1)	Bachelor (12)
30 %	1	–	–	–
50 %	4	2	–	2
70 %	2	2	–	2
90 %	1	4	–	2
100 %	4	5	1	6

Use Case Scenario I. The first step is to book a meeting the first week with all new students for a face-to-face seminar. During that meeting upcoming seminar is booked. In addition to the face-to-face seminars, I respond asynchronously via SciPro Forum and book individual meetings as well as use distance technology for synchronous voice interaction. SciPro provides notifications to my e-mail if students post something in the SciPro forum or add files etc. This semester I have had 595 notifications and provided the same number of written feedback messages to students in the SciPro forums for each thesis project either direct via my e-mail (e-mail SciPro reply) or as logged in SciPro. Total number of asynchronous interactions via SciPro is about 1200 during the semester.

This course period I have had ten face-to-face seminars of about total 30 h, six individual face-to-face meetings, four Skype supervisions and nine face to face final seminars, a total of 13, 5 h. In three final seminars participants have been participating via Skype from different countries. For each thesis an external reviewer is assessing the thesis quality in two stages, as rough draft and if it is ready for final seminar (fulfilled all grading criteria). The communication between reviewer and supervisor is internal in SciPro. This means that for 25 students at least 50 interactions will be taking place between reviewer and supervisor. Then the grading interaction will be conducted meaning another 25 interactions at least, between both grading professors. This means that student get a lot of feedback in a structured way, both in an informal and highly formal way. Generous time needs to be allocated initially when students are exploring options and deciding on problem, research question, and methods. This process is best done face to face and with peers in a brainstorming and informal way. Once the project design is in place, interaction can be conducted via written feedback and with the instructions, guidelines and support already provided by SciPro. At the second phase students get feedback from their peers by using the peer review functionality in the system. Two peer reviews (mandatory) for each student are required. No supervisor time is needed to facilitate this process. I also include co-supervisors in the supervision. Their role and contribution varies a lot, some do it as part of their lecturing, others as volunteers only because it is a topic they are interested in, others are external to the university and are included in order to create a participatory approach. They providing expert knowledge, contextual information or by providing "preventive supervision".

Use Case Scenario II – Group and Individual Supervision. This model characterizes of a focus on blending of group and individual supervision. Since I have a strong research agenda and suggested a set of topics for the Idea Bank to be used in the matching process. From that pool students select topics that may want to use for their thesis. However, the students themselves may also develop their own topics for thesis projects. Each topic heading is followed by a short description and specific requirements if needed in order to be able to fulfill the task. The description also includes other aspects that may be of importance for both the supervisors and the students, linked to the topic. In my model, most students did choose one of my topics.

In my model, we follow the supervision process of 4 groups with similar topics. I started with a first group meeting. The reason for this is to more effectively handle basic administrative issues at the same for all students. A first group supervision is also beneficial in creating awareness between supervisor and students regarding research area chosen. This may hopefully lead to that the students initially share information and knowledge [8] with each other. In this case, I used a supervision strategy that involved four meetings once a week, in which all four pairs of students participated. This is to give the students a good and firm base before they set out on their own research process. During the first meeting I the overall writing process was discussed as well as the different milestones involved in thesis process. I also declared what I expected from the collaboration with the students and gave written instructions and documentations for progressing through the thesis process. Each student also gave a brief overview of the topic, upon which I gave a first verbal feedback. As described above, SciPro provides notifications if students or the reviewer post something in the SciPro. I have had 91 such notifications with approximately the same number of responses. The main task of the second meeting was to discuss the topic, the problem and the research question and narrow it down to a realistic and doable level and to provide a full project plan. All other participants were invited to comments and discuss. Alternative research strategies and suggested readings were also discussed. During the third meeting, the students presented an extended and elaborated plan and an outline of the "rough draft" ready for the first review. This is an important milestone, since the rough draft should contain a readable version of the introduction, the problem and the research question and a description of the intended methods of collecting and analyzing data. The students may during this meeting argue and reason for their choices. In the fourth and last joint and collaborative meeting, the goal was to finalize a final version of the "rough draft", since this is a 'threshold' stage. The supervisor and an examiner have to approve the outline and if approved, the student can proceed with the study. At this stage, I start to supervise each thesis individually. The main reason is that, based on my experience, each work have reached such a specific level of independency as regard to focus of topic, theory use and utility of methodology, that it is better that I supervise them one by one hereafter. The students now manage the thesis work more by themselves and the feedback is now given individually. At the end of the project process, when I, as supervisor, and the examiner have approved it, a final seminar is created and the thesis is uploaded to SciPro to be read by the opponents. After the defense of the thesis, the students have the possibility to make minor adjustments before the final grading is done.

4 Discussion and Conclusion

Based on the two different models of thesis supervision, SciPro system adds value when it comes to the management and supervision of bachelor and master theses. It is now possible to supervise more students, but also increase the quality of the end product, the final thesis. One important step is the matching of students and supervisors based on research topics/ideas. This provides a strong motivation and provides the necessary personal driving force for both parties. Since students get most basic information through the SciPro system, engaged and motivated supervisors as well as students, is an essential aspect. As seen in the case descriptions the IT support system does not reduce the level of interaction with the supervisors, on the contrary, there is probably more interaction now than before the system was introduced since the communication is more focused, aligned to course objectives and faster. So, what issues are problematic? We experience a very heterogeneous student group nowadays; international, different backgrounds and different pre-knowledge, and different personalities. The same is true for supervisors. A general observation is that the students who are requiring the least supervision are the fastest and often perform well at the end. Who these are, is evident very early in the seminars. The self-study information in the system makes these students very independent once they have the general approach and project plan in place. There are other students that are not that fast. In fact these students might be the most innovative, dedicated and interesting. However, they are not progressing in the same speed as others, reasons could be (1) not enough language skills (foreign mother tongue), (2) not enough pre-knowledge about research methods, (3) not used to independent work, (4) not used to a creative work style; creating own ideas, critical and creative analysis, (5) not used to writing, and finally (6) unmotivated students. Based on our observations, we can extract six categories of students, who might need other types of support in their thesis work. To start with these special needs groups has to be identified early in the process, and pro-active interventions implemented in parallel to the standard supervision. We suggest a refined thesis process to include a pool of dedicated supervisors who supports the six identified special needs groups and that tools, instructions and special seminars are designed for these groups. If special needs support could be implemented more students will finish their theses in time, and thesis quality will improve to the benefit of students, supervisors, the department and the society as a whole. A mean to accomplish that is to utilize collaboration [9] and information/knowledge sharing through group supervision among supervisors and students. Utilizing the group-supervision model and strategy for also calls for a shift in practical and pedagogical procedures. For example, the knowledge hand-over between students in the group as well as between supervisors and students could be beneficial in several ways: each student gets an information update from both fellow students and supervisor, they learn about resources and references from others, they can discuss about the application of different data collection and analysis methods. This way the students get both peer reviews/feedback and feedback from the supervisor during the meetings. This also shows that the group-supervision also is a learning process in itself.

References

1. Muilenburg, L.Y., Berge, Z.L.: Student barriers to online learning: A factor analytic study. Distance Educ. **26**(1), 29–48 (2005)
2. Aghaee, N., Hansson, H.: Peer portal: quality enhancement in thesis writing using self managed peer review on a mass scale. Int. Rev. Res. Open Distance Learn. **14**(1), 186–203 (2013)
3. Hansson, H., Moberg, J.: Quality processes in technology enhanced thesis work. In: Proceedings of the 24th ICDE World Conference (2011)
4. Schön, D.A.: The Reflective Practitioner: How Professionals Think in Action. Basic Books, New York (1983)
5. Fook, J.: Developing critical reflection as a research method. In: Creative Spaces for Qualitative Researching: Living Research. Sense Publishers, Rotterdam (2011)
6. Bradbury, H., Reason, P.: Action research: an opportunity for revitalizing research purpose and practices. Qual. Soc. Work **2**(2), 155–175 (2003)
7. Gibbs, G.: Learning by Doing: A Guide to Teaching and Learning Methods. FEU, London (1988)
8. Talja, S., Hansen, P.: Information sharing. In: Spink, A., Cole, C. (eds.) New Directions in Human Information Behavior. Information Science and Knowledge Management Series, vol. 8, pp. 113–134. Springer, Dordrecht (2006)
9. Hansen, P., Järvelin, P.: Collaborative information retrieval in an information-intensive domain. Inf. Process. Manage. **41**(5), 1101–1119 (2005)

Analysis of Tools and Methods for Describing and Sharing Reusable Pedagogical Scenarios

Marina Kurvits, Mart Laanpere(✉), and Terje Väljataga

Tallinn University, Narva Road 25, 10120 Tallinn, Estonia
mart.laanpere@tlu.ee

Abstract. Even without rigorous empirical research, we know that some teachers are more effective in their teaching approaches than others. We can hypothesise that part of their success can be attributed to the pedagogical methods or scenarios they use, and that these scenarios could also be re-used by other teachers. But it is quite complicated to describe good teaching practices, methods and approaches so that these can easily be adopted by other teachers. Today, several different tools and methods exist for describing and sharing effective pedagogical scenarios, but their biggest disadvantage is a low rate of acceptance among teachers. The paper provides an overview of the state of the art in the domain of software tools for building and sharing pedagogical scenarios, using a two-dimensional analytic framework. As an outcome of this analysis, design guidelines for an alternative scenario-building tool are proposed.

Keywords: Pedagogical scenarios · Pedagogical scripting · Design-based research

1 Introduction

Technology and social media have not only become a part of school life, but have also begun to have a significant effect on the forms and methods of teaching and learning. Traditional pedagogy that is focused on a transition of knowledge is not always effective in the modern changing world [1] because it leads to isolated knowledge, which is difficult to apply in contexts outside of school [2]. A teacher is no longer the only source of knowledge and information for a student [3]. Therefore, it is self-evident that teachers should change both their teaching strategies and their activities related to teaching. But despite of the availability of modern technology in the classroom, and a generous amount of educational web resources that can support teaching and learning, large-scale uptake of educational innovation is hindered by a number of barriers, one of such barriers being teachers' "resistance to change" [4]. Even well prepared educational reform initiatives often fail to achieve the intended results in changing teacher pedagogical practices [5]. Various studies [1, 6, 7] have demonstrated that one possible key to successful educational innovation is timely pedagogical guidance for teachers on designing the learning activities with ICT and using new learning environments. Even if some innovative teachers successfully adopt the new approaches and methods, disseminating innovative teaching practices to the majority of teachers is not a trivial task, and the modification

F.W.B. Li et al. (Eds.): ICWL 2015, LNCS 9412, pp. 251–257, 2015.
DOI: 10.1007/978-3-319-25515-6_24

of existing teaching and learning practices remains one of the most difficult challenges in the domain of education today [7].

Therefore, this paper focuses on the following research problem: how can good teaching practices, methods and approaches be described and adopted by other teachers?

To address this problem, we provide an overview of the state of the art in the domain of software tools for building and sharing pedagogical scenarios, followed by a critical analysis of these existing tools that leads us to stating the design guidelines for a new online tool for describing and sharing pedagogical scenarios. But first, we will give a brief historical overview of the approaches to reusable pedagogical designs.

2 Re-usable Pedagogical Designs: An Historical Overview

In the 19th century, the German philosopher Johann Friedrich Herbart, pointed out the importance of instruction in the formation of representations [8]. According to Herbart's instructional model process, instruction consists of four phases: clearness, association, system and method. His four-step model was one of the first systematic approaches to teaching and has been used in various forms by educators for many years. Later, Robert M. Gagne developed the idea of task-skill hierarchies that provide guidance through sequencing [8]. With Leslie Briggs, Gagne developed a theory of instruction [8] where they indicated nine events in instruction that support the learner's internal process. Different combinations and sequences of these instructional events can be implemented as the main structural elements when describing reusable pedagogical scenarios in a narrative, yet well-structured form of lesson plans.

In 1983, M.D. Merrill and his associates developed a scientific and practical instructional development guide [9] designed to clarify and extend the Gagne-Briggs theory [8], which is called "Component Display Theory" (CDT). CDT provides the needed operational procedures for an instructional designer to use in the process of developing effective and appealing instruction practices [9]. None of the pedagogical design frameworks described above have been supported by relevant software applications.

Based on our own observation data gathered from a large number of in-service courses for Estonian teachers, we claim that most teachers still work with the guidance systems from pre-computer era, such as those described above. To be able to design, implement, study and share innovative pedagogical approaches using ICT successfully, teachers need a new framework and corresponding software tools.

3 The Concept of Pedagogical Scenarios

As it happens often in educational sciences, there exist several competing vocabularies for describing pedagogical scenarios or designs, among others: instructional designs, didactic designs, pedagogical scenarios, learning scenarios, learning stories and scripts. We have tried to understand and define the differences and similarities between these vocabulary sets, searching for a common ground and harmonized view.

A teacher's task is to create conditions for learners that will facilitate them in the learning process. To facilitate specific types of sense-making, interaction and collaborative activities, Schneider et al. [1] suggested the creation of pedagogical scenarios. According to this, the main building blocks of a pedagogical scenario are the student activities mediated by various artifacts (blackboard, textbook, maps, presentations etc.). Schneider et al. define a pedagogical scenario as an orchestrated sequence of learning activities [1]. It is very important to note that a pedagogical scenario should be compiled in a generic and de-contextualized manner, allowing re-use by different teachers in the context of various school subjects, age groups and lessons topics. Every teacher can derive several contextualized learning scenarios from one generic pedagogical scenario. Hereby we define a learning scenario as guide for learners that directs and supports their learning, regardless of the learning environment (virtual or physical). It consists of the list of the activities that students are expected to follow and the resources they should use. In the field of computer-supported collaborative learning (CSCL), such scenarios are called scripts [10], defined as "*a story or scenario that the students and tutors have to enact, as actors enact a movie script*" [11].

It is also known that teachers already describe sometimes their own successful teaching practices and experiences through personal blogs or in forums/journals maintained by professional communities. We call such descriptions that are composed after the learning event, in a narrative and reflective manner the learning stories [12].

Based on the literature review summarized above, we have mapped the key concepts associated with learning scenarios in the form of a concept map (Fig. 1).

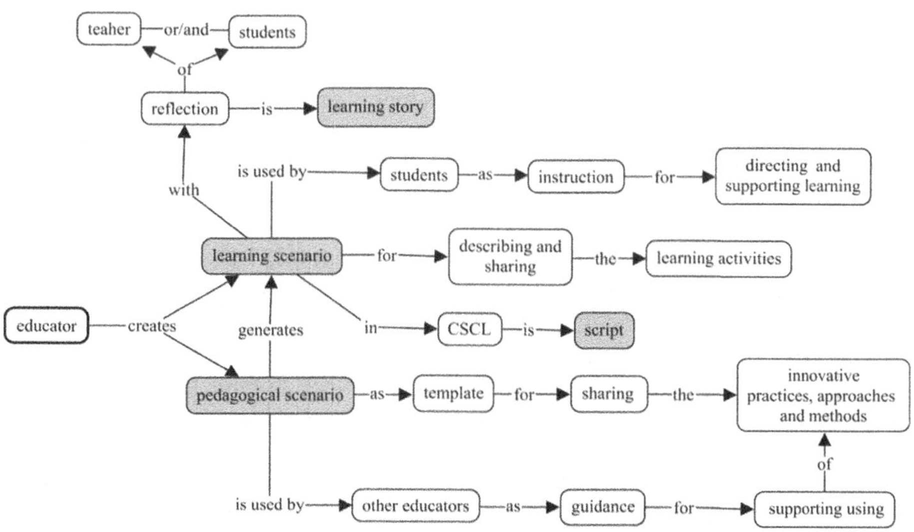

Fig. 1. Relationships between the concepts of a pedagogical scenario, learning scenario, learning story and script

Learning scenarios can be used not only for disseminating innovative teaching and learning practices among teachers (top-down approach), this construct is also useful when analysing and generalizing the learning stories of students and teachers (bottom-up approach).

4 Review of Existing Software Tools and Services

The issue of making creation and sharing of innovative pedagogical scenarios more systemic and helpful for teachers has been addressed by several software development projects within last two decades. This chapter provides a short comparative and critical analysis of existing scenario building tools.

The most traditional formalisations of pedagogical scripts are templates that should assist an (inexperienced teacher) in writing narrative pedagogical scenarios in a structured manner, e.g. lesson plan templates. There are some software tools that include such templates: for example, Lesson Plans[1] or Lesson Builder[2]. The similar toolkit Scenario Development Environment (SDE) was developed during the iTec project, with a view to helping teachers design and change their teaching practices [13].

There also exist several other structured approaches to describing, documenting and analysing pedagogical scenarios. We will describe a few of these below.

IMS Learning Design (IMS LD) is a technical specification of a meta-language for describing learning designs in a machine-readable format (e.g. XML or RDF). The main rationale behind IMS LD is to provide a framework of different elements to describe any design of the learning process in a formal way [14]. There exist several software tools for producing and sharing formalized pedagogical designs fully compatible with IMS LD specification, e.g. ReLoad, ReCourse and Prolix.

Conole and Fill [6] have created an online learning design toolkit that could be used for three main purposes: as guidance to support practitioners in the creation of activities; as a collection of existing learning activities and practices; and as a "mechanism for creating meta-models for e-learning" [6]. This tool is not available today.

One of the most popular tools in this niche is the Learning Activity Management System, or LAMS, which provides teachers with a visual environment for creating sequences of learning activities. LAMS enables users to determine learning pathways, monitor the activities of learners, and most importantly to adapt the learning sequences of other educators [15]. LAMS is loosely compliant with IMS LD, and it has been integrated into learning management system Moodle.

Bower et al. [16] claimed that tools such as LAMS and the Learning Management Systems (LMS) did not require the teacher to consider the pedagogically important aspects of the learning design process, making it difficult to implement activities that facilitated innovative teaching approaches. To address these issues, they developed a software application - Learning Designer.

Based on the fact that the adoption of tools for creating a learning scenario by teachers is still low, Sobreira and Tchounikine [17] recently presented an innovative approach to designing pedagogical scenarios – the table/tree pivotal model approach. Based on this approach a simple model – the T^2 model – was designed. The main task of this model is to provide a base for creating and editing scripts.

We have outlined the descriptions of various tools for describing, planning, preparing and sharing learning activities including: Lesson Plans, Lesson Builder, The SDE,

[1] http://lessonplanspage.com/.
[2] http://thelessonbuilder.org/welcome.

DialogPLUS Toolkit, LAMS, Learning Designer and the T^2 model. In this chapter we will compare these tools in a different way. First of all, we have analysed the existing tools on the basis of a two-dimensional framework (see Fig. 2). The framework identifies two key dimensions: the way of representing the scenario (either an unstructured narrative, or a visual, structured view of the scenario); and the purpose of the tool from the perspective of its scenario (a learning scenario as guidance for students that directs and supports learning, or a pedagogical scenario that guides and support teachers in their creation and sharing of innovative practices).

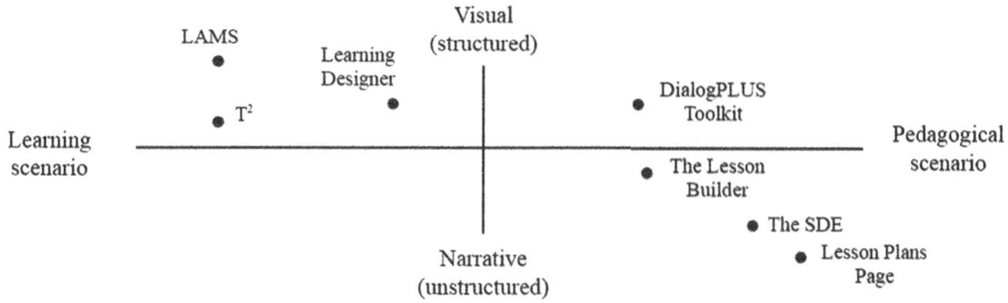

Fig. 2. Classification of the tools

The vertical axis separates the intended user for whom a scenario is created, and illustrates who can use the tool. Is it a learning scenario (on the left half of the axis) or a pedagogical scenario? The horizontal axis separates different representation of scenario: the narrative, unstructured form (bottom half) and the visual, structured form. As we can see, most of the tools that allow for the creation of pedagogical scenarios are in the bottom right quadrant, and almost all scenarios are presented in a narrative manner. Of course, this is more usual for teachers, but the limitation of narrative scenarios is that they can contain long blurred descriptions, that sometimes do not give specific instructions for the implementation of a scenario. The DialogPLUS Toolkit is an exception, but unfortunately an online version of this toolkit is no longer available.

Some of the tools for describing learning activities were more structured and visual, and this is quite logical, because these scenarios were created to work not only with teachers, but also with students. Students used these tools as guidance and instructions for learning.

Now, we will compare these tools in relation to their popularity among teachers and the age of the tool. However, there are no exact statistics available on the usage scale for each of these tools. We did find some information on The Lesson Plans Page (on the Lesson Plans Page website it is indicated that the site has over 4,000 lesson plans) and statistics about LAMS from the LAMS Community[3] (in 2012, the number of sequences created was 1094). Eventually, some of the points on the horizontal axis are results of an "educated guess".

---

[3] http://lamscommunity.org/dotlrn/clubs/educationalcommunity/forums/message-view?message_id=1479910.

Figure 3 shows that most of existing tools for describing and sharing teachers' practices are not popular among teachers. It is understandable for DialogPLUS Toolkit and T^2 that were made as analytic tools for researchers, and at the end of the research project these tools were no longer supported. Based on the fact that the authors of Learning Designer have proposed embedding a Learning Designer layer in learning platforms such as LAMS, Moodle and Blackboard [16], it can be assumed that the number of re-used Learning Activities will grow. Also LAMS has been integrated with several widely-used Learning Management Systems, (e.g. Moodle) that will certainly increase the number of Learning Sequences.

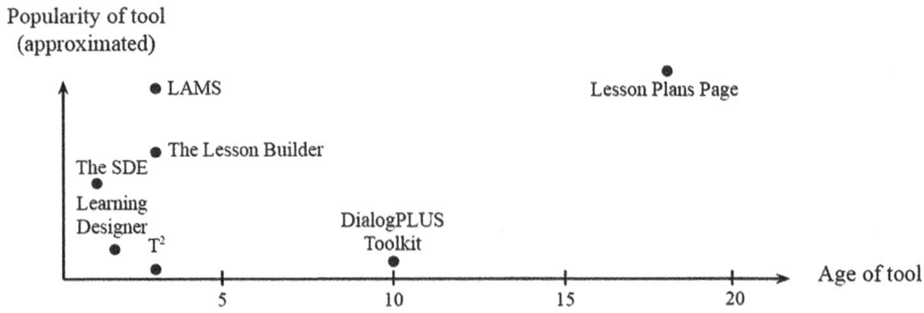

Fig. 3. Comparison of popularity among teachers and the age of the tools

5 Discussion and Conclusion

The purpose of this paper was to review and analyse current scenario-building and sharing tools, and also to describe the differences between the concepts of pedagogical scenarios, learning scenarios, learning stories and learning scripts. We analysed the existing tools such as LAMS, Learning Designer and T^2, that allow the user to create a learning scenario or script. Lesson Plans, Lesson Builder and the Scenario Development Environment (SDE) are some tools for creating pedagogical scenarios and learning stories. However, to support teachers in changing their approach and in using innovative methods and systems, there should be a fundamentally different tool for creating and sharing pedagogical scenarios. It should use a simple visual language for representing structure and components of scenarios (artefacts, tasks, roles, workflows, activity types). It should be easy-to-use and allow lightweight integration with common web tools used by teachers (e.g. Google Docs). It should also allow creating sub-versions and remixes of validated "template scenarios". And finally, it should link semantically the generic pedagogical scenarios with contextualized learning scenarios and *ex post facto* teaching and learning stories together with learning analytics data gathered during the lesson that was implemented in accordance with the scenario. The scenario building and sharing tool LePlanner that is developed in line with these requirements is currently in alpha stage.

References

1. Schneider, D., Synteta, P., Frété, C., Girardin, F., Morand, S.: Conception and implementation of rich pedagogical scenarios through collaborative portal sites: clear focus and fuzzy edges. In: International Conference on Open and Online Learning, University of Mauritius (2003)
2. Illeris, K.: Towards a contemporary and comprehensive theory of learning. Int. J. Lifelong Educ. **22**(4), 396–406 (2003)
3. Churches, A.: 21st century pedagogy (2008). http://edorigami.edublogs.org/2008/08/16/21st-century-pedagogy/. Accessed 10 July 2015
4. Bingimlas, K.: Barriers to the successful integration of ICT in teaching and learning environments: a review of the literature. EURASIA J. Math. Sci. Technol. Educ. **5**(3), 235–245 (2009)
5. Le Fevre, D.: Barriers to implementing pedagogical change: the role of teachers' perceptions of risk. Teach. Teacher Educ. **38**, 56–64 (2014)
6. Conole, G., Fill, K.: A learning design toolkit to create pedagogically effective learning activities. J. Interact. Media Educ. **8**, 1–16 (2005)
7. Häkkinen, P., Mäkitalo-Siegl, K.: Educational perspectives on scripting CSCL. Scripting Comput. Support. Collaborative Learn. **6**, 263–271 (2007)
8. Saettler, P.: The Evolution of American Educational Technology. IAP, Charlotte (1990)
9. Choi, S.: Application of component display theory in designing and developing CALI. CALICO J. **3**(4), 40–45 (1986)
10. Dillenbourg, P., Tchounikine, P.: Flexibility in macro-scripts for CSCL. J. Comput. Assist. Learn. **23**(1), 1–13 (2007)
11. Dillenbourg, P.: Over-scripting CSCL: the risks of blending collaborative learning with instructional design. In: Kirschner, P.A. (ed.) Three worlds of CSCL. Can we support CSCL, pp. 61–91. Open Universiteit Nederland, Heerlen (2002)
12. iTEC Scenarios: (2013) http://itec.aalto.fi/. Accessed 10 July 2015
13. Toikkanen, T., Keune, A.: Designing Edukata: a method for educators to create learner centered activities. In: Proceedings of WCEMT 2014, pp. 1476–1483 (2014)
14. Caeiro, M., Anido, L., Llamas, M.: A critical analysis of IMS learning design. In: Wasson, B., Ludvigsen, S., Hoppe, U. (eds.) Designing for Change in Networked Learning Environments, vol. 2, pp. 363–367. Springer, Netherlands (2003)
15. Dalziel, J.: Lessons from LAMS for IMS learning design. In: Sixth International Conference on Advanced Learning Technologies, pp. 1101–1102 (2006)
16. Bower, M., Craft, B., Laurillard, D.: Using the learning designer to develop a conceptual framework for linking learning design tools and systems. In: International LAMS and learning Design Conference, pp. 61–71 (2011)
17. Sobreira, P., Tchounikine, P.: A model for flexibly editing CSCL scripts. Int. J. Comput. Support. Collaborative Learn. **7**(4), 567–592 (2012)

Learning to Assemble Building Blocks with a Leap Motion Controller

Juncong Lin, Wei Yang, Xing Gao(✉), and Minghong Liao

Software School, Xiamen University,
Xiamen 361005, Fujian, People's Republic of China
{jclin,gaoxing,liao}@xmu.edu.cn

Abstract. Playing toy blocks can greatly help children develop various abilities such as spatial, mathematical, creative problem solving etc. Developing a computer-aided block building system would benefit a lot in recreational and educational applications. Providing a natural user interface to increase the user's sense of immersion is very important for the success of such kind system. In this paper, we develop a virtual toy block assembly system targeting on children's preschool education. With the help of leap motion controller, child only need to make various hand gestures to play toy blocks similar to how they do in real scenario. A block snapping interface is designed to help quickly place block at the appropriate position. Our system demonstrate great potential in education area.

Keywords: Toy block assembly · Leap motion · Hand gesture · Snapping interface

1 Introduction

Block building is a very beneficial activity which can help children develop various skills, such as spatial, mathematical, creative problem solving etc. Developing a computer aided system for block building is desirable for recreational and educational applications. With such a system, users (especially kids) are given a lot of freedom so they can enjoy the process of imagining, designing and constructing with blocks freely. They can easily try different sets of building blocks with no or little additional cost.

Providing comfortable user experience is fundamental for such system. Traditional direct manipulation style with mouse and keyboard could be awkward. In [6], the authors presented a Kinect framework for virtual assembly of building blocks. Body gestures are used to provide an intuitive user interface. However, it is not so nature as toy blocks are manipulated with hands in reality. Besides, the hardware setting and manipulation manner in their system let user feel distant from the blocks which is quite uncomfortable.

In this paper, we presented a computer-aided toy block building system. Equipped with a leap motion controller, our system allows users to manipulate

F.W.B. Li et al. (Eds.): ICWL 2015, LNCS 9412, pp. 258–263, 2015.
DOI: 10.1007/978-3-319-25515-6_25

blocks in the virtual scenario in a free-hand style, providing them a natural experience. A set of hand gestures is carefully designed for manipulation of blocks. To help place the block in the scene accurately and quickly, we also realize a snapping interface which considers various factors (such as distance, alignment, symmetry, balance etc.) to determine the optimal position. Our system provide an effective and low-cost manner for preschool education of children. Compared with body gesture based method [6], our system are more similar to the real scenario, and thus providing a more immersive environment (Fig. 1).

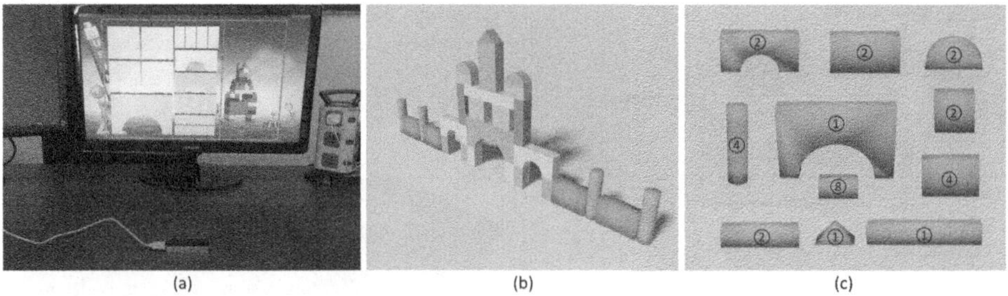

Fig. 1. Playing toy blocks with a leap motion controller: (a) Toy block assembly scenario; (b) A virtual castle constructed by the user; (c) The set of blocks for the castle. The value on each block indicates the number of blocks used in this virtual assembly.

2 Previous Work

2.1 Recreational Graphics

Recreational application are very popular in graphics community in past decade. In [3], Mitani et al. described a method for producing unfolded papercraft patterns of rounded toy animal figures from triangulated meshes. Xin et al. [9] generalized the 6-piece orthogonal burr puzzle to design and model burr puzzles from 3D models. Mori et al. [13] introduced an interactive system to help nonprofessional users to design their own plush toys. Li et al. [12] proposed an automatic algorithm for generating paper architectures given a user-specified 3D model.

2.2 Free-Hand Interaction

Free-hand interaction has been explored for various applications such as games [4], immersive 3D modeling [5], mobile augmented reality applications [2] etc. Gesture data fetching is the, prerequisite of these systems. Compared with glove-based methods [10] or vision-based methods [1], depth sensor based methods [8] are much more stable and efficient and thus attract more and more attentions recently. Gesture recognition is another important step. Gesture can be static or dynamic. There are many different methods for recognizing static hand gestures [7, 11].

3 User Interface

Our system has three modes: selection, building, adjustment. In the selection mode (Fig. 2(a)), the user can browse all the building blocks from the database and then select one block which is going to be assembled in the virtual environment. In the building mode (Fig. 2(b)), the user moves the block towards the desired position and release the block. During navigation, user can also switch to further adjust the orientation or position of the block which has been released and placed on the initial position suggested by the snapping interface.

Fig. 2. User interface of our block building system: (a) Selection mode; (b) Building mode.

3.1 Gesture Set

We design a set of hand gestures for operations involved in the three modes.

Selection Gestures are used in the selection mode allowing the user to browse all the available building blocks and select one of them. User first make a fist with the right hand to activate the selection mode (Fig. 3(a)). Then he can manipulate the cursor on the display screen by move the fist vertically in the air. He finally make a confirm gesture with right hand (Fig. 3(j)) to select current-pointing block and switch to navigation mode.

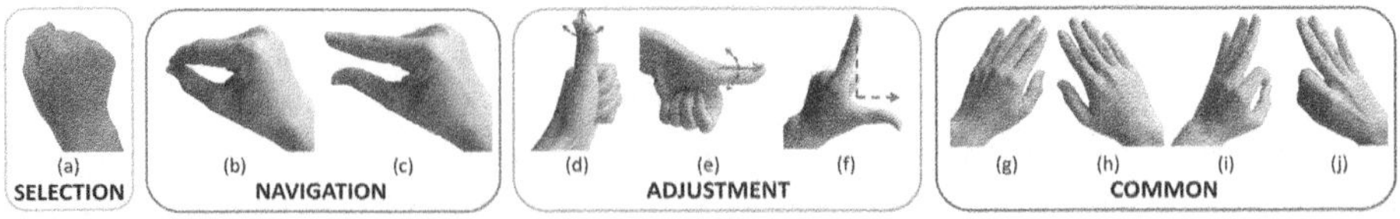

Fig. 3. Hand gesture set for our system: (a) Selection mode activate; (b) Grasp block; (c) Release block; (d) Rotate around up direction; (e) Rotate around right direction; (f) Translate; (g,h) Neural; (i,j) Confirm.

Navigation Gestures are used to help the user assemble current block to the appropriate position. The user firstly makes a grasp gesture with his right hand by putting the tips of thumb and index finger closed (Fig. 3(b)) to activate the navigation mode. Keeping the grasp gesture, he can then move the right hand horizontally in the air, and the block will move accordingly. The user finally make a release gesture (Fig. 3(c)).

Adjustment Gestures are used to further adjust the orientation or position of current block. The adjustment mode can be activated either in navigation or when the block is released. The user firstly make the rotation gestures (Fig. 3(d,e)) or translation gesture (Fig. 3(f)) statically with his left hand to activate adjustment mode, then he can either rotate around the thumb or translate horizontally to adjust the orientation and position of current block.

3.2 Snapping Interface for Block Assembly

Although our hand gesture based interaction style provide users a natural experience. However, the lack of reference and the imprecise nature of gesture based interaction [6] present great challenge for user to place block in the appropriate position quickly. Thus, the snapping interface described in [6] is used in our system to help user quickly assemble block.

The solution of optimal snapping position is formulated as an energy minimization problem. And the target function is defined as the weight combination of distance energy E_d, alignment energy E_a, contact energy E_c, balance energy E_b and symmetry energy E_s:

$$F(\mathbf{p}, \theta) = w_d E_d + w_a E_a + w_c E_c + w_b E_b + w_s E_s \tag{1}$$

The optimization problem can finally be solved with a hierarchy strategy: An orientation filtering step is performed firstly to filter out invalid θ; Constraints are combined to reduce search space; Stochastic optimization method is finally used to find the optimal position with Monte Carlo sampler employed to explore the cost function. More details can be found in [6].

4 Experimental Results

We have implemented a prototype system with C++. The whole system runs smoothly on a laptop with standard configuration (Intel Core Duo CPU 2.4 GHZ, 8 G RAM). The gesture fetching and recognition are all done in real time. The snapping algorithm usually converges within 20 iterations. And it takes about 0.2 s to find the optimal position for each assembly operation. Figure 4 shows more examples of the building blocks constructed by our system.

Fig. 4. Building block examples constructed with our system.

5 Conclusions

In this paper, we present a computer aided block assembly system. Equipped with a leap controller, our system allow child to assemble blocks fully with their bare hands. A set of hand gestures are carefully designed for various tasks during the assembly process. Besides, a snapping interface is implemented to help user place block quickly in appropriate orientation and position. In the future, we will further improve the immersion of our system and popularize the system in preschool education.

Acknowledgment. This work was supported by the National Natural Science Foundation of China (No. 61202142), the National Key Technology R&D Program Foundation of China (No.2015BAH34F00/F01), Joint Funds of the Ministry of Education of China and China Mobile (No.MCM20130221), and Key Technology R&D Program of Xiamen (Nos.3502Z20140059,3502Z20141009)

References

1. Bröckl-Fox, U.: Real-Time 3D interaction with up to 16 degrees of freedom from monocular image flows. In: Proceedings of International Workshop on Automatic Face and Gesture Recognition, pp. 172–178 (1995)
2. Datcu, D., Lukosch, S.: Free-hands interaction in augmented reality. In: Proceedings of the 1st Symposium on Spatial User Interaction, pp. 33–40 (2013)
3. Mitani, J., Suzuki, H.: Making papercraft toys from meshes using strip-based approximate unfolding. ACM Trans. Graph. **23**(3), 259–263 (2004)
4. Kim, D., Hilliges, O., Izadi, S., Butler, A., Chen, J., Oikonomidis, I., Olivier, P.: Digits: freehand 3D interactions anywhere using a wrist-worn gloveless sensor. In: Proceedings of the 25th Annual ACM Symposium on User Interface Software and Technology, pp. 167–176 (2012)
5. Kim, H., Albuquerque, G., Havemann, S., Fellner, D.W.: Tangible 3D: hand gesture interaction for immersive 3D modeling. In: Proceedings of the 11th Eurographics Conference on Virtual Environments, pp. 191–199 (2005)
6. Lin, J., Sun, Q., Li, G., He, Y.: SnapBlocks: a snapping interface for assembling toy blocks with XBOX Kinect. Multimedia tools and applications **73**(3), 2009–2032 (2014)

7. Patwardhan, K.S., Roy, S.D.: Hand gesture modelling and recognition involving changing shapes and trajectories, using a predictive eigentracker. Pattern Recogn. Lett. **28**(3), 329–334 (2007)
8. Penelle, B., Debeir, O.: Multi-sensor data fusion for hand tracking using Kinect and Leap Motion. In: Proceedings of the 2014 Virtual Reality International Conference, p. Article No. 22 (2014)
9. Xin, S., Lai, C.F., Fu, C.W., Wong, T.T., He, Y., Cohen-Or, D.: Making burr puzzles from 3D models. ACM Trans. Graph. **30**(4), 97 (2011)
10. Sturman, D.J., Zeltzer, D.: A survey of glove-based input. IEEE Comput. Graph. Appl. **14**, 30–39 (1994)
11. Triescha, J., von der Malsburg, C.: Classification of hand postures against complex backgrounds using elastic graph matching. Image Vis. Comput. **20**(13–14), 937–943 (2002)
12. Li, X.Y., Shen, C.H., Huang, S.S., Ju, T., Hu, S.M.: Popup: Automatic Paper Architectures from 3D Models. ACM Transactions on Graphics **29**(4), 1–9 (2011). Article No: 111
13. Mori, Y., Igarashi, T.: Plushie: an interactive design system for plush toys. ACM Transactions on Graphics **26**(3), 45 (2007)

A Generic Software Framework for Intelligent Integrated Computer-Assisted Language Learning (iiCALL) Environment

Harald Wahl[1(✉)], Rudolf Galler[1], and Werner Winiwarter[2]

[1] Department of Information Engineering and Security, University of Applied Sciences Technikum Wien, Vienna, Austria
wahl@technikum-wien.at, galler.r@gmx.at

[2] Research Group Data Analytics and Computing, University of Vienna, Vienna, Austria
werner.winiwarter@univie.ac.at

Abstract. Intelligent Integrated Computer-Assisted Language Learning (iiCALL) describes various approaches in the field of second language learning. The term ''Integrated'' refers to approaches which operate inside established workspaces such as Web-browsers and e-mail clients, whereas the term ''Intelligent'' relates to appropriate methods from the field of computer linguistics. The iiCALL environments are composed of several single systems, which are developed by specialists from different domains with specific background-knowledge (e.g. didactic experts, linguists, or software developers). High-quality solutions of such learning environments are characterized by solid technical delivery and proper language content. Both demand semantic interoperability between these systems as well as flexibility and scalability of the entire environment. Similar challenges exist in healthcare. Hence, the idea of the Health Level Seven V3 standard is adapted to meet the requirements for iiCALL. This paper addresses this challenge and presents a development framework for the conception of iiCALL, as well as a software framework for generic and transparent information exchange within those environments.

Keywords: Computer-assisted language learning · iiCALL · Web-based learning · Natural language processing · NLP · Integrated learning

1 Introduction

Computer-Assisted Language Learning (CALL) was introduced in the late 90s by [3] and designates the search for and study of applications of the computer in language teaching and learning. As a result of innovations in the field of computer linguistics and artificial intelligence, CALL systems became more intelligent which led to the notion of Intelligent CALL (ICALL). A comparison of several systems can be found in [1]. Besides enhancing CALL with intelligent approaches, there are efforts to integrate language learning in common and well-established working environments, such as e-mail-clients or Web browsers. The main goal is to enable language learning at any time and in any place so that it accompanies daily life and daily business. [5–7] explore

F.W.B. Li et al. (Eds.): ICWL 2015, LNCS 9412, pp. 264–270, 2015.
DOI: 10.1007/978-3-319-25515-6_26

various approaches referring to the design of such language learning environments and introduce the designation Intelligent Integrated CALL (iiCALL). A first prototype of a Web-based and integrated language learning platform is shown in [8, 9]. The prototype realizes context-related vocabulary training. The architecture is similar to the current prototype visualized in Fig. 1.

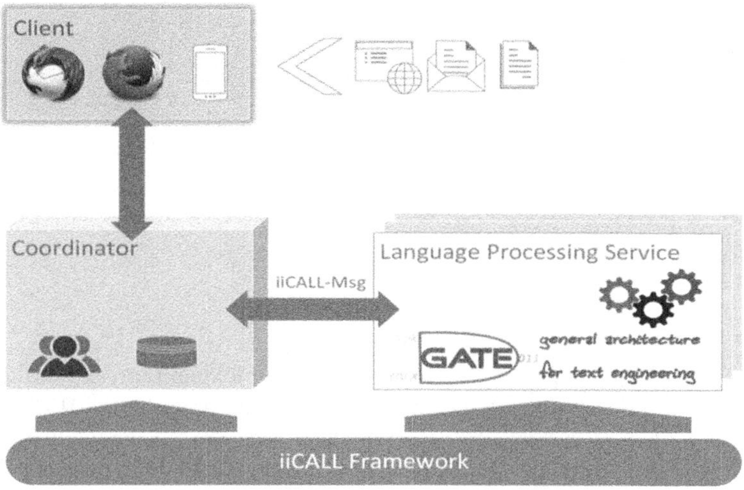

Fig. 1. Protoype architecture

The Web browser of the user acts as a client und holds various user settings, such as present language skills and language subjects or language contexts, which the user aims to learn. The contents of visited websites will be sent to a server (coordinator). The server analyses the provided content with regards to context and language. For this purpose it will utilize appropriate tools which are capable of tasks in the field of Natural Language Processing (NLP) and Information Extraction (IE). If the result of this analysis matches the user-presets, the server will create a multiple-choice vocabulary test and transmit it to the client, so that the user may solve it. It was evaluated in [4] to use the General Architecture for Text Engineering (GATE) for NLP and IE tasks. There will be several systems within such an environment which are developed by different parties with distinct backgrounds. Consequently, such a setup demands semantic interoperability. This implies that all parties which are involved in the conception of such systems need to have a consistent and uniform understanding of exchanged information. Also, the several systems need to have a consistent perception of exchanged data. The Health Level Seven (HL7) V3 standard [2] addresses similar challenges related to semantic interoperability within the health-care domain. [11] follows the idea of certain key elements of this standard and present a Generic Data Model (GDM) as well as a development process to obtain a generic iiCALL environment. Based on this most recent research and the findings of further investigations of the HL7 V3 standard, this paper proposes an adapted methodology for the conception of an iiCALL environment.

2 iiCALL Development Framework

This section provides a rough overview on the revised methodology and the generic data model, which was primarily presented in [11]. It is shown in Fig. 2 and involves three main phases: Concept, Design and Implementation. The analysis of use cases and associated requirements for a language learning environment constitute the beginning of the concept phase.

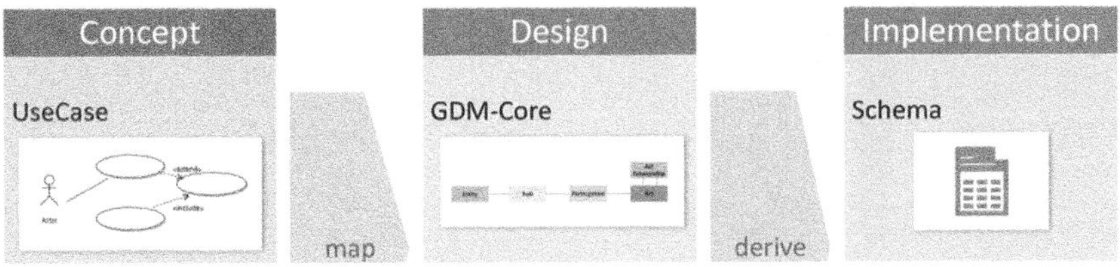

Fig. 2. Methodology

The requirements are initially captured in verbal or textual form and further formalized as use case models utilizing the Unified Modelling Language (UML). Interactions between participating systems for a certain use case are documented by sequence diagrams. Activity diagrams note the behavior of each system with respect to a specific use case. This involves actions that cause the transmission of an iiCALL message (similar trigger-events in HL7 V3) as well as the expected behaviors and the duties of a system which are associated with the receipt of an iiCALL message (similar to application-roles in HL7 V3). The formalized use cases, interactions and behaviors constitute the basis for the design phase. In this phase, the models are mapped to the GDM. The major aim is to map all information, which is exchanged between the systems that participate on a certain use case. For this purpose, relevant data attributes are assigned to the classes of the GDM core, and then further mapped on sub classes, which are specialized from these parent classes. In the third phase, an XML Schema Definition (XSD) is derived from the refined GDM. This schema declares the structure of all classes of the GDM for a specific iiCALL environment, including their attributes and permitted attribute values. Based on that schema, a software framework is generated automatically. This framework handles information exchange within the language learning environment by exchanging iiCALL messages which are structured according to the GDM.

2.1 The Generic Data Model (GDM)

The top layer of the data model for a generic iiCALL environment basically corresponds to the backbone of the Reference Information Model (RIM backbone) of the HL7 V3 standard. It will be addressed as GDM Core and is shown in Fig. 3.

Entities can be seen as objects of any kind that may occur within the language learning environment. These entities appear in Roles. As such, they can participate in a certain manner (Participation) in specific activities (Act). Several activities can be concatenated by using ActRelationships, which enables the description of workflows.

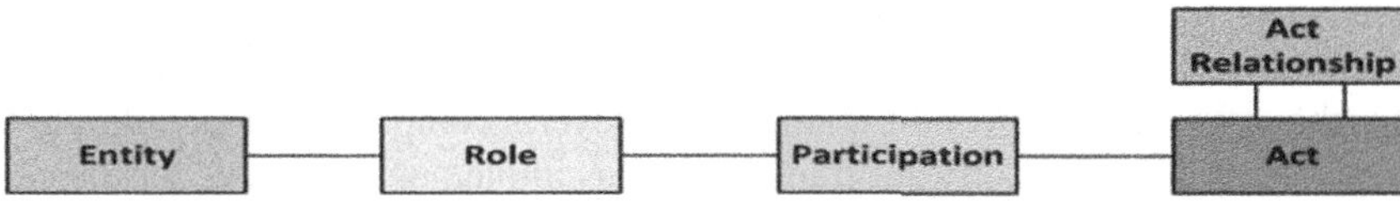

Fig. 3. GDM core

The GDM core serves as a consistent and superior data model which ensures interoperability between the participating systems of an iiCALL environment and even on a basic level between different language learning environments. Therefore, its structure should not be changed and remain steady. To consider the several use cases within a language learning environment in the data model, three elements of the GDM core can be specialized. This affects Entities, Roles and Acts. The underlying concept is similar to the concept of inheritance from the object-oriented world. Figure 4 shows the result of this process, as suggested by the methodology in Sect. 2.1.

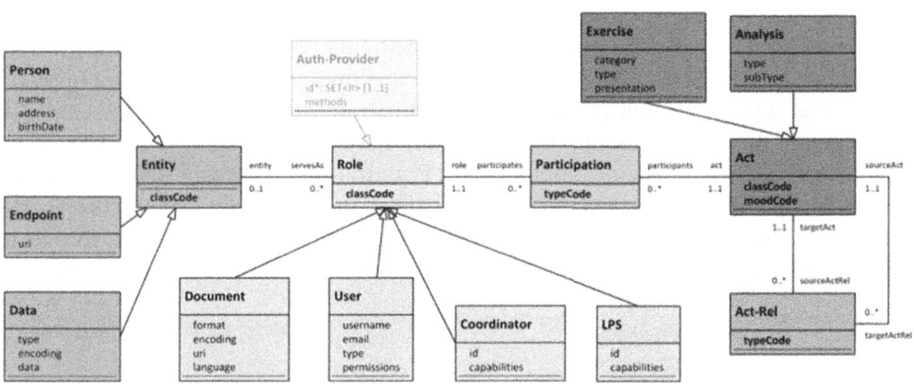

Fig. 4. Refined GDM

Compared to the HL7 V3 standard, the GDM core abandons links between roles, since there is no application in iiCALL environments as per current state of research. Additionally, compared to the data model proposed in [11], the GDM core does not involve any state or any connector element. The state element was intended to contain the user's skill level or learning progress. The connector element was considered to link to external standards, such as the Typed Feature Structure (TFS) or the Lexical Markup Framework (LMF) (also refer to [5]). From the current point of view, there is no need to consider separate elements for a user state or for a connector, since both can be mapped by specialized classes in the refined GDM.

3 The Software Framework

The main task of the software framework is to manage the information exchange between the several systems of an iiCALL environment, such as coordinators or language processing services (LPSs). It supports information exchange, so that the required steps for sending and receiving iiCALL messages are transparent to the users of the framework, particularly to developers of applications. To provide corresponding means, the software framework is composed of several components with different tasks und responsibilities. The software framework was implemented in Java for the current prototype. The components are as follows:

Schema. The GDM, as proposed above, serves as superior data model for the information exchange inside the iiCALL environment.

GDM. The mapping of the GDM is an essential aspect in the development of a framework for a generic iiCALL environment. The process of mapping has to occur in an automated manner based on the schema.

Connector. Connectors act as flexible links between the participating systems in an iiCALL environment. A connector receives messages and forwards them to the hub of the framework. Vice versa, messages will be accepted from the hub of the framework and transmitted to opposite connectors of other systems. For this purpose, a connector determines the parameter for communication, particularly with respect to transmission protocol and message encoding format. Connectors organize communication in such a way, so that it becomes transparent to users of the framework.

Figure 5 illustrates this approach. App A may communicate with App B via Connector X. This connector employs HTTP as transport protocol and encodes the messages containing GDM data in JSON format. On the other hand, App A corresponds with App C by utilizing Connector Y, which transmits messages in XML format by applying the SMTP transport protocol.

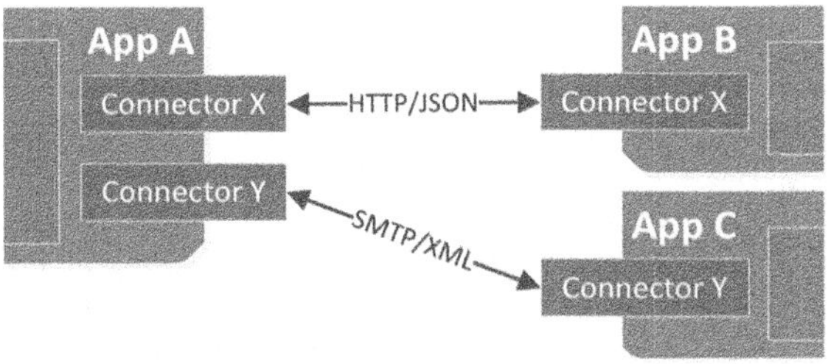

Fig. 5. Message exchange via connectors

Act-Handler. Act-Handlers offer the possibility for users to implement expected behaviors and duties which are associated with a certain activity.

Hub. The hub acts as an intermediary for acts and messages between connectors and act-handlers.

Configuration. Two layers of configuration are offered to adapt the framework to the demands of users. One lists connectors and act-handlers which are utilized for a certain framework instance, the other includes parameters for the several components.

Utils. Utility classes support framework developers as well as framework users by providing helpful methods for general routines.

4 Conclusion

The present paper outlined a revised data model and methodology for a web-based iiCALL environment that overcomes heterogeneity of participating systems and ensures semantic interoperability between them. The proposed data model and methodology are based on ideas of the HL7 V3 standard and consider experiences of the latest research in this field. The implementation of a corresponding prototype proves that the approaches are basically useful for certain use cases. However, several points need to be considered for future work. Firstly the prototype needs to be enhanced and studied with a broader range of use cases [12]. Finally, it is a challenge to implement the framework using different technologies like .NET or JavaScript.

References

1. Gamper, J., Knapp, J.: A review of intelligent CALL systems. Comput. Assist. Lang. Learn. **15**(4), 329–342 (2002)
2. HL7 Standards Product Brief - HL7 Version 3 Normative Edition (2014) [Online]
3. Levy, M.: CALL: Context and Conceptualisation. Oxford University Press, Oxford (1997)
4. Wahl, H., Winiwarter, W., Quirchmayr, G.: Natural language processing technologies for developing a language learning environment. In: 12th International Conference on Information Integration and Web-based Applications and Services (iiWAS2010), pp. 379–386. ACM, Paris, France (2010)
5. Wahl, H., Winiwarter, W., Quirchmayr, G.: Towards an intelligent integrated language learning environment. Int. J. Pervasive Comput. Commun. **7**(3), 220–239 (2011)
6. Wahl, H.; Winiwarter, W.: A technological overview of an intelligent integrated computer-assisted language learning (iiCALL) environment. In: World Conference on Educational Multimedia, Hypermedia and Telecommunications (ED-MEDIA) 2011, Chesapeake, Lisbon, Portugal, pp. 3832–3837, 27 June–1 July 2011
7. Wahl, H., Winiwarter, W.: The intelligent integrated computer-assisted language learning (iiCALL) environment – work in progress. In: 13th International Conference on Information Integration and Web-Based Applications and Services, pp. 426–429. ACM, Ho Chi Minh City, Vietnam (2011). ACM ISBN 978-1-4503-0784-0
8. Wahl, H., Winiwarter, W.: A prototypical implementation of the intelligent integrated computer-assisted language learning (iiCALL) environment. In: Popescu, E., Li, Q., Klamma, R., Leung, H., Specht, M. (eds.) ICWL 2012. LNCS, vol. 7558, pp. 328–333. Springer, Heidelberg (2012)
9. Wahl, H., Winiwarter, W.: A context-related vocabulary trainer in the integrated intelligent computer-assisted language learning (iiCALL) environment. In: 14th International Conference on Information Integration and Web-Based Applications and Service, Bali, Indonesia, pp. 356–359 (2012). ACM ISBN 978-1-4503-1306-3

10. Wahl, H., Winiwarter, W.: Educational impacts of the intelligent integrated computer-assisted language learning (iiCALL) environment. In: World Conference on Educational Multimedia, Hypermedia and Telecommunications (EdMedia) 2013, Victoria, Canada, pp. 420–425. AACE, Chesapeake, VA (2013)
11. Wahl, H., Winiwarter, W.: Towards a generic model for the integrated intelligent computer-assisted language learning (iiCALL) environment. In: 15th International Conference on Information Integration and Web-Based Applications and Services, Vienna, Austria, pp. 729–733 (2013). ACM ISBN 978-1-4503-2113-6
12. Wahl, H., Winiwarter, W.: Exemplary use cases based on the generic data model for the integrated intelligent computer-assisted language learning (iiCALL) environment. In: 16th International Conference on Information Integration and Web-Based Applications and Services, Hanoi, Vietnam, pp. 27–34 (2014). ACM ISBN 978-1-4503-3001-5

Modelling Factors Influencing Digital Readiness: A Case of Teachers in Ghana's Basic School System

James Sunney Quaicoe(✉) and Kai Pata

School of Digital Technologies (Centre for Educational Technology),
Tallinn University, Narva mnt 29, Tallinn 10120, Estonia
{paasanni,kpata}@tlu.ee

Abstract. This study explored the factors involved in developing teachers' digital readiness towards ICT integration in basic schools. A survey with teachers in the Western Ghana was carried out; a sample (N = 85) teachers from 17 schools selected from the urban, peri-urban and rural areas participated. We used Valsiner's Zone of Free Movement (ZFM) and Zone of Promoted Action (ZPA) to model the factors in which teachers' digital readiness is formed as the final level of Vygotsky's Zone of Proximal Development (ZPD). In our hypothetical model, ZFM comprised factors related with surrounding ICT environment in schools, and teachers' culturally defined predispositions related to ICT use and issues; ZPA an intervention-related factor projected teacher actions within ZFM to facilitate learning in the range of ZPD. The hypothesised model was evaluated with SEM-Path analysis – using regression analysis. The final path model indicated that the ZFM factors related with ICT environment in schools and the culturally defined predispositions related to ICT use; constrained the intervention-related ZPA factor that in turn has impact on teachers' digital activities. In addition, ZFM factors directly influenced at what level of digital knowledge, -application, -skills and -confidence teachers arrived, and what their projections in using ICT were in the final stage of ZPD.

Keywords: Teacher digital readiness · ICT integration · ZPD · ZFM · ZPA

1 Introduction

Integrating technology into teaching and learning in today's' classrooms is necessary to promote proactive digital learning environment. ICTs in education has extensive advantages to both teachers and pupils [5]. Teachers are seen as digital change agents in schools, who should be equipped with the relevant digital literacy orientation on tools and pedagogical approaches towards their professional practice [10] to obtain digital readiness. Digital readiness may be measured through teachers' digital knowledge, -skills, -confidence and how they are undertaking digital activities in school [4].

In turn, we posit in this paper that the proactiveness of school environment (digital facilities and digital culture) may influence directly, and through training interventions at what level of digital readiness teachers would arrive. School as an organisation has

F.W.B. Li et al. (Eds.): ICWL 2015, LNCS 9412, pp. 271–277, 2015.
DOI: 10.1007/978-3-319-25515-6_27

its culture, that centres on both human and material resources in school [6]. Various factors - institutional, cultural, environmental and teacher beliefs and competence among others have been identified as expedient towards integrating ICTs in education [4]. ICT integration needs to be understood in the context of external and internal struggles in the schools, considering the technical and cultural setup as enablers or inhibitors to change [3].

We suggest the Valsiner's [14] Zone of Free Movement (ZFM) and Zone of Promoted Action (ZPA) and Zone of Proximal Development (ZPD) [15] as a suitable theoretical framework for investigating how school's digital environment and –culture, and the training interventions impact jointly on developing teachers' digital readiness.

In his works Vygotsky [15] defined ZPD as the distance between a learners' independent problem solving capacity and prospective higher-level performance to be attained because of interventions and further orientation by human facilitator. As an extension to Vygotskian ZPD, Valsiner [14] intimated that ZPD is influenced by other structural, human, and material factors that potentially would enable or inhibit the learner in the acquisition of the new skills. He [14] distinguished two zones, Zone of Free Movement (ZFM) and Zone of Promoted Action (ZPA). ZPA is defined as the approach or activities promoting opening for advancement of the learner capacity. It could be in the form of training, orientation, and tutorials offered to learn and serving as interface between ZFM and ZPD [7]. In our study, the Zones are:

1. ZFM comprises: (i) the environmental variables in school – digital equipment, -support systems and - agenda; and (ii) the culturally predisposed beliefs variables - digital projections, digital opinion on using ICT for educational purposes, digital attitude, digital obstacles and perception on digital impact on teachers' work.
2. ZPA is defined as the targeted intervention in the ZPD, ZPA occurs within the ZFM constraints, and comprises in our study the ICT training factor.
3. ZPD comprises the internal factors accounting for digital readiness as influenced by ZFM and ZPA. These are teachers' digital confidence, digital knowledge, digital skills, digital activities, and digital application.

The teachers in Ghana have had capacity development in computer usage generally and innovative teaching and learning practices occasionally – by government and other funding institutions such British Council and Microsoft; Intel and other corporate institutions. Coupling these training and workshops are deployment of laptops to schools [8, 9]. Studies [1–3, 12] refer to several ICT and digital related factors acting as inhibitors of digital readiness. This study therefore sought answers to the following research questions; RQ1: How are teacher digital readiness (ZPD factors - digital confidence, digital knowledge, digital skills, and digital application and digital activities) factors influenced by the school environment and cultural (ZFM) factors? RQ2: How is ZPA (digital training) factor for readiness influenced by schools' digital environment and culture? RQ3: How is ZPA (digital training) factor influencing teachers' digital readiness (ZPD factors - digital confidence, digital knowledge, digital skills, and digital application and digital activities) factor?

2 Methodology

Participants of the study were drawn from the various basic school levels (lower primary, upper primary, and Junior High Schools) from selected school location (exclusively urban, peri-urban, and rural) schools in Ghana. The subjects were 85 teachers with average teaching of experience of 17 years. Teachers voluntarily responded to paper-based questionnaire. Rubrics for the survey were adopted – with some level of customisation from [13] and [4]. The entire data collection procedure recorded 98 % returning rate.

The Hypothesised Model's design was informed by the theories of Vygotsky's and Valsiner [14, 15]; namely Valsiner's Zone of Free Movement (ZFM) and Zone of Promoted Action (ZPA) and Vygotsky's Zone of Proximal Development (ZPD). Based on our theoretic underpinnings of interrelations of ZFM, ZPA, and ZPD, a path matrix as our initial hypothesised model was created (Fig. 1).

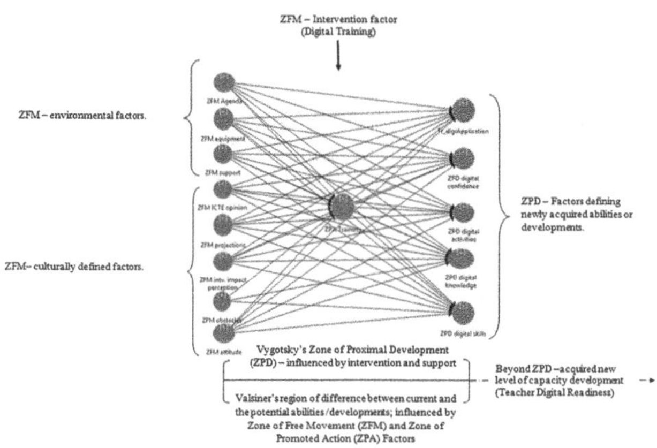

Fig. 1. Hypothesised model (factors influencing digital readiness of teachers)

3 Results

We defined six regression layers (L1–L6) that were analysed for regression coefficients; which defined the path weights and effects.

L1: ZPD (digital application) as the criterion, with ZPA and ZFM as the predictors.
L2: ZPD (digital activities) as the criterion, with ZPA and ZFM as the predictors.
L3: ZPD (digital confidence) as the criterion, with ZPA and ZFM as the predictors.
L4: ZPD (digital knowledge) as the criterion, with ZPA and ZFM as the predictors.
L5: ZPD (digital skills) as the criterion, with ZPA and ZFM as the predictors.
L6: ZPA (digital training) as the mediating, criterion with ZFM as a predictor.

We tested this model with using Structural Equation Modelling (SEM)–Path Analysis with Regression. The scope was unidirectional influence of the ZFM and ZPA

Table 1. Test results of the path analysis for the various regressions layers

Regression Layers (Paths)	r	R^2	e	variance accounted for in the layer
ZFM ▶ ZPA ▶ ZPD (digital application)	0.536	0.288	0.843	84.30%
ZFM ▶ ZPA ▶ ZPD (digital activities)	0.536	0.352	0.804	80.40%
ZFM ▶ ZPA ▶ ZPD (digital confidence)	0.493	0.244	0.869	86.90%
ZFM ▶ ZPA ▶ ZPD (digital knowledge)	0.357	0.278	0.849	84.90%
ZFM ▶ ZPA ▶ ZPD (digital digital skills)	0.572	0.327	0.820	82%
ZFM ▶ ZPA (digital training)	0.676	0.457	0.736	73.60%

factors on the ZPD factors. Resultantly, we concentrated on the strong influencers in the path to generate the final path model (see Table 1 and Fig. 2).

To summarise, the answers to our research questions were the following (Fig. 2):

(i) RQ1: We found that the ZFM variables digital opinion on ICT in education and digital intervention impact had no statistical significant effect in the model; consequently, they were dropped out of the model. The ZFM surrounding environment factors - digital agenda, and digital support had statistically significant positive effect on the ZPD factor (digital activities); while ZFM culturally defined factor (digital projections) had a statistically significant negative effect on the ZPD

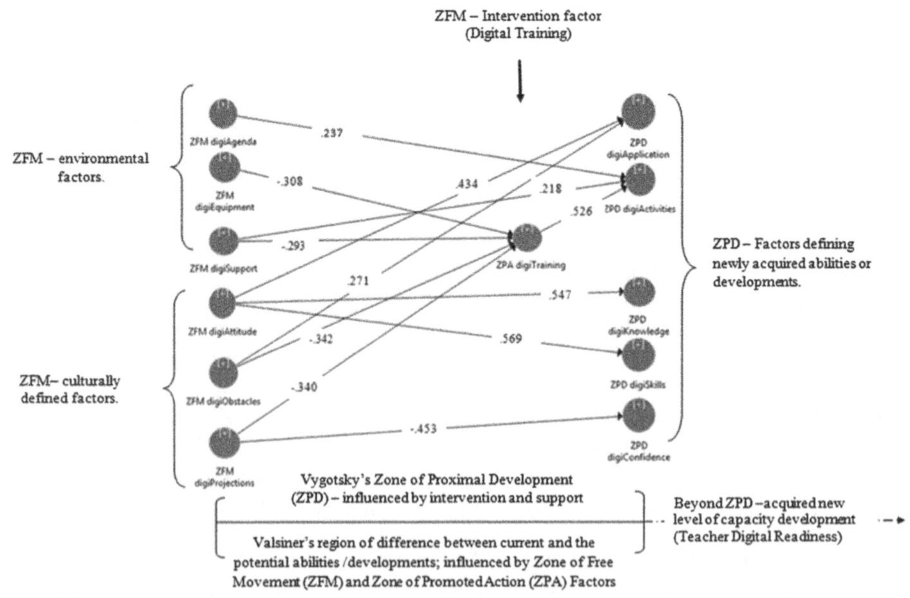

Fig. 2. Hypothesised reduced model – factors influencing teacher digital readiness

factor (digital confidence). Furthermore, ZFM culturally defined factors digital obstacles and digital attitude had a direct positive effect of the ZPD factor (digital application). In addition, digital attitude stood out as a strong influence in the model as it positively influenced ZPD factors teachers' digital knowledge, digital application and digital skills significantly.

(ii) RQ2: The ZFM surrounding environment factors (digital equipment and digital support) and ZFM culturally defined factors (digital projections and digital obstacles) had a statistically significant direct, but negative effect on ZPA intervening factor (digital training).

(iii) RQ3: ZPA (digital training) factor had a significant positive effect on the ZPD factor (digital activities).

4 Discussion

A multifaceted variable assessment is essential to address the issue of ICT integration in schools using teachers as change agents. This study therefore explored the effects of both the external and internal digital and/or ICT related variables on the perceptions teachers have about their digital readiness towards ICT integration in schools. The study thrived on the zone theories; ZPD by Vigotsky [15]; and ZFM and ZPA by Valsiner [14]. In the study, we found that ZFM factors may inhibit the digital readiness development of teachers; which is in accordance with Valsiner's [14] assumption of the role of the surrounding environmental factors and cultural factors influence the development within the ZPD. In our model, representing the factors influencing teachers' digital readiness – the ZFM inhibitors were directly influential and constraining the ZPA factor digital training. Several ZFM factors appeared not to be mediated by training and had direct strong positive effect on the ZPD factors (teacher digital readiness).

In Ghana ICT, integration in schools was introduced to teachers in the basic schools in 2007; when Ghana rolled out its New Education Reform (NER). Over the years and most recently, implementation of ICT policy in schools have focussed extensively on deployment of ICT equipment and training workshops for basic schools teachers [8, 9]. It is generalised from the path analysis that training as an intervention factor had influenced teachers, particularly their digital activities. It can be assumed that digital environmental factors at school must be mediated by training to have positive effect on teachers' digital application of ICT. In other words, equipping schools with computers without providing training will not result in teachers using ICT in teaching.

It should be noted that external factors digital equipment, digital support, digital obstacles and digital projection affected negatively on training; therefore, to increase teachers' digital readiness in the classroom training needs to be embedded within the specific ZFM factors from the schools the teachers originate from. For example, the training groups could be composed considering the similar ZFM factors in schools, or the training could be provided in the school facility.

Furthermore, it is worth noting that digital agenda directly influenced digital activities positively, yet it was not mediated by training. The suggestion is that emphasises on digital trainings should be on the need for the well-drawn school ICT plan or digital agenda; in this teachers' readiness in digital application could be promoted.

Teachers' digital attitude equally stood out as the only factor with multiple direct influence on ZPD Factors - teachers' digital readiness factors (digital knowledge, digital skills, and digital application). The implications of this outcome is that training should incorporate the components that address teachers' digital attitudes to project them to a level of accepting their new role as agents of technology change and accept the paradigm shift in the teaching profession. Stakeholders in education need to appreciate that deploying ICT resources and equipment; and conducting "snapshot" ICT workshops and orientation training for teachers alone do not represent sufficient means for technology integration in schools [11].

5 Conclusion

On the bases of our findings, we advocate for school's ZFM-embedded interventions for increasing digital readiness of teachers. The proactive digital environment and digital culture of specific schools may positively mediate the development of teachers' digital readiness. Jointly developing schools' digital agenda with the teaching staff and promoting school's digital culture should be incorporated into training agendas. The findings of this study will be validated on a bigger scale with the same collected in all regions in Ghana.

References

1. Bingimlas, K.A.: Barriers to the successful integration of ICT in teaching and learning environments : a review. Eurasia J. Math. Sci. Technol. Educ. **5**(3), 235–245 (2009)
2. Boakye, K.B., Banini, D.A.: Teacher ICT readiness in Ghana. In: Toure, K. et al. (eds.) ICT and Changing Mindsets in Education. pp. 1–8, ERNWACA/ROCARE, Mali (2008)
3. Buabeng-Andoh, C.: Factors influencing teachers' adoption and integration of information and communication technology into teaching: a review of the literature. Int. J. Dev. using Inf. Commun. Technol. **8**(1), 136–155 (2012)
4. European Union: Survey of Schools: ICT in Education, Benchmarking Access and Attitudes to Technology in Europe's schools, Belgium (2013)
5. Fu, J.S.: ICT in education: a critical literature review and its implications. Int. J. Educ. Dev. using Inf. Commun. Technol. **9**(1), 112–125 (2013)
6. Fyksen, S.: A Digital literacy for the future: ICT as separate subject. Int. J. e-Learn. Secur. **1**(3/4), 71–80 (2011)
7. Galligan, L.: Using Valsiner. In: Goos, M. et al. (eds.) 31st Annual Conference of Mathematics Education Research Group of Australasia, pp. 211–218, MERGA Inc. (2008)
8. GBN: Government donates one thousand laptops to Western Region schools. https://www.ghanabusinessnews.com/2015/02/26/government-donates-one-thousand-laptops-to-western-region-schools/
9. GNA: Strengthen capacity of teachers in ICT. http://www.ghanaweb.com/GhanaHomePage/regional/artikel.php?ID=344131. Accessed 20 Mar 2015 (2015)

10. Lund, A., et al.: What does professional digital competence mean in teacher education? Nord. J. Digit. Lit. **9**(4), 281–299 (2014)
11. Mckenney, S.: Designing and researching technology -enhanced learning for the zone of professional implementation. Res. Learn. Technol. **21**, 1–9 (2013)
12. Quaicoe, J.S., Pata, K.: Factors determining digital divide in ghana's basic schools. In: Cunningham, P., Cunningham, M. (eds.) IST-Africa 2015 Conference Proceedings. pp. 4–11. IST-Africa, Lilongwe (2015)
13. UNESCO-IICBA: ICT-enhanced Teacher Standards for Africa (ICTeTSA), Addis Ababa (2012)
14. Valsiner, J.: Culture and the Development of Children's Actions a Theory of Human Development. Wiley, Chichester (1997)
15. Vygotsky, L.S.: Interaction between learning and development. In: Gauvain, M., Cole, M. (eds.) From: Mind and Society, pp. 79–91. Reprinted in: Readings on the Development of Children, pp. 30–36. W. H Freeman and Company, New York (1978)

Erratum to: Blogging Activities in Higher Education: Comparing Learning Scenarios in Multiple Course Experiences

Elvira Popescu[1(✉)], Zuzana Kubincová[2], and Martin Homola[2]

[1] University of Craiova, Craiova, Romania
popescu_elvira@software.ucv.ro
[2] Comenius University in Bratislava, Bratislava, Slovakia
{kubincova, homola}@fmph.uniba.sk

Erratum to:
Chapter 18: F.W.B. Li et al. (Eds.) Advances in Web-Based Learning - ICWL 2015 DOI:10.1007/978-3-319-25515-6_18

The following acknowledgment should have been included in the paper starting on page 197 of this volume:

Acknowledgement. This work was supported by a grant of the Romanian National Authority for Scientific Research and Innovation, CNCS – UEFISCDI, project number PN-II-RU-TE-2014-4-2604.

The online version of the original chapter can be found under DOI 10.1007/978-3-319-25515-6_18

F.W.B. Li et al. (Eds.): ICWL 2015, LNCS 9412, p. E1, 2015.
DOI: 10.1007/978-3-319-25515-6_28

Author Index

The manufacturer's authorised representative in the EU is Springer Nature Customer Service Centre GmbH, Europaplatz 3, 69115 Heidelberg, Germany. If you have any concerns regarding our products, please contact ProductSafety@springernature.com

Printed and bound by CPI Group (UK) Ltd, Croydon, CR0 4YY
30/09/2026
02225195-0017